The New Illiterates

The New Illiterates

—And How You Can Keep Your Child From Becoming One

SAMUEL L. BLUMENFELD

ARLINGTON HOUSE   NEW ROCHELLE, N. Y.

Second Printing, April, 1974

Copyright 1973 Arlington House.

Library of Congress Catalog Card Number 73-78654

ISBN 0-87000-184-1

Manufactured in the United States of America

To the memory of

RHODA

A wise man devoutly thanks God that the price of knowledge is labor, and that when we buy the truth, we must pay the price. If you wish to enjoy the prospect at the mountain's summit, you must climb its rugged sides.

—Boston Schoolmasters, 1844

Contents

Foreword

The purpose of this book is to expose to the American public, in terms as clear and unequivocal as possible, the extent of the reading problem this country has and the incredible educational malpractice which has caused it. It is not my intention to disparage textbook publishers or ruin professional reputations. My intention is to defend the American child's right to sound instruction in the most elementary of his learning skills: reading. The very fact that the federal government has had to launch a Right-to-Read program is enough to indicate that there is something desperately wrong with the reading instruction which is being dispensed in our schools at a cost of billions each year. Never have so many children spent so much time in school, and never have we had so much functional illiteracy. Pouring more money into the public schools will not change a thing unless the crucial matter of instruction methods is dealt with in as honest and forthright a manner as possible, regardless of the vested interests of any publisher or group of textbook writers who also happen to be professors of education. To continue to evade the issue will only compound the problem much to our own detriment.

In the course of researching this book, I made a shocking, incredible discovery: that for the last forty years the normal children of America have been taught to read by a method originally conceived and used in the early 1800s to teach the deaf how to read, a method which has long since been discarded by the teachers of the deaf themselves as inadequate and outmoded. Yet, today, the vast majority of normal American children are still being taught to read by this very method. The result has been widespread reading disability.

Until present no one has identified the conceptual origin of the sight-vocabulary method, which is the prevalent method still being used throughout our public schools to teach children how to read. Historians have been very vague about its beginnings. In writing this book, I decided that once and for all I would end the mystery and find out in whose mind the sight-vocabulary method was conceived. The reader will find the unexpected results of that search in this book.

But there is much more than that within these pages, although that revelation in itself would be enough for one book. I have proceeded to expose, often to my amazement and disbelief, a case of educational malpractice on a scale that can only stagger the imagination and shock the American people. I believe this exposure will require some deep soul-searching on the part of everyone involved in elementary education, particularly since it involves a very real conflict of interests among teachers who write textbooks within the framework of a publicly financed school system. This problem must be faced if we are to begin straightening out the pedagogical mess of public education.

Most people will not believe that seventeen years after Rudolf Flesch ignited the phonics vs. sight-reading controversy, that that controversy is still raging today as strongly and bitterly as ever. True, changes for the better have begun to take place, due mainly to the efforts of Dr. Jeanne Chall and the linguists. But the present confusion in reading pedagogy is so great, that only the experts can make heads or tails of it. For that reason, I have written this book in such a manner as to make a reading expert of anyone who will take the trouble to read it—the average parent, the grade-school teacher, the college student, the student-teacher—even the professor of education.

I am not a professional educator. This book could never have been written by one. He would have been too close to the scene, too inhibited by fears concerning his own career, too involved with the very people and methods he would have had to criticize. It had to be written by someone outside the profession, someone who felt deeply enough about the subject to be willing to do the kind of research that was required. I found myself eminently qualified for the task. I have spent all of my professional life with the written word. As an editor and a writer I have watched with horror the steady decline of real literacy in this country. We are turning out thousands of high school and college graduates who will never read a book once they leave school. This situation must be reversed, and it must start where the most serious damage is being done—in grades one, two, and three. It is my fervent hope that this book will provide the necessary knowledge to make the drastic changes in beginning reading instruction which will put this country firmly back on the course of literacy.

Never has more been written on learning disabilities, remedial teaching, reading problems and the like. Never has there been greater confusion among those who rely on the establishment leadership for the right answers. The reason for the confusion is obvious: the establishment leadership is as confused as the people they are supposed to lead. That is why this book was written: to make things as clear and unconfused as possible.

To produce such a book required research and labors I did not believe I could accomplish. Fortunately, I was helped in the task by many good people. Among them I wish to thank Mr. Watson Washburn, chairman of the board of trustees of the Reading Reform Foundation, Mrs. Kathryn J. Diehl of the Reading Methods Research Association, and Mr. Malcolm C. Hamilton, head of public services at the Monroe C. Gutman Library of the Harvard Graduate School of Education. My thanks must also go to the Lesley College Curriculum Library in Cambridge, Massachusetts, for permitting me to use their facilities, and to the staff of the Boston Public Library for facilitating my research in that excellent institution. To the late Shirley Goodstone, a remarkable friend, must go my gratitude for encouraging me to undertake a task which she did not live to see completed. Special thanks must also go to Timothy Reynolds of Boston University for assistance in trying out the primer section and to my friend Stephen P. DuMont for his good suggestions. Without the cooperation and assistance of all these people, this book would not have been possible.

S. L. B.

Boston,
November 1972

The New Illiterates

1

The Scope of the Crisis: Or, Why

Johnny Still *Can't Read*

Most Americans are unaware of how serious the illiteracy problem is in the United States. They do not realize that it has reached the level of a national disaster—a disaster that could remain with us well into the twenty-first century and from which we may never completely recover. Is this an exaggeration? Consider the evidence. On May 20, 1970, the *New York Times* carried a front page story which conveyed the staggering suggestion that about 50 percent of the American people over the age of twenty-five were probably functionally illiterate. The story is worth reading as it was published:

> Washington, May 19—Half of the nation's adults may lack the literacy necessary to master such day-to-day reading matter as driving manuals, newspapers and job applications, according to a study just published at Harvard University.
>
> This strong suggestion, advanced by David Harmon, an Israeli adult education expert now at Harvard, was supported today by officials of the United States Office of Education.
>
> The official estimate of the Census Bureau is that 8.3 percent of the population over age 25 is functionally illiterate. Mr. Harmon, writing in the *Harvard Educational Review*, challenges that figure, contending it is a gross understatement.

"In fact, over half that group may be functionally illiterate," the article says.

Mr. Harmon's challenge takes two forms. One is that present common definitions of functional illiteracy are based only on whether individuals have completed the fourth or fifth grade.

But there is no assurance that individuals retain this level of education, Mr. Harmon says, contending that even if they do, it is inadequate.

In an interview today, Mr. Harmon said his studies indicated that much essential reading material required "at least 10th grade and perhaps 11th grade education. And if you include more sophisticated things like tax returns, the level is even higher."

Mr. Harmon's study included analysis of materials, like driving manuals in 30 states. He found that these were written at approximately an 11th grade level.

"No one says that such material can't be written at fourth-grade levels," he said today, referring to the present illiteracy definition, "but the fact is that it is not."

The Census Bureau estimates that in 1968, half the population over age 25 had less than a 12th grade education.

In his article, Mr. Harmon cited a second basis for his challenge, the results of the few field studies that have been conducted.

He referred to a Chicago study in 1963 and a national survey in 1967, both among disadvantaged adults which showed that about half those with sixth-grade education or higher were functionally illiterate.

Mr. Harmon urges the elimination of the grade-level definition of functional illiteracy. It should be supplanted by a true functional definition, he says, based on whether individuals can in fact read materials necessary to daily life.

Mr. Harmon's article was reviewed prior to publication by the United States Office of Education.

"We found no fault with it," said Paul Delker, director of adult educational programs.

"He and I are in complete agreement on the problem of definition," Mr. Delker said. "These materials often require a good deal more than 8th-grade reading skills. And an adult who is not able to handle such materials is not able to function properly in our society."

"If you can't read a job application, you're in trouble," Mr. Delker went on. "If you can't read a driving manual, even when you know how to drive, you're in trouble."

16

The important point of the story is that total illiteracy is not the real problem in the United States as it is, say, in India or Africa. Semiliteracy, or functional illiteracy, is. The ability to read under a tenth-grade level is simply insufficient for an individual if he is to function in our society to his own maximum benefit. Moreover, it is insufficient if this society is to maintain the level of technological civilization we have reached, a level which rises each year as technology advances. We must do much better than we are doing. Yet our public schools seem to be doing worse each year.

Most knowledgeable Americans have been aware of the literacy problem ever since Rudolf Flesch's famous book, *Why Johnny Can't Read*, published in 1955, exposed the poor job our schools were doing in teaching children how to read. But few of us ever conceived that the literacy crisis would reach the proportions revealed by the *Times* story. But the fact is that Johnny, who was between the ages of seven and sixteen when the Flesch book first appeared, is now an adult of between twenty-three and thirty-three. This is the age group of the newlywed, the young executive, the young parent, the management trainee, the new teachers, the new generation of young adults of which 50 percent, it is estimated, may be semiliterate or functionally illiterate.

It was naively expected by many Americans that the mere publication of Mr. Flesch's book and the enormous controversy it generated over the issue of phonics vs. the whole-word method in teaching children how to read would correct a deplorable situation. But it did no such thing. Opposition by the professional educators to the teaching reforms advocated by Flesch and others was so adamant and so successful, that no significant reform took place in teaching methods in the public schools. In fact, the situation proceeded to get worse as the consequences of the whole-word methodology spread into the secondary school level.

The result is that Johnny *still* can't read. Yes, he managed to get through high school, and even college, reading just enough to get by and doing a good job of covering up his deficiency. But now that his formal schooling is behind him, he reads as little as possible, and takes little interest in how Johnny, Jr., is learning to read. Johnny, Sr., watches a lot of television, forms his opinions on the basis of what he sees there, and lets it go at that.

You would think that television newscasters would be delighted with this situation of a captive semiliterate audience totally dependent on the boob tube for enlightenment. But they are not. Walter Cronkite, writing in the May 1970 issue of *Signature* magazine, expressed his alarm concerning viewer illiteracy. He said:

The most severe problem is that television is all-pervasive; that it is watched by millions of people who either do not read at all or do not read well. Of the television audience, a number we cannot begin to estimate—tens or hundreds of thousands, millions perhaps—seldom read a newspaper or news magazine and never read a journal of opinion.

Yet on the network evening news broadcasts that are relied upon as the principal news source by more people than any other medium, the *amount* of news provided is skimpy. The total number of words spoken on any half-hour news broadcast is considerably less than the total number of words printed on any standard newspaper front page. . . .

There is not time to develop, in any single day's broadcast, every argument on all sides of an issue. Thus, the viewer who is not watching or listening closely may well receive an erroneous or merely sensory impression of the actual facts rather than derive an intelligent, cohesive picture from them. . . .

Meanwhile, because of economic competition, the number of newspapers and magazines serving the American public is dwindling. . . .

The result of all this is a genuine crisis in communications. Since a democracy cannot flourish if its people are not adequately informed on the issues, the problem becomes one of the nation's survival.

Indeed it is. Literacy is so important to this nation's survival that even the federal government has recognized the problem by launching a Right-to-Read program. In soliciting funds for the program, James E. Allen, Jr., then U. S. commissioner of education, brought the following facts to the attention of the Congressional Committee on Education and Labor in October 1969:

One out of every four students nationwide has significant reading deficiencies.

In large city school systems up to half of the students read below expectation.

There are more than three million illiterates in our adult population.

About half of the unemployed youths, ages sixteen to twenty-one, are functionally illiterate.

Three-quarters of the juvenile offenders in New York City are two or more years retarded in reading.

In a recent U. S. armed forces program called Project 100,000, 68.2 percent of the young men fell below grade seven in reading and academic ability.

Thus, the government has been able to measure the scope of the problem, but as of this writing, the Right-to-Read program has yet to develop beyond the rhetoric stage. The government, however, has been instrumental in putting the spotlight on the reading problem in one area under its control. It was the U. S. Army, in fact, which came up with the notion of functional literacy when, during World War II, it defined illiterates as "persons who were incapable of understanding the kinds of written instructions that are needed for carrying out basic military functions or tasks." In those days, the army merely rejected such functional illiterates because there were enough literates to make up for those rejected. But in the Vietnam War, with its heavy manpower demands, the army adopted a different attitude. Because of the many college deferments, the army was forced to lower its literacy standards and accept thousands of functionally illiterate men. To make use of them it was necessary to institute a crash program of remedial reading to bring the men up to acceptable literacy standards. *Newsweek* of October 30, 1967, reported the situation in terms which left no doubt as to where the responsibility for this illiteracy lay:

> The military draft has exposed the dismal performance of U. S. public schools: fully one-third of the 1.5 million men turning 21 each year fail to meet the minimal mental and physical draft requirements. Disturbed by these failures and pressed by the increasing manpower demands of the Vietnam war, Defense Secretary McNamara last year lowered draft standards to take recruits with the equivalent of just a sixth-grade education. Then, using its by-the-numbers techniques, the army began pilot programs to give these "drop-in" recruits remedial reading and writing classes.

How did the army manage to teach young men whom the public schools had considered hopeless how to read? By using the phonics techniques which Rudolf Flesch had advocated and which were resoundingly rejected by the professional educators. But more about methods later.

Commissioner Allen's findings concerning juvenile offenders—that three-quarters of them had serious reading problems—was particularly significant. It is said that beneath the surface of every juvenile delin-

19

quent is a functional illiterate—a youngster who could not learn how to read in school. We can judge the seriousness of the problem by the enormous increase in juvenile crimes in the past decade.*

To what extent does a youngster's illiteracy contribute to his delinquency? No one, of course, knows for sure. But a youth who cannot read must feel particularly trapped in a society where advancement depends to a great degree on one's education. The frustration that illiteracy can cause, the sense of being trapped it can engender may be enough to drive a great many youths toward crime, not only as a means of obtaining material possessions, but also as a means of getting back at a society that requires education as a means of self-advancement but is incapable of teaching the basic educational necessities to those youths who need them most.

The connection between the reading problem and crime has not escaped some of the people in our judicial system. Chief Justice Warren Burger of the United States Supreme Court has said, "The percentage of inmates in all institutions who canot read or write is staggering. The figures on illiteracy alone are enough to make one wish that every sentence imposed could include a provision that would grant release only when the prisoner has learned to read and write."

The Chief Justice's remarks can perhaps be understood better in the light of a recent survey conducted by Dr. Garland Waller, head of education for all federal prisons. The survey revealed that the average inmate in a federal prison had nine years of public education, but a reading level between fourth and fifth grades.

School vandalism is another manifestation of delinquency which may have its origins in the reading problem. A school which cannot teach

---

* In 1960, 325,700 cars were reported stolen in the United States; in 1970 that figure was up to 921,400. Of the 127,341 arrests made concerning stolen cars, 56.1 percent, or 71,456, involved youths under eighteen years of age. Hundreds of thousands of other juvenile car thieves were never caught. In 1960 there were 506,200 cases of larceny over $50 reported; ten years later there were 1,746,100. Of the 616,099 larceny arrests made in 1970, 50.7 percent involved offenders under eighteen. The increase in burglaries has been equally spectacular, with 897,400 cases reported in 1960 and 2,169,300 reported in 1970. Of the 285,418 burglary arrests in 1970, 148,296, or 52 percent, were of youths under eighteen.

In 1968 there were 149,052 youths between eleven and seventeen arrested as runaways. In 1970 the number was up to 179,073. As for narcotics violations, in 1968 43,200 youths under eighteen were arrested on such charges. Two years later, in 1970, the figure had reached 77,756. Of the 5,616,839 people arrested in 1968, 1,457,078 were under eighteen. Of the 6,570,473 arrested in 1970, 1,660,643 were under eighteen. The statistics tell a very harrowing story about a significant portion of American youth.

20

a child how to read is certainly not going to be an object of endearment to that frustrated youth. He will find some way of getting back at the school, usually through an act of destruction or vandalism. According to the *American School Board Journal* of January 1972, more than $100-million was spent in 1972 repairing the damage inflicted on school property by vandals. "The school vandal," reported the *Journal*, "is a student between the ages of eight and fourteen, surveys by public school officials have discovered. The F.B.I. crime report states that of the 100,000 recent arrests for vandalism, 77 percent of the vandals were under 18 years of age and the largest number were from 12 to 14 years of age."

Another problem which plagues the taxpaying citizen is the high cost of welfare. How much illiteracy contributes to the welfare recipient's predicament, we do not know. But obviously illiteracy is an important contributory factor in the tremendous increase in the number of welfare recipients and the burgeoning costs of such programs to the taxpayer. A cursory look at the statistics for illegitimate births shows the trend. In 1961, 93,200 unwed mothers between the ages of fifteen and nineteen bore illegitimate children. In 1968, the number of unwed mothers in that age group had risen to 158,000. This increase is startling when measured against the general decline in the national birthrate. Thus, although fewer children are being born, the percentage of illegitimate births is higher.

Then there is the dropout problem, the many thousands of youths who leave their high schools before graduation because they can't read and can get nothing further out of their "education." Almost every dropout has a reading problem. In fact, the heart of the program created by Dropouts Anonymous, a movement started in Rosemead, California by Mary Stewart, a housewife, is teaching the dropouts to read—by phonics.

The *Times* story we quoted at the beginning of this chapter was not the first to sound the alarm. The same newspaper had printed another story seven months earlier (October 11, 1969) with this very explicit headline: "Illiteracy Considered Nation's No. 1 Educational Problem." The story reported that according to a United States Office of Education estimate, 24 million Americans eighteen years of age and older had never learned the basic reading, writing and arithmetic skills needed to function in an increasingly sophisticated and technological society. The story went on:

In addition to the adult illiterates, an estimated 8 million to 12 million children now in school (the exact figures are not available)

21

have such serious reading problems that they are headed toward functional illiteracy as adults.

"Illiteracy is really a much greater functional handicap than is the loss of limbs," says Dr. Grant Venn, Assistant United States Commissioner for Vocational and Adult Education.

Unskilled jobs, the salvation of the functionally illiterate, are continuing to disappear. Dr. Venn cites projections showing that the trend to automation will reduce unskilled workers to 5 percent of the labor force by 1975, compared with 17 percent today.

Twenty-five years ago, he pointed out, 30 percent of available jobs were for unskilled workers.

"If a kid didn't learn to read and dropped out of school, that was okay because we had this need for unskilled labor," he explained. "But it's a new ball game now. Educational quality now ought to be determined by how well you take in all kids and get them to read."

Although the greatest concentration of nonreaders and poor readers are in the black slums, the rural South and Appalachia, the Office of Education maintains that virtually every school district in the country—rich and poor—has its share of problem readers.

Yes, the middle-class youngster of normal intelligence and health with a case of "dyslexia"—a fancy word for reading problem—is now a fact of American life. Some of these youngsters go on through college and then get jobs in large corporations where their reading disability becomes a problem for industry. For example, General Motors recognized the reading problem as early as 1952 when it organized a Reading Improvement Program to increase the reading efficiency of its management personnel. Since 1964 some 332 managers have participated in the program. These men have come from the operations, financial, and legal staffs which have a great deal of paper work.

Thus we find the new illiterates not only among the poor and unskilled but among the supposedly well-off and educated. We even find illiteracy among the so-called literates in college. Karl Shapiro, eminent poet, critic, and university professor, commented on this new phenomenon at a meeting of the California Library Association in 1970. He said:

I wish to report to you my version of the degeneration of the literary intelligence and its attendant confusions everywhere in our lives. . . .

For example, I have been engaged in creative writing programs for 20-odd years, virtually from the beginning of this kind of teaching. These programs have corroded steadily and today have reached the point of futility. . . . Students in similar programs today, according to my experience all over the United States, can no longer spell, can no longer construct a simple English sentence, much less a paragraph, and cannot speak.

We have the most inarticulate generation of college students in our history, and this may well account for their mass outbreaks of violence. They have no more intelligent way to express themselves.

But what is really distressing is that this generation cannot and does not read. I am speaking of university students in what are supposed to be our best universities. Their illiteracy is staggering. . . .

I use *illiteracy* in the proper sense: the inability to read and write. As this condition becomes endemic in the American educational system, the value and meaning of literature becomes obscured, literature falls into desuetude.

As far as I can tell, the high school has now reached the level of the grade school; the college is at high school level; the graduate school at college level. . . .

We are experiencing a literary breakdown which is unlike anything I know of in the history of letters. It is something new and something to be reckoned with.

Is the picture clear? In the last twenty years the United States has undergone a staggering degeneration of its literary skills, on all levels of society, affecting small children in school, high school students, college students, factory workers, corporation executives, from ghetto dropouts to suburban middle-class youths.

How did all of this come about? Is there anything we can do about it? With the $50 billion we spend on public education each year, with compulsory attendance laws, how is it possible for a nation to produce such poor results on such an incredible scale?

Rudolf Flesch identified the cause of the problem back in 1955. In *Why Johnny Can't Read*, he argued cogently that the problem had been caused by a massive switch in the methods of teaching children how to read in our public schools. Educators had switched from the traditional alphabet, or phonics, method which had been used to teach children how to read since the invention of the alphabet, to the whole-word method contrived by nineteenth-century educators and introduced into the primary schools in the 1920s and '30s. The change took place without fanfare, without the general public even knowing that it was occurring. By 1940 virtually every American public school was teaching children how to read by this new, untried whole-word method. By 1955, the poor results of that method were so much in evidence, that Flesch's book was widely acclaimed by the general American public which had become aware of the reading problem but could not identify its cause. But Flesch was a layman. And so he got virtually nowhere with the professional educators. They continued to use the same methods, producing the same results. However, in 1967, Jeanne Chall, a professional educator from the Harvard Graduate School of Education, wrote *Learning to Read: The Great Debate*, which virtually corroborated Mr. Flesch's position. Miss Chall's book was also enthusiastically received by the general reading public but was rejected by a large portion of the teaching establishment. The reviewer in the *Journal of Reading** wrote:

> What prevents Chall's study from achieving respectability is that many of her conclusions are derived from a consideration of studies that were ill-conceived, incomplete and lacking in the essentials of suitable methodological criteria. In her eagerness to clarify these studies she allowed her personal bias toward a code emphasis to color her interpretation of the data. . . .

Thus, despite two authoritative books, plus other books as well on the subject, and the overwhelming evidence of the serious damage the whole-word method is doing to the national intellect, 75 percent of our schoolchildren are still being taught to read via the whole-word method! In a period of about twelve years, only 25 percent of the public schools have returned to the alphabetic principle. If we understand what this means in statistical terms, we can see that the literacy disaster will be with us not for just another twenty years, but well into the twenty-first century, unless something is done about it soon and on a large scale.

The statistics are important. As we pointed out, the students Flesch wrote about are now adults. The four million six-year-olds who in 1971 were being taught the whole-word method, will be the semiliterate adults of the 1980s and '90s. Those who were six in 1955 will be the functionally illiterate senior citizens of the year 2015. Those who were six in 1971 will be sixty-five in 2030. Since it is estimated that it will take twenty years before the whole-word method is replaced by an alphabetic method in all the public schools, we can see how far into the future the effects of this illiteracy will be felt. In 1970 there were about 36 million children enrolled in grades one through eight. If, because of the present teaching methods, one out of three becomes a

* Harold Newman, *Journal of Reading*, January 1969, pp. 313-315.

functional illiterate, that means we can expect twelve million children now in school to swell the ranks of the illiterates.

Thus, the problem must be seen not only at the primary school level, where immediate conversion to an alphabetic method can save these youngsters from functional illiteracy. But something must also be done about those who have already been taught by the whole-word method. Some of this reeducation is being done in industry, by the army, by private volunteer agencies. But there are far too many functional illiterates who will not be reached, unless a national campaign of very wide acceptance is launched.

Yet, resistance to this drive for literacy will come mainly from the educational establishment, which has such a vested interest in error, that it would be naive to expect any real cooperation from them in correcting the situation. It is of course ironic that the strongest opposition to literacy should come from the professional educators. But this is simply another one of those incredible absurdities which characterize life in the twentieth century. If any swift progress is achieved, it will be due to the efforts of laymen and nonprofessionals who can circumvent and surmount the bureaucratic and political obstacles standing in the way of change in the public educational system.

Can we expect any success to result from the federal government's Right-to-Read Program? Unfortunately, no. As of this moment the Department of Education has decided not to get involved in the controversy over methods. It does not want to offend the teaching establishment, although it is aware that a national disaster exists. Since you cannot possibly solve a problem without first identifying it, the Right-to-Read program does not inspire the confidence and optimism it should.

Nor are the professional educators and their publishing allies the only obstacles to literacy in this country. There is a growing number of educational philosophers who, in attacking the "system," identify literacy as a form of social and cultural oppression. The late Paul Goodman, a liberal critic of the system, wrote:

> Perhaps in the present dispensation we should be well-off if it were socially acceptable for large numbers not to read. It would be harder to regiment people if they were not so well "informed"; as Norbert Weiner used to point out, every repetition of a cliché only increases the noise and *prevents* communication. With less literacy, there would be more folk culture. Much suffering of inferiority would be avoided if youngsters did not have to meet a perhaps unnecessary standard. . . .

Given their present motives, the schools are not competent to teach authentic literacy, reading as a means of liberation and cultivation. And I doubt that most of us who seriously read and write the English language ever learned it by the route of "Run, Spot, Run" to *Silas Marner*. . . .

A great neurologist tells me that the puzzle is not how to teach reading, but why some children fail to learn to read. Given the amount of exposure that any urban child gets, any normal animal should spontaneously catch on to the code. What prevents? It is almost demonstrable that, for many children, it is precisely going to school that prevents—because of the school's alien style, banning of spontaneous interest, extrinsic rewards and punishments. . . . Many of the backward readers might have had a better chance on the streets.*

Goodman seems to be contradicting himself. He seems to favor *less* literacy, but then criticizes the schools for preventing children from learning how to read. He dismisses the methods controversy by referring to a "great neurologist" whom he declines to identify. Such criticism, of course, tends to confuse the public which is being told different things by different sides. Of course, the whole-word method is a part of the constraining system which Goodman wants to abolish. But then he seems to consider literacy itself as some sort of undesirable constraint.

Neil Postman, New York University professor and author of *Teaching as a Subversive Activity*, is another critic of the system who sees in literacy a form of political oppression. He participated in the same literacy symposium sponsored by the *Harvard Educational Review* which was the subject of the *Times* article cited at the opening of this chapter. He wrote:

Print is not dead, it's just old—and old technologies do not generate new patterns of behavior. For us, print is the technology of convention. We have accommodated our senses to it. We have routinized and even ritualized our responses to it. We have devoted our institutions, which are now venerable, to its service. By maintaining the printed word as the keystone of education, we are therefore opting for political and social stasis. . . .

Electronic media are predictably working to unloose disruptive social and political ideas, along with new forms of sensibility and

* *Compulsory Mis-Education* (New York: Vintage Books, 1964), pp. 25-26.

expression. Whether this is being achieved by the structure of the media, or by their content, or by some combination of both we cannot be sure. But like Gutenberg's infernal machine of 450 years ago, the electric plug is causing all hell to break loose. Meanwhile, the schools are still pushing the old technology; and, in fact, pushing it with almost hysterical vigor. Everyone's going to learn to read, even if we have to kill them to do it. It is as if the schools were the last bastion of the old culture, and if it has to go, why let's take as many down with us as we can.

Postman isn't entirely negative in his views. He has a vision of the school of the future. He suggests that it resemble "an electric circus," with TV cameras, film projectors, computers, audio and video tape machines, radio, and photographic and stereophonic equipment. "The major effort of the school would be to assist students in achieving what has been called 'multi-media literacy.' "

Liberal critics like Postman and Goodman do not affect the attitude of the general public, which has a pretty good idea what literacy and illiteracy are. But their influence is greatest among educators, particularly young educators, who are disillusioned with the system and associate a drive for literacy with the system's much-condemned oppressiveness. Thus, we are no longer merely dealing with disagreements over methods in teaching children how to read, but with philosophical arguments over the value of literacy itself. Teachers who are primarily interested in the philosophical arguments over literacy are only secondarily, if at all, concerned with methods. But method is at the heart of the problem. Either you can read or you can't. Either you can read well or not so well. The content of what you read is irrelevant. Either you can translate symbols on paper into sounds coming out of your mouth, or you can't. That's all we ought to be concerned with in dealing with literacy per se. What a person does with his literacy is another matter.

We ought to be concerned with the effects this widespread illiteracy has had on the quality of our national life. Karl Shapiro suggested that this illiteracy might be the cause of the campus violence this country has been experiencing on such a large scale. "They have no more intelligent way to express themselves," he said. No one has been able to prove that illiteracy has caused the violence, but certainly one can attribute the new disrespect for the printed word to the subliminal hatred of reading which so many young people seem to have.

"Who would have thought," wrote Shapiro, "at least since the defeat of Hitler, that American professors would begin to remove their notes and files from their offices and take them home; that they would begin to remove their best or their irreplaceable volumes; that libraries would begin the reduplication of indexes as a safety measure; that specifically trained police and guards and firemen would replace the old innocuous campus cop?"

If illiteracy, or semiliteracy, or functional illiteracy has caused the frustration which, in turn, has caused the violence in our universities, how much violence has it been responsible for in the ghettos? In 1968 Christopher Jencks, executive director of the Center for Educational Policy Research at Harvard, wrote:

> The public school system of New York City is on the brink of collapse. . . . The origin of the crisis is simple. The public schools have not been able to teach most black children to read and write and to add and subtract competently. . . . The fact that the schools cannot teach black children basic skills has made the rest of the curriculum unworkable and it has left the children with nothing useful and creative to do for six hours a day. Ghetto schools have therefore become little more than custodial institutions for keeping the children off the streets.*

But what happens when the children get back onto the streets, as eventually they must? Is it not possible that the frustrations caused by illiteracy is responsible for some of the violence we read about in the newspapers?

What about drugs? Who would deny that this country has among its youth the greatest drug problem any civilized, industrial nation has ever experienced? Is it not possible that the supposed insights which the drug experience is alleged to provide these youths is a substitute for the insights they should have been able to get through reading? What other reason could there be for the incredible widespread use of drugs among high school and college students?

Other indicators of youthful suffering are even more frightening. The incidence of heroin addiction among high school students is shocking when you consider that only a few years ago such addiction among teenagers was unheard of. Obviously, school failure brought on by the reading problem can be an important contributory cause to such desperate acts of self-destruction.

As we try to assess the effects of illiteracy on a national scale, we ought not to forget the amount of suffering and frustration which an

* *New York Times Magazine*, November 3, 1968.

illiterate undergoes in a lifetime, day after day, when he is faced with situations in which his inadequacy determines a choice he must make, prevents him from taking an opportunity to better himself, or influences the pleasures he can or cannot enjoy.

Anyone who has ever known or lived with an illiterate knows how it will affect a person's life style, his career, his future well-being. But all of these individual situations create a cumulative national situation, a real *but* invisible national disaster. And simply because it is not as visible in its totality as a hurricane, or an earthquake, or an economic depression does not mean that its effects are not as destructive and painful. In fact, they are probably more so because of the time span involved.

Thus, if we wanted to understand the full scope of the illiteracy disaster, we would have to understand its relationship to the enormous dropout problem with its hard-core unemployables, the delinquency problem with its costs to the public in crime and ruined lives, the increase in welfare costs, the drug problem and the enormous suffering it has caused, the growth of campus violence, the deterioration of the literary arts and the decline of literary standards, the dependency of large numbers of adults on television as their sole source of information, the so-called generation gap, the growth of underground countercultures.

We would also have to understand that the new philosophical opposition to literacy is also a direct result of the literacy problem. If so many youngsters weren't having so much trouble learning how to read via the whole-word method used in the vast majority of public schools, there would be no need to question the value of literacy. But if learning to read can cause so much suffering and frustration among youngsters, people are bound to wonder if learning to read need be that important. But the truth is that an adult illiterate in our society suffers just as much as a child learning how to read via the whole-word method. But there need not be this suffering at all. The fact is that under a phonics, linguistics or alphabetic method, learning how to read is not difficult at all. It is the whole-word or sight-vocabulary method which is causing all the distress, and in the chapters to follow I shall demonstrate exactly why this is the case.

2

How Johnny Was Taught to "Read," Or,
Getting Hooked on 17 Words

There is probably no way more calculated to confuse, discourage, and finally frustrate a child than teaching him to "read" via the whole-word method. Not only does this method not teach the child to read, but it places almost insurmountable obstacles to his ever learning to read. The amazing thing is not how many children fail to learn how to read by this method, but how many manage to circumvent the method and learn to read despite it.

Perhaps the best way to demonstrate the absurdity of the method and the damage it can do is to lead the reader through the very course itself as it is given to the child. It is the only way to become fully aware of its horrors. I have read no description of the whole-word method by Rudolf Flesch or anyone else, which adequately exposes its incredible absurdities. Only an analytical and detailed look at the course of study itself can do the subject justice.

The course we shall review was perhaps the most widely used in the public schools in the forties, fifties, and sixties, when most of today's young adults were in primary school. It is entitled *The New Basic Readers, Curriculum Foundation Series*, better known as the Dick and Jane reading program, published by Scott, Foresman and Company. It is still one of the most widely used systems in this country in its various editions. The particular text I shall refer to, *The New Pre-Primers, Teacher's Edition*, bears a 1951 copyright, with previous copyrights in

1940, 1941, and 1946. There have been two editions since 1951, one in 1956, and the latest in 1962. I prefer to review the 1951 edition because this was the edition most widely in use when Flesch wrote *Why Johnny Can't Read*, and it was the edition that a great many of our functionally illiterate adults were taught by. If you can understand how they were taught to "read," you may be able to understand why they cannot read today. We shall deal with the later editions in a subsequent chapter to see how the method has been "improved" after so much public criticism. But the 1951 edition was published before the public had the vaguest idea of what was going on. It is the pre-exposure edition, the whole-word method in its pure, uncorrupted state.

In following the child through this course of study, we shall assume that the school has adopted the complete Dick and Jane program, from the Pre-Readers, through the Pre-Primers, right into the Primers. The program begins with the *Before We Read* books. These are picture books without any words at all which are supposed to prepare the child for the first pre-primer. In these picture books, the child becomes acquainted with the fictional characters and their pets he will read about in the *New Pre-Primers*. He meets Dick and Jane, Sally, Puff, Spot, and Tim. He also hears the words he will be "reading" when he gets to the pre-primers. In other words, he is given an oral and pictorial introduction to what he will later encounter with printed words. According to the teacher's *Guidebook*:

> In the new *Before We Read*, the child interprets a series of pictures in sequence—pictures that present the story setting, characterizations, and action without printed words. . . . Though he has not encountered a single printed word the authors try to give the child the illusion that he has read a story.

Before We Read is described by the publisher as a reading readiness program, but actually it is no such thing. It is a clue readiness program in which the child is given a preview of the context in which the first printed words will be used. By the use of pictures he is taught how to compare objects to find those that are alike. "They can now apply these methods of visual analysis in discriminating between words," explains the *Guidebook*. In other words, the child is being prepared to look at a word as a whole single object which he is expected to compare to other whole single objects, be they other words, pictures, desks, windows, or his fellow pupils. Also, according to the *Guidebook*, "Pupils have learned to listen carefully to the sounds of words and to be aware of rhyming words and of words that begin with the same sound.

32

. . . This, in turn, prepares pupils for the simple types of phonetic and structural word analysis that follow at later levels of reading." All of this sounds as though some instruction in phonics will be given, except that nowhere in all of this reading preparation is the alphabet mentioned or taught. In any phonics- or linguistics-oriented reading course, the letters of the alphabet are taught first before the child is exposed to words. In the Dick and Jane pre-reading program, the alphabet is not taught, mentioned, or referred to. There is a complete taboo on it.

Thus, the child is being prepared to "read," and all of his hopes have been built up. The child is saying to himself, "I am finally going to learn how to read. I can hardly wait." But actually nothing in the pre-reading program prepares the child for learning to read. He has not been taught to identify the separate letters of the alphabet. He may know them if his parents taught them to him at home. But if no one has taught him the alphabet, to recognize the twenty-six different symbols that make up the words he will be "reading," he is really not ready at all to start reading. But the child does not know this. He assumes that his teachers know what they are doing and he has complete confidence in them. But unless you understand from the very beginning that the teacher who follows this methodology has no intention whatever of teaching this youngster really how to read, you will not be able to understand the cause of the child's later disappointment, frustration, and failure. The cause can be summed up very simply: this is a method which extravagantly promises to teach a child to read but actually does no such thing. The subsequent letdown can only be understood in terms of the tremendous sense of expectation and anticipation which the method engenders in the child. With this in mind, let us proceed into the reading course.

The child is now ready to start reading the first Pre-Primer, *We Look and See*, a 48-page reader, with 46 full-color illustrations and a vocabulary of 17 words. The *Guidebook* gives the teacher the following instructions on how to introduce the book to her pupils:

> Display a copy of *Before We Read* and the picture cards or cutouts of Dick, Jane, and Sally. Ask, "What are the names of the children that we read about in this book?" [Note that the children are being told that they "read" something when all they actually did was look at pictures and talk about them. Why start the children off on this false premise?—S.L.B.] "What pets do they have? What were some of the funny things the children and their pets did?" If necessary, turn to a few of the picture-stories and aid pupils' recall. Next hold up a copy of *We Look and See* and remark: "Here

is a new book for us to read. The name of this book is *We Look and See*. It has many more stories about Dick, Jane, Sally, and their pets. And in this book you will be *reading* what the children say as they play. Who is here on the cover? What is Sally doing? What is Puff doing? There's a funny story in this book about Sally and the big black umbrella." The picture on the title page showing Sally chasing a butterfly should also be displayed and discussed.

Next call attention to the new *Our Big Book* and explain, "This is *Our Big Book*. Some of the first stories in *We Look and See* are in this book, too." Place the word cards *Dick, Jane,* and *Sally* in the pocket chart and call attention to pages 7, 11, and 15 in *Our Big Book*, which show the three children and their names. Pupils will enjoy reading the names below each picture. Turn to other pages and observe that the pictures show what the children are doing and the words tell what they are saying as they play. Then distribute individual copies of *We Look and See* and let pupils look at the pictures by themselves.

There may be some children who are not familiar with the three story characters. A brief, informal conversation about pupils' own play activities with their brothers, sisters, pets, and toys will set the scene for introducing Dick, Jane, and Sally. Following this discussion, the teachers might say, "You have been telling us about your fun. Now we're going to read about the fun some other children have. Here are pictures of our three new friends. They have such good times that you'll laugh right out loud over the things that happen."

Place the picture cards from the Unit Card Set or the cutouts of Dick, Jane, and Sally in the pocket chart. If the pictures are not available, show pages 7, 11, and 15 of *Our Big Book* or of the first Pre-Primer. Encourage comments about the three story characters and make the most of remarks that individualize Dick, Jane, and Sally. To give each story character a personality, such comments as the following may be helpful: "This boy's name is Dick. He is seven years old and goes to school. He often has to help his two sisters when they are playing games. Jane is younger than Dick—she is six years old. She is just about your age and much like the girls in our room. And there is Sally. She is Dick and Jane's little sister. Sally is always doing something funny, just the way your own little brothers and sisters do."

Thus, the only use the illustrated materials have is merely to acquaint the pupils with Dick, Jane, and Sally. The child has still not been taught to recognize a single letter of the alphabet, but his head has been crammed with details about the lives of the three fictional characters. In addition, he has been told that looking at pictures is the same as reading. He is not at all sure what reading consists of. Presently, the first reading lesson begins. The name of the story is "Look," and it covers pages 3 through 6 of the Pre-Primer. The first page of the text reads: "Look, look." The second page reads: "Oh, oh, oh." The final page of the story reads: "Oh, oh. Oh, look." Thus, the first story introduces the child to two words: *look* and *oh*. Each page has an appropriate full-color illustration depicting the action of the story. The *Guidebook* explains to the teacher how she should teach the child to read *look* and *oh* in the following manner:

Presenting vocabulary: Acquainting children with the form, sound, and meaning of printed symbols will be facilitated by the use of the blackboard, a pocket chart, and the new Unit Card Set. To avoid confusion, in early lessons it is best to remove a line from the chart or blackboard after children have read it several times and before a new line is presented. As used in this *Guidebook*, the word *present* means that the new word, phrase, or sentence should be placed in the pocket chart or written in manuscript on the blackboard as it is spoken by the teacher.

Since many six-year-olds have limited visual adaptation, it is difficult and taxing for them to make constant shifts of eyes from blackboard to book and vice versa. Therefore, it is best to keep all books —*Our Big Book* or copies of *We Look and See*—closed and not to refer to them during the presentation and checking of vocabulary. Word and phrase cards placed in the pocket chart or words written on the blackboard should be used for these activities.

The following procedure may be used to introduce the vocabulary for "Look." "The first story in our book is about Sally and Dick. Sally wants Dick to watch her do something, and she calls to him. This is what she says to Dick when she wants him to look at her." Use the tone of calling to someone as you present the phrase *Look, look*. Then reread the line aloud, sliding your hand rapidly from left to right under the phrase to establish the correct left-to-right movement of the eyes. Ask children to read the line by looking at the words and thinking them to themselves but not saying them aloud. Explain that this is called "reading to yourself." After several pupils have read the line aloud, point to or frame one of the words and say, "This word tells what Sally wants Dick to do. What is the word? Sally wants to be sure that Dick sees what she is doing;

so she doesn't just say 'Look.' What does she say?" Have the entire line reread and remove it from the pocket chart.

Explain that something unexpected happens to Sally in this story. She is so surprised that she says *Oh, oh, oh.* Present the phrase by reading it aloud in a manner that shows Sally's surprise. Have the sentence read silently and orally. Point to *Oh* and say, "We often say this word when we are surprised or excited. What is the word? Sometimes when we say 'Oh,' we hold our breath and make it a long 'Oh-h-h.' Sometimes, we do what Sally does and say the word over and over. Can you read all the words the way you think Sally says them when she is excited?"

Place the line *Oh, look* in the pocket chart and explain that this is something else Sally says to Dick. Add that pupils can read the line by themselves, because it has two words they know. After the line has been read silently and orally, ask: "What does Sally want Dick to do when she says this? Put your hands around the word that tells what Sally wants Dick to do. Is there a word here that makes you think Sally is surprised? Show it to us." Remove the lines from the pocket chart.

Checking the presentation: "What does Sally want Dick to do when she says this to him?" Place *Look, look* in the pocket chart. "Read the line just the way you think Sally says it." Next place *Oh, oh, oh* in the pocket chart or on the blackboard, have the line read silently, then ask, "Who can read these words the way he thinks Sally says them?" Continue in this manner with *Oh, look.* In this last line, have various pupils frame the word that shows Sally is surprised and the word that tells what she wants Dick to do.

So far, the children have not been taught to read the two words *look* and *oh*. They have simply been told what the words say and to repeat what the teacher has told them. They have not been taught the difference between an *l* and an *o*, or a *k* and an *h*. It is hard to imagine what these words must look like to a child who has no knowledge of the alphabet. How is he to remember what the words say? The whole-word method relies heavily on story interpretation to provide clues. But much of it is pure guesswork, which is why so many critics of the whole-word method call it the "look-and-guess" method. However, for each story, the *Guidebook* provides a section on story interpretation to give the illusion that it is equipping the child with the rudimentary skills needed to evaluate literature. Considering the meagerness of literary content, one might ask what is there to interpret in a story of two words? Here is how much the authors can say about *look* and *oh*:

The first six stories in *We Look and See* are duplicated in the new *Our Big Book*, which should be used for the first reading of these stories. Individual copies of *We Look and See* may be used for the rereading of each story.

Before opening *Our Big Book* to page 3 you might say, "One day Sally became tired of playing with her toys. So she looked and looked for something to do. Finally, she went into the hall near the front door. There on the floor she found some things she thought would be fun to play with. The picture on the first page of our story tells what Sally found." Welcome any spontaneous comments before guiding the picture interpretation and the reading of the story title.

Page 3: Interpreting the pictured action can begin by having children tell what Sally found, what she is doing with the rubbers, and whose rubbers they might be. "Do you think Sally can walk in the big rubbers when she gets them on her feet? How do you suppose she will have to walk to keep them on? The word under the picture tells the name of the story. Who can read it for us?"

Page 4: Sally is obviously on her way! Link the first picture with the second by guiding children's comments and responses so that an explanation similar to the following is expressed: "After Sally finished putting the rubbers on her feet, she wanted to see if she could walk in them. So she stood up, opened the front door, and walked very, very slowly outside. Dick was in the yard, and Sally wanted him to see her. Sally walked past the red wagon and down the sidewalk to where Dick was standing."

Next talk about what Dick is doing and how the sidewalk got wet. Continue with: "What is Sally doing now? How can you tell that the water is splashing? Is Sally having fun? What makes you think so? What do you think Sally is saying to Dick? You can find out by reading the line under the picture."

Let someone tell what Sally is saying and then guess why she wants Dick to look at her. "How do you think Sally feels? Can you read what she says in a happy way?"

Page 5: Now Sally has a problem. As children look at the picture, encourage speculation about what has happened and about what Sally was going to do before the rubber came off her foot. Emphasize the surprised look on Sally's face with: "Do you think she knew this would happen? How would you feel if you were Sally? Let's read the line under the picture to ourselves to find out what Sally is saying. Who can read the line so that we all know how surprised she is?"

Help anticipate the outcome by asking, "Where is Sally standing? Why do you think she walked into the puddle? What do you think may happen if Sally tries to put her foot back into the big rubber? What is Dick doing? Why do you suppose he has moved away from Sally? What makes you think he knows what is going on? Do you think he will help his little sister? What could he do? Let's turn the page and see."

Page 6: "How do you think Sally feels now? Why do you suppose she looks so surprised? How did Dick help her?" Make Dick's action clear by helping pupils see that Dick got the wagon and pushed it up behind Sally. Thus, to Sally's surprise, she fell not into the puddle but into the wagon that she didn't know was there!

"The two lines on this page tell us what Sally is saying to Dick. Find the line that tells the first thing Sally says." Have the line read silently and ask, "How does Sally feel about what has happened? What does she say to show us she is surprised? Now read to yourself the next thing Sally says. What does she say to Dick?" Next ask several pupils to read the two lines just as Sally might say them. Conclude with surmises of how Sally will get back to the front door.

After providing such an elaborate context for the simple two words and after interpreting the story to death, it is still not clear how the child is expected to know *look* from *oh* except on the teacher's say-so. So much time has been spent on irrelevant questions about every detail of this so-called story, that it is highly likely that the child forgets that this is a lesson in learning how to read two words. Such forgetting may require rereading, and the *Guidebook* immediately provides instructions for that, too:

Rereading: Distribute copies of *We Look and See* with the comments: "We read the first story in *Our Big Book*. Now let's find the same story in our own books. This time we will read it all the way through."

Be sure, in the oral rereading of a page of an entire story, to help children interpret the picture content as a setting for the verbal text. Here is a partial example of the type of rereading that might be worked toward for pages 3 and 4: "Sally has found some big rubbers, and she thinks she might be able to walk in them. She takes off her own little shoes and puts on the big rubbers. Sally wants everyone to see her in the big rubbers. She says 'Look.' That's why the name of the story is 'Look.'

"Now Sally decides to go outside. Dick is watering the grass in the yard. There is a big puddle on the sidewalk. Sally goes over to the puddle and puts one foot in it. Splash, splash! Sally wants Dick to see what she can do with the big rubbers. So she says, 'Look, look.'"

Because the story is different with each reader, not only will interest be maintained, but the story will grow in zest and detail with each rereading. If, by chance, youngsters omit interesting or amusing picture details, you might highlight these points by asking such questions as: "What do you see in this picture that might help Sally? How would you feel if the big rubber had fallen off your feet? Can you read this line to show us how surprised you would be if this were happening to you?"

When several children have given their versions of this story, promise: "Tomorrow we will read about Sally's sister, Jane. Something funny happens to her, too."

It is apparent from the above that the child is being taught to read pictures rather than words. The printed words seem to be almost incidental to everything else taking place during the lesson. However, the lesson is by no means over. There is a section immediately following the one on rereading entitled, "Extending Skills and Abilities," in which printed type is compared to manuscript writing. The instructions read as follows:

To aid children in recognizing words in either book type or manuscript writing and to develop the habit of scrutinizing words from left to right, place the word *look* in the pocket chart and have it read. Move your hand from left to right under the word and ask children to look at the word carefully to notice how it looks at the beginning, in the middle, and at the end. Then explain that you are going to write the word *look* on the blackboard. "This is the first part of the word. (Write *l* on the blackboard in manuscript.) This is the middle part. (Write *oo* after the *l*.) And the end of the word looks like this. (Add *k*.) The word I have just written says the same thing as the word in the chart." Hold the word card under the manuscript form and have both words pronounced. Clear the chart and blackboard and repeat the procedure with the word *oh*.

Finally, place the word cards *look* and *oh* on the chalk ledge and write one of the words on the blackboard. Have children select the word card that matches it. [Note how the *Guidebook* assiduously avoids referring to the letters as letters, as if such knowledge were taboo. Why? The *Guidebook* never explains.—S.L.B.]

Exercises of this kind in which children compare printed type and manuscript writing are valuable in developing fluency in reading material presented on the blackboard, bulletin board, or in experience chart form. [Here is another potential source of confusion. The child has not yet been taught the individual letters of the alphabet, but now he is expected to learn how to recognize a selected few letters in printed type and manuscript form in whole words. Note that the teacher never names the letters she writes. In addition, both capital and small letters are used, as well as commas and periods, which are never explained to the child—S.L.B.] They are also an important step in building a background of readiness for *We Talk, Spell, and Write*, Book 1. This first book in The Basic Language Program of the Curriculum Foundation Series includes a new type of readiness material for manuscript writing and for spelling. It is designed for use when children are well advanced into the Pre-Primer or even Primer Level of *The New Basic Readers*.

Noting correspondence of oral and printed words: This exercise is designed to strengthen awareness of the point-by-point correspondence between spoken and printed words and to promote the habit of careful observation of individual words in one-line reading units. [How can you promote careful observation by not teaching letter names?—S.L.B.] In this exercise the child must identify word wholes separated by spaces and he must hear word wholes within the sequence of sounds. Successful tallying of this type is evidence that he understands that a printed word represents a spoken word.

Write in a column in manuscript the following four lines: *Look look look look. Oh oh oh oh. Oh look look look. Oh oh look look.* Ask one child to pronounce all the words in the first line, framing each as he says it. Then explain that everyone is to listen carefully as you say some of these words. Say "Look look" and ask someone to draw a line under just what you said. Continue by pronouncing these words in the other lines: *Oh oh oh. Oh look look. Oh oh look.*

Thus, the child is expected to rely on his memory alone to recognize the difference between *look* and *oh*. How he chooses to remember the difference is entirely up to him. The pair of o's in *look* may remind him of a pair of eyes. Or he may use some other device of memory. The publishers, however, are by no means finished teaching the child how to "read" *look* and *oh*. They have a section called "Extending interests," which provides the following instructions to the teacher:

> Sharing experiences: A volunteer might show the class how he walks when he is wearing shoes that are much too big. Then one of the girls could demonstrate the mincing steps she must take when she puts on her mother's high-heeled shoes.
>
> Art Activities: The experiences the children relate during conversation time may be drawn or painted for a bulletin-board exhibit called "Look!" For such an activity, children might work at easels or on newspapers spread on the floor. As the paintings are completed, have each artist describe what he wants his friends to "look" at.

Now you have some idea of how Flesch's Johnnies were taught how to read. You may think that this elaborate, confusing, laborious, misleading, and irrelevant methodology is used only to teach the first two words of the story. But such is not the case. Each additional word is given the same lengthy treatment, ad nauseam, until the children have exhausted every possible idea, thought, and action which Dick, Jane, and Sally can possibly have or commit. All this to learn seventeen words of no particular distinction by memory.

Is so elaborate a context needed to get children to recognize the configurations of seventeen words? Why spend so much time on the life details of these fictional characters if the sole objective is learning to recognize seventeen words? Why not simply provide the child with a list of the seventeen words to memorize? This, of course, would not teach the child how to read. But neither do the Dick and Jane stories. A simple list to memorize would be an honest, direct way to teach whole words. But there is no money to be made for the publisher in providing schools with simple lists of words. And there is a modest fortune to be made in creating an elaborate, illustrated context with all of its accompanying paraphernalia merely to teach seventeen words, six of which are the names of the publisher's fictional characters and their pets.

In case you're curious about the seventeen words, here they are in the order they are taught: *look, oh, Jane, see, Dick, funny, Sally, Puff, jump, run, Spot, come, Tim, up, and, go, down.* To teach these seventeen words, the publisher provides a 48-page Pre-Primer with 45 expensive, full-color illustrations, and 57 pages of instructional commentary in the *Guidebook*, plus *Our Big Book*, which is the easel edition of *We Look and See*, plus a Unit Card Set. The real clincher, however, is that once sold on the first seventeen words, you are locked into the whole Dick and Jane program, because all of the pre-primers and primers that come after *We Look and See* are built on the same innocuous "controlled" vocabulary. Since the whole-word method depends on memory, context clues, and constant repetition for its success, the school must adopt the entire program once it gets started.

Other whole-word series do the same, hooking the teacher and pupils on an initial arbitrary list of words. For example, the *Alice and Jerry Basic Reading Program* (published by Row, Peterson and Company) begins with these seventeen words: *Alice, and, Jerry, brown, come, here, I, little, said, see, something, a, down, look, looked, saw, she.* Only five of these words—*and, look, see, come, down*—are to be found in the Dick and Jane first seventeen. Considering the amount of work involved in learning each word, a child who has started with the Dick and Jane first seventeen words would lose time if he were switched to another series in midstream. The *Guidebook* itself makes this point in the introduction (p. 52):

> If the books are not used in sequential order, or if the sequence is broken by the use of unrelated Pre-Primers, the values of vocabulary control and of the gradual step-up in sentence length and complexity, and in page length are lost. Moreover, to interrupt this program at any point destroys the value of the sequential program of skill development.
>
> Just as the introduction of other readiness books between *Before We Read* and *We Look and See* will destroy the child's sense of security in his beginning reading experiences, so the use of unrelated pre-primers that introduce new characters at the point where he is beginning to feel at home with Dick, Jane, and Sally destroys his sense of security and presents problems that may block growth in reading ability.

Thus, it is not only a question of losing time should the child be switched from Dick and Jane, but of losing his sense of security. If the child's sense of security were based on his own knowledge of the alphabet and a knowledge of how words are constructed from letters

42

which represent sounds, that security would not be threatened by a switch from one primer to another. He would know how to read any book on his age level. But too many publishers are not interested in developing that kind of security based on the child's own independent knowledge. Instead they create in the child an artificial dependency on their product, much in the same way that drug pushers create a dependency in their customers for *their* products. In this sense, these publishers are like drug pushers. Both want to hook the users and create dependency.

Since whole-word learning depends heavily on repetition of words, once you get hooked on the first seventeen words, you are clearly motivated by the desire not to waste time to keep going on with the same series. For example, in *We Look and See*, the first Dick and Jane pre-primer, the initial seventeen words are repeated 335 times. In the second Dick and Jane pre-primer, *We Work and Play*, those first seventeen words are repeated 438 times, while the additional twenty-one new words are repeated only 394 times. Thus, the vocabulary of the first pre-primer accounts for more than half the wordage in the second pre-primer. In the third pre-primer, *We Come and Go*, the first seventeen words are repeated 581 times, the second twenty-one words are repeated 448 times, and the new twenty words are repeated 417 times. Thus, out of a total wordage of 2,613 for the three pre-primers, the first seventeen words account for 1,354 of them. That is why the publisher is so anxious to hook the pupils on those first seventeen words.

It is interesting to see which of the seventeen words are repeated most often, and in the table on the following page we show the number of repetitions of each of the words in each of the pre-primers.

Please note that the names of the publisher's fictional characters and their pets, the source of the child's sense of security, account for 430 of the repetitions, about 20 percent of the total wordage of the three pre-primers.

If anything, the statistics bear out the contention that the whole-word method is extremely inefficient. *Oh* is repeated 138 times and *see* 176. Repetitions of these two words alone almost equal the entire wordage of the first Pre-Primer. What a slow, tedious, monotonous way to learn two simple words! Obviously the trouble with this method is that it makes no use of the advantages the alphabet provides in learning how to read. For example, in a linguistic, or phonics-oriented, method, words are taught in families, first words with regular spellings, then words with irregular spellings. For example, in any alphabet-based reading course, the word *fun* would be taught with other words in the same family, such as *bun, gun, nun, pun, run, sun*. There would be no need

	1st Pre-Primer	2nd Pre-Primer	3rd Pre-Primer	Total repetitions
Look	34	48	28	110
oh	35	47	56	138
Jane	11	17	45	73
see	37	70	69	176
Dick	12	25	39	76
funny	17	18	17	52
Sally	16	28	63	107
Puff	12	20	12	44
jump	32	13	18	63
run	14	14	13	41
Spot	18	19	32	69
come	12	22	23	57
Tim	13	14	34	61
up	24	13	23	60
and	15	32	51	98
go	18	15	41	74
down	15	23	17	55

to repeat a word like *run* forty-one times, as it is repeated in the three Dick and Jane pre-primers. In addition, a word like *look* would be taught in conjunction with words like *book, cook, hook, nook, took.* *Jump* would be taught with *bump, dump, hump, lump, pump*, etc. But note that the Dick and Jane readers do not teach words in such families. In fact, in all three pre-primers, many of the words seem to have been chosen deliberately because they do not relate to other words in families.

For example, in the second pre-primer, such irregular and difficult words as *work, something*, and *mother* are introduced, when in a phonics course they would be introduced much later. The child gets the impression, from the very beginning, that words have little relation to one anther linguistically, that they are all separate objects, like pictographs, which must be learned one by one. The prospects of learning to read thousands of words by sheer memorization must come as a staggering realization to some children as they proceed through the three pre-primers. Somewhere along the line they decide that the undertaking is simply beyond their capacity and they give up, while their friends, who have learned the alphabet at home on grandmother's knee, seem to pick up reading with little or no trouble.

44

Is any use of the alphabet made in the first pre-primer? Let's have a look. We have already seen how *look* and *oh* are taught. The next words offered are *Jane* and *see*. Here's how the *Guidebook* teaches them:

> Presenting vocabulary: Introduce the vocabulary by saying, "Today's story is about *Jane.*" Place *Jane* in the pocket chart under the picture card or write the word on the blackboard and have it read. "Jane was riding her tricycle on the sidewalk. Dick and Sally were watching her. Suddenly, Dick saw that something was going to happen. He was so excited that he called to Jane. He wanted her to do something. This line tells us what Dick said to Jane." Present *Look, Jane, look* and have it read silently and orally. Clear the pocket chart.
>
> "Then Jane did something funny, and Dick wanted Sally to see Jane. This line tells what Dick said to Sally." Display *See Jane* and read it aloud as you sweep your hand under the words. Have pupils read the line silently before you call on someone to read it aloud. Next point to the word *See* and remark, "This word tells what Dick wanted Sally to do. What is the word? Whom did Dick want Sally to see? Frame the word that tells us." Remove *See Jane* and present *See, see*, explaining that this tells something else Dick said. Have the line read silently and orally and then clear the pocket chart.
>
> Checking the presentation: To check ability to identify the words *see* and *Jane*, place *Oh, see* in the chart and say, "Dick said something more to Sally. See if you can read this line to yourself. What did Dick say?" Add the word *Jane* and have this line read silently and orally.

Then the *Guidebook* "interprets the story," devoting over a thousand words to explain a story with a vocabulary of four words. The *Guidebook* offers an interesting rationale for their incredibly detailed *explication de texte* (p. 74):

> In the interpretation of this page, emphasis is placed on questions to help children formulate opinions or infer the intent or emotional reactions of story characters. All responses to such questions should be respected. As the story develops, these opinions can be checked by the pupils themselves. Throughout this *Guidebook*, a balance is maintained between fact questions that require specific answers and the "What-do-you-think?" or "What-do-you-suppose?" type of question that encourages children to formulate opinions or to make

inferences. The thinking skills thus developed are basic in the interpretation of all literature and should be given careful consideration from the earliest levels.

It is interesting that the authors of Dick and Jane discard the alphabet, as if it were too much for a young mind to absorb, but they are willing to burden the child who has barely learned four words with "the interpretation of literature." The "literature" he is supposed to "interpret" in this story consists of:

Oh, Jane.
Look, Jane, look.
Look, look.
Oh, look.
See Jane.
See, see.
See Jane.
Oh, see Jane.

What the child interprets, really, is not literature, but the pictures accompanying the text. It is probable that some children are not quite sure whether they are reading words or pictures. The distinction is not made clear in Dick and Jane. Again, the child is confronted with both capital letters and small letters, commas and periods. The *Guidebook* takes up the matter of capitalized and uncapitalized words as follows:

Comparing capitalized and uncapitalized word forms: To promote the ability to recognize words in either capitalized or uncapitalized initial-letter form, write on the blackboard in a column *Oh, see, Look, See, oh,* and *look.* Place on the chalk ledge the word cards for the two forms of each of the three words. Explain, "When we are excited or surprised, we sometimes say 'Oh.' Who can find all the word cards that say *Oh*? Now find this word on the blackboard. Draw a line under all the words on the blackboard that say *Oh*." Continue with *look* and *see.* "When Dick wants Jane to look at something, he says 'Look.' When Dick wants Sally to see what is happening to Jane, he says 'See Jane.' "

Did you detect in that paragraph any mention of the reason why a word is sometimes capitalized and sometimes not? The child is simply presented with the word in both its capitalized and uncapitalized forms and told that they are the same word. The child must then decide in

46

his mind that the same words for totally unknown reasons sometimes look a little different. He is not told that there is something known as a letter, which is capitalized at the beginning of a sentence or a proper name. Why this information is withheld is a mystery. But the authors are so obsessed with the idea of teaching whole words as separate whole objects, that they will do or say nothing that might draw the child's attention to the fact that words are made up of individual letters, each one of which stands for a sound. They prefer to let the child rely on memory of whole objects, and, in fact, immediately following their nonexplanation of capitalized and uncapitalized letters, they have a section on developing memory based on association. It reads:

> To strengthen the ability to make associations and to form visual images for the purpose of remembering, place in a row on a desk or table three such easily associated objects as a needle, a piece of thread, and a piece of cloth. Point to the first object on the left and have it named. "What is in the middle of the row? What is at the end? What could we do with all these things?" Have a child begin at the left and point to and name each object. Then say, "Look carefully. Do you think you can remember these things we use for sewing?
>
> "Close your eyes now. Can you see those three things just as they are on the desk? See if you can tell us what is at the beginning of the row. What is in the middle? What is at the end?" Repeat the procedure with other rows of objects: a piece of paper, pencil, and eraser; a cup, saucer, and spoon; a hammer, nail, and piece of wood.

Thus, the child is being trained to remember the configurations of words as he would the configurations of objects. What is treacherous about this kind of training is that it is difficult to unlearn this habit of looking at words as objects when the time comes to look at them linguistically or phonically. This is the kind of bad habit deliberately given the child which forever stands in his way of becoming an effective reader.

What we also encounter in the Dick and Jane program are all the convolutions one must go through when trying to teach someone to read without teaching him the alphabet. It's like trying to teach an individual to walk without him using his legs, or to write without him using his fingers. The handicap creates an absurdly abnormal situation. If you want to "walk" without using your legs, you can be taught to drag yourself around on your elbows. That is not "walking," but it is

47

a form of body locomotion. Without hands, you may be able to write with a pencil between your teeth, but the result will hardly be the same as if you were writing with the pencil between your fingers. The same is true with teaching someone how to read without the alphabet. You teach someone to memorize word objects, but that is not reading.

Another serious fault of this method is that when you teach children to look at words as whole objects you fight the idea that words should be read from left to right. Since the main stress in this method is on the word as a whole object, the left-to-right pattern can only apply itself to the reading of a sentence, because a child may learn each word by using some clue of memory which may involve the first letter in some words, the last letter in others, or the center letters in still others. Since the child must devise his own means of memorizing words, there can be no control whatever over how he looks at the whole word. Moreover, if you are asked to look at separate objects, you don't necessarily look at them from left to right. You may look at them from the center out, or simply as two direct objects, neither from left to right nor right to left. The idea that you can get a child to "read" from left to right by the teacher sliding her hand rapidly from left to right under whole words is preposterous. The child has not been told that the words are composed of letters of the alphabet. He has no idea what the letters stand for or that their sequential arrangement is of any relevance to the word. The only sure way you can get a child to read a word from left to right is to make him aware of the fact that the word is composed of letters in a sequential arrangement or spelling pattern representing an appropriate sequence of vocal sounds.

The next two words presented are *Dick* and *funny*. The *Guidebook* introduces them as follows:

> Presenting vocabulary: So far, children have read stories about Sally and Jane. When these have been mentioned, hold up the picture card of Dick and say, "Today we are going to read a story about Sally and Jane's brother. Who knows his name?" Place the word card *Dick* below the picture in the pocket chart and have the word read.
>
> "Sally and Jane were outside watching Dick. Sally thought he was very funny. This is what Sally said to Jane." Place *Oh, see Dick* in the chart and ask children to read the line to themselves before reading it aloud. "Then Sally said *Funny, funny Dick.*" Present this line by reading it aloud as you sweep your hand under it from left to right. After the silent and oral reading of this second line, have both read aloud. If a comment is made on the difference

in appearance of the two forms of funny, explain, "Yes, they do look a little different. Sometimes the word looks like this (point to *Funny*), and sometimes it looks like this (point to *funny*)."

That is another example of nonteaching. Note that it is not suggested the teacher explain why one *Funny* is printed with a capital *F* and another *funny* with a small *f*. The teacher mentions the difference only *if* a comment is made by a pupil about it, only *if* a pupil notices a difference. And if the difference is noticed, the teacher simply explains that sometimes it looks like this and sometimes it looks like that, for no earthly reason whatever. Is it not obvious that after a number of such nonexplanations to legitimate questions, the pupil must conclude that the differences between words are purely arbitrary, that he will be required to guess what the printed word actually says, and that an element of uncertainty will always plague him as a reader? Why couldn't the child simply be told that at the beginning of a sentence the first letter of the first word is capitalized? But since the system deliberately withholds any information regarding the existence of individual letters, that explanation is not given. The *Guidebook* goes on:

> Checking the presentation: "Look at the first line in the chart. Find the word that tells us that Sally was surprised or excited. Now frame that word." Continue by asking other pupils to frame and say the words that tell them whom Sally wants Jane to see and how Dick looks.

The framing method, of course, is calculated to make the pupil look at the word as a whole object, and a series of words as a series of objects with no linguistic relationship to one another. Each must be viewed as a separate picture in its own frame, like pictures on a wall. This probably accounts for the staccato, hesitant reading style of sight readers when they are asked to read aloud. They are looking at words as a series of pictures within frames instead of a continuum of vocal sounds.

The next section of the *Guidebook* is devoted to interpreting the story. It consists of the same kinds of questions asked in learning the previous words, relying more heavily on the pictures which accompany the text than the text itself. The story text consists of the following:

Dick
Look, Jane.
Look, look.
See Dick.

See, see.
Oh, see.
See Dick.
Oh, see Dick.
Oh, oh, oh.
Funny, funny Dick.

Four full-page illustrations accompany the text, so that the child is given plenty of visual aids in trying to figure out what the words say. The *Guidebook* then offers an exercise in memorizing:

> Memory based on visualization: This exercise is designed to strengthen the ability to visualize pictured action for the purpose of remembering the sequence of events in a story. Ask pupils to look carefully at the picture on page 11 and try to remember everything they see there. After a few seconds, say, "Now close your eyes. Can you see this picture in your mind? Tell us what you see." Use the same procedure with pages 12, 13, and 14.
>
> Then suggest that it is fun to see who can start at the beginning and tell the whole story without looking at his book. In preparation, have everyone look carefully through the story to note what happened first, next, and so on. Later, several children may retell the story from memory.
>
> This exercise prepares for page 7 of the *Think-and-Do Book*, which checks the ability to remember story characters, setting, and action.

There is, of course, no intellectual value for the child whatever in learning the Dick and Jane stories by memory. The stories are supposed to serve as vehicles for teaching the child to read words. But since he is actually not being taught to read independently, he must be made dependent on the stories themselves and his memory of their details for clues to the words he has been shown. Thus, slowly but surely, the child is being told that reading is simply a process of memorization. The better his techniques of memory, the better "reader" he will become. If he has poor memory ability, he is condemned to be a poor reader. Since adults have problems remembering things, you can imagine the trauma this must be for children in trying to remember so much with so little developed brain power. The *Guidebook* then provides an exercise in meaning associations:

Strengthening meaning associations: To strengthen meaning associations with the word *funny*, display pages 11 and 14 in *Our Big Book*. Place the line *Funny, funny Dick* in the pocket chart, have it read, and ask one of the youngsters to point to the picture in which Sally might have said this about Dick. Then have a child tell why he thinks Dick is funny in this picture. (If *Our Big Book* is not available, the picture card of Dick and page 14 of the Pre-Primer may be displayed.) Repeat by using the line *Funny, funny Jane* and pages 9 and 13 of *Our Big Book*, or the picture card of Jane and page 9 of the Pre-Primer. Continue by alternating names and using different pictures.

The use of page 6 of the *Think-and-Do Book* will further strengthen meaning associations with the word *funny* and will give each child an opportunity to apply the thinking skills required in the above exercise.

The above exercise, of course, is totally useless and a waste of time. Any child knows what the word funny means, and simply to show him pictures of Dick and Jane doing something funny will in no way increase his comprehension of the word, nor will it enable him to remember what the whole-word looks like. This is not only another example of nonteaching but also one of nonrelevance. What the exercise really does is simply highlight the complete intellectual emptiness of the whole-word method. It is another meaningless device, of which there are many in the *Guidebook*, calculated to give the impression that some sort of learning is going on when in reality none is going on at all.

The whole-word method is really a contradiction in terms. The authors of the method know that you really can't teach a child to read and spell thousands of different words without a knowledge of the separate letters. So they attempt to focus on the separate components within a word only as means to help the child recognize the whole word, not to understand its internal sound-symbol construction. To accomplish this perverted bit of pedagogy, the *Guidebook* follows up the paragraph on meaning associations with these two paragraphs:

Memory of word form: Careful observation of detail in left-to-right serial order and clear visual imagery are essential to memory of word forms. To strengthen these abilities, write the word *look* on the blackboard. Point to the *l* and identify it only as the beginning, *oo* as the middle, and *k* as the end of the word. Say, "Now watch while I write the word *look* on the blackboard. It begins like this. (Write *l.*) Here is the middle of the word. (Add *oo.*) And this is the way the word ends. (Add *k.*) Look at the word again; then close your eyes. Can you see the word *look* just the way it is on the blackboard? Can you see the beginning of the word? The middle? The end?" Repeat the procedure with the word *see*, pointing out *s* as the beginning and *ee* as the end.

Ask children to close their eyes and try to see *look* and *see* as you say them. Pronounce each word slowly. Erase the words from the blackboard, write an *l*, and ask, "In which word did you see this?" When pupils answer correctly, add the remaining letters of the word. Erase *look* and repeat with *see*. Next write *oo* on the blackboard. "In what word did you see this?" Complete the word and continue with such combinations of letters as *l, oo, loo, ook, s, ee.* If children have difficulty with this exercise, give additional training in serial memory as suggested on page 77 of this *Guidebook.*

Thus, we are presented with a new concept, that of serial memory, in which the child is supposed to remember what individual letters look like in the order they appear in a word without being told that they are letters which stand for certain sounds. As far as the child is concerned, the letters are simply odd shapes arbitrarily strung together to make a whole word. It is like asking a child to look at the beginning, the middle, and the end of the picture so that he has a grasp of the details of the whole. To do that with thousands of words would simply burden a child's mind beyond its capacity. It is assumed that some of the teachers who used this *Guidebook* were intelligent enough to ignore its taboo on naming letters and in that way helped children learn how to read. Only the most moronic teachers would have followed this *Guidebook* to the letter. Note, also, how recognition of many more words could be accomplished if words were taught in families, if *see* were taught with *bee, fee, tree,* and *look* were taught with *book, cook, took,* etc. But that would require teaching the children the letters first, which the whole-word method bends over backward to avoid. After all, with such knowledge of the letters, the child would no longer need Dick and Jane and a "controlled" vocabulary.

The lengths to which the whole-word advocates go to avoid mentioning the letters of the alphabet must have its effects on the child's mind. To keep skirting the issue of separate letters and their sounds must produce in the child a kind of unconscious dread of that which is taboo. As we know from the study of primitive cultures, taboos play an important part in the primitive psyche's mythology of fear. To what degree the taboo regarding the letters of the alphabet and their sounds is instilled in the child's mind in these early reading lessons we have no way of knowing. But certainly the difficulty some of these children later have in responding to remedial reading may be a result of it.

Under the heading of "Extending Interests," the *Guidebook* provides even more instruction in nonteaching. Here is what the *Guidebook* recommends in this lesson:

> Rhythms: As an appropriate group activity, let children "skate" to music. The "Skater's Waltz," by Waldteufel, played on a piano or phonograph, is particularly suitable. If a piano is used, mark the waltz rhythm by accenting the first beat in each measure and swaying from side to side. Children quickly get the feel of the waltz and will join in, even though not everyone will move to the same side at the same time.
>
> As the music continues, ask children to try to see someone skating slowly and easily down a street. "Can you show us how you would skate to this music?" Responses may vary somewhat, but most pupils will probably slide one foot forward on the first beat and glide (keeping weight on the forward foot) on the last two beats of every measure. (If the story "Dick" is reread after this rhythmic activity, pupils' kinesthetic images of Dick's ride on skates will be more vivid.)

We have no objection to lessons in music appreciation or dancing, but how the pupils' kinesthetic images of Dick's riding on skates will teach them how to read: *Dick. Look, Jane. Look, look. See Dick. See, see. Oh, see. See Dick. Oh, see Dick. Oh, oh, oh. Funny, funny Dick.* is not explained. Obviously, this exercise teaches nothing at all as far as reading is concerned.

All of the foregoing has supposedly taught us to read the words *look, oh, Jane, see, Dick, funny*. The next word we are introduced to is *Sally*, the third fictional character. As a word it has little linguistic interest for a child learning how to read because it does not belong to a family of regularly used words. *Dally, rally, tally* are not the kind of words found in the vocabulary of a six-year-old. So the purpose of getting the child to learn the proper name Sally is merely to hook him on the Dick and Jane readers and their fictional characters. In the course of the three pre-primers, the word *Sally* will be repeated 107 times, giving it the fourth highest frequency of any word in the three pre-primers. Here is how *Sally* is presented:

Presenting vocabulary: Display the picture card of Sally with her name below it. "Here is a picture of Sally, and this is her name. Often the things Sally does turn out to be funny because she is not really big enough to do them. Once when Sally was playing at being grown-up, she wanted Dick and Jane to see what she was doing; so she said *See Sally*." Present the line and explain that when Sally is telling others what she is doing, she often calls herself by name. Have the line read silently and orally. Continue, "Suddenly something surprising happened. Sally thought it very funny. She said this about herself." Place *Funny, funny Sally* under the first line in the chart and see if children can read it without help. Ask several pupils to read both lines silently and orally.

Checking the presentation: Refer to the two lines already in the chart and ask, "Can you find the line that tells what Sally wanted Dick and Jane to do? Read it for us." Point to the other line and again mention that Sally was talking about herself. "What does this line tell you about Sally? Can you frame and say the word that tells us Sally thinks she is funny? Do you see that word again? Show it to us." Finally, have someone find and frame Sally's name.

The next fifty-seven lines of the *Guidebook* are devoted to interpreting the story, which, again, entails a detailed study of the four pictures and only an incidental reference to the words. The text of the story reads:

Sally
Look, Dick.
Look, Jane.
See Sally.
Oh, oh, oh.
Oh, Dick.
See Sally.
Look, Jane.
Look, Dick.
See funny Sally.
Funny, funny Sally.

Again, the *Guidebook* suggests an exercise in developing memory on the basis of observation, with this particular lesson devoted to identifying the three fictional characters by their pictures and names. All of this is pure book salesmanship, with the sole intent on the part of the authors and publisher of getting the pupil hooked on the entire expen-

54

sive Dick and Jane program. This lesson also has the *Guidebook's* first reference to anything resembling phonics, but it actually has nothing to do with phonics. It is headed "Developing phonetic skills" and reads as follows:

The following exercises are designed to promote accurate auditory perception of the initial-consonant sounds *d, j,* and *s:*

1. Suggest a listening game. "Our ears are going to help us in this game. We'll see just how carefully we can listen. Who knows the name of the boy in our book? Let's all say the name *Dick* and listen to how it sounds at the beginning." Call on children whose names begin with this same initial-consonant sound and ask each one to say his own name and Dick's name. Point out that these names sound alike at the beginning. Ask, "Can you think of any other boys' or girls' names that begin with the same sound as *Dick?*" Such names as *Danny, Dorothy, Donna, Donald, Don, Douglas, Doris, Dale, David* may be contributed. Continue in the same manner with the names *Jane* and *Sally.*

2. Set B of the Speech Improvement Cards will be useful for developmental work on many of the skills introduced in The New Basic Pre-Primer Program. (This set may be purchased separately, if desired.) For the convenience of teachers who have early printings of the Speech Improvement Cards, which are not numbered, the numbering system used is explained below. Since the cards have probably been cut, it is suggested that the teacher first number the Key Sheet and then mark the numbers on the faces of the corresponding cards in Set B. . . .

Begin with the first group at the top of the Key Sheet and number the cards, group by group, from left to right. The first group in the second row of the Key Sheet will begin at the left with the number 37. The first group of cards in the bottom row will begin at the left with the number 91. When all the cards have been numbered in this manner, the numbers will be consecutive within each group as follows: *s,* 1-18; *sh,* 19-27; *l,* 28-45; *k* or *c,* 46-63; *f,* 64-81; *g,* 82-99; *th,* 100-117; *r,* 118-135; *ch,* 136-144.

Select the Speech Improvement Cards numbered 1 (suits), 2 (circle), 4 (soup), 7 (soap), 8 (sign), 9 (circus), 30 (doll), 56 (doctor), and 60 (desk). Identify and discuss the picture shown on each card. (Reference to the Key Sheet for Picture Cards will give the specific words to be used in identifying the various objects.) Naming all the pictured objects in the *d* group and in the *s* group will increase awareness of both initial-consonant sounds. The key words for

Speech Improvement Card 8 (policeman with a motorcycle standing before a stop sign) comprise a repetitive sound pattern established in *Before We Read*. This card is particularly helpful in developing an awareness of the sound of *s* and in indicating the children who have difficulty reproducing this sound. (See the suggestions given in the section "Meeting individual needs.")

Continue by putting the Unit Card Set pictures of Dick and Sally in the pocket chart. Shuffle the *d* and *s* Speech Improvement Cards and ask children to place the pictures whose names begin with the same sound as *Dick* under his picture in the chart. The pictures whose names begin like *Sally* should be placed in the chart under Sally's picture.

If the Speech Improvement Cards are not available, use magazine pictures of objects beginning with the consonant sounds of *d*, *j*, and *s*.

Meeting individual needs: Of the three initial-consonant sounds presented in the preceding exercise, the sound of *s* is the most difficult for young children to reproduce. With these girls and boys, you may wish to use the testing procedures suggested in *Speech in the Classroom*, the Teacher's Manual accompanying the Speech Improvement Cards. After the test has been completed and interpreted, follow the retraining suggestions given in the manual.

I have quoted this excerpt to reveal some of the pedagogic claptrap in the Dick and Jane reading program to which millions of children have been and are being subjected. Let us analyze what the above is about. The exercises are supposed to promote "accurate auditory perception of the initial-consonant sounds of *d*, *j*, and *s*." To do this, the children are shown pictures, provided through some gimmick known as Speech Improvement Cards, of objects which begin with the same sound. The child is not shown other words which begin with these sounds, because the only words he has learned so far are *look, oh, Jane, see, Dick, funny,* and *Sally*. Only *see* and *Sally* begin with the same letter, but curiously enough this is not mentioned in the *Guidebook*. So the child still has no idea that a particular letter is the symbol of a particular sound. All he has been told is that a lot of words sound alike at the beginning, which, as information, is incomplete if he is not told *why* these words sound alike at the beginning: that it has something to do with the sound value of the initial letter. Remember, the child, so far, has been taught nothing about an alphabet and its twenty-six symbols. He still doesn't know that an individual letter stands for something. Again, the unnecessary complexity of the whole-word system is only matched by its ineptness as a teaching method. This is more nonteaching, designed to fill the child's mind with confusing incomplete information and to increase the sales of additional gimmicks for classroom use. We must remember that before Dick and Jane came into being, millions of children learned how to read with the simplest classroom tools. All of the paraphernalia of Dick and Jane were unavailable and unnecessary; consequently, education was much less expensive and the results much better. Parents would probably be happy to bear the expense of the Dick and Jane method if it produced results. But never has a method which cost so much taught so little. In fact, the method seems to be an elaborate evasion of teaching what has to be taught.

The next words taught are *Puff, jump,* and *run.* They are all taught in the same elaborate, endless, complicated manner as the previous words, with no reference to the families of words from which they come. The text of the story is as follows:

Puff.
Jump, Puff.
Jump, jump, jump.
Jump, Puff, jump.
Run, Puff.
Run, Puff, run.
Run, run, run.
Jump, jump, jump.
Oh, Puff.
Oh, oh, oh.
Funny, funny Puff.

Nearly two pages of text in the *Guidebook* are devoted to interpreting that literary gem. Also, more use is made of the Speech Improvement Cards in exercises designed to "promote auditory perception and accurate auditory imagery of the initial-consonant sounds *d, s, j,* and *p.*" Still no mention of the alphabet, or letters, or letter sounds.

The next words taught are *Spot* and *come.* About 360 words are used to present these two new words, and 600 more are used to "interpret" the story, which consists of:

Spot.
Come, come.
Come, Spot, come.
Run, run, run.
Jump, Spot.

Jump, jump.
Jump, Spot, jump.
Oh, Spot.
Oh, oh, oh.
Funny, funny Spot.

In the section devoted to "memory of word form," we are given this interesting exercise:

> To develop the habit of scrutinizing words from left to right and to promote the ability to visualize word forms, write *Spot* on the blackboard in manuscript and have it read. "Look at the word carefully to see how it looks at the beginning, in the middle, and at the end." Write the word again, slowly, and draw attention to the way it looks: "I am going to write *Spot* again while you watch. This is the beginning of the word, this is the middle, and this is the end." Use the same procedure as pupils note the beginning, middle, and end of the word *Sally*. "Now close your eyes and try to see each word as I say it." Then erase both words from the blackboard, write *y*, and ask, "Which word ends like this? Yes, you see it at the end of the word *Sally*." Write Sally. Write *t* and proceed with *Spot*. Write *S* and ask, "Which word do you think of when I write this?" Show that both *Sally* and *Spot* begin this way.
>
> Write the word *See* beside *Sally* and *Spot* and have *See* pronounced. Lead children to notice that *See* looks like *Spot* and *Sally* at the beginning, but that each word ends differently. Develop the idea that most of the time you must look beyond the beginning of a word to identify it. Then write *t* on the blackboard, ask which word ends this way, and complete the word as children reply. Repeat with *ee* and *y*.

It is easy to see the harm and misconceptions conveyed by this kind of deceptive teaching in which letters are taught not as letters with specific phonetic functions, but merely as configuration clues to pictographs. Why aren't the letters identified by their names? They have names for the purpose of easy identification. Yet the child is deprived of this information and told that a word "looks like this" at the beginning or at the end. How is he expected to remember the shape of something never identified by name or function? To use the letters as mere configuration clues is a gross misuse of them. In addition, the exercise is supposed to teach children to look at a word from left to right. But if four words look the same at the beginning, the child may look at the end of the word for his clue. He's liable to remember the word *Sally* not by the *S* at the beginning but the *y* at the end. After all, the child will use any device of memory available to him. Besides, the teacher has provided him with no real reason for reading from left to right. The sequence of letters has no meaning to him, and the teacher has made no mention of letters having sound values. So why should he adhere to an arbitrary rule to read a word from left to right when all that is really needed is a clue in the word to identify its meaning, and any clue that does the job is legitimate. If we look at the first seventeen words we can imagine that some children will remember *look* by the *oo*, *oh* by the *h*, *Jane* by the *J*, *see* by the *ee*, *Dick* by the *D* or *k*, *funny* by the *y*, *Sally* by the *ll*, *Puff* by the *ff*, *jump* by the *m*, *run* by the *r*, *Spot* by the *S*, *come* by the *c*, *Tim* by the *T*, *up* by the *p*, *and* by the *d*, *go* by the *g*, and *down* by the *w*. Other children may find the clues in other letters. But certainly this is no way to learn how to read. Yet this is what the Dick and Jane whole-word method teaches, and that is why so many children subjected to this method never learn how to read, write, or spell to any effective degree. Perhaps the most damning sentence in the exercise is this: "Develop the idea that most of the time you must look beyond the beginning of a word to identify it." How far beyond we are not told. I suppose only as far as the child has to, in order to remember. And the American people have paid good money for this kind of teaching!

In the section devoted to "developing phonetic skills," the following exercise is suggested (p. 96):

> To check auditory perception of initial consonant sounds, ask riddles that contain pairs of words very much alike in total sound pattern but not in the initial-consonant sound. "Which one can you bounce, a hall or a ball? Which do you wear, a bat or a hat? Which do you eat, a tie or a pie? Is Puff a kitten or a mitten?

That is the extent of the exercise. Again, it teaches nothing since the child will not see those rhyming words or know why they rhyme until he encounters them sometime in the future. No phonetic skill of any kind is developed since the child hasn't the faintest idea why the words rhyme. He simply has been made aware that some words almost sound like other words, just as he has been taught that the word *look* sometimes looks like *Look* and sometimes *look*. It is somewhat amazing how assiduously the whole-word method avoids teaching the child anything and spends so much time doing it.

The next story introduces the next three words: *Tim, up, and,* and the story after that introduces the final two words of the first seventeen: *go* and *down*. All of these words are introduced as elaborately as the previous ones, much of it consisting of pure nonteaching, bad teaching, or bogus teaching. For example, there is an exercise in "experiencing sensory images" in the *Guidebook* in which the child is asked to close his eyes and think of the pictures in the story he has just "read" and feel the sensations of the story's action (p. 99). In what way this contributes to the child's ability to read words is not known.

Another example of bad teaching in the *Guidebook* (p. 101) is an exercise "to strengthen auditory perception of the initial-consonant sounds *d*, *p*, and *s*." The words used for the *s* sound are *suits, circle, soup, soap*, and *circus*. Of course, the child is only shown pictures, but he is bound to be confused about *s* and *c* having the same sound, unless he has been taught the letters and knows that *c* often also sounds like *k*. One of the difficulties of the English alphabet is that its twenty-six letters stand for about forty-five sounds, and unless you introduce this knowledge to the pupil in an organized, step-by-step way, with the simplest and most regular words first, and the most difficult and irregular words last, you are bound to create great confusion in the young mind. But in whole-word methodology, the entire concept of the alphabet is so obscured, so fragmented, so mutilated, that a great deal of damage is easily done to the child's later learning capabilities. It takes years, sometimes, to straighten out a child who has become so confused in that first year.

Another time-wasting, nonteaching exercise suggested in the *Guidebook* is a game to develop the "ability to remember objects in serial order" (p.101):

> Place three toys—a block, a doll, and a ball, for example—in a row. Call attention to the first toy at the children's left, to the toy in the middle, and to the last toy. After everyone has closed his eyes or the toys have been covered, ask, "Which toy is last in the row? First in the row? In the middle? Who can begin with the first toy and name the others just as he remembers seeing them?" Later, add another toy and rearrange the row for another try.

It would be one thing if the child were being asked to remember the sequence of letters in a word he will be using and reading for the rest of his life. It would help him learn something about spelling. But to waste his time on a meaningless exercise is criminal. It is only of value to learn things in "serial order" if that serial order has some meaning, such as letters in a word, or words in a poem one is memorizing, or numerals in one's Social Security number. In the case of this game it has absolutely no meaning. One is amazed at the kind of pedagogical claptrap that fills this *Guidebook* and makes it the most expensive, most wasteful, and most inefficient method ever devised for teaching children "how to read."

3

On the Road to Functional Illiteracy

In the preceding chapter, we examined how the first seventeen words of the child's "sight vocabulary" are taught in the first Dick and Jane pre-primer. The twenty-one words of the second pre-primer and the twenty words of the third pre-primer are taught in exactly the same manner, with a comparable amount of bad teaching, bogus teaching, and nonteaching. For example, there are a number of exercises in the *Guidebook* devoted to "strengthening the auditory perception of rhyme," in which the examples given are so irregular, that a child may become quite confused in understanding our language's spelling patterns. Here are some of the rhyming patterns the child is presented with: *my, tie, high; one, run; come, drum; oh, snow, toe*. What purpose can possibly be served by presenting such irregular rhyming patterns to beginning readers? The child cannot read the rhyming words, and therefore they do not add to his reading vocabulary. At this early stage in reading, rhymes are used to teach children to recognize the various regular spelling patterns that most of our one-syllable words follow. But these Dick and Jane exercises to promote "auditory perception" are of no value at this stage in the child's learning, and they will only confuse him later when he must learn to spell.

At this point, the child still knows nothing about letters and their sound values. He does not know the phonetic reason why words rhyme. If he were to be taught why words rhyme, the logical way would be to start with the simplest, most regular of our rhyming patterns and show them to him so that he could benefit from such exercises by learning how to read and spell many more words than the sight method permits. For example, instead of rhyming *fun* with *one*, he would rhyme it with *bun, gun, sun*. Instead of rhyming *snow* with *toe*, he would rhyme it with *bow, low, row, tow*. After becoming familiar with the regular rhyming patterns based on regular spelling patterns, he would then be introduced slowly to the irregular rhymes. Since our spelling patterns are somewhere between 80 and 85 percent regular, it is the height of pedagogical folly to start a beginning reader with materials which require a sophisticated knowledge of the language's irregularities without having taught the child the language's most elementary regular aspects. We all admit that English spelling has many odd irregularities. But that is all the more reason why the irregular aspects of the language should not be introduced until the child has mastered the regular ones.

In the teaching of any subject, we proceed from the most elementary to the most complex. In the sight method, there is no such teaching organization at all. We start with whole words, which are a big step ahead of individual letters, deliberately withhold elementary alphabetic information from the child, then skip and jump around among complex, irrelevant concepts. For example, before the child has the simplest knowledge of the letters, he is presented with an exercise on "formulating sentences" (p. 174). That exercise is followed up by another on words and sentences (p. 202):

> Comprehending sentence meaning: To strengthen the understanding that a sentence is a meaning unit and to promote ability to use context clues as an aid in checking word recognition, begin by placing on the chalk ledge several word cards for *want, see, for, go,* and *look*. Write the sentence *Dick and Jane   something* and ask, "Can you tell which word is left out?" When someone answers "want" or "see" ask him to find that word on the chalk ledge and show where it belongs in the sentence. "Is there another word that would fit in this sentence?" Repeat by using such sentences as *Sally sees something (for) Tim. See Something (for) Sally. I (want or see) something.*

Note that the teacher deals with the concepts of word and sentence quite freely in this exercise. The child is expected to understand these sophisticated concepts, but the more elementary concepts of alphabet letter and syllable have not as yet been taught. There are, of course, a number of exercises in the *Guidebook* which draw dangerously close to revealing something about the alphabetic principle, but the teacher is specifically told to withhold that information. For example, one of the exercises devoted to "developing phonetic skills" is probably the most shameless example of deliberate, calculated nonteaching in the *Guidebook* (p. 240):

> To check auditory perception of initial-consonant sounds, write *baby* and *ball* on the blackboard. Have the words pronounced and observe with youngsters that they begin with the same sound. If someone mentions that these words also look alike at the beginning, agree with him but do not name the letter or try to teach association of a sound with a letter at this time. The visual-auditory perception (association of sound and symbol) of initial consonants is presented first at Primer level. However, observation of likenesses in form as well as in sound is an indication of the child's growing readiness for the next level.

It is obvious that the reason why the teacher is advised not to name the letter or teach association of a sound with a letter is because that would give the child information which might prematurely make him independent of a controlled sight vocabulary, independent of the publisher's product. Knowledge of the letters is made in such piecemeal, fragmentary fashion, that only the smartest children, and those who have had alphabet training at home, can figure out the phonetic construction of words and read on their own. There is no sound pedagogical reason to withhold the alphabetic concept from a child who is being taught the concepts of word and sentence. Yet, believe it or not, the alphabet itself is not introduced to the pupil in this reading program until he is in fifth grade! And then it is not taught as an aid to reading, but as an aid to using the dictionary. At least this is what is recommended by William S. Gray, chief author of the Dick and Jane program, in his book *On Their Own in Reading*.

There are many instances throughout the pre-primer program when it becomes almost imperative to draw the pupil's attention to the alphabetic principle, but the authors of Dick and Jane manage to avoid it. For example, in the *Guidebook* we are given an exercise in "structural analysis" so that the child can be taught to recognize whole words in their plural forms (p. 177). Some whole-word experts think that the plural forms of words should be taught as separate whole words. But the authors of Dick and Jane have worked out some complicated formula whereby they use a process of "structural analysis" as a means of identifying parts of words which form "meaning units." The rule is stated as follows: "The root word is the meaning unit for the child in an inflected form of a known word." In other words, you don't tell a child that by adding the letter *s* to a word you make it plural. That's too simple. You tell him that he is looking at an inflected form of a root word which he supposed to know by sight. Here is how the child is introduced to the plural form in his first encounter with it in Dick and Jane:

> To develop the ability to recognize words formed by adding *s* to the root form, write *boat* on the blackboard. Have the word pronounced and say, "I am going to do something to this word." Add an *s* to boat and have the word pronounced. Erase the initial letter *b* and substitute *B*; have *Boats* pronounced. Remove the *s* and have *Boat* pronounced. Repeat the procedure with the words *car*, *cars*, *Cars*, and *Car*. Stress the total appearance of each word, not the letters that change it.

Is it not possible that in the constant way the child's mind is deliberately diverted from the alphabetic principle, he may, as a result, develop a kind of automatic avoidance of the obvious? He is forbidden to infer that the letter *s*, which he merely recognizes as a marking without a specific name, may stand for a sound. He knows that when you add *s* to a word, the word changes in sound and meaning. But he does not know why, and somehow he gets the feeling that *he is not supposed to know why*. When you add this deliberate avoidance of the alphabetic principle to the one mentioned earlier in this chapter and to all the other subtle avoidances in lesson after lesson, exercise after exercise, you are bound to create in the child a learning block built on an unconscious taboo. This learning block, implanted in the first grades, may make it impossible for the child to ever learn how to read with any fluency, thus guaranteeing his future failure as a student.

Thus, by the time the child has acquired his sight vocabulary of fifty-eight words with the completion of the three Dick and Jane pre-primers, he has also acquired a very real taboo regarding the alphabetic principle. The letters have not been named for him and their separate, distinct identities are very vague in his mind. The words he has learned to recognize have virtually no phonetic or linguistic connection with one another, except that they are all in the English language. They are words deliberately chosen because they obscure or hide the alphabetic principle best. The great emphasis of the lessons has been on talking about pictures, getting involved in the lives of Dick and Jane, learning to rely on memory. The *Guidebook* makes it clear that the goal of the

66

pre-primers is to make the child dependent on the Dick and Jane context for his reading advancement. It does not pretend to teach the child to read independently of that context. The parent can get a good idea of what kind of reading skill his child is expected to have by the vocabulary test given at the end of each pre-primer. In the *Guidebook*, we are given the vocabulary test for the first pre-primer as well as the instructions which are to be used for the other two tests (pp. 118-120). The form of the test is simple. There are five rows of squares—four squares to a row—in which three words appear in each square. Here is how the test appears in the *Guidebook*:

Puff	Come	and	*Puff*
Spot	Jane	see	Jump
Look	*Tim*	*run*	Look
Run	and	Funny	up
Go	*up*	Jump	jump
Tim	go	*Sally*	*down*
Look	Up	Dick	look
Dick	*Oh*	Run	*see*
Spot	Go	*Down*	run
funny	down	Oh	*Jane*
down	*come*	Up	Jump
jump	run	*Go*	Down
Down	Puff	*and*	oh
Look	*funny*	down	*go*
Dick	jump	run	up

The instructions are equally simple. In the child's copy of the test, none of the words are italicized. The teacher calls out the italicized word in the first square of her *Guidebook* copy of the test, and the pupils underline the word they think is correct in that square on their papers. She does this with each square in each row, from left to right, until all the squares have been covered. Then she collects the papers and evaluates the results. Interpreting the errors is the most interesting part of the test because it exposes the worthlessness of the whole-word method as a way of teaching children how to read. The *Guidebook* says:

> If a pupil's score is low, the teacher should make a careful diagnosis of the errors and give the guidance necessary to reteach the words that were missed. . . .
> Suggestions for discovering the causes of error in word recognition and for correcting poor habits of word perception follow:

1. If the child has marked the word *oh* when *go* was pronounced, it is possible that he did not hear the word clearly. Check on his ability to hear and discriminate between sounds.

2. If the word *see* is marked for *run*, the child may be noting only the general configuration of a word. If he reads fairly well from the book, he may be overdependent on context clues or may remember the stories verbatim. One or both of the other words in each square of the test may resemble the word tested in number of letters, in length, in general form if superimposed, or in general form if reversed (as in the case of *go* and *up*.) If the errors indicate confusion of words similar in form in these respects, check on memorization of the stories and on habits of scrutinizing word forms. Tracing of large words placed on paper or on the blackboard, or letting pupils observe the teacher as she writes words will be helpful.

3. If the word *up* is marked for *down*, or *Go* is marked for *Run*, confusion in associating meanings with the word forms is revealed. If this tendency was not noted in reading from the book, the pupil may be overdependent on context clues or may have memorized the stories. Practice in reading from the chart or blackboard new sentences containing these words will be helpful. . . .

4. If *Jump* is marked for *Jane*, or *Dick* for *Look*, or if the words *Puff*, *jump*, and *funny*, or *down* and *and* are confused, the pupil may be directing all his attention to only one letter of a word. Note that these examples represent similarities in initial, final, and medial letters, as well as the mere recurrence of a given letter. Tracing words or observing words as they are written by the teacher may correct such confusions.

Of course, there is one sure way to correct such confusions: teach the child the letters of the alphabet and the alphabetic principle, and he will not mistake *up* for *down*, or *Dick* for *Look*. But that solution is much too simple for the authors of Dick and Jane. They would rather the child struggled with an impossible method and remained the unwilling slave of Dick and Jane indefinitely. Thus, the authors of Dick and Jane are willing to admit the kinds of incredible "reading" errors a child can make when being taught a sight vocabulary. Why not call a spade a spade? A child who cannot distinguish between *up* and *down* can't read. Whatever words he manages to distinguish correctly merely becomes a matter of expert guessing. It involves no reading skill at all. A sight vocabulary only serves the purposes of the publisher who wants to make children dependent on his books. The authors admit that some

68

of the errors might be the result of overdependence on context clues. But how do you make an overdependent child into merely a dependent one? How much dependence is good, how much is bad? The point is that the child need not be made dependent at all on any particular context for his ability to read. A sight vocabulary contributes nothing to the child's intellectual growth; in fact, it is a hindrance, a retarding agent, calculated to delay for as long as it suits the publisher, the pupil's ability to read independently.

Any school which insists that a child master a sight vocabulary before teaching him to read on alphabetic principles is not only wasting the child's time, but endangering his sound intellectual development. Teaching a child a sight vocabulary is, by definition, teaching him to recognize words without knowing the letters of the alphabet or their sound values. This makes it impossible for him to achieve any degree of reading proficiency and independence until he has the knowledge denied him. He becomes totally dependent on a set of books with a controlled vocabulary, thus limiting his reading scope to only those books containing those words he can recognize on sight or in a specific context. Placing such artificial limits on the young mind for no sound pedagogical reason is criminal. Placing such limits on the young mind for the sake of enriching a few authors and publishers is likewise criminal.

In the Dick and Jane program, the whole-word method does not end with the completion of the three pre-primers. The method is used through the primer and the subsequent readers in the series right up to the sixth grade. However, beyond the pre-primer and primer stage the method is augmented by the addition of so-called word attack skills. The authors of the Dick and Jane program admit that there are gross inadequacies in the whole-word method. They say so in the pre-primer *Guidebook* (p. 35):

> As the child's growing stock of sight words increases and carries him into wider reading at Book One level, he will inevitably encounter new words when the teacher is not at hand to tell him what they are. It is at this point that the effectiveness of a sight vocabulary breaks down and the need for word-attack skills becomes obvious. In The New Basic Reading Program the child is carefully guided first to develop a basic sight vocabulary and then to acquire skills and understandings that will give him new independence in word attack.

We shall examine these word-attack skills later in this chapter and see them for what they are: additional means for guessing at words rather than reading them. It is significant, incidentally, that the whole-word proponents should have concocted a phrase like "word attack" to describe what they do to words. If you can't recognize the word on sight, you "attack" it. You don't sound it out, decipher it, or decode it. You engage in an act of violence against it, as if the word were an enemy. Yet, there is no simpler way to figure out an unknown word than by separating it into syllables and sounding out each syllable in its proper order. You don't have to attack anything, and you don't have to remember much more than twenty-six letters and their forty-five sounds.

What is important to emphasize at this point, however, is that the acquisition of a sight vocabulary is not considered preliminary to learning how to read via alphabetic principles. As far as the authors of Dick and Jane are concerned, it is *the* basic way to read. This is made quite clear in Gray's own words in *On Their Own in Reading*:

> At the outset in learning to read, the child becomes familiar with symbols for words already in his speaking vocabulary by having the printed forms of the words presented to him as wholes in meaningful context. Words learned in this way are usually referred to as sight vocabulary. Obviously, . . . a child's success in reading depends upon his ability to master a basic stock of sight words. The necessity for building a sight vocabulary does not, however, end with the early stages in learning to read. Even though the method of learning new words as wholes is later supplemented by word-analysis techniques, the development of an ever-increasing body of sight words remains an important task throughout the primary grades.

Thus, the child is to be completely dependent, right through to junior high school, on controlled-vocabulary books, written essentially by the same authors who got him hooked on the first seventeen words. Gray makes that clear when he writes further:

> Clearly, the problem of developing mastery of sight vocabulary is not an easy one nor one that can successfully be met without the help of carefully prepared reading materials at all grade levels. To bring words first encountered as sight words to the level of instantaneous perception, we must give the child many opportunities to meet these words over and over in meaningful context. Thus there is a need for basic reading materials written with a con-

trolled vocabulary in which words, once they have been presented, are frequently repeated. . . .

Similarly, the desirability of exerting control over the number and placement of new words becomes obvious. When a new word that is introduced in basic reading materials is dropped in among familiar words, the meaningful context helps the child recognize it accurately each time he encounters it.

Obviously, the whole concept of "meaningful context" defeats the whole idea of learning how to read. You learn how to read on alphabetic principles so that you can decipher any word in any context or in no context. But if you are taught by whole words, books have to be printed to accommodate your limited ability to word-guess. Thus, a whole publishing industry, devoted to producing books with "meaningful contexts" for sight-vocabulary slaves, is created, and the authors, publishers, and salesmen share the prosperity of a captive market, made captive by an innocent-looking pre-primer of seventeen words.

Of course, when the child finishes school and is forced to read books or an insurance policy, or on-the-job training material in which he encounters new words in unfamiliar contexts, he is in trouble. The word-attack skills are supposed to come to the rescue, but if you've ever taught in high school and encountered some of these helpless sight readers struggling with unfamiliar words in an unfamiliar context you know that word-attack skills on top of a shaky sight vocabulary are not very effective. The child, having never learned to read by way of alphabetic principles, is simply lost and has already given up, not in the sixth grade, but in the third grade. Gray, nevertheless, is quite adamant about not making alphabetic principles the basis for reading, arguing as follows:

Unless the child has been taught some simple techniques of word attack, his only alternatives are to guess at the words, to seek out the teacher and demand help, or to skip the new words without attempting to determine what they may be. Since none of these ways of responding to unfamiliar words is satisfactory as a general method, the need for definite instruction in usable methods of word analysis is obvious. Skill in word analysis should be built on the basis of the child's experience with sight words. It is not necessary to give drill on meaningless word elements as has been assumed by those who have recently proposed teaching word analysis before actual reading begins.

71

In other words, the child's experience with sight words becomes the sole basis on which his word analysis skills are developed. He is never to learn how to read independently on alphabetic principles. The trouble with the whole-word method is that some children never really acquire a very efficient sight vocabulary on which their later "word-attack" skills can be developed. If a child does not master a sight vocabulary, as many children never do, he is lost, really lost. Gray writes:

> To give children real power in word perception, we must see that they master a sight vocabulary and we must also teach them how to attack new words in various ways. They must learn to combine meaning and word-form clues with a more detailed analysis of structural and phonetic elements in a word, and eventually they must learn how to use a glossary or dictionary.

The vocabulary test previously cited has already shown us some of the horrendous errors in reading some children make when learning a sight vocabulary. It has also revealed the weakness of the corrective measures recommended by the authors. Gray admits that "the problem of developing mastery of sight vocabulary is not an easy one." The truth is, and the rate of functional illiteracy proves it without a doubt, that many children *never* master an adequate sight vocabulary—a sight vocabulary that can take them beyond the controlled reading materials of the third or fourth grades. That is what functional illiteracy is all about: *the inability of about half the children taught to read via Dick and Jane to acquire an adequate sight vocabulary that can take them beyond the controlled reading materials of the third or fourth grades.* The tragedy is that no measures were taken in junior high school or high school to undo the damage done to these children in elementary school. Today, of course, children read only controlled-vocabulary books right through high school! The inadequacies of elementary training are perpetuated right through high school with new history and social science textbooks written with a controlled vocabulary, with literary classics rewritten by whole-word experts to accommodate the limited sight vocabularies of the students.

Gray's word-attack skills are woefully inadequate. For one thing, they place additional burdens on the child's already overburdened memory. If the child has had problems acquiring his sight vocabulary, the word-attack skills are like the Chinese torture: they compound bad teaching methods with worse teaching methods, expecting an already confused mind to absorb even more confusing "information." Let us scrutinize the word-attack skills as taught in the Dick and Jane program beyond the pre-primer level.

Assuming that a child has successfully mastered the fifty-eight-word sight vocabulary of the three pre-primers, he goes on to the primer, *Fun with Dick and Jane*. If he has had trouble mastering those first fifty-eight words, the publishers have provided a remedial primer called *Guess Who*, which more intensively tries to get the poor child to recognize and remember those fifty-eight words.

In *Fun with Dick and Jane*, a 157-page primer, the child has to learn to recognize one hundred additional new words, giving him a total sight vocabulary of 158 words at its completion. In the spirit of the controlled context, the first fifty-eight words are all reintroduced in the first forty-one pages of the primer, and the new words are introduced at a rate of one per page. There are the usual repetitions. Each word is used a minimum of twelve times in the primer.

When we examine the new words chosen for the primer, we can easily see that they too were selected because they best obscure the alphabetic principle. Of the hundred new words added to the child's sight vocabulary, only a few are related to one another, or to the already learned fifty-eight words, in spelling pattern. The child would have to be a linguistic genius to infer any phonetic principles from that list of words. One gets the impression from the choice of words that the authors were determined to deprive the child of any easy road to phonetic knowledge.

For example, out of the 158 words in *Fun with Dick and Jane* (1951 edition), we find the following groups of phonetically related words which have the same spelling patterns: *see, three; jump, bump; run, fun; Spot, not; go, so; can, ran; me, she, we, he; ball, all; duck, cluck; new, mew; cow, bow-wow, now; that, cat; black, Jack, quack; hop, stop; come, some.* But the child is also confronted with such irregular groups as: *two, to, blue, who; four, for; said, red; this, is; play, they; a, the; but, put; come, home; one, fun.* This deliberate mixing of words from regular phonetically consistent spelling patterns and those with irregular spelling or pronunciation patterns can only confuse the young child who is trying to organize in his mind the knowledge he must have to master reading. Add to this confusing mess single words like *pretty, hello, little, cookie, good-by, rabbits, friends, laughed, chickens*, etc., and the child is easily convinced that the groupings of letters in words have no consistency or logical meaning at all.

But since there are only twenty-six letters in our alphabet and about forty-five different identifiable sounds in our language, it becomes increasingly difficult to distinguish hundreds and hundreds of words without making use of a knowledge of the individual letters. Even the authors of Dick and Jane, much to their chagrin, realized that they would have to teach the child something about the letters, for the poor child could never remember the configurations of hundreds of whole words on visual or context clues alone. But you could be sure that they would give the child only enough information to keep him moving forward within the Dick and Jane strait jacket, never enough to get him out of it so that he could read anything he wanted independently. So in the primer the child is finally introduced to some of the letters of the alphabet.

He is taught the names of seventeen consonant letters and their sound values only as they appear at the beginnings of words. What phonetic value they have in the middle of words is neither considered nor discussed. The letter is taught merely as a phonetic clue to the word—one clue among several taught as word-attack skills. In fact, the child is not encouraged to use a phonetic clue until he has first exhausted context and word-form clues. If these fail him, then he is to try the phonetic clue of the initial-consonant sound. Here is how the first letter is introduced to the child in the Teacher's Edition of *Fun with Dick and Jane* (p. 75):

> Developing phonetic skills: This exercise is the beginning of a sequential program for helping children learn to associate the speech sounds with the appropriate letter symbols. This phonetic skill, known as visual-auditory perception, is essential for independence in both word attack and spelling. . . .
>
> To promote visual-auditory perception of the initial consonant *f*, write the following words in a column on the blackboard: *fun, for, funny, family*. Underline the word *fun*. Have the first two words pronounced and ask, "Do *fun* and *for* begin with the same sound? Now say the next word softly to yourself. What is it? Does it begin with the same sound as *fun*? What is the last word? Do *fun* and *family* begin with the same sound? Now say each of these words to yourself and think how each sounds. Do they all sound alike at the beginning? Let's look carefully at the beginning of each word. Do they all look alike at the beginning?"
>
> Comment, "All these words begin with the same sound; they also begin with the same letter. These words begin with this letter. (Write the letter *f* above the column of words.) The name of this letter is *f*."

Start a second column by writing the capitalized form *Fun* opposite *fun* and have both forms pronounced. Establish the idea that the two forms are the same word; then point to *Fun* and comment, "This begins with the letter *F*, too; but this (point to *F*) is a capital letter *F*." (Write *F* above the second column.) Then say, "I am going to write *For* and *Funny* and *Family* over here with a capital letter at the beginning of each." Have children pronounce each pair of words and compare the forms. Continue, "If words look like this (point to *f* at the top of the column) or like this (point to *F*) at the beginning, we say they begin with the letter *f*."

Write *Father* on the blackboard and remark, "Here is another word. What is it? Do *Father* and *fun* begin with the same sound? With what letter does *Father* begin?" Next write *yes*, have *yes* and *fun* pronounced, and ask pupils whether these words begin with the same sound. (It is unnecessary to call the letter *y* by name. All that need be said is that *yes* does not begin with the letter *f*; it begins with a different letter.) Continue with the words *For, Mother, here, family.*

Since the purpose of teaching the child the identity and sound of the letter *f* is merely to supply him with an additional clue to word-guessing, there is really no attempt in that lesson to teach the child how written words are built on alphabetic principles. The child is then introduced to sixteen other initial-consonant letters in the course of this primer, merely to supply him with phonetic clues. The use of consonants in the middle of words is not discussed. Thus, by the time the child completes reading *Fun with Dick and Jane* he knows the names and sound values of *b, c* (as *k*), *d, f, g, h, j, k, l, m, n, p, r, s, t, w, y* as initial consonants. He is not, incidentally, taught them in alphabetical order. He is introduced to them in this order: *f, b, m, c, w, s, h, t, r, g, y, n, k, l, p, d.* Naturally, if the child were taught the identities of the letters in alphabetical sequence, he would have to be made aware of the concept of the alphabet, and in the Dick and Jane program he is hardly ready for that. Thus, it can hardly be said that by introducing the child to the seventeen consonants only as they appear at the beginnings of words and in a completely arbitrary sequence, that the authors are anxious for him to gain any clear concept of the function and value of the alphabet. They are merely supplying more clues to word-guessing to bolster a method of word recognition that is so inadequate and so limited that the letters must finally be referred to. As yet, he knows nothing about the vowels *a, e, i, o, u* or the consonants *q, v, x,* and *z*. Thus, out of his sight vocabulary of 158 words at the completion of *Fun with Dick and Jane*, he can apply his phonetic "knowledge" to about seventy of the words which begin with one of the consonants learned in the course of reading the primer. But obviously, knowing the first letter of a word is hardly enough to be able to read it. The child still depends on the other clues used by sight readers.

Meanwhile, it should be emphasized that this fragmentary phonetic knowledge is given to the child in the overwhelmingly antiphonetic context of a sight-reading program. All of the new words in the primer are taught and learned as sight words, with lengthy, involved story interpretations accompanying each lesson, and there are as many exercises devoted to the memory of word-forms as to the developing of so-called phonetic skills.

There are, as a matter of fact, about fifteen additional types of exercises throughout the *Guidebook* to *Fun with Dick and Jane* promoting word-recognition "skills" which have nothing to do with phonetics. I will list them so that the reader can see what the pitifully inadequate and fragmentary phonetic exercises must compete with: 1. Comparing capitalized and uncapitalized word forms; 2. Memory based on observation, to promote the habit of careful observation of detail and attention to sequence for the purpose of remembering story plots; 3. Strengthening meaning associations through visual imagery; 4. Experiencing sensory images; 5. Strengthening awareness of correct language structure; 6. Comprehending sentence meaning, to strengthen the understanding that a sentence is a meaning unit and to promote ability to use context clues as an aid to word recognition; 7. Classifying, to strengthen the ability in simple classification; 8. Making judgments, to strengthen the ability to make judgments; 9. Memory based on sequence, to help children organize ideas for the purpose of remembering; 10. Recognizing motives of story characters; 11. Making inferences; 12. Formulating sentences; 13. Perceiving relationships, to strengthen the ability to recognize cause-effect relationships and to express these relationships in complete sentences; 14. Perceiving place relationships; 15. Memory based on association.

None of these exercises contribute in the slightest to the child's ability to read on alphabetic or phonetic principles. But the most antiphonetic exercises in the program are those devoted to the "memory of word forms." They tend to cancel out any understanding the child may acquire of alphabetic principles. A typical example is the word-form exercise on page 99 of the *Guidebook*. This is worth examining because it shows how these exercises negate the phonetic exercises given elsewhere in the book:

76

Memory of word form: To promote the ability to visualize word forms that begin with the initial consonants *f*, *m*, and *b*, suggest, "Close your eyes and try to see the word *big*. Is it a long word or a short word? Does it look like this at the beginning (write *m* on the blackboard), or does it look like this (write *b*)? Now close your eyes again and think how the word *big* looks." While the youngsters' eyes are closed, write *b--l* (ball) on the blackboard. Have children open their eyes. Then point to the *l* and ask, "Is this the way the word *big* looks at the end?" When everyone agrees that it is not, write the word *big*. "Does *big* look like this?" Return then to *b--l* and ask, "Can anyone think of a word that does look like this at the beginning and at the end?" When the word *ball* is given, fill in the missing letters. Next place *b--y* (baby) on the blackboard. "Can anyone think of a word that begins with *b* and looks like this at the end? (Point to *y*.)" Complete the word *baby*. Other words that may be used are *for, find, funny*.

Since the youngsters do not yet know any really long words beginning with *b*, the foregoing exercise simply strengthens ability to visualize the beginnings and endings of fairly short words. To carry this exercise a step further and bring out word length as a significant aid to memory of word form, write the following words in a column on the blackboard: *m-* (me), *M-----* (Mother). Point to *m* and *M* and ask, "What is the name of this letter? Now close your eyes and try to see the word *me*. Can you see it? Is it a long or a short word? Try to see the word *Mother*. Is it long or short? Now open your eyes. Who can show us where these words, *Mother* and *me*, will fit?" Complete both words. Below Mother write *m--e* (make) and say, "I am thinking of a middle-sized word that begins with *m* and ends like this. (Point to *e*.) Can you close your eyes and see a word like this?" Complete *make*. Then repeat the procedure outlined for *me* and *Mother*, using the following pairs of short and long words: *fun, Father; for, family*.

In a sight-vocabulary program, the size of a word, of course, is important. It is an aid to memory. *Big* is remembered as a little word and *little* is remembered as a middle-sized or big word, depending on what is considered big or middle-sized. In a reading program based on alphabetic principles, it isn't the size of the word that counts, but the number of syllables. *Big, ball, for, find, make* are all one-syllable words. You learn them as single phonetic or pronunciation units in easily identifiable spelling patterns. You don't divide them arbitrarily into three parts: a beginning, a middle, and an end. In that way you lose the entire concept of what a syllable is. For example, with the word *ball*, the significant phonetic components are the initial consonant *b* and the pronunciation unit *all*, which follows a common spelling pattern found in such words as: *all, ball, call, fall, gall, hall, mall, pall, stall, tall, wall*. But by drawing the poor child's attention to the initial consonant *b* and the final consonant *l*, you fragmentize the word beyond any phonetic recognition. In addition, you deny him the facility of learning a whole group of phonetically related words which follow a regular spelling pattern. The same is true of *make*, with its *ake* pronunciation unit, found in such words as *bake, cake, fake, Jake, lake, quake, rake, sake, take, wake*.

The important difference between *me* and *Mother* is not that *me* is short and *Mother* is long, but that *me* is a one-syllable word and *Mother* a two-syllable word. By fragmentizing *Mother* into three parts—*M* at the beginning, *r* at the end, and everything else in the middle—you lose the significance of its two-syllable construction. This arbitrary three-part division of all words, regardless of their number of syllables or pronunciation units is a pure sight-vocabulary invention, and serves no other purpose than to conceal from the child the alphabetic principles on which written words are constructed.

But again the authors of the Dick and Jane program reveal the shortcomings of their sight-vocabulary technique by openly admitting the kinds of errors children will make when taught to "read" by this method. This *Guidebook* also includes a vocabulary test similar to the one cited earlier, and here is what it says about interpreting some of the children's errors:

1. If the child has marked the word *run* when *fun* was pronounced, it is possible that he did not hear the word clearly. Check on his ability to hear and discriminate between sounds.

2. If the word *you* is marked for *yes*, the child may be noting only the general configuration of a word. If he reads fairly well from the book, he is overdependent on context clues or has memorized the text. One or both of the other words in each box of the test may resemble the word tested in number of letters, in length, or in general form if superimposed. If the errors indicated confusion in words similar in these respects, it would be wise to check on habits of scrutinizing internal characteristics of words and on directional procedure in reading.

3. If *funny* is marked for *family*, if *get* is marked for *eat*, if *pretty, little*, and *yellow* are confused, the pupil may be giving too much

attention to one letter of a word. Note that these words represent similarities in initial, final, or medial letters, as well as recurring letters.

Perhaps nothing better proves the value of knowing the alphabetic principles than the kinds of errors children make when trying to "read" without knowing them. In a whole-word program, nothing the child does can be completely right. If he diligently tries to remember the general configuration of a word, he may mistake *you* for *yes*. If he memorizes the text or becomes "overdependent" on context clues, he may fail to differentiate between similar-looking words out of context. The child has obviously tried hard to do as the teacher has told him, yet he has failed. What a disappointment this must be to the child. How is he to know how dependent he should be on context clues? He is expected to scrutinize the "internal characteristics" of words, to look for configuration clues in the middle if the initial and final letters are of no help. He does not know yet how to divide a word into manageable syllables or pronunciation units which he can easily read. Then, what about the child whose ability to "read" consists of nothing more than remembering one letter in a word? How much of a sight vocabulary can he master? Is he not doomed to illiteracy?

From the primer in the Dick and Jane program, the child proceeds to the Book One level, a reader entitled *Our New Friends*, written by the same group of authors responsible for the previous books. "The moment the child opens *Our New Friends*," states the introduction, "and sees the well-loved characters, Dick, Jane, and Sally, his feeling of security is strengthened." And well it ought to be, since the child has nothing to show for all of his previous labor except a shaky ability to recognize 158 sight words in a "meaningful context" and a detailed knowledge of the private lives of Dick and Jane. Let's face it. Without Dick and Jane, the child would be lost, and the authors and publishers know it because they deliberately arranged the program so that this would be the result.

"In the new *Our New Friends*," explains the introduction, "the 58 Pre-Primer words and the 100 Primer words are again carefully reintroduced and maintained. This book introduces only 177 new words, with no more than two new words on any given page." Thus, the "meaningful context" is maintained.

Again, the selection of vocabulary seems to be based on how well the new words conceal the alphabetic principle. Of the 335 words learned by the completion of *Our New Friends*, only about a third of them can be grouped as phonetically consistent with regular spelling patterns. The rest—two-thirds of the vocabulary—are single words which must be learned by sight without any phonetic clues, except perhaps by the identification of an initial or final consonant.

In *Our New Friends* the child enlarges his phonetic knowledge by applying what he knows about initial consonants to the ends of words. He is taught to substitute one initial consonant for another if the word "looks the same" in the middle or at the end. He learns to do the same type of substitution with the final consonant of a word if the word "looks the same" at the beginning. He is also introduced to two-letter consonant clusters representing one sound, such as *ch, sh, th,* and *wh.* He is still not taught anything about vowels or the function of consonants in the middle of words or about syllables. Many phonics experts consider it to be extremely bad phonics to teach children the sound values of letters without demonstrating their use in full syllabic pronunciation units. But in Dick and Jane, we must remember, a letter is merely a clue. So the child's "phonetic knowledge," by the time he completes *Our New Friends,* is still not sufficient to make him independent of Dick and Jane. At the same time he is still being given exercises in word-form memory, in which all words, regardless of their number of syllables, are fragmented into three parts, thereby negating the syllabic construction of words. The words are broken up and put together like jig-saw puzzles rather than looked at as sequences of decipherable symbols representing sequences of vocal sounds.

Again, the letters of the alphabet are brought in only as an aid to sight reading. The authors carefully avoid drawing the child's mind to an understanding of alphabetic principles. For example, there are many single words in that vocabulary list which could open the door to hundreds of additional words from their spelling families. One such word is *Dick,* which was introduced in the first pre-primer. Yet, words like *brick, hick, kick, trick, quick, pick, sick, tick* could have easily been introduced if the authors had wanted to take advantage of the alphabetic principle. The same could have been done with such words as *splash, dear, eat, came, nest, old, night,* and others from similar common spelling families. A few words are introduced in this manner, such as *last, let, take, sat,* and *book.* But they are introduced as words which can be recognized on sight if the initial consonant is substituted in an already known sight word such as *fast, get, make, cat,* and *look.* The child, as yet, has no clear idea of the sound values of the letters beyond the initial or final consonants. And he is still being taught to look at words as wholes.

Here is an example of some of the whole-word nonsense to be found in the *Guidebook* to *Our New Friends*. This memory of word-form exercise designed to promote "careful observation and visual imagery" of the words *way, man, last*, reads, in part, as follows (p. 72):

Point up specific details through such comments and questions as "One of these words has a letter below the line and no tall letters. Which word is it? (*way*) Close your eyes and try to see this word. One word has no tall letters, no letters below the line. Which one is that? (*man*) One word has a tall letter at the beginning and another tall letter at the end. Which word is it? (*last*) Close your eyes and try to see the word *last.*" Then erase all three words and ask, "Can you see the word *man*? Does it have any tall letters? any letter below the line? What letter is at the beginning? at the end? (Write *man.*) Can you see the word *last*? Does it have any letter below the line? Does it have any tall letters? Where are the tall letters? What tall letter is at the beginning? at the end? (Write *last.*) Now, can you see the word *way*? Does it have any tall letters? a letter below the line? Where? What letter is it? (Write *way.*)

This is the kind of pedagogical aberration you get when trying to get a child to recognize whole words by their configurations rather than by their spelling. *Man, last*, and *way* are simple words which can easily be learned if they are taught in conjunction with other words of the same spelling families, if the letters, their individual shapes and sound values are learned before whole words are taken up. But to teach a child to remember a word because one of its letters is tall or below the line is shoddy teaching at best. Yet millions of children have been subjected to such "teaching."

The test instructions in the *Guidebook* provide an insight into the kinds of errors the children are still making after the completion of *Our New Friends*. The authors suggest the reasons for some of the errors:

1. If the child has marked the word *find* when *five* was pronounced, it is possible that he did not hear the word clearly. . . .

2. If a child consistently makes such errors as marking *get* for *let* or *Tim* for *Jim*, he may be noting only the configuration of the last part of the word. More work should be given on noting initial consonants.

3. If *mew* is marked for *man* or *talk* for *take*, the pupil may be

directing too much attention to the initial letter of a word, and more practice is needed in careful observation of the beginning, middle, and end of word forms.

If *last* is marked for *lost* or *white* for *which*, the child may be using context clues effectively in reading but failing to perceive word forms accurately. In such cases, further work on careful observation of word forms is needed.

Notice that all of the corrective suggestions are for the teacher to teach more of the same nonsense. The child doesn't know whether to read a word from its end or its beginning. He must look for his phonetic or configuration clues wherever he finds them. No wonder remedial reading teachers are surprised when they discover that the failing child does not read words from left to right. How can he? He's looking all over the lot for tall letters, short letters, letters below the line, beginning letters, end letters—any clues that will give him enough of a hint as to what the word says.

4

Scrambling the Alphabet in Dick and Jane

By now Johnny has a sight vocabulary of 335 words; that is, he can recognize by word form and other whole-word recognition clues 335 words. The pre-primers gave him his first 58 words, *Fun with Dick and Jane* gave him 100 more, and *Our New Friends* added another 177. The next reader in the series is entitled *Friends and Neighbors*, written by the same group of dedicated authors. It is a second-level reader, first part, with an additional 229 new words, which, on completion, brings the child's total reading vocabulary to 564 words. It is, of course, not easy for a six- or seven-year old to learn 229 new sight words on top of the 335 he is still struggling to remember, and so the "meaningful context" or "controlled vocabulary" methodology is applied in this reader as it is in all of the other books in the series. The Teacher's Edition tells us (p. 268):

> No page introduces more than two of the 229 new words, and no new words are introduced in the first unit of the book. The first five uses of each of the 229 new words are bunched for easy mastery, with no gap of more than five pages between any two of these first five uses. At spaced intervals, at least five more uses of each word occur.

There is something new, however, in the way that new words are presented in this reader. Of the 229 new words, 137 are presented as sight words to be learned as wholes, while the other 92 can be learned either by sight or by applying some word-attack or word-analysis skill the child has learned. The *Guidebook* explains this departure (p. 69):

New words followed by an asterisk are words that pupils should be able to attack independently through phonetic and structural analysis. These words need not be presented as sight words. Under the heading "Application of Word-Analysis Skills," the method to be used as the basis of word attack is shown in parenthesis after the starred word.

Upon examination, however, it turns out that 90 percent of the words starred for attack are simple ones like *train, got, full, stop, stay, by* which can be learned by substituting the initial consonant in an already known sight word such as *rain, not, pull, hop, day, my*. This is assuming that the child can recognize a similarity in word-form between the known word and the new word. He still must learn words like *neighbors, balloon, telephone, handkerchief, people, Halloween, break-fast, potatoes, Christmas,* etc., as whole words. Considering how "phonetic skills" are arbitrarily introduced in the middle of remembering whole words, they may appear to hinder more than help. One wonders about the other word-analysis skills which the child is expected to apply. For example, the *Guidebook* suggests that the words *Tommy, Johnny,* and *digging* be "attacked" by pointing out that these are "root words" with the "final consonants doubled, plus suffix." When you consider how much the child has to remember, and how many different word forms already crowd his mind, you wonder what good it is to single out a few words among hundreds and draw attention to *their* double consonants when other words with double consonants are ignored. Also, why throw in the difficult concept of suffix before the child even knows what a syllable is? But this is typical of how phonetic knowledge is introduced in the Dick and Jane books, in a manner most likely to confuse the pupil and make it impossible for him to grasp.

In *Friends and Neighbors*, the child is finally introduced to his first vowel letters. The *Guidebook* details this momentous development this way (p. 126):

Phonetic analysis: To promote visual-auditory perception of the vowel *i*, both long and short sounds, follow these procedures:
1. Write the sentence *I like apples* and have it read. Ask a child to point to and pronounce the first word. Say, "This word has only one letter in it, and the name of the letter is *I*. Can you hear the

84

sound of this letter in the next word?" Then write *I* and *i*; at the left write in a column *find, side, high, white, tie, kind, sign, five.* Have pupils pronounce the words and underline the letter *i* in each. Explain, "Sometimes the letter *i* stands for the sound you hear in these words. We call this the 'long *i* sound.' "

2. Then explain that in many words the letter *i* stands for another sound. In a second column at the right write the words *in, is, it, if* and have them pronounced. Have pupils point to the parts of the words that look and sound alike. Then ask, "What is the name of this letter? Often the letter *i* stands for the sound you hear in these words. We call this the 'short *i* sound.' " To the second column add the words *did, thing, sister*; have them pronounced and the letter *i* underlined in each.

3. To give practice in discriminating between the long and the short *i* sounds, pronounce the words *fire, miss, string, right, fish, pile, mind.* Then ask children to tell whether they hear the long *i* sound or the short *i* sound in each word.

4. This step is designed to promote the ability to blend consonant and vowel sounds into pronunciation units. Write the unknown word *hit.* Explain, "The letter *i* in this word stands for the short *i* sound. What is the word?" Continue with *chin* and *hid.* Next write the known word *sat.* Tell pupils that you are going to make a new word by changing one letter. Change *a* to *i.* Explain that the *i* stands for the short sound. Have the word *sit* pronounced. Continue by rapidly substituting initial or final consonants as indicated: *sit, sip, tip, lip, hip, hid, lid.*

Next write the word *child.* Explain that in this word the *i* stands for its long sound. See whether children can pronounce the word. Continue with the words *wild* and *mind.*

This is a tremendous amount of phonetic information to cram into the child's head at once. Logic would dictate that the child master the more regular short vowel forms before tackling the less regular long-vowel forms. Besides why should the child bother to identify an isolated letter sound—vowel or consonant—in a word he supposedly can already read as a whole word? If he already knows the word by a word-form clue, he may be confused by having his attention drawn to a single letter for no particular reason that makes sense to him. Also, he is shown the long and short *i* in single words from so many different spelling patterns, that this will hardly help him to recognize the most common spelling patterns in which the long *i* and short *i* appear.

It should be remembered that this phonetic information is being given

85

for the purpose of providing additional word-recognition clues, not to establish any organized understanding of alphabetic principles or change the child's whole-word reading habits to new reading habits based on a mastering of syllabic pronunciation units. That is why the child must feel, when being given this phonetic information, that little, if any of it, will be very useful to him. Since the information applies to about 15 percent of the words in the total vocabulary of the book, most of which he has already learned as whole words, one wonders if the child will make the effort to understand what he is being taught when he is so busy trying to learn the word forms of 137 new difficult, multi-syllabic sight words. The phonetic information becomes just so much more miscellaneous information to file away in a mind already crammed with word forms, association clues, story details, and other aids to "reading."

Actually, there is more phonetic information in *Friends and Neighbors* than in all the previous books in the Dick and Jane series put together. But it is important to understand that this phonetic information is to supplement whole-word learning, not replace it. The *Guidebook* makes that clear when it states (pp. 50, 49):

> Mastery of a basic sight vocabulary is essential (1) if at early levels children are to read fluently and with enjoyment and (2) if children are to generalize principles of word attack.

And

> It is important that children be able to call up accurate visual images of known words from memory. The ability to visualize known word forms is essential to effective use of initial- and final-consonant substitution in attacking unknown words, because the new word must be compared with the child's mental picture of a word he knows.

In other words, the mastery of a sight vocabulary is still the basis on which everything else—including the phonetic elements—is to be learned. But as we noted in Chapter 3, the trouble with the future functional illiterate starts with his initial inability, for one reason or another, to master a sight vocabulary, making it impossible for him to integrate the phonetic and structural-analysis information he is given. He is trying to grapple with whole words as whole words. Now he is asked to look for arbitrary phonetic details in words which he is trying to remember

86

as wholes. Naturally, this will interfere with his other memory clues regarding a particular word.

In addition, the phonetic information is not made simple. He is told about the long *i* and the short *i* vowel sounds as they appear in a wide variety of spelling patterns all in one lesson. The other phonetic lessons are no better. For example, there is an exercise "designed to strengthen the concept of the *r* sound as a consonant blender and to develop the ability to use *r* blends in substitution" (p. 83). The teacher is then told to write the word *brown* on the blackboard, pronounce it, erase the initial letter *b*, substitute it with *c*, and have *crown* pronounced. The only thing wrong with that lesson is that the child hasn't learned anything about the vowel *o* yet, and he is looking at the word *brown* not as a sequence of phonetic elements, but as a pictograph, a whole word. For all we know, his way of remembering the word *brown* may be by the letter *w*, or the letter *r*, or the *b* at the beginning and the *n* at the end. Since there is no way of controlling what devices or gimmicks of memory a child will use in remembering any specific word, there is no way of knowing how the new phonetic information will be used by him.

The test results, of course, confirm this. The *Guidebook* tells us (p. 104):

> If a child consistently makes such errors as marking *get* for *let* or *Tim* for *Jim*, he may be noting only the configuration of the last part of the word. More work should be given in noting initial consonants.
>
> If *mew* is marked for *man* or *talk* for *take*, the pupil may be directing too much attention to the initial letter of a word, and more practice is needed in careful observation of the beginning, middle, and end of word forms.
>
> If *last* is marked for *lost* or *white* for *which*, the child may be using context clues effectively in reading but failing to perceive word forms accurately. In such cases, further work on careful observation of word forms is needed.

Again, the cure is no better than the disease—more exercises in word forms, in dividing one-syllable words into three arbitrary parts, in still looking at words as pictographs. Thus, despite the fact that *Friends and Neighbors* has more phonetic exercises than the previous books, the mistakes some children make are still as bad as those made on previous levels.

However, by the time the child has completed *Friends and Neighbors*, he is supposed to know the short, long, and variant sounds of vowels *i* and *a*, what happens to *i* and *a* when followed by various consonants, how *y* stands for *i* at the ends of some words. He also now knows that one of two like consonant letters in a word is usually silent, and how silent consonant letters like *gh* may be meaning or phonetic clues, or how silent vowel letters are visual clues to vowel sounds. He is also supposed to know about inflectional variants or derivatives formed by doubling the final consonant before an ending or a suffix, inflectional variants formed by changing *y* to *i* before an ending, and derivatives formed by adding the suffix *y* with no change in the root word. He also has had exercises in consonant substitution, consonant blending, and consonant and vowel blending.

The impression one gets in reading through all these phonetic and structural-analysis exercises is that the pupil is confronted with so many rules and exceptions to rules governing the sounds of letters, that he may decide that it is not worth the effort to learn them at all, especially since he can apply this knowledge to so few words in his reading vocabulary. Even an adult, thoroughly versed in phonetics, would find himself disturbed by the needless complexity of the presentation. It is needlessly complex because the authors are not interested in presenting the pupil with an organized approach to alphabetic principles. Their approach seems to be more designed to discourage mastery of the alphabetic principles rather than to facilitate it. But this is in keeping with their methodology from the very first pre-primer.

From *Friends and Neighbors*, the child moves on to *More Friends and Neighbors* and more of the same methodology. He is presented with 315 new words to add to his vocabulary, some to be learned completely as sight words, others to be "attacked" with the help of word-analysis skills. The latter are for the most part easy words that can be learned by initial or final consonant substitution, or vowel substitution. What is especially interesting about these 315 new words is that about two-thirds of them are the simple, regular, one-syllable words which a child usually learns in his first reading lessons in a program based on alphabetic principles. After struggling with such formidable sight words as *beautiful, breakfast, Christmas, Halloween, handkerchief, merry-go-round, neighbor, something, telephone, tomorrow*, and *umbrella*, the child is finally exposed to *bad, bag, bite, cap, dime, dust, face, fix, gay, hay, jay, lay, leg, men, need, pan, rub, sad, tap, wag, wet*, and over a hundred fifty other such words. The other third of the vocabulary consists mainly of regular two-syllable words like *became, chatter, even, follow, given, matter, oven, penny, river, sudden, won-*

der, etc. The child is also taught the rest of the vowel sounds in this reader.

It must finally dawn on some alert children that the spelling patterns of the English language are not quite as irregular and arbitrary as they had been shown to be in their first year and a half of reading. As a result, by the time the children reach the end of the second level of the program, they may indeed begin to grasp something of an understanding of alphabetic or phonic principles, despite the program's total emphasis on sight reading. However, it may already be too late for other children still struggling desperately to digest the first 564 sight words and thoroughly confused by the phonetic information fed them.

From *More Friends and Neighbors* the child moves on to his first third-level reader, *Streets and Roads*. By now he has a vocabulary of 879 words, mostly sight words known by their total word forms and not by their phonetic structure. The methodology of this third-level reader is basically the same as the previous readers, except that in this one child may be overwhelmed by the staggering amount of phonetic information presented to him. He is given 401 new words, 118 of which are sight words to be learned as wholes, the other 283 being "attack words" to be learned by applying one or more word-analysis skills in "unlocking" them. The introduction encapsulates the program's methodology:

> If the child is to be free to respond to the ideas presented in books, he must master an increasing stock of words that he can identify instantly, and he must have a growing ability to apply word-attack skills as a part of the total reading process. These goals can be achieved if sight words are carefully presented and all words are used many times in meaningful context, if the child develops methods of remembering word forms, if he grows continuously in his ability to use word-form and context clues, and if he develops efficiency in structural and phonetic analysis.

Thus, the emphasis, on the third level, is still on remembering word forms and using structural and phonetic knowledge as a supplementary means of reading. Whereas the phonics or linguistics methods teach a child to read by only *one* method, based exclusively on alphabetic principles, the Dick and Jane program teaches a child to read by several methods at once: by remembering the general configuration of a word, by knowing one or more of the phonetic elements in a word otherwise recognized by its general configuration, by knowing all of the phonetic elements in a word. Thus, the child must hesitate at each word he encounters in order to decide which "reading" method to apply to it. His mind is constantly shifting gears to find the right method or combination of methods to apply to the next word he sees. This is why children taught to read by whole-word methodology read with such hesitation and lack of fluency.

Spoken language is a stream of vocal sounds broken by meaningful pauses. Written language, as represented by letters arranged in sequential pronunciation units, is a symbolic representation of the same stream of vocal sounds, punctuated by the same meaningful pauses. When a child learns to read either by a phonics or linguistics method, he translates into vocal sounds a sequence of written pronunciation units, which he has learned to decipher first as single syllables, then as groups of syllables, until his reading pattern is as continuous as his speech pattern. True, when we are adult readers, we can scan a page of words quickly and skip what we don't want to read. But before we can do this we must develop the fluency which makes such quick comprehension possible.

The whole-word method makes it impossible to attain this fluency, simply because it concentrates on word forms and word-form details rather than on a moving sequence of easily learned pronunciation units. In whole-word methodology, a phonetic element is merely a word-form detail, a clue, not the basic element of words. It is extremely important to understand this distinction, because whole-word teachers will contend that they do teach phonetics, and indeed the second- and third-level readers of the Dick and Jane series will prove this. However, it is the way the phonetics is taught, in what context it is taught, and for what purpose it is taught that counts and makes the important difference.

A good example of how phonetics is integrated into whole-word methodology for the mere purpose of supplementing it is provided by a description of the "structural analysis" procedures given in the introduction to *Streets and Roads*.

Structural analysis is the means by which the child identifies meaning units or pronunciation units within a word. This type of analysis is based on visual scrutiny of the total word form. At preceding levels the child has learned to study the word form, looking for a meaning unit in it; this unit may be the root word, or a suffix. At Book Three level he learns to look for a prefix as a meaning unit, and he learns to look for pronunciation units—that is, syllables within the word whole. If through visual scrutiny he identifies a root word, prefix, or suffix as a meaning unit or if he identifies syllables as pronunciation units, he has analyzed the structural pattern of the word.

Thus, the child is expected in some instances to apply both whole-word and phonetic methods to the "reading" of a single word. In a method based on alphabetic principles, the word would be read phonetically from beginning to end, simplifying the entire process. All words would be read in the same phonetic manner, thus eliminating all of the complicated thought processes which are required of the child in "structural analysis." It is these thought processes which make children hesitate so often when reading via the whole-word method. They are stopping to think of how to "attack" the word, instead of just reading it one syllable at a time starting with the first. Some sight readers may eventually learn to do this. But many do not, as the early habits of looking at all words as wholes and remembering word forms is not easily discarded. Besides, since the pupil has 118 new sight words to learn in this reader, he is by no means encouraged to discard his word-form memory habits. The *Guidebook* describes how a pupil is supposed to combine word-form and phonetic methods in figuring out a word (p. 49):

> At preceding levels the child has learned to apply structural analysis to identify the root word in simple inflected forms and those in which the final consonant is doubled before an inflectional ending or suffix is added. For example, visual analysis of the total form of *flapping* reveals that it has an *ing* on the end. The child who mentally "takes off" the *ing* and notes the double *p* has identified the structure of the word-root with final consonant doubled plus an ending. He is then ready to apply phonetic analysis to the root word *flap*.

One could hardly think of a more complicated way to decipher the word *flapping*. In the first place, it requires the student to read the word from right to left, to start with the *ing* and work backward to the *flap*. Then, when the child gets rid of the *ing* and one of the double *p*'s, he is ready to "attack" the root word by applying phonetic analysis. Note how all this runs contrary to the idea that a word should be read from left to right. If the child had been taught at the start to look at words syllabically, as pronunciation units, by a phonics or linguistics method, he would have little trouble figuring out *flapping*. He would

91

not think in terms of "attacking" the word as if it were a difficult enemy, but deciphering it and getting to know it as a friend, easy to know and not withholding anything. He would read it, as it should be read, from left to right, recognizing immediately that *flap* is from the regular spelling and pronunciation pattern which includes such common one-syllable words as *cap, lap, map, trap, strap,* and that *ping* was from the *bing, ring, sing, thing* family. He would not look at the *ing* as an "inflectional ending" to a "root word," but as a simple pronunciation unit. Whatever other function the *ing* has in the word is irrelevant at this stage. And he would recognize the double *p* as a common spelling pattern, including a large number of words like *betting, petting, napping, snapping, Betty, petty, happy, snappy.* He would use the same method to decipher all words into vocal sounds, with only a handful of exceptions, too few to worry about. But the trouble with the whole-word method is that virtually every word must get exceptional attention.

It is in *Streets and Roads,* this third-level reader, however, where the mixture of whole-word and phonetic methods creates such confusion, complexity, and pedagogical chaos that many of the pupils simply stop learning to "read." They give up, and begin that elaborate game of avoiding the necessity to read, pretending to read, and getting through school the best they can without reading. Their lack of ability to read becomes a constant and potential source of embarrassment, a serious obstacle to scholastic achievement. Unless their parents find out about it or a teacher takes an interest in the child and recommends remedial reading, the child begins to enter a period of emotional troubles, delinquency, scholastic failure, or simple disinterest in school. In any case, he becomes the functionally illiterate adult of the future—an adult who cannot read material written above the fourth-grade level.

The reason why so many children cannot catch on to the phonetics is that the authors manage to create almost as many phonetic rules as there are words. So the child has the choice of trying to remember the word as a whole or remembering the phonetic rule applicable to the specific word. Thus, his memory is taxed regardless of the method he chooses with which to learn a word. It is true that most phonetic rules apply to large numbers of words, but in the whole-word method the child is exposed to such a small sampling of words illustrating any particular rule, that he simply cannot learn it well enough. In a method based on alphabetic principles, the sampling of words illustrating a particular phonetic formation is large enough and read often enough so that whatever the child is supposed to learn he learns well. That, of course, is the purpose of drill, which the whole-word proponents abhor. Yet, before a pianist can play a piece of music well, he spends years drilling the scales over and over again. The same is true in learning to read. One does not jump from illiteracy to literacy without the intermediate step of word drills necessary for making certain elementary phonetic knowledge automatic. To present the child with an endless list of phonetic rules with a few word samples to illustrate them will not teach him how to read fluently, particularly if the rules are negated by whole-word habits. Curiously enough, the whole-word proponents do not object to the constant repetition of a word as long as it is the same word. But to drill a child on common pronunciation units which enable him to learn hundreds of words easily and with a minimum of effort is considered abhorrent.

The reason why so many children break down in the third level is because, like Pavlov's dogs, they are confronted with conflicting instructions and information: explicit phonetic information which conflicts with what is now the implicit whole-word information of previous levels. Up to the third level they have been taught to look at words as wholes, to remember word forms, to see all words as having a beginning, a middle, and an end. They have been taught to use every device of memory in order to associate a printed word with a vocal word. We have seen by the examples of the vocabulary-test errors how inefficient memory can be in the process of acquiring a sight vocabulary. By the third level, the child has had to learn about 520 pure sight words and about 350 other sight words with the help of some phonetic clue or word-analysis skill. Thus, his total vocabulary of about 870 words is basically a sight vocabulary. It takes no great intelligence to realize that many six-, seven-, and eight-year-old children will have difficulty memorizing 870 words, regardless of what techniques are used. If the same feat would easily tax an adult's memory, it will certainly tax a child's. That is why in an alphabetic-oriented reading program, word drills in the early stages, when the child is learning the sound values of the letters, play so important a part in the learning process, in order to reduce the number of things a child must remember. By making responses to syllabic pronunciation units completely automatic, the child can reserve his memory for those exceptional and irregular formations which must be committed to memory.

The whole-word method, of course, tries to help a child acquire an automatic recall or recognition of a word through many repetitions in a controlled context. But the child is still learning only one whole word at a time and required to learn that word by its own total shape and, later on, by a phonetic clue or word-attack skill. Instead of repeating common syllabic pronunciation units which occur in many different words, the child must repeat each new word he learns over and over again before his recognition of it, based on memory and association use, will become instant and automatic.

However, on level three, the child is suddenly swamped with a heavy load of phonetic information, which basically contradicts every reading habit he has been previously taught. This in itself is bad enough, but nowhere is the child told that his reading habits are wrong. He still must use whole-word techniques to learn his 118 new sight words, and many of the 283 attack words which have root words he has already learned by sight or look like root words he already knows. But what is even more horrifying is that the phonetic information, as presented, is calculated to tax the child's memory even more painfully than it has already been taxed.

Let us review, first, how phonetic information has been given the child before the third level. No phonetic information is imparted at all in the pre-primers. The vocabulary, in fact, deliberately obscures the phonetic structure of written words. In the primer, *Fun with Dick and Jane*, the child is taught to identify seventeen consonant letters, as they appear at the beginnings of words, as phonetic clues. In *Our New Friends*, the first level, second part, reader, he is taught to identify the consonant letters as they appear at the ends of words. He is also taught to identify a few two-consonant blends at the beginnings and ends of words. The middles of words, however, are still a big mystery, and the remembering of word forms is still the child's basic way of acquiring his reading vocabulary.

So far, however, the phonetic information, which consists basically of identifying consonant letters and their sound values at the beginnings and ends of words, is consistent with the whole-word method of chopping words into three parts—beginnings, middles, and ends—regardless of their syllables or pronunciation units. In fact, the fragmentation, or mutilation, of words is continued with complete disregard for the phonetic structure of the word and in a manner to make the child not see it. This, of course, is consistent with the plan to keep the child locked in the series by the controlled vocabulary which runs through all of the books.

In *Friends and Neighbors*, the second-level reader, part one, the child is taught more two-consonant blends at the beginnings and ends of words, and there is still heavy emphasis on memory of word forms. However, in this reader the child is introduced to the vowels *i* and *a* in their short, long, and variant occurrences. These vowels and their sounds are taught as more phonetic clues, and their relation to the consonants that follow become "visual clues" to their particular sounds.

They are still not taught as syllables or common pronunciation units, but as vowels acted on by adjoining separate letters. Thus, the concept of a pronunciation unit is negated by the way the child is taught to regard the consonant as a visual clue to the preceding vowel. Of course, what the child is being taught is not wrong as phonetic knowledge. But as an aid to reading, it is the wrong approach. As a means of understanding vowel variants it is valid to an adult studying the phonetics of the English language. But as a means of teaching a child to read, it is much too complex and requires too much thought.

However, it is this adult approach to phonetics which the child is given throughout. For example, here are the phonetic rules the child is taught to remember in this second-level reader: one of two like consonant letters is usually silent; silent consonant letters may be meaning or phonetic clues; silent vowel letters are visual clues to vowel sounds (*a* followed by *i* or *y*); vowel letters stand for more than one sound; when *i* or *a* is followed by *r*, usually the vowel sound is neither long nor short; when *a* is followed by *l* or *w*, usually the *a* stands for the sound heard in *call* or *saw*; the letter *i* is usually used to represent an *i* sound in the middle of a word; the letter *y* is used to represent an *i* sound at the end of a word.

Thus, when a child encounters an *i* or an *a* in an unknown word, he must stop and think which rule applies, *if* he can remember the rules. Most likely he will not, if he is trying to remember the word forms of 500 words on top of that. He will try to learn the word by sight rather than apply a phonetic rule.

In a phonics- or linguistics-oriented reading program, the child learns to recognize a common pronunciation unit automatically without stopping to think of a phonetic rule. He has seen the spelling pattern of this pronunciation unit in so many simple one-syllable words that he easily recognizes it in a two- or three-syllable word. Since the printed word will already be in his speaking vocabulary, he will not have to rely on his knowledge of a phonetic rule to figure out the word, but on his ability to recognize a sequence of common pronunciation units which will sound like a word he already knows and makes sense in the context he is reading it.

In the second-part reader of the second level, *More Friends and Neighbors*, the child is introduced to the remaining vowels *e*, *o*, and *u* and confronted with more phonetic rules governing their variant sounds. His head is being filled with phonetic rules, but he is still looking at words as wholes, learning more sight words, and dividing words into beginnings, middles, and ends. He has been made aware of the alphabetical sequence, to prepare him for later dictionary skills. But he is still not aware of the syllable or the concept of a pronunciation unit. If a word is not divided into three parts, it is divided, via "structural analysis," between the root word—which is a meaning unit—and an inflectional ending, still consistent with whole-word methodology.

However, it is in the third-level reader, first part, *Streets and Roads*, that the child is finally told that there is such a thing as a syllable—a pronunciation unit—and for the first time he is made aware that long words can be divided into syllables, rather than beginnings, ends, and middles. Here is how the child is introduced to the syllable, two years after he has been "reading" multisyllabic words and compound words, and knows about sentences, root words, inflectional ends, contractions, and a host of interpretative skills. Here is the lesson in the Teacher's Edition (p. 94):

> Structural analysis: Structural analysis is the means by which the child identifies the parts of a word that form meaning units or pronunciation units within the word. At preceding levels in The New Basic Reading Program, the child has learned to identify derived or inflected forms of words and to identify a root word as a meaning unit within a whole word. He is now ready for the level where he learns how to determine, through structural analysis, the parts of the word that make up pronunciation units, or syllables. Unlike the structural elements in derivatives and compounds, the syllable forms a pronunciation unit but not a meaning unit in the whole word.

Let us stop and look critically at that paragraph. It is interesting that syllabication in whole-word methodology should come under the heading of "structural analysis" rather than "phonetic analysis." This is another arbitrary reorganization of knowledge in a way that can only delay or obstruct understanding. The syllable, the pronunciation unit, is the heart of the word. It is what the child must master before he can read anything fluently. That is why in phonics the child is taught to recognize and vocalize common one-syllable words and a host of nonsense syllables which later turn up in multisyllabic words *before* he is ready to read for meaning and enjoyment. In whole-word methodology, he has been "reading" multisyllabic words for two years without knowing that they are composed of pronunciation units. His mind has been directed toward interpreting literature before he knows the most elementary phonetic components of a word. Is that not really putting the cart a few miles before the horse? The lesson continues:

At preceding levels the child has learned to identify most of the vowel sounds in our language and to associate these with appropriate letter symbols. He has developed some understanding of how consonants and vowels function in our spoken and printed language and has learned to apply these understandings in attacking one-syllable root words. The same skills and understandings will enable the child to apply phonetic analysis to a syllable within a word.

It is important here to recall that the child was introduced to the letter sounds in a highly fragmented way: first initial and final consonant sounds, then vowel sounds in long, short, and variant forms, all in the context of already known whole words. The stress has been on the separate sounds of the separate letters, rather than on the sounds of the letters together, except in the case of consonant blends. The letters have been regarded as "phonetic clues." Let's see if there is an improvement in this approach. The lesson continues:

> To develop the ability to hear syllables and to promote the understanding that a syllable is a pronunciation unit, write the words *cap, me, go, not, bus, cut, it,* and *met* on the blackboard. Have pupils pronounce each word and tell what vowel letter they see and what vowel sound they hear in each. Through discussion develop the idea that there is at least one vowel letter and one vowel sound in every word in our language. . . .

You may ask, what's wrong with that? Nothing, basically, except that it should have been taught in the pre-primer or *Before-We-Read* stage, not now. The child is being told to look at words, which he already knows as wholes, as pronunciation units, as syllables. He may ask, "so what?" If he can already "read" these words by their configurations, the significance of this knowledge will escape him, because its usefulness will not be apparent to him. He learned to read these words without knowing that they were one-syllable, so why bother him about it now? He is already struggling to remember thirty-four new sight words introduced in this reader up to this lesson. Moreover, he is involved with "recognizing the emotional reactions of story characters," also part of the lesson. So, it is unlikely that he will consider the information being given of any importance. In a phonics course he would not have to contend with such distractions while learning the basics of reading. Also, when a child is taught to read by a phonics or linguistics method, the significance of what he is taught is apparent because it is put to immediate use and its contribution to the child's mastery is obvious to him. In this case it is not. Let us proceed:

Then write the words *same, sail, feet, seat, time, please, nose,* and *use* and have pupils tell how many vowel letters they see and how many vowel sounds they hear in each.

Write the word *baby*, pronounce it, and ask pupils to tell what vowel sound they hear in the first part of the word. Pronounce *baby* again and ask pupils to tell what vowel sound they hear in the last part (short *i*) [*sic*]. Repeat with *sandwich, fancy, yellow, tiny, funny,* and *hungry*.

Explain that a word or part of a word in which we hear one vowel sound is called a *syllable*. Review the first list of words (*cap, we, go,* etc.) and develop the idea that these are one-syllable words. Have pupils pronounce the second list of words (*same, sail,* etc.) and develop the idea that since we hear only one vowel sound in each, these are also one-syllable words. Review the third list of words (*baby, sandwich,* etc.), asking pupils to pronounce each word and tell how many vowels they hear. Develop the idea that if we hear two vowel sounds, the word has two syllables. Pronounce *night, Friday, bunch, bunny, hall, always, stick, picnic,* and *angry*. Have pupils tell how many vowel sounds and how many syllables they hear in each word.

Thus, the child has been introduced to the concept of syllable. Of course, this does not affect the way the child looks at the one-syllable words he already knows, or the new ones he's likely to learn. He still sees them as word forms rather than pronunciation units composed of a vowel, or a vowel and a consonant, or a vowel and several consonants. He is still being taught new multisyllabic words as sight words. Syllabication is merely taught as another attack skill, a convenient way to divide up a word so that it can be attacked by applying one of the child's growing number of phonetic rules. For syllabication to be of any use to him, the child must know these principles about vowels, which are taught him through a number of exercises in *Streets and Roads*:

A single vowel letter usually has its short sound unless it comes at the end of the word or an accented syllable.

If there are two vowel letters together in a word or an accented syllable, the first stands for a long vowel sound and the second is silent.

If there are two vowel letters in a word or an accented syllable, one of which is final *e*, usually the first vowel letter stands for a long vowel sound and the final *e* is silent.

If the only vowel letter in a word or syllable is followed by *r*, the sound of the vowel is usually controlled by the *r* sound.

The child is also expected to understand these principles regarding syllabication if he is to use syllabication in word attack:

In words of two or more syllables, one syllable is stressed or accented more than the other or others.

Accent affects vowel sounds in syllables.

In most two-syllable words which end in a consonant followed by *y*, usually the first syllable is accented and the second unaccented.

In variants and derived forms the accent usually falls on the root word.

If the first vowel letter in a word is followed by two consonants, the first syllable usually ends with the first of the two consonants.

If the first vowel element in a word is followed by a single consonant, that consonant usually begins the second syllable.

If the last syllable of a word ends in *le*, the consonant preceding the *le* begins the last syllable.

Thus, even if the child becomes proficient at dividing words into syllables, he must remember these generalizations. If he does not, then syllabication is not very useful to him. And it is obvious that many children will have trouble remembering these rules or generalizations, particularly if they have already had problems acquiring their sight vocabulary. Also, since each rule applies to only a handful of words in the child's vocabulary, he is not likely to burden himself with remembering them. These children will rely more and more on their brighter classmates to provide the answers when they need them. However, their ability to become independent readers is severely handicapped. They are not going to carry a book of phonetic rules around with them wherever they go, and if they have little reason to divide words into syllables, since they cannot put the syllables to use, they will continue to look at all words as wholes.

Thus, the extensive exercises in phonetics and syllabication throughout the *Guidebook* will not undo the bad habits inherent in whole-word methodology. In some respects they will reinforce them. The child will decide that it is probably easier to learn all words as wholes than to try and figure any of them out phonetically, except for simple consonant or vowel substitutions.

The phonetic principles cited above are not the only principles the child must learn if he is to become efficient in "independent" word attack. He must also apply "structural analysis" in attacking new words. He must know how to recognize words formed by doubling the final consonant, dropping the final *e*, or changing *y* to *i* before adding an ending or a suffix. He must know how to recognize contractions, as well as words formed by adding such prefixes and suffixes as *un-, -y, -ly, -er, -ish, -ful*, etc. He must know how to identify root words in inflected and derived forms.

"Word attack" is not all the child must be concerned with in reading on the third level. Understanding the story is considered as important as reading the words, and in each lesson from one-half to two-thirds of it is devoted to the development of interpretive skills. Here is a list of such skills with which the child must concern himself:

Interpreting the main idea.

Recognizing emotional reactions, motives, and inner drives of story characters.

Interpreting ideas implied but not directly stated.

Making inferences.

Recognizing story or plot structure.

Comprehending phrase and sentence meanings.

Interpreting figurative, idiomatic, and picturesque language.

Forming sensory images: visual, auditory, kinesthetic, touch, smell, taste.

Anticipating outcomes.

Identifying and evaluating character traits.

Making judgments and drawing conclusions.

Generalizing.

Perceiving relationships: time, place, sequence, part-whole, cause-effect, class.

Comparing and contrasting.

Rereading to locate specific information, verify an opinion, or prove a point.

Identifying and reacting to the mood or tone of a passage, story, or poem.

Projecting idea, mood, or tone in oral interpretation.

Strengthening memory based on: observation, association, visual imagery, auditory imagery, sequence, cause-effect relationships, part-whole relationships.

Summarizing and organizing ideas for the purpose of remembering.

I have listed all of these skills to make the reader aware that the third-level child at whom all this is being thrown is, at the same time, just being introduced to the concept of alphabetical sequence and to that of the syllable! One could hardly imagine a greater pedagogical *mis-*organization than this. For the child it means intellectual chaos, and we cannot blame him for failing to make heads or tails of what he is supposed to be learning.

5

The Making of a Dyslexic

From *Streets and Roads*, in which the child is virtually buried in an avalanche of phonetic rules, we go on to *More Streets and Roads*, the third-level, part-two reader of this basic reading program. This particular reader has 498 new words, 357 of which are "attack" words, with the remaining 141 to be learned as pure sight words. All of these words when learned will give the child a total reading vocabulary of 1,778 words. It should be noted at this point that the child, at the completion of this reader, will be burdened with remembering the word forms of about 625 pure sight words, as well as the word forms of about 1,100 attack words, most of which required a knowledge of an already known sight word in order to have been properly "attacked." For example, many of the attack words are learned by simple consonant or vowel substitution of an already known sight word. Thus, most of the child's vocabulary at this point has been acquired by pure sight learning, which depends entirely on the memory of word forms. If a child has a weak or even a normal memory, his "reading" ability will show it.

As noted in the previous chapter, the acquisition of attack skills also relies almost entirely on memory: remembering a large number of somewhat complicated phonetic rules which govern letter sounds, inflectional endings, etc. Thus, again, the child with a weak memory will have difficulty learning these rules on top of the sight words he must also remember. Taxing a child's memory so greatly in the early stages of development is extremely poor pedagogy and leads in so many cases to disastrous results.

In *More Streets and Roads* the same methodology is employed with the same intensity. The sight words are learned by remembering their overall forms, the attack words are learned by applying a phonetic rule or principle of "structural analysis" if one can remember the right rule. There are exercises in syllabication, in the use of visual clues in determining accented syllables in unknown words, in prefixes, etc. An exercise in the Teacher's Edition, on two-letter consonant symbols (*th, ch, sh*) is supposed to lead pupils "to form the generalization that when the first vowel element in a word is followed by a two-letter consonant symbol, this symbol is not broken when the word is divided into syllables and may go with either the first or the last syllable" (p. 199). How a child is supposed to remember that generalization while at the same time remembering over a thousand whole words and the many details of a story interpretation, we are not told.

A typical lesson in this reader can be found on pages 79 to 86 of the Teacher's Edition. The story is entitled "A Great Day of Long Ago" and is about the visit of President-elect George Washington to a small town. The hero of the story, a small boy, is given the task of dropping a crown of leaves on the President's head as he passes under a big tree. The story itself is interesting, simply written, and runs for eight pages in the reader, with five full-color, half-page illustrations. The pupil is introduced to fourteen new words in this story: seven as sight words, and seven as attack words. The new sight words are: *journey, president, Washington, soldiers, visitors, women, direction*; the new attack words are: *greet, hail, Betsy, candles, fresh, flags, sir*. The sight words, which must be memorized on the basis of their whole forms, are clearly the more difficult. Of the attack words, *greet* and *hail* are to be attacked by figuring out the sound of the two vowel letters together; *Betsy, candles, fresh*, and *flags* are to be attacked by noting the "position of single vowel letter," and *sir* is learned by remembering the generalization about what happens to a vowel sound when it is followed by the consonant *r*. Since the child must learn seven rather complex words by sight, we can assume that some children will dispense with the attack procedures and learn the attack words by sight as well, since they are simpler than the sight words. In other words, there is no real control over how pupils will learn the fourteen new words in this story. They will learn them any way they can.

The first page of this lesson is devoted to establishing the story background and presenting the new vocabulary. The next four full pages are devoted to interpreting the story in profuse detail. Then follows a half-page exercise in "perceiving relationships." The apparent purpose of the exercise is to help pupils determine what came before and what came after, for example, "the year 1953 or the year 1945" or what invention came first, the truck or the airplane. "Such discussions are sure to stimulate pupils to talk with older people about life in earlier times and to share their findings with the class," theorizes the *Guidebook*. After this an exercise "combining structural and phonetic analysis" runs for about three quarters of a page. The *Guidebook* states: "This exercise strengthens the concept that the soft, unstressed vowel sound known as the 'schwa' is heard in the unaccented syllables of most words in our language. It also promotes the understanding that the syllable *tion* is unaccented and is pronounced shan or chan." The phonetic symbol a is used for the schwa sound in a number of dictionaries.

After this phonetic exercise there follows another under the heading of "Meeting individual needs," in which is reviewed "the basic understanding that the visual clue to the vowel sound follows the vowel letter in a word or syllable." This exercise runs for about a third of a page. Then comes a reference to an exercise in the *Think-and-Do-Book* which "emphasizes the importance of using picture details as an aid to visualization."

Then there is a full-page section on "extending interests." Half of this is devoted to "enjoying literature" by suggesting other books which the pupil might read about George Washington, and the other half suggests how to arrange an "Early-Days Corner" in the classroom in which the children are to display old kitchen utensils, relics, keepsakes, and other "unbreakable objects belonging to their families and friends." All of this is to enhance an understanding of earlier times.

Thus, of a lesson comprising almost eight full pages in the *Guidebook*, about a page is devoted to the phonetic structure of words, and that exercise is far above the rest of the lesson in complexity and difficulty. It is completely adult in approach, whereas everything else is appropriately scaled to the mind of the third-level reader.

Thus, from the very first lesson in the first pre-primer, in which as much of the lesson was devoted to interpreting the story as to the learning of vocabulary, to this lesson in the third-level, part-two reader, we find that whole-word methodology is pursued with a consistency and pattern that is both unrelenting and uncompromising. The child never learns to read on alphabetic principles. He must rely more and more on his memory, and apparently, for the future functional illiterate, the memory breaks down in the fourth grade. The child's mind can absorb just so many sight words. He cannot remember enough of the rules and generalizations of phonetics and structural analysis to develop the "attack" skills required to increase his reading abilities beyond the fourth grade.

The child's problem is also compounded by the fact that in the fourth grade he must use arithmetic, science, history, geography, and social science textbooks in addition to his readers. William Kottmeyer, assistant superintendent of instruction in the St. Louis public schools, in his *Teacher's Guide for Remedial Reading*, describes the impact of this problem when the child with reading difficulties enters the fourth grade and is confronted with so many new books:

> These textbooks suddenly multiply the vocabulary with which the pupil must deal. They have relatively uncontrolled sentence structure and are predominantly expository, in contrast to the primary readers, which are entirely narrative. Now these pupils can no longer get by on sight vocabulary alone; and, if they have not mastered the word perception skills the primary readers were to produce, they are in trouble. Their handicaps are sometimes further obscured because many middle-grade teachers depend heavily upon silent reading assignments and do not quickly discover the appalling helplessness of their pupils with books.

Thus, the fourth grade is the turning point in the scholastic career of the budding functional illiterate. Now that we've reached that point, let us review everything in the methodology which makes this result not only possible but inevitable. First, there is the lack of instruction in learning the letters of the alphabet, their names and shapes, or their sound values as a preparation for learning how to read whole words. This contributes to later confusion and inability of many children to differentiate between such similar letters as *d* and *b*, or *p*, *g*, and *q*, or *f* and *t*. Second, there is the deliberate obscuring of the alphabetic principle in the very choice of pre-primer vocabulary, which includes some of the most highly irregular words in the language. Third, the child is taught to look at a word as a whole, not as a sequence of letters with sound values. He is taught to divide words into three parts—beginnings, middles, and ends—which further obscures the phonetic structure of words. He is supposed to remember word-form details without a knowledge of the separate letters and their shapes. This cultivates the habit of looking at words from all directions, thus contributing to his later failure to read words from left to right. Fourth, the great emphasis on story and picture interpretation distracts the child from the sufficiently difficult task of mastering words. Fifth, an unconscious taboo against the alphabetic principle is inculcated as the letter names are

106

studiously avoided and not mentioned in the pre-primer stage, although the child may want to know them. None of the experts has yet identified or evaluated the psychic damage done by this deliberate withholding of information which would facilitate the child's understanding of the alphabetic principle. Some children are extremely susceptible to subliminal suggestion, and the implicit suggestion that they must not learn the letters may become embedded in their unconscious, creating a later resistance to learning the alphabetic principle on their own. Sixth, the child is taught about whole words and sentences before he knows anything about individual letters, thus reversing the natural and logical order of learning. Making the child master the complex before he has mastered the simple only contributes to his confusion. Seventh, he is deliberately made dependent on a controlled context for his ability to read, which makes him insecure and helpless when confronted with books without a similarly controlled context.

Already, in the pre-primer stage alone, we have enough to set the child on the road to functional illiteracy and dyslexia before we even get to the attack skills. The pre-primers, with their first fifty-eight sight words, inculcate all the bad habits the child needs to prevent him from becoming a good reader.

When he gets to the primer he is finally introduced to the names of seventeen consonant letters and their sound values merely as phonetic clues to whole-word reading. The phonetic structure of a word beyond its first letter is ignored. He must still rely on the memory of word-forms to increase his vocabulary. In the Book One reader, the child is taught how to apply his knowledge of consonant letters to the ends of words, and he is taught the sounds of initial and final consonant clusters. The child is still using consonant letters as phonetic clues to whole words.

Not until the Book Two level does the child encounter his first vowel letter. He already has had to learn 335 words by sight without knowing about vowels. These vowel letters and their sounds are given the same function as the consonant letters in this whole-word context: that is, as phonetic clues. By the completion of the second-level readers, the child has been taught the identities and sound values of all the letters of the alphabet. But as yet he only knows them as phonetic clues to whole words. The alphabetic principle behind the structure of all words is still unknown to him. He is still being given exercises in remembering whole word-forms. He does not yet know what a syllable is, although by the completion of the second level he has ostensibly increased his sight vocabulary to 879 words.

Finally, at level three, he is introduced to the concept of the syllable, the pronunciation unit, and the rules governing the syllabication of words. After two years of dividing words into three pictorial parts, he is told of a new way to divide words that conflicts with the old way. Since the child, on the third level, is still required to learn new words by sight, he cannot possibly abandon the old way of dividing words. Thus, the child is placed in the unenviable position of having to comply with two different methods of looking at words and wondering which to choose. It should not be forgotten that while he is trying to retain old sight words and learn new ones, remember a host of phonetic rules governing letter sounds as well as trying to apply the rules of syllabication to word attack, he is still spending most of his time interpreting the stories. His confusion is undoubtedly obscured by the method's great preoccupation with story interpretation. Confusion begets confusion. And, by the time the fourth level is reached, the child whose memory cannot keep up with the additional burdens placed on it simply gives up.

Of course, some children give up even before the fourth-grade level. These children become known as "dyslexic"—a fancy medical term coined especially to describe the perfectly normal, intelligent youngster who can't learn how to read by the whole-word method.

As we commented earlier in this book, what is surprising is not how many children fail to learn how to read by the whole-word method, but how many succeed. The latter are usually children with very good memories, or photographic memories. However, success in reading is a highly disputed concept. Whole-word experts measure success according to their own standards. If a child can successfully read the controlled vocabulary of his reading level, that is considered success. But what if we applied more demanding academic standards? Would these same "successful" readers be as successful? In the last ten years, the entire reading content of secondary education has had to be scaled down to reading levels considered "successful" by whole-word standards. But are these standards adequate? A report in the *New York Times* of February 3, 1972 sheds some light on the problem. It concerns a survey conducted to find out how well young people write. Its relevance to reading ability is obvious, but more important, it reveals the difficult problem of setting standards of judgment when standards in general are deteriorating. Here is the article:

Washington, Feb. 2—Young Americans' mastery of the form and mechanics of written English ranges from adequate to almost nil, according to the first nationwide survey attempt to find out how well Johnny can write.

The finding is contained in the latest report of the National

Assessment of Education Progress, a series of studies described as a censuslike survey of "what Americans know and can do." The project was initiated and is financed by the Federal Government. The writing report, made public here today, makes the following assertions:

Nine-year-olds show almost no command of the basic writing mechanics of grammar, syntax, vocabulary, spelling, sentence structure and punctuation.

By the time most students reach the age of 17, their mastery has improved markedly. More than half of the 17-year-olds display a "sound grasp of the basics of written language," except for spelling and word choice. Only 15 per cent show a serious lack of ability in those basics. But even the best teen-age writers seldom display any special flair or facility by moving beyond "basic constructions and commonplace language."

Young adults of 26 to 35 show markedly better ability in the rudiments of written expression than the teen-agers. But while the best adult writers use a sophisticated and precise vocabulary, their constructions are usually simple, basic and somewhat journalistic in style, reflecting, perhaps, the influence of mass media.

The findings were based on uniform writing exercises administered during the 1969-70 school year to 86,000 children aged 9, 13 and 17 in 2,500 schools in every section of the country and to nearly 8,000 young adults in their homes. The sample was intended to represent accurately the nation as a whole.

The results were not broken down on the basis of race, sex, region or type of community, but a future report is to deal with such matters.

"Only four or five people in the whole assessment had a really good command of the English language," said Dr. Henry Slotnik, the author of the 150-page report, at a news conference in the Sheraton-Carlton Hotel.

He said he meant that these writers were not limited to simple construction and that they demonstrated flexibility and judgment in matching constructions and words precisely to the thoughts they wanted to convey.

An earlier report on the overall effectiveness of written communication, based on the same survey, found that although students could generally write adequate business letters and personal notes, their writing usually lacked imagination, vitality and detail. . . .

The report on writing mechanics was criticized by Dr. John Maxwell, assistant executive secretary of the National Council of

Teachers of English, who was one of five expert panelists who commented on the findings here today.

He said the writers in the sample had had no particular reason for writing what they were writing, that they were not instructed to edit or proofread their work and that the results therefore might not reflect the writers' best efforts. Consequently, he said, the findings of the survey should be interpreted cautiously.

In the writing exercises, 9-year-olds were shown a picture of a forest fire and given 15 minutes to write about what they saw or imagined: 13-year-olds and 17-year-olds were asked to write about a person they admired.

Young adults were asked to write a letter to a public official opposing or supporting a proposed highway interchange for their community. The teen-agers and adults had 30 minutes to complete the exercise.

The exercises were scored on over-all quality and specific writing mechanics by English teachers.

The scoring was said to have shown steady gains in writing ability as children grew older. No opinion was offered as to whether this was because of schooling or maturation.

The following samples from the writing exercises were adjudged as being among the best in their age categories:

Nine-year-olds—"A man was in the forest he was smoking a sigar. Then he dropped it. He did not know it starled a fire. First it got big and bigger and all at once gave a big boom. All the forest animals tried to get away from the fire, some did and sone did not."

Thirteen-year-olds—"I admire Glen Cunningham because when he was little he burned his leggs in a school trying to get his brother out. Most kids when they get hurt they will acept what the doctor says about it."

Seventeen-year-olds—"The first person that comes to my mind is a man who the whold school loves as I do, a man who can stand the pressures of sports, a man tough as nails, a man to whom failure is unknown; Central High Schools own Coach Paul Baldwin."

Young adults—"As a resident of Windsorville, Va., I would like very much to express my views concerning the proposed additional interchange on the expressway between Market Beach and the State Capitol."

All errors are as they were in the original text.

The worst papers, especially in the younger age groups, were described as "all but unintelligible."

Obviously success is a relative term when you ask, "according to whose standards?" The best writings in that survey were simply the best in that group. But did they measure up to any particular standards of excellence? The same could be said of reading. A successful reader, based on whole-word standards, would not be considered a successful reader on phonics-based standards. This writer's teaching experience bears this out. For eighteen months during the years 1970 and 1971, I served as a substitute English teacher in the high schools and junior high schools of a large Boston suburb. After listening to hundreds of students read, I concluded that there were basically three kinds of readers in my classes. There was, first, the small minority of very good readers, those who read very fluently with virtually no errors of any kind. Then there was another minority at the other end of the scale, those who read very poorly, bordering sometimes on illiteracy.

The majority, however, were in the middle. They seemed to read with an adequate speed, but they made many errors along the way. They would drop words, read words that weren't there, sometimes rearrange the words in a sentence. They were never aware of their errors and never stopped to correct themselves, unless someone was there to point out the errors. If not, they would read on, even when their error altered the meaning of the sentence. My point is that these readers were considered successful by whole-word standards. But they could not compare in quality with that small minority at the top who read fluently and accurately. Since I did not know how any of these students had been taught to read in the first three grades, I could not attribute their present abilities to any method. However, the errors the majority of the middle group made were typical of whole-word reading habits. Since these students were of an age-group which had been predominantly subjected to a Dick and Jane type of program, one could assume that their reading carelessness was a result of sight-vocabulary training.

I was inclined to believe that the fluent minority on top had been taught to read by phonics. I could tell by their inflections and rhythms that they read in that continuous unbroken stream of sounds which can only be achieved by learning to read words as a continuum of pronunciation units.

Although some children learn to read adequately according to whole-word standards, a significant number of normal, intelligent youngsters never learn to read by the whole-word method and consequently must be given special remedial reading courses if they are ever to advance scholastically. These children are known as *dyslexic*, and their symptoms will not seem strange to anyone who has read the preceding three chapters carefully. In fact, chances are that any normal child who is taught to read by the method described earlier would emerge dyslexic to some degree. According to Dr. Rudolph F. Wagner, in his *Dyslexia and Your Child: A Guide for Parents and Teachers*:

> The overt symptoms of a child with a specific reading problem are known to anyone concerned with the education of these children: they are poor readers in spite of good intelligence; they are easily discouraged by their failures; they often reverse letters and whole words; they are sometimes held back a grade in school; they are not disturbed in the pathological sense; they are usually in as good health as most of their classmates; and they have no access to the world of the written word with its literary treasures.

He then cites a case history:

> The story of Henry and his reading problem is typical of many youngsters in this country and abroad. Henry had normal intelligence, a healthy body, concerned parents, formal reading instructions in school, a nice teacher—yet he could not learn how to read.

Note how casually Dr. Wagner glides over "formal reading instructions in school." If Henry reverses letters and whole words, maybe it is because he hasn't had sufficient instruction in identifying the individual letters of the alphabet. If taught to look at words as wholes, the errors of the dyslexic child are the errors of a child with a poor memory compounded by poor instruction. How many are there like Henry? According to Dr. Wagner:

> Statistical surveys tell us that the percentage of children like Henry ranges anywhere from 3 to 5 percent of the entire school population in the United States, excluding the illiterates found among adults, and some surveys place the figure as high as 40 percent, depending on how the term *reading problem* is defined.

The dividing line between the functionally illiterate and the dyslexic is very fuzzy. In fact, the experts on dyslexia have difficulty identifying the "illness." As Dr. Wagner notes:

> Professionally used diagnostic categories likewise are myriad and colorful, to say the least: dyslexia, alexia, learning disability

112

(congenital or developmental), aphasoid, language impairment, strephosymbolia, and many more. To top it all, we even find a fancy Latin name, *amnesia verbalis visualis*, a sort of forgetting visually presented words.

In other words, if you have difficulty remembering your sight vocabulary, your whole-word expert will say you are afflicted with a terrible condition known as *amnesia verbalis visualis*! Dr. Wagner cites another symptom:

> The child shows poor ability to associate sounds with corresponding letter symbols. He knows and speaks the "hissing sound," *s*, but cannot relate it to the letter S.

Maybe the child was too busy "interpreting literature" the day the class worked on the *s* consonant. Maybe his teacher didn't stress phonetic clues too strongly. Dr. Wagner, however, like all the experts on dyslexia, tends to look more deeply for the causes of such symptoms:

> Beyond the observation that children with reading problems have larger numbers of reversals than normal children it is further assumed that the cause of reversals in poor readers may be due to perceptual difficulties, lack of spatial orientation, and possibly underlying neurological deficiencies of a milder borderline nature.

What Dr. Wagner doesn't seem to understand is that when a child is taught to read whole words without first being taught the identities and names of the individual letters constituting the words, he will *inevitably* have problems differentiating similar-looking letters in whole words, particularly if he has no idea that the letters have sound values and are not just arbitrary markings on paper. After all, why be so fussy about the minute details of the individual letters when all one needs to remember a word is one clearly recognizable word-form clue?

We get another bit of enlightenment about dyslexia from another book, *Developmental Language Disability: Adult Accomplishments of Dyslexic Boys* by Margaret B. Rawson:

> The term "dyslexia" is used here in its extended meaning, as synonymous with "specific developmental *language* disability," called "strephosymbolia" (twisted symbols) by S. T. Orton because of the prevalence of orientation and sequence confusions among the

persons we now call "dyslexic." Or, as a ten-year-old rendered it with Anglo-Saxon simplicity, "What's *wrong* is my *words*. I forget them!"

We have commented on the incredibly heavy burden the whole-word method places on the memory of young children. Yet dyslexia experts seem to be unaware of this. Miss Rawson made her study of dyslexic children in a private "progressive" school in Pennsylvania, and describes the teaching methods used:

> Reading instruction offered in the classrooms from 1930 through 1947 was based on the commonly used experience-chart and sight-word method, with some phonetic instruction always included. In practice the methods used in the early grades were almost identical with those now generally recommended in texts on beginning reading with basal readers.

With that she dismisses the problem of methods. She did not look for the cause of dyslexia in the teaching method itself. Instead, she concluded that dyslexia was caused by a "neurological organization factor, often familial."

Some of the most interesting writings on reading disability came out of a conference on dyslexia held at the Johns Hopkins Medical Institutions in 1961. The results of that conference were compiled in a volume entitled *Reading Disability: Progress and Research Needs in Dyslexia* edited by Dr. John Money, head of the Johns Hopkins Reading Clinic. Among the papers included was one by Roger E. Saunders, a psychologist, who offered the best description of the symptoms of dyslexia I have found:

> It is not uncommon to find, particularly in dyslexic children below the fourth-grade level, regardless of their age, words read in reverse, for example *was* as *saw*, *on* as *no*. A single letter may be reversed, as in *dig* for *big*. Often also there may be a transposition of some of the letters within a word, for example, *abroad* for *aboard*, *left* for *felt*, *how* for *who*. General confusion of words which have only a slightly different configuration abounds, for example *through, though, thought*, and *quit, quiet, quite*. . . . Guesses are frequent, in view of the inability to handle the sounds-symbol system. They grasp for the meaning of unknown words on the basis of a few clues the rest of the printed material has furnished. It

114

is also possible that, while working out a difficult word, there may be such a long pause that the meaning of the previously read words will escape them.

What Saunders so accurately describes are the usual kinds of errors any normal child is bound to make when taught to "read" by the whole-word method. If you haven't been taught to read by the sound-symbol system, why should you be expected to do so? The assumption is that children figure it out for themselves if they are not taught it. But as we have seen, whole-word methodology creates obstacles to learning to read by a sound-symbol system. But rather than criticize the method, the child is held to be suffering from an illness caused by his own deficiencies rather than the method's. We have amply demonstrated in previous chapters how the whole-word method produces the dyslexic child. Getting rid of dyslexia requires getting rid of the sight-vocabulary method causing it. Sight-reading taxes the child's memory too heavily. Dr. John Money, in this same book, nearly hit the nail on the head:

> [The dyslexic] is perhaps a person weak in visual imagery and visual memory of all types, the opposite of the person with eidetic imagery and photographic memory.

What Dr. Money should have said is not that the dyslexic is a person with a weak memory, but merely a person with a normal memory. Our contention is that only a child with an exceptionally good memory can learn to read *well* by the sight-word method.

But Money had identified the problem as being essentially one of memory. He knew that some children had more difficulty than others in distinguishing and remembering the different letters of the alphabet. But since no investigation had been made of the method whereby the child had been taught to read, he attributed the dyslexic child's memory problem to a difficulty in establishing concepts—the difficulty of remembering letters or understanding their symbol-sound relationship in words. He wrote:

> The dyslexic's conceptual confusion does not end with the alphabet but is further compounded by the vagary with which the shapes of letters are assembled into words. The word is a visual image that takes on meaning not by reason simply of the presence of its component images, but by reason of their sequential arrangement in space. Reversal or rearrangement of the same few letters

totally destroys the conceptual constancy and identity of the entity, that is, the word.

But how can Money, or any other expert in dyslexia, expect a child to learn to distinguish the letters of the alphabet or discover the alphabetic principle in the phonetic structure of words if he is taught to read by way of a sight-vocabulary method which deliberately obscures the alphabetic principle, withholds information about the separate letters, avoids naming the letters for the first year, and fragments words arbitrarily into three nonphonetic pictorial parts?

One particular group of children particularly harmed by whole-word methodology, sometimes beyond repair, are those who are ambidextrous or left-handed. Such children need careful and strong guidance in getting the habit of reading words from left to right. This can be easily done in a phonics program, because the child learns to read by following the left-to-right sequence of letter-sounds in words. But in whole-word reading, he looks for any visual clue he can find in the word. In some instances he may actually read some words backward—from right to left. Why not? The left-to-right sequence of letters has no particular relevance if the letter sounds are not known; and in the reading program we've covered, the child is taught to unlock or attack a word on the basis of any clue—phonetic or otherwise. If one phonetic clue is sufficient to unlock a word, what difference should it make to the child whether that clue is read from left to right, right to left, or discovered in the middle? But if the child has been taught to read *all* words, from the very first lesson, as simple pronunciation units or sequences of pronunciation units, made up of known letters representing specific sounds, he would read from left to right as a matter of course simply because *it would be impossible to read in any other way*.

Money obviously suspected as much when he wrote:

> For experimental purposes, it would be of interest to try teaching a totally phonetic script to a group of dyslexic children, and an ideographic or rebus script to another group.

Since he had written this in 1962, I was curious to find out if such an experiment had indeed been conducted. Its findings would be of great interest in determining the classroom causes of dyslexia. So, on February 29, 1972, I telephoned Dr. Money at his office at the Johns Hopkins University Hospital in Baltimore. I was able to reach him quite easily. After identifying myself and telling him the reason for my call, I asked him if the experiment he had suggested had been carried out.

116

He replied that it had not. He explained that the Johns Hopkins Reading Clinic had gone out of business in 1964 because its funding had been discontinued by the Department of Health, Education, and Welfare. I asked him if he knew of any experiments in methodology which might have been conducted anywhere to identify the causes of dyslexia. He replied that he knew of none. "There's been no really serious experimental work done in the field of dyslexia in general," he said. I asked why. "It is caused," he said, "by the institutionalization of vested interests. It's extraordinarily difficult to cross institutional lines when it comes to public education and public money. The government will provide funds for all sorts of fads and hoopla, but not for any really serious work. They won't get down to brass tacks." What was the reason, I asked. It was a lack of understanding of the scientific approach and the scientific method, he explained. There were too many do-gooders in the field who were not really scientists.

I then asked him if we could expect any good results to come from a government program such as the Right-to-Read Program. His reply was that he did not think so. Bureaucratic rigidity would not permit it.

Thus, it was obvious from what Dr. Money had told me that research in dyslexia had gotten no further in the last ten years than what had been published in his report of 1962. In other words, all that the experts knew were the symptoms, not the causes. No research or experiments had been conducted with the teaching methods to see whether the child or the method was at fault. Since most of the experts on dyslexia and remedial reading were teachers committed to whole-word methodology to some degree, you could be sure that the method would not be found at fault. Some experts were even involved in creating the whole-word basal systems, and obviously they would be the last to find the cause of dyslexia in their methods. There had to be something wrong with the pupils who could not learn how to read via their pedagogical creations. Thus, terms like "minimal brain damage," "learning disabilities," and "hypersensitivity" were invented to describe pupils who couldn't learn to read by way of sight-vocabulary techniques, and these hair-raising terms have been bandied about by teachers confronted by concerned parents wanting to know why Johnny was having such a devil of a time learning to read. The teacher's solution to the problem? An increased dosage of sight-word instruction.

However, many teachers of remedial reading have no vested interest in any method. They measure their effectiveness by how well they can straighten out the child. Consequently, many of them rely heavily on phonics-oriented remedial reading materials. Most of these materials

117

have only been available on the market since 1965. But how many poor readers ever get any remedial attention? The children who are referred to the reading clinics are usually in such bad shape that they can in no way hide their deficiencies from their teachers or parents. The clinics and remedial reading courses only see the worst cases. They do not bother with the millions of children who get by in their reading, who read enough to get through school, but never pick up a book once they get out. These students simply relieve themselves of the burden of reading once they leave school.

6

The Sight-Word Establishment and
Some Significant History

In the preceding chapters we described in detail the methodology responsible for the present crisis in functional illiteracy. We also described how after the publication of Rudolf Flesch's *Why Johnny Can't Read* in 1955 very little changed in teaching methods in the next ten or fifteen years. The reading professionals would simply not take Flesch's book seriously, and they convinced most public school educators not to take it seriously either. Moreover, the sight-word establishment had an economic and professional interest in upholding the methods they had developed. The result was that for the next ten years after the Flesch book was published the sight-vocabulary cancer spread into the secondary-school level where standards had to be lowered and textbooks rewritten with simpler vocabularies to accommodate the poorer reading ability of the students emerging from the elementary schools. Anyone who has taught at the high school level in recent years will be familiar with the comic-book simplicity of many high school textbooks.

How did the sight-vocabulary establishment get such a stranglehold on the teaching profession? It was a simple process of institutionalizing vested interests. Those vested interests included the professional educators who created the sight-word basal systems, on the success of which their professional reputations depended; the publishers who invested millions of dollars in the publication of these systems; the school administrators who spent millions of the taxpayers' money to buy these books. Thus, while the whole-word basal systems have been an incalculable pedagogical failure, they have been an incredible commercial success, with authors and publishers not only making millions for themselves, but encouraging others to imitate them. Thus, Dick and Jane soon had to compete with Alice and Jerry and other basal series using the same methodology. It was the commercial success of Dick and Jane which made the creation of a sight-vocabulary establishment inevitable. There was too much of economic value at stake, and since it would take years before the long-range effects of whole-word methodology would make themselves known, the commercial success of the basal systems was enough to keep publishers deliriously happy until Flesch's book exploded on the scene. By then, however, the professional hold of the whole-word proponents on elementary education was firm enough to withstand the pressures for change called for by Flesch's book.

Who are, or have been, the leading lights in the sight-vocabulary establishment? They have been, of course, the authors of the basal systems—the beneficiaries of enormous royalties. A look at their careers will give the reader an idea of how individuals with so great an economic and professional stake in their methods can institutionalize their interests to the degree that change becomes virtually impossible and necessary reforms are greatly delayed despite increasing pressure from all sides.

The most powerful lobby in the United States for the whole-word method is the International Reading Association (IRA), which was founded in January 1956 at a meeting in Chicago by a merger of two organizations: the International Council for the Improvement of Reading, headed by Dr. William S. Gray, and the National Association of Remedial Teaching, headed by Dr. Ruth M. Strang. Dr. Gray, professor of education at the University of Chicago, was, of course, the senior author of the Dick and Jane basal readers, and Dr. Strang was a veteran expert on whole-word methodology and a prolific author of books on reading. The merger committee was chaired by Helen M. Robinson of the NART and Albert J. Harris of the ICIRI. Dr. Robinson was closely associated with Dr. Gray at the University of Chicago and is also an author of Scott, Foresman's New Basic Readers, New Cathedral Basic Readers, and the most recent Scott, Foresman Reading Systems. In royalties alone, she and Dr. Gray had a great deal to protect, as well as the investment of their publisher. Dr. Harris was an author of another whole-word basal reading program for the Macmillan Company. It should be noted that the founding of the IRA took place

120

the year after *Why Johnny Can't Read* was published, perhaps as a defensive measure, or perhaps just coincidentally. Dr. Robinson reviewed *Why Johnny Can't Read* in the October 1955 issue of *Elementary School Journal*, unfavorably, of course. A new edition of Dick and Jane was being published and a lot of money was at stake.

Thus was the IRA born. Its list of presidents reads like a roster of the Basal Readers Authors' Guild. Dr. Gray served as first president (1955-56). Dr. Harris served as third president (1957-58). Dr. A. Sterl Artley, coauthor of Dick and Jane, served as fifth president (1959-60). Mary C. Austin, coauthor with Dr. William D. Sheldon of the Sheldon Basic Reading Series published by Allyn and Bacon, served as sixth president (1960-61). Dr. Sheldon served as seventh president (1961-62). Nila Banton Smith, editor of *Best of Children's Literature*, published by Bobbs-Merrill, was ninth president (1963-64). Her books were advertised as supplementing the basal reading programs, with vocabularies closely correlated with the vocabularies of the most widely used basal readers. Dr. Theodore Clymer, senior author of Ginn's basal reading program, became tenth president (1964-65). Dorothy Kendall Bracken, coauthor with Ruth M. Strang of *Making Better Readers*, became eleventh president (1965-66). Mildred A. Dawson, author of a series for the World Book Company, became twelfth president (1966-67). H. Alan Robinson, an author with Scott, Foresman, publisher of Dick and Jane, became thirteenth president (1967-68). Leo C. Fay, author of Lyons and Carnahan's Young American Basic Reading Program, became fourteenth president (1968-69).

In other words, the leadership of the IRA was composed of the authors of America's best-selling whole-word basal reading programs. They had gathered together not only to defend their professional interests but their considerable economic interests as well. That is what is known as the institutionalization of vested interests. It is as simple as that. The influence of the IRA among teachers of reading has been quite significant. There are 40,000 members in the IRA which has been run largely as a private lobby for the authors of the sight-vocabulary basal systems. The same people manage to be chairmen of the most important committees and editors of the IRA's influential publications, *The Journal of Reading* and *The Reading Teacher*. They pan the books they don't like and praise the ones they do. They keep the phonics people at a comfortable distance.

What has made the position of these authors so formidable in the face of tremendous criticism has been their professional status in their respective institutions. Dr. Gray, until his death in 1960, was considered the foremost authority on reading at the University of Chicago.

Helen M. Robinson replaced him in that position. Albert J. Harris has been director of the Office of Research and Evaluation at the City University of New York. Dr. Artley is a professor of education at the University of Missouri. Mary C. Austin is a professor of education at Case Western Reserve University. William D. Sheldon is director of the Reading and Language Arts Center, Syracuse University. Nila Banton Smith is a professor at Glassboro State College. Theodore Clymer is a professor of education at the University of Minnesota. Dorothy Kendall Bracken is a professor at Southern Methodist University. Mildred A. Dawson is a professor at Sacramento State College. H. Alan Robinson is with the University of Chicago, and Leo C. Fay is a professor at the Indiana University School of Education.

Thus, you are dealing with authors who can exert great influence throughout the teaching profession through their positions in the various schools of education. However, even such a formidable lobby cannot resist the pressures for change indefinitely. They were able to ride out the storm created by Rudolf Flesch and a couple of other critics in the fifties and early sixties. Their position, in fact, seemed impregnable until 1967 when Professor Jeanne Chall of the Harvard Graduate School of Education published her book, *Learning to Read: The Great Debate*.

Before we consider the impact of Miss Chall's book on the sight-word establishment, we ought to have a brief look at the history of how children have been taught to read since the alphabet was invented. It will give us the historical perspective we need to see present trends within a larger context. The best book which can serve as a guide to this task is Mitford M. Mathews' *Teaching to Read: Historically Considered* (1966). Mathews takes us through about three thousand years of history in less than two hundred pages.

The alphabet, it appears, was invented by the Phoenicians some three thousand years ago. The Phoenicians, who lived in the area we now call Lebanon, spoke a Semitic language and were neighbors of the Greeks with whom they traded. The Phoenicians used their writing system to help record many of their commercial transactions. The Greeks were intrigued by the facility acquired by the use of a sound-symbol system and they tried to use it for their own language. But Greek was quite different from Phoenician in its sounds and it took a great deal of experimentation before the Greeks devised a complete set of symbols or letters with which they could represent every sound of their language. To facilitate the learning of the alphabet, each letter was given a distinct name, borrowed from the Phoenicians in most cases, in which the sound of the letter was given. Thus, we got *alpha, beta, gamma,* etc. The important point to note here is that the name of the letter was quite distinct from the letter's sound value, and there was no confusion in the minds of the Greeks about the two.

In those days there was no such thing as a dictionary or spelling guide. This was long before printing. If you knew the alphabet and wished to use it you simply sounded out each word you wanted to write and then set down the letters representing the sounds in the same sequence as the sounds themselves were uttered. This seems like so obvious a procedure, yet two thousand years later we shall find professors of education doubting its simple validity. At first, you used the alphabet in any direction you wanted. The Phoenicians wrote from right to left as do those who write Hebrew today. But eventually the Greeks settled on a left-to-right direction.

Before the invention of the alphabet, writing was ideographic. Language was represented by picture-symbols which required a great deal of memorization and was never very accurate. It was easy enough to represent commonplace objects and simple actions by picture symbols. But when it came to communicating complex philosophical abstractions or great subtleties, ideographs were inadequate. The alphabet was a tremendous improvement. Once you mastered the sound-symbol system, you could write down any thought in precisely the manner you wanted it to be conveyed. This enabled the Greeks to expand the mind's capacity to think and work, and it permitted a tremendous advance in man's intellectual development.

According to Mathews:

> Other peoples, such as the Babylonians and the Egyptians, had caught glimpses of the desirability of having signs represent *sounds*, not *things*, but they were never able to break with convention to the extent of setting aside picture writing in favor of letter writing. The fundamental defect of picture writing was that it was not based upon sounds at all. Greeks saw this basic weakness and by avoiding it achieved everlasting distinction.

How were the Greeks able to "break with convention"?

> The secret of their phenomenal advance was in the vividness of their conception of the nature of a word. They reasoned that words were sounds, or combinations of ascertainable sounds, and they held inexorably to the basic proposition that writing, properly executed, was a guide to sound.

123

Perhaps this is one reason why the Greeks produced such great dramatists: their infatuation with and love of the spoken word, and their determination to capture it as accurately as possible for themselves and future generations. It is worth noting that much of the ancient Greek literature we enjoy today was written in the form of dialogues.

At first Greek writing was not separated into words but was set down in solid lines and read as a continuum of sound. Eventually, the solid line was spaced out into separate words. By then the writing system had been perfected.

Teaching children to read was fairly simple. The pupil was first taught to master the names and forms of the letters, which were then still handwritten. He learned the letters in alphabetical order, and various exercises were devised to facilitate this learning. The next step was to learn the sound values of the letters. This was done by learning syllables, first such simple consonant-vowel combinations as ba, be, bē, bi, bo, then three-letter groups, such as ban, ben, bēn, bin, bon, etc. Because of the perfect matching of the Greek language sounds with the alphabetic symbols, this was the simplest way to learn how to read. The child was drilled in syllables until he knew the sound values of every letter and could form words by putting the letters together. Having learned all this, he then read words.

Mathews tells us something else which is quite amusing when seen in the light of today's debates. He points out that a schoolmaster in ancient Greece and Rome was regarded with great disdain and contempt. "There must have been a reason for this universal attitude toward elementary teachers among people as intelligent as the Greeks and Romans," he writes. "The most probable explanation of it is that teaching to read was widely recognized as something anybody could do. There was nothing difficult about it. Its acceptable execution called for neither learning nor talents; no distinction could be attained in such a mediocre occupation."

I doubt that the distinguished members of the sight-word establishment would take too kindly to this description of their profession. But judging from their pedagogical performance, these professional "educators" fit the description perfectly.

From Greece we go to Rome. The Romans got the alphabet from the Etruscans who got it from the Greeks. Somewhere in the transfer, the Greek letter names got lost. So the Romans created new ones by using the sounds of the vowels to serve as their names and the consonant sound accompanied by a vowel sound to name the consonants. Since the word *consonant* signified "sounding with" in Latin, it indicates that the Romans understood the vocal difference between consonants and vowels. However, by making the names of the letters resemble their sound values so closely, the Romans opened the way for the mistake so many people would make centuries later in confusing the letter names with the letter sounds. Despite this change of letter names, Roman children learned to read virtually in the same way as the Greeks. Meanwhile, in the course of Roman expansion, the Latin alphabet was applied to other languages in Europe.

It was Christian missionaries in England who applied the Latin alphabet to the English language somewhere around the seventh century. It was not a perfect match and in the centuries that followed, both language and symbols underwent changes. There were no such things as dictionaries, and people wrote phonetically as they pleased, as long as they were understood. Literacy, it should be remembered, was not widespread. But children were taught to read basically as had been the Greek and Roman children: letter names first, then letter sounds through work on vowel-consonant combinations; and finally words. However, there were now new difficulties. The language sounds were changing and there were no single letters to represent these new sounds. So scribes used all sorts of combinations of vowels to represent some of these new sounds. In addition many words were borrowed from other languages. However, when printing came in, spellings became somewhat fixed, despite inconsistencies of all kinds.

Meanwhile, in the seventeenth and eighteenth centuries pedagogy began to develop its own aberrations, as teachers confused letter names with letter sounds and did not understand the distinction between the two. Children suffered greatly as a result. In describing this period, Mathews notes that:

> As letters became progressively less and less dependable indicators of sounds, as spellings became less and less alphabetical, and as confusion between the names and the sounds of letters came more and more to prevail, difficulties increased for those trying to learn to read and for teachers undertaking to guide them.

The situation called for reform and there were many proposals for improving the alphabet, including one to increase it to 34 letters, but all of them failed. Meanwhile children were taught to read in the traditional way handed down from the Greeks.

In Germany, however, where elementary teachers faced the same problems as in England, one Valentin Ickelsamer thought he had found a better way to teach reading. He taught the children to identify the letters by their sounds, not their names, and in 1527 he prepared a primer to show how it was done. His new method found little support, but it had the distinction of being the first departure from the traditional ABC method, which would go unchallenged until the Enlightenment in the late eighteenth century.

The Age of Enlightenment ushered in a scientific approach to all things. The "supernatural" of theology was replaced by the "natural" of science, and the concept of natural law was expounded with considerable enthusiasm. For the field of education it meant that the traditional methods of teaching reading would be regarded critically. The idea of forcing children to learn the alphabet and drilling them on syllables was considered very unnatural by some of the enlightened.

The first pedagogue to apply the concept of the "natural" to reading instruction was Friedrich Gedike, a leading Prussian educator, who thought it was unnatural to start with the elements, that is, the letters, and proceed to the whole, that is, the word. It was natural, he contended, to start with the whole word and proceed to the elements. In his primer, published in 1791, he described a whole-word method of teaching. He criticized the traditional method because it was tough on the children. In turn, Gedike was criticized by most of his colleagues who found fault with his new method. Several other educators in Germany tried to advocate a whole-word approach, but they gained little support, and none of their works were published in the United States.

The next innovator was Jean Joseph Jacotot, a professor of French literature at Louvain University in Belgium, who around 1823 originated the idea of teaching a child to read by first reading an entire book to the student, then dismantling it into its parts, then into sentences, then into words, and finally into letters and their sounds. This was in keeping with what was considered to be the natural order of learning: to start with the whole, which was then reduced in degrees to its ultimate basic elements.

Several German pedagogues seized the idea and toyed with it. They decided that starting with a whole book was too impractical. A whole sentence? That too seemed like too much. They finally settled on just a whole word. Basically what the method did was teach the child the sounds of the individual letters by analyzing the syllables of the whole word. This was not a sight-word approach, for the child was not supposed to memorize the words or learn a sight vocabulary. The whole word was merely used as a vehicle for learning letter sounds, and once the letter sounds were learned, the word was put aside. From that point on, reading instruction proceeded in the traditional manner.

This was the method in use when Horace Mann, Secretary of the Massachusetts Board of Education, visited Prussia in 1843 to inspect

126

its compulsory public school system. He visited a class in which he saw the method demonstrated and he brought back to Boston a glowing report about it. Actually, Mann knew about such new methods some years before he visited Prussia. During the 1830s there had been considerable discussion in the United States among educators concerning the problems of teaching children to read. A number of new approaches were suggested and some were being used in the Boston school system at the time Mann visited Prussia.

The first primer in this country to depart from the traditional method was *Worcester's Primer* published in 1826. Samuel Worcester, a textbook writer, modeled his primer on the method used at the Edinburgh Sessional School. It required the student to know the alphabet before starting the primer, and Worcester provided elaborate instructions on teaching the alphabet in his introductory material. From the letter names, the child was to proceed directly into whole words whereby the sounds of the letters were learned. In his directions to the teacher, Worcester wrote:

> In teaching this and the next Lesson, the instructor must name the words, and let the scholar repeat them after him. Then the letters, of which each word is composed, must be learned, and the scholar must be shown what those letters make when sounded together, and the meaning of the word must be illustrated by the Cut, and by remarks and anecdotes tending to amuse and interest the child.

Thus, there was no departure from the concept of a sound-symbol system being mastered. It was simply a new technique of by-passing the nonsense syllables of the traditional method and proceeding directly to whole words which were already in the child's speaking vocabulary.

During this same period, however, another New England educator, dealing with entirely different pedagogical problems, conceived of the notion of teaching a child to read by first having him learn a sight vocabulary of about fifty words before introducing him to the letters. This educator was the Rev. Thomas H. Gallaudet of Hartford, Connecticut, director from 1817 to 1830 of the American Asylum at Hartford for the Education of the Deaf and Dumb. Gallaudet was an unusual teacher who brought to the instructional problems of the deaf and dumb great empathy and a talent for innovation. He thought he could apply to normal children some of the techniques used to teach deaf-mutes to read. Since deaf-mutes could not learn a sound-symbol system of reading, they were taught to read by a sight method consisting of pictures and whole words. They then learned the manual alphabet—known as dactylology—which permitted them to spell out the words they knew with their fingers and thus "speak" to others. For this purpose, the written language, a sound-symbol record of normal man's spoken language, was conveyed to the deaf-mute as ideographs rather than "phono"-graphs. The deaf child learned the meaning of *cat* by being shown a picture of the animal along with the word. The totally deaf child could have no conception of language until he first *saw* written words. In fact, learning to read for the deaf was synonymous with learning the language.

During his thirteen years as director and teacher at the Asylum, Gallaudet observed closely how the deaf learned to read. He thought he had discovered some important principles of learning which could be applied to the needs of normal children. He was keenly aware of the current interest in improving reading instruction and thought he might contribute a new point of view. Gallaudet knew that deaf children learned to read words by sight alone. Moreover, he had tested his methods on his own children, who were normal although his wife was deaf, and found them satisfactory. At the time of his resignation from the Asylum, in 1830, the principal pedagogical journal in the country was the *American Annals of Education*, edited by William C. Woodbridge, an associate of Gallaudet's who had also taught at the Asylum from 1817 to 1821. Gallaudet sent Woodbridge an account of his method in the form of a letter which Woodbridge published in August 1830. Both men had taught deaf-mutes and saw the possibilities of applying these methods to normal children. This is what Gallaudet wrote:

Mr. Editor—No one who has attended to the early instruction of children, can fail of having noticed the difficulties of teaching them to read, owing to the numerous and singular irregularities which attend the orthoepy and orthography of our language. That great improvements are yet to be made in this department of primary education, I have no doubt. In the books which are used for this purpose, there are still many striking defects. I rejoice to see, however, that they are diminishing, and improvements taking place, which, it is to be hoped, will, ere long, result in a system of instruction more true to nature, and adapted to the actual progress and development of the infantile mind.

If parents and instructors, who are interested in this subject, would communicate the results of their observation and experiments to the public, through the medium of your Journal, in a concise and practical form, an amount of experience would be

128

accumulated, that would serve to direct the efforts yet to be made in the accomplishment of this desirable object.

Education, like every other science, is to be perfected by a course of patient and elaborate experiments; and the sooner these experiments, with their results, can be collected, the sooner will the principles which they develope be ascertained, and a practical application of them be successfully made.

Mind, like matter, can be made subject to experiment. If, in this way, chemistry has arrived to a degree of perfection, as a science, which commands the admiration of all the lovers of true philosophy, what may not be expected, also, in the science of education, if the same inductive process is pursued, of eliciting, comparing and arranging the phenomena, which is presented by the subject under examination?

In pursuance of these suggestions, permit me to state the mode which has been pursued in my own family for seven years past, to make my children acquainted with the power and use of letters.

The words *horse, dog, cat* are written, in a very plain and legible hand, on three separate cards. One of them is shown to the child, and the name of the object pronounced; and then the second and the third in the same manner, *without any reference to the individual letters which compose the word.* After repeating this a few times, the child is asked, 'what is that?' holding up one of the cards, and so of the rest. Let the cards then be placed together, and the child required to select those denoting the several objects, one after the other. Vary the order of doing this until the child becomes perfectly familiar with the words; which will be in a very short time.

The next day, another card containing the name of some other familiar object, may be added, and the child practised in the same manner upon the four cards. The number of cards may soon be increased to six, to ten, to twenty, to fifty.

Here I have been accustomed to stop, and begin to teach the child the letters of which the words are composed in the following manner. Take the word *horse*, and covering all the rest, show the letter *h*, giving its name. Do this with the other letters in succession, repeating the process, until the child is perfectly familiar with the four [sic] letters. Then lay down the fifty cards in order, and ask the child to find the letter *h* among them, then *o, r, s,* and *e*. This will readily be done. He has thus learned four [sic] letters of the alphabet. Vary the order in which the cards are laid, and

129

require the child to point out again the letters, *h, o, r, s, e.* Let this be done till he is familiar with them. Pursue the same course with the card containing the word *dog,* and so on, until the child is perfectly acquainted with all the letters on the cards. They may then be written down in the order of the alphabet, and the child taught to repeat them in that order.

A few lessons will enable him to know the same letters, and the same words, in their printed form.

The interest which this mode of instruction has excited in the mind of the little learner, (while the common one is so dull and tedious,) and the success that has attended it, have more than equalled my expectations. There is a great advantage, too, in the child's becoming acquainted with the written characters. The parent can thus *pursue* the course of instruction, and devise new lessons of words, and of short and simple phrases and stories, teaching the child to read and to learn to spell them, both by inspection and from memory. The child, also, can derive great pleasure and improvement from learning to write the same words and lessons, with a slate and pencil, with which every child should be furnished as soon as he discovers the least inclination to make a single mark.

In this way I have found not the least difficulty in teaching a child to read both written and printed characters at the same time.

Should my leisure permit, I hope to prepare a *Primer* for children, on the plan above described. In the meanwhile, should the hints that I have suggested, throw any light on this interesting step of infantile education, which will be of use to others, and serve also to draw forth from your correspondents, accounts of similar experiments, I shall hope that some benefit may have resulted even from this trifling contribution to the important cause in which you are engaged.

As the reader can see, Gallaudet was quite cautious in putting forth this new sight-word method, and it would take six years for him to prepare his *Primer.* However, from a historical point of view, this is the first account we have in the United States of how to teach a child to read up to fifty words by sight before introducing him to the letters of the alphabet. Its significance, as we shall see, is not so much in its description of the method, but its source. Only a man who had spent so much time dealing with words as ideographs could have conceived of this new approach. In subsequent issues of *American Annals of Education,* Gallaudet revealed how deeply his teaching experience with the deaf and dumb had influenced his thoughts about language and how we learn it. When you taught a deaf person to read, you were also teaching him language for the first time, and Gallaudet was able to observe the process of how a person learns to understand his first words:

> The word *hat* must have originally derived its meaning from the actual sight of a hat, or from a picture of it, or from its appropriate delineation by certain motions of the hands, describing its shape and use, or by a definition, all the words of which must themselves have been explained by the presence of some objects or pictures, or by the exhibition of bodily signs and gestures. . . .
>
> Thus it is true, that the elements of language must be found either in the *actual presence of objects, or in their expression by symbolical signs.* . . . It matters not, whether this language consists of audible signs addressed to the ear, or of visible signs presented to the eye. Both are alike unmeaning, without aid of *observation*, on the one hand, and of *consciousness* on the other.
>
> We are apt to attribute a sort of magical power to speech. . . . The sounds addressed to the ear . . . are quite unintelligible, unless accompanied with a simultaneous explanation . . . some assemblage of visible circumstances.

What Gallaudet had done was adopted to a great extent the point of view of the deaf-mute who had to learn to make his way in the world without the benefit of sound or spoken language. But it led to a serious confusion in Gallaudet's thinking concerning two very different learning processes: that of learning to speak one's native language and that of learning to read it. It was easy to see the source of his confusion. In teaching the deaf to read by sight, he was also teaching them language by sight for the first time. They underwent two learning processes at the same time. But a normal child came to school already with a knowledge of several thousand words in his speaking vocabulary, with a much greater intellectual development which the sense of sound afforded him. In learning how to read, it was not necessary to teach him what he already knew, to repeat the process of learning to speak. It was only necessary to help him master the sound-symbol system, so that he could translate written words into spoken ones. The normal child did not learn his language by learning to read. He learned to read in order to help him expand his *use* of language, and this could only be done by adhering strictly to a sound-symbol system.

Deaf-mutes, devoid of their hearing sense, obviously learned quite differently from normal children. Because of their deficiency they compensated by use of their other senses and sometimes learned by sight even better than normal children. Gallaudet had learned how to teach the deaf and dumb in Paris in 1815 under Abbé Sicard, director of the Royal School for Deaf-Mutes. The Abbé's predecessor, the Abbé de l'Epée, had originated the techniques Gallaudet was to improve on. A contemporary admirer of de l'Epée wrote:

> The Professor for educating Deaf and Dumb persons at Paris has contrived a methodical art, extremely simple and easy, for the language of Signs, by which he gives his pupils ideas of every species; ideas, I do not hesitate to say, more exact, more precise, than those commonly acquired by the medium of the ear. As we are left to judge of the signification of words, in our infancy, by the circumstances wherein we hear them uttered, it often happens that we take hold of their sense but by halves, and we content ourselves with this by halves all our life. But such is not the case with the Deaf and Dumb instructed by (de l'Epée). His method of giving them ideas which do not fall under the senses is entirely by analyzing, and making them analyze along with him. He thus conducts them from sensible to abstract ideas by simple and methodical analyses; and we may judge what advantage his language of action possesses over the articulate sounds of our school-mistresses and preceptors.*

That is exactly what Gallaudet felt when he thought of applying to normal children the teaching methods he had used so successfully with deaf-mutes. The methodical analyses used to enlarge the vocabularies of the deaf and dumb could, he theorized, be used with normal children. Thus, in 1830, he published his first book for normal children, *The Child's Picture Defining and Reading Book.* There are few copies of this book still in existence, but I located one in the rare book department of the Boston Public Library. On the copyright page there is this notice:

> This little volume, although originally prepared for the Deaf and Dumb, will be found to be equally adapted to the instruction of other children in families, infant schools, common schools, and Sunday schools.

---

* Christopher A. Garnett, Jr., *The Exchange of Letters Between Samuel Heinicke and Abbé Charles Michel de l'Epée* (New York: Vantage Press, 1968).

But it was Gallaudet's Preface which stunned me, and I reproduce it here unabridged:

This little book was originally designed for the use of some of the younger classes in the Institution with which the author is connected. His experience, for a long course of years, in the instruction of the Deaf and Dumb, has fully convinced him, that most, if not all, the principles on which the gradual development and cultivation of *their* powers, both intellectual and moral, is conducted, may be applied, with equal success, in the education of children and youth who can *hear* and *speak*. That enthusiasm in his profession, which it is well suited to inspire, has led him to go still further in his speculations, and to think, that *if these principles were thus applied*, a new era would commence in the whole process of education, from its earliest stages upwards; and that a system of instruction might be devised, with *a regular series of books* corresponding to it, more true to Nature, and better adapted to the rapid and successful cultivation of both the mind and heart, than any other now in existence. While, within the last half century, so many astonishing discoveries and improvements have been made in the various sciences and their practical applications to the business of life, does it comport, either with the past history, or the future prospects, of our species, to suppose, that the science of education, on which, in fact, *these very discoveries and improvements* depend, has already attained to that degree of excellence of which it is susceptible?

In all the arts and sciences, experiment has led the way to improvement. Results have been laboriously obtained and carefully examined; then compared, arranged, and classified. Thus *Genius* has embraced within its scope of clear and extensive vision a host of particulars, noticing with rapid and intuitive glance their respective resemblances, and differences, and relations; and perceiving these few and simple principles by which the causes of the various phenomena that they exhibit, are to be explained. *Invention* takes these principles and applies them to the production of new and wonderful results. Is not this the only way in which the science of education can ever be elevated to an equality of rank with other sciences, and have its *elementary principles* accurately defined and successfully applied? Why, too, it may be asked, is the discovery of elementary principles in every other science—in Geometry, for instance, considered as entitled to rank among the highest efforts of genius, while those that relate to the science of Education continue to be so much overlooked and neglected?

But the preface of a child's book, is hardly a suitable place for a philosophical disquisition; and the remainder of it must be devoted to stating the *object* for which this little work is designed, and the *manner* in which the author would recommend it to be used. It is formed on two simple principles,—that children almost immediately refer to some sensible object, or visible occurrence or transaction, in their first efforts to acquire the meaning of words, and even those whose import is of an intellectual and elevated kind; —and that the language of pictures, being founded in Nature, and thus a Universal Language, may, like the signs and gestures and pantomime employed in the instruction of the deaf and dumb, be used, as a key or translation to illustrate and explain written or printed language, and this probably to an extent that has, hitherto, scarcely been imagined.

The first part of the book is intended to show, how a reference to some sensible object, with a suitable explanation on the part of the teacher, is vastly better adapted to give a child the precise import of terms, than the common, and very absurd mode of attempting this by *definitions in a dictionary*. The youthful mind needs illustrative examples, and a gradual induction of particulars, in order to enable it to understand the meaning of words.

It will be seen, that with each of the pictures of sensible objects, are associated an adjective, a verb, and a short phrase in which most of the pronouns and prepositions are introduced, and the various tenses of verbs illustrated. These should all be made intelligible to the child, by *oral explanation* on the part of the instructor. For instance, suppose we refer to the word tent. The child sees the picture of a tent. This will aid him in forming a just conception of it. But this is not enough. Let the materials out of which a tent is formed be described to him; the manner of erecting it; its size, and its design. Then explain to him, that a tent is a *temporary* dwelling; unlike the house in which he lives for months and days and years; that it is put up often only for a night; and so on, referring to all the particulars which constitute the correct import of the word. Give him another example of the use of the word temporary, and another, and another; endeavoring all the while, to make these examples of a more elevated and general kind. Then ask *him* to furnish some examples. If they are well chosen, let him know it; if they are not, correct his mistakes. Proceed in the same way to explain the word *remove*; illustrating its meaning, at first, by

134

the removal of a tent, and then, of other objects. After this, as before, let the child furnish illustrative examples. Explain the import of the little phrase. Then a variety of questions may be asked with regard to each of the single objects, of which some examples will be found prepared, at the end of the first part, as a specimen.

The first part of the book may also be used for lessons in spelling; the child learning to spell the names of the objects, the adjectives, the verbs, and the words in the phrases. He may thus, also, easily be taught the different parts of speech, by being told which are called nouns, adjectives, verbs, etc.

It will be noticed that most of the adjectives are contrasted with each other,—a very useful mode of teaching their meaning, as is abundantly exemplified in the instruction of the deaf and dumb.

The second part of the book consists of reading lessons, each explained and illustrated by an appropriate picture. Let the child attempt the reading of these lessons, without any assistance on the part of the teacher in regard to the *import* of the words contained in them. The object here is, to exercise the thinking powers and ingenuity of the child, in endeavouring to understand the story, by the mere inspection of the picture. After he has done this, the inquiry should be made, if there are any words or phrases which he does not fully understand. If so, they should be explained to him by illustrative examples, as in the case of the pictures of single objects. Then let a variety of simple questions be put to him, with regard to the agents, the actions, and the occurrences described; such as, "Who is that man?" "Where is he?" "What is he doing?" "Why is he doing it?" and the like.

A regular set of questions has not been prepared for the stories in the second part of the book. The author should rather leave this to the ingenuity of the teacher. Such questions, when printed, are too often so mechanically arranged, and made to correspond to the various parts of the narrative, that, on the principle of *juxtaposition*, they can often be readily answered without any exercise of reflection on the part of the child, and without affording any evidence that he understands either the question or the answer.

It is not improbable, that at first sight this little book may be considered as containing *nothing new*, and as *too simple* to furnish any thing like improvement in the early stages of education. Its value, if it should prove to possess any, will principally depend on its simplicity, and, in no small degree, on the ability, and patience, and fidelity of the instructer in *using* it. There is no greater mistake than to suppose, that when a new book is put into the hands of a child, *it alone* is to answer the purpose for which all books for children should be prepared. They must, certainly, in the first steps of education, be accompanied with judicious *oral* explanations, or they will all be comparatively useless.

It ought to be stated, that this book is intended for such children as are already able to read what is written in a very simple and easy style.

Should this experiment prove to be conducive to the object which the author had in view, he may attempt a *primary* book, on the same plan, and, indeed, a *series of books*, embracing subjects of a more elevated and important kind.

The significance of this preface is that it outlines for the first time and for the use of normal children basic whole-word methodology, with its extensive use of pictures as a means of having children look at words as representing objects, or ideas, rather than sounds. What is, in fact, so striking is the similarity between the methodology used to teach the deaf and dumb as presented here by Gallaudet and the methodology used in Dick and Jane. Both use sight reading and ideographics as the central means of learning, with oral explanations as supplementary and secondary to the primary role of sight. In Dick and Jane the letter sounds serve as phonetic clues to sight learning. In Gallaudet's *Picture Defining Dictionary* oral explanations, which are used in place of sign language, supplement sight learning. The role of sound, and the sound-symbol system, in both Gallaudet and Dick and Jane are relegated to secondary supplemental roles, when actually with normal children—and even with deaf children, some experts believe—they should be primary. It should be remembered that the written language was devised to help develop and expand the spoken language, which is the principle vehicle of our thoughts and concepts. We think in terms of language, we speak to ourselves, we formulate our thoughts in terms of language. True, we often cannot find the right words to describe what we feel and think, but eventually, with effort we do find them, and once we do, we pin down and concretize that which is so elusive. Thought can only be anchored by words.

Among the many things of interest in Gallaudet's preface are his characterization of education as a science to which could be applied the same inductive techniques applied to chemistry, and his belief that he had discovered the elementary principles of primary learning. His enthusiasm led him to believe that "if these principles were thus applied, a new era would commence in the whole process of education." They would indeed be applied a century later, but the "new era" would hardly evoke celebration. At the time, however, he really felt that he had discovered something important, something more in harmony with the current enlightened enthusiasm for the natural. Did he not say that his system was "more true to nature"? And do we not find whole-word experts in the twentieth century saying the same thing? As for his notion of education being a science, we will find this same scientific label being applied to the whole-word method a hundred years later, but without any history or record of experimental use to support it.

Thus, for all practical purposes, we have identified the source of the sight-vocabulary method. The development of this method, so contrary to sound-symbol principles, was not a chance invention made by a tinkering educator as Rudolf Flesch and others have erroneously believed. Its pedagogical basis is the elaborate, complex system developed to educate the deaf and dumb. How this method—slightly abridged for normal children—became detached from its source and entered the mainstream of pedagogical practice in the primary education of normal children is still a mystery. The missing link is Gallaudet's primer, *The Mother's Primer*, published in 1836. I have made a considerable effort to locate a copy, but there seems to be none in existence. However, we do know, from another source, what it's first line was:

Frank had a dog; his name was Spot. (!)

7

From Thomas H. Gallaudet to William S. Gray

If it weren't for the incredible dispute which arose between Horace Mann and the Boston schoolmasters in 1844 over the matter of his Seventh Annual Report, in which the teaching of reading was one of the points of contention, there would be virtually no record of Thomas H. Gallaudet's sight-vocabulary primer. But we know from a notice in the August 1835 issue of *American Annals of Education* that *The Mother's Primer* by Gallaudet was published that year. The notice included this description of the book:

> In the first number of this work, we published a letter from Mr. Gallaudet, stating the plan he had adopted of teaching his children to read by commencing with *words* instead of *letters*. This plan has been found successful with the members of his own family; and after long trial, has been published in the little book before us. The results of years of experiment, by one of the ablest analysts of the infant mind, are of great value to every parent and teacher; and we are confident, that those who will adopt this little book as a manual, will spare themselves and their children, much irksome and useless labor.

This was quite a recommendation by Gallaudet's editor friend Woodbridge. In those five years between that original letter and publication

139

of the primer, Gallaudet's name had appeard in *American Annals of Education* quite frequently. He was by then well known to its readers. However, there is evidence that he was considered an authority on education even before his first appearance in the *Annals*. In Heman Humphrey's biography of Gallaudet there is a letter from Gallaudet to one John Tappan, Esq., of Boston, dated March 27, 1828, outlining a plan for a model school very much like the one established by John Dewey three-quarters of a century later. Here is just a short excerpt from that letter:

> Suppose, in a city like Boston, some ten or twelve families should unite and establish a private school for the instruction of their children under six or seven years of age, and I should take charge of it for one year, devoting to it five hours a day, and having sufficient vacation for relaxation.
>
> In such a school and in such a time I could apply the principles in teaching the deaf and dumb, and devise, arrange, and mature, a new, and permit me to say, more rational mode of instruction than now in operation. I speak of a private school, because I had rather begin in a noiseless way, and have the best opportunity of being able to present to the public, with a good degree of confidence, a system of instruction for such young minds.

Gallaudet's confidence that he could apply to normal children the principles used in teaching the deaf and dumb was expressed as early as 1820 in an address delivered at the third anniversary of the founding of the Hartford Asylum:

> If I mistake not, simplicity, method, and the abandonment of a great deal of the unintelligible jargon of the schools, which nothing but long use has rendered sacred, will make that delightful to the youthful mind which is now irksome, and that comparatively easy which is now difficult. But all this can only be effected by a patient course of experiment, and by a careful analysis of the human mind. . . .
>
> Perhaps there are no circumstances under which the mind is placed, more singularly propitious for such experiments and analyses, than those in which we find an untaught deaf and dumb person. He is as nearly the child of nature as we can ever hope to find one. And possibly the simplicity and patience with which he must be taught, the absolute intelligibility which must illuminate every step that is taken in his education, and the singular and inter-

esting aspects under which his mind is continually presenting itself, may furnish a course of observations and experiments which will have an important bearing upon the education of those who are in possession of all their faculties. At any rate, it is pleasant to think that we may thus be indebted to these very children of misfortune, for some of the future benefits which our youth may enjoy in the task of acquiring knowledge.

Thus, we have a very clear idea of the conceptual genesis of Gallaudet's primer. On August 2, 1836, the Boston Primary School Committee decided to adopt the primer on an experimental basis. The teachers using it were asked to give the committee their opinion of the primer's value within a year. On the basis of that opinion, the committee issued the following report on November 7, 1837:

> They have carefully examined the Mother's Primer, and caused the experiment to be made in several of the schools, and from the favorable reports which have been received from the teachers of the success they have met with in advancing the children from the fourth to the third class, your committee are induced to recommend its adoption in our Primary Schools; believing as they do that it is easier as well as more expeditious and interesting to the pupil, than the old, unintelligible, and irksome mode of teaching them to call certain arbitrary marks, or letters, by certain arbitrary sounds.
>
> Your committee have been informed by one of the teachers, who has for the last year adopted this proposed mode of teaching, that pupils taught in this way, are enabled, in four months to read very well in plain reading, and spell words of one syllable, even with silent letters; whereas it generally takes a longer period of time, by the old method, to teach them the alphabet of large and small letters.

The teachers were reporting a phenomenon we are all well aware of today. A child can learn an initial sight vocabulary faster than he can learn the alphabet and letter sounds. However, this initial success is deceptive because it does not provide the foundation for learning thousands of additional words, and therefore it is in the second and third years in which the sight readers' problems become evident. Moreover, the language of the report reflects the writer's bias against the alphabet method. To refer to the alphabet as a set of "arbitrary marks" designating "certain arbitrary sounds" betrays a complete ignorance of the

141

nature and advantages of a sound-symbol system over an ideographic one.

Horace Mann became Secretary of the Massachusetts Board of Education on June 28, 1837, several months before the Gallaudet primer was adopted for use throughout the primary schools of Boston, and he approved of it. Keenly interested in the new method, he endorsed it in his Second Annual Report issued in 1838. His endorsement encouraged other textbook writers, namely J. M. Bumstead and Mann's own wife, Mary Tyler Peabody, to write primers imitating Gallaudet's. But his dispute with the Boston schoolmasters did not occur until 1844, eight years after Gallaudet's primer, as well as other word-method primers, had been in use in the Boston school system. By then there would be plenty of evidence to prove or disprove the value of the new method.

Mann, who is considered the father of our compulsory education system, is often hailed as the first spokesman in America for the whole-word method. He was certainly not the first, but he was undoubtedly the best known and perhaps the most eloquent. The *American Annals of Education* provided a ready platform for the critics of English orthography and the alphabet method. One could find such opinions as the following in its pages:

> If it is true, that so long as we cling with intense fondness to the deformities of our orthography—with a fondness like the mother's love to her offspring, enhanced by deformity—much time is, and must be, wasted over the elementary books of reading and spelling. It becomes the friends of education to examine the facts, and act with energy, as men living in an age of reform. (April 1832, p. 173)

> He [the child] should read his lessons as if the words were Chinese symbols, without paying any attention to the individual letters, but with special regard to the meaning. . . . This method needs neither recommendation nor defense, with those who have tried it: and were it adopted, we should soon get rid of the stupid and uninteresting mode now prevalent. (October 1832, p. 479)

> The ABC is our initiative tormentor, requiring much time and herculean effort, altogether thrown away. (November 1833, p. 512)

There were even articles claiming that too much studying caused insanity! There was a climate of revolt against traditional academic discipline, and for many reformers the alphabet seemed to symbolize that discipline. In reality, the rebellion against the ABC was more emotional than rational. It was more philosophical than scientific. It finally led to the bitter quarrel between Mann and the Boston schoolmasters, with Mann representing the liberal forces of rebellion and reform and the schoolmasters representing tradition and conservatism. Today that peculiar ideological alignment still seems to persist when it comes to teaching to read. Yet, one would assume that liberals were just as interested in sound pedagogical methods as conservatives.

At this point it might be useful to sketch in a few details about Mann, his beliefs, and the kind of philosophical climate which prevailed when all of these changes were taking place. Mann was born in Franklin, Massachusetts in 1796 and grew up in the afterglow of the Age of Enlightenment. He graduated from Brown University, taught school for about three years, then entered law. He served as a member of the Massachusetts state legislature until his appointment in 1837 to fill the newly created position of Secretary to the Massachusetts Board of Education. He brought to the job all the enthusiasm, dedication, and spirit of a crusader. As a liberal, Mann firmly believed in the necessity for a compulsory public education system supported by the taxpayer. He also firmly believed in the tenets of natural law and in the doctrines of phrenology. Few accounts about Mann bother to mention this last detail. But I believe it is important if we are to understand the kind of philosophical emotionalism which spurred much of the educational reform of the time.

Phrenology was a pseudoscientific school of thought developed in the early 1800s by a German physician named François Joseph Gall who in the course of his work with the insane became convinced that the brain was the organic seat of what we would now call personality development. As George H. Calvert, an enthusiastic American phrenologist wrote in 1832:

> Gall arrived at the conclusion, that different portions of the brain were dedicated to the manifestation of particular faculties, by observing the unfailing coincidence between the unusual prominence of particular parts of the cranium, and the existence in more than common strength of particular feelings or talents.

By dissecting and examining hundreds of skulls and brains, Dr. Gall worked out a map of the brain in which, he was convinced, he was able to identify the exact organic locations of such personality traits as combativeness, destructiveness, love of approbation, benevolence, conscientiousness, etc. He identified several dozen such traits, which were

143

then called "propensities, temperaments, and talents." He reasoned that the degree of temperament and talent depended on the size of that portion of the brain which was its seat. Thus, intelligence was located in the frontal lobes. A person with a high forehead was inherently intelligent. If he became a compulsive murderer, it was because that part of the brain which was the seat of destructiveness was larger than the other parts. The harmonious personality was one in which all of the parts of the brain were of such proportions as to work harmoniously together.

It was impossible for Gall to prove his theory by showing exact cause and effect. But then, as now, only the most exacting scientists demanded such proof. Many people believed in phrenology because it offered a plausible "scientific" explanation for human behavior when only traditional Biblical ones existed. In traditional beliefs a person committed murder because he was evil or possessed by the devil. Now, according to phrenology, he was merely unfortunate enough to have been born with a brain disproportionately large in the destructiveness area. Had someone recognized this in the person's childhood, by noting the bump on his head in that area devoted to destructiveness, he could have been saved by being given training or exercises to offset that personality propensity. That's where the importance of education came in.

Gall and his associate, John Gaspar Spurzheim, a French physician, started publication of their definitive work in Paris in 1809. It was impressively entitled *The Anatomy and Physiology of the Nervous System in General, and of the Brain in particular, with observations upon the possibility of ascertaining the several intellectual and moral dispositions of Man and Animals by the configurations of their Heads.* Publication of the four-volume work was completed in 1819.

As early as 1807 news of Dr. Gall's work had spread to England, and in 1815 Gall's associate, Dr. Spurzheim, journeyed to Edinburgh, the Athens of science, where phrenology had been dismissed as the unscientific nonsense it was. Spurzheim lectured, made friends, and converted to phrenology one George Combe, a young lawyer, and his medical-student brother Andrew. The result was the creation of the Edinburgh Phrenological Society and Combe's lifelong association with the new "science," of which he eventually became chief spokesman after the death of Spurzheim in 1832.

Phrenology seems to have reached the United States soon after its introduction in England. But its major impact here came with the publication in Boston in 1829 of Combe's *The Constitution of Man.* In it Combe wrote, "Phrenology appears to me to be the clearest, most complete, and best supported system of Human Nature, which has hitherto been taught."

The real breakthrough for phrenology in the United States came in 1832 when Spurzheim visited this country and delivered a series of lectures in Boston and at Harvard. According to an eyewitness of the time: "The immediate results of Spurzheim's lectures in Boston and Cambridge were most gratifying to him and the public. Their effect upon the minds of leading men and editors produced an excitement throughout the country." Spurzheim visited schools, insane asylums, studied a few heads and spoke about the importance of fresh air and natural foods. His views on schools, prisons, insanity, and dieting were basically the prevailing liberal views. Then, suddenly, on November 17, 1832, he died at age 71. It was said that exhaustion, caused by the schedule of his work, killed him.

His death was mourned in Boston, with the city's dignitaries attending the funeral. Spurzheim was the first to be interred in the new Mt. Auburn cemetery. On the day of his funeral a group of Bostonians founded the Boston Phrenological Society. Similar societies were organized in other parts of the country. Spurzheim's visit saw the beginning of a veritable flood of books in the United States devoted to every aspect of phrenology.

In 1832, when Spurzheim had come to Boston, Horace Mann was a member of the Massachusetts State Legislature. But six years later, when George Combe came to the United States and lectured in Boston, Mann had already been Secretary of the Massachusetts Board of Education for a year. On October 8, 1838 the two men met and it was the beginning of a lifelong friendship. In noting the occasion in his diary, Mann described Combe as "the author of that extra-ordinary book, 'The Constitution of Man,' the doctrines of which, I believe, will work the same change in metaphysical science that Lord Bacon wrought in natural."

Mann attended all of Combe's lectures and invited the Scotsman to attend a common school convention in Taunton. In his own account of the occasion, Combe wrote: "Mr. Mann, in his official capacity of Secretary to the Board of Education, read an address to the people, showing the necessity of education for improving the human mind, and its nature and objects. . . . I never listened to a more sound, philosophical, comprehensive, practical, eloquent, and felicitous composition."

Mann became an ardent phrenologist, and he and Combe were in complete agreement on the matter of education: that there should be universal, compulsory, state-supported, secular education; that subject matter should not be limited to the three R's, which were only the tools of learning; that the curriculum should be expanded to include practical courses; that normal schools should be created in which to train teachers; and that new enlightened methods should be tried.

Although Combe did not advocate any specific way of teaching children to read, he criticized the traditional method which emphasized reading facility rather than reading for understanding. For example, after a visit to a school in Philadelphia in 1839, Combe wrote:

> The great object aimed at, is to teach the children to read fluently. They read long passages with ease, without understanding the meaning of them. One of the female teachers, to whom I remarked this circumstance, acknowledged the fact, and said, in explanation of it, that the parents insisted on the children being rendered great readers; that they complained to the directors of the time spent in explaining words and teaching objects as being "lost;" and that the directors, to satisfy them, desired her to make them "read," and not waste time in giving explanations. She obeyed, and certainly the children read with great fluency; but the meaning of the words is to a great extent unknown to them.

Thus, the desire to change methods was inspired more by philosophical considerations than any real scientific understanding of how children best learned to read. Mann and Combe assumed that the traditional methods were a result of traditional attitudes toward discipline and learning rather than of an understanding of how children can be taught to master a sound-symbol system. Neither Mann nor Combe had spent any time teaching children to read, and thus, they did not have the practical experience to temper their philosophical enthusiasm.

Both Combe and Mann admired the Prussian state-controlled system of compulsory education. And American educational journals were filled with articles about every facet of the Prussian system, all of which seemed worthy of duplication in this country. In February 1842, Mann wrote to Combe, who had returned to Europe in 1840, asking him to furnish him "with a series of letters in relation to the German schools —their courses of studies, modes of instruction, discipline, order, qualifications of teachers, attainments of scholars, results, etc." In May 1843 the Manns finally went to Europe. They first visited schools in England, Scotland, Ireland, France, and Holland, then went on to Prussia. Mann spent about six weeks touring the schools in Prussia and Saxony. In August, he and his wife and the Combes had a reunion in Leipzig.

On November 4, 1843, the Manns returned to Boston. Shortly after his return he wrote his famous Seventh Annual Report which was released on January 1, 1844. The report covered his entire European tour but concentrated mainly on the Prussian system's organization, modes of instruction, teacher training, discipline, physical aspects, etc. He unabashedly praised the system. His only criticisms were that religious instruction was included in what he thought should be a completely secular education; that compulsory education ended too soon at age fourteen; and that there were no school libraries. Had the report, however, been limited merely to a glowing account of Prussian methods, it perhaps would not have provoked the reaction it did. However, throughout the report, Mann had interwoven a very disparaging critique of the Boston school system, and this the Association of Boston Masters could not possibly ignore. Besides, antagonism between the reformer secretary and the more conservative schoolmasters had been festering for years. The Seventh Annual Report merely brought the situation to a head.

Thus the Association of Masters, representing thirty-one Boston schoolmasters, decided to issue a full-scale critique of Mann's report. They were sure that if the report went unchallenged, it would be assumed that Mann's critical comments on the Boston schools vis à vis the Scotch or Prussian schools would be accepted as truth. What rankled the schoolmasters especially was the fact that Mann had hardly visited their schools in the five years of his tenure as secretary, and that he was not only unfair in his criticism, but ignorant of what was happening in the schools. Moreover, these schoolmasters, men of considerable intellectual ability, resented being downgraded.

Concerning the subject of teaching to read, Mann used the Seventh Annual Report to present his views again:

> I am satisfied that our greatest error in teaching children to read, lies in beginning with the alphabet;—in giving them what are called the 'Names of the Letters,' *a, b, c,* etc. How can a child to whom nature offers such a profusion of beautiful objects,—of sights and sounds and colors,—and in whose breast so many social feelings spring up;—how can such a child be expected to turn with delight from all these to the stiff and lifeless column of the alphabet? How can one who as yet is utterly incapable of appreciating the remote benefits, which in after-life reward the acquisition of knowledge, derive any pleasure from an exercise which presents neither beauty to his eye, nor music to his ear, nor sense to his understanding?
>
> Although in former reports and publications I have dwelt at length upon what seems to be the absurdity of teaching to read

by *beginning* with the alphabet, yet I feel constrained to recur to the subject again,—being persuaded that no thorough reform will ever be effected in our schools until this practice is abolished.

Mann went on for some pages, describing the method he had seen used in the Prussian schools, reviewing the problems of English orthography and the difficulties our alphabet posed for the child, and endorsing the new methods being used in the Boston schools.

The schoolmasters' challenge to Mann was published in August 1844 under the title, *Remarks on the Seventh Annual Report of the Hon. Horace Mann, Secretary of the Massachusetts Board of Education.* The Association of Masters had assigned Samuel S. Greene, the thirty-seven-year-old principal of the Phillips Grammar School, the task of challenging the secretary on the subject of reading. They couldn't have chosen a more lucid and intelligent mind for the task. Greene's critique of the whole-word method remains a classic. (The full text from the *Remarks* is reprinted in the appendix to this book.)

The new method had been in use in the Boston primary schools for about six years, and in that time the shortcomings of the whole-word method had become quite apparent. Greene wrote:

> After repeated inquiries made in many of the primary schools of the city, we are persuaded, that the teachers have taken full amount of license allowed them, by the author of the books which they use. Some begin with the alphabet; others require the children to learn eight or ten words, from which they teach the several letters, though not in the order in which they are arranged in the alphabet. Some carry the process of teaching words to a greater extent, yet require the child to learn to spell, before teaching him to read. Others, as will appear, teach the children to read, without making them at all acquainted with the letters. One evil, resulting from this want of system, is a great neglect of spelling. It is the opinion of those masters who have been longest in the service, and can therefore compare the results of the two systems, that in respect to spelling, among the candidates for admission from the primary schools, there has been a great deterioration during the trial of the new system; a period of about six years. . . .
>
> And, here we may remark, that the testimony of able primary school teachers themselves, who have tried both systems, is adverse to this mode of teaching reading. They declare that in the end, nothing is gained, but much is lost; that the task of teaching the alphabet, and the art of combining letters into words, are more

148

difficult, and less satisfactory, than if the child had begun with the letters.

When we reread the documents of 1844, we are reminded of what Santayana said about those who ignore history being condemned to repeat it.

The dispute between the Association of Masters and Horace Mann did not end with the publication of the *Remarks*. Before the year was up, Mann answered with a *Reply to the "Remarks" of thirty-one Boston schoolmasters on the Seventh Annual Report of the Secretary of the Massachusetts Board of Education*. It was an emotional and bitter reply in which Mann accused his critics of misrepresenting him, quoting him out of context, insulting his intelligence. But it is in this *Reply* that we find the reference to the first line in Gallaudet's *Primer*: "Frank had a dog; his name was Spot" (p. 98). Mann also made it clear that the new method originated with Gallaudet. He wrote:

Such is a very brief, and perhaps therefore, imperfect, sketch of the "new method," as I know it to have been most successfully practised, in many schools. It was advocated,—with the exception of learning the *powers* of letters,—by Mr. Gallaudet, in the Annals of Education, as far back as 1830. Soon afterwards he prepared a "Primer" on the plan. Mr. Worcester soon followed him, though not wholly on the same plan. Since that time several works have been prepared, more or less in accordance with these views; but all abandoning the "old system."

Thus, we have it in Mann's own words that Gallaudet was the originator of the new sight-vocabulary technique. That Mann's defense of the new system was more emotional than scientific is obvious when you read the *Reply*. Describing the situation to George Combe in a letter dated December 1, 1844, he wrote:

The orthodox have hunted me this winter as though they were bloodhounds, and I a poor rabbit. . . . They feel in respect to a free education, that opens the mind, develops the conscience, and cultivates reverence for whatever is good without the infusion of Calvinistic influence, as the old monks felt about printing, when they said, "If we do not put that down, it will put us down." . . .

I wrote a 'Reply to the Boston Masters.' In this Reply, you will see of how much service your letter and others have been to me.

The schoolmasters at this point were not about to play dead. There was too much at stake in this dispute, and they were determined to keep the public record straight. They met in December 1844 and chose a committee to draft a rejoinder, which was published by the Association in mid-1845. The *Rejoinder to the "Reply" of the Hon. Horace Mann, Secretary of the Massachusetts Board of Education to the "Remarks" of the Association of Boston Masters upon his Seventh Annual Report* consisted of the commitee's general report, together with separate replies by the writers of the three articles in the *Remarks*.

From the point of view of the historian, the *Rejoinder* is as important as the *Seventh Annual Report*, the *Remarks*, and the *Reply to the Remarks*, because it helps to clarify the origin of the whole-word method. It cites Gallaudet's Primer as the *first* sight-vocabulary primer. By 1841, there was already some confusion among educators as to how the new method had all started. Some thought it had begun with Worcester's *Primer* in 1826 which was based on the Edinburgh method, which used words to teach letters but was by no means a departure from teaching reading as a pure sound-symbol system. It was Gallaudet, however, who introduced the idea of delaying the teaching of the letters until about fifty words or so were known by sight. Therefore to him must go the honor of having originated the first sight-vocabulary primer. His *Mother's Primer* was adopted for regular use throughout all the Boston primary schools in 1837. The introduction of later primers by Bumstead and Miss Peabody confused the scene. But it was Samuel Greene who took the cue from Mann in the *Reply* and set the record straight in his article in the *Rejoinder*. He saved the best for last when he wrote:

> I will allude to but one subject more, and that is the support which Mr. Mann claims for the method, on the score of authority. True, there are learned and good men who have favored this method of teaching. And a system in which, nominally, words are taught first, has been introduced into a number of towns in the State, but Mr. Mann has omitted to mention that in several of these, the plan has been rejected and the old one restored. He mentions, among others, Mr. Gallaudet, as one of its advocates. It is well known that this gentleman was formerly at the head of the Asylum for the Deaf and Dumb at Hartford. He taught reading, to a class of persons to whom letters cannot be the representatives of sound. Letters, to the mute, are all *silent*. Words themselves are silent. Thoughts may live and burn in his breast, but he cannot utter them; yet he can communicate them by signs. Nay, more;

aided by these, he may learn the written symbols of ideas. Hence, to him the letters are nothing but a certain number of "marks"—the very term Mr. Gallaudet applies to them in the "Mother's Primer." The mute must, therefore, be taught to associate the printed word with the idea, and not with the spoken word which it represents.

When the word is thus learned, it may be resolved into its "marks;" and spelling with the mute consists in arranging these "marks" mechanically, in the proper order to reproduce the picture which he has learned to associate with some idea. Now it is not difficult to discover in all this, a striking resemblance to the "new system," as it has been heretofore advocated. Indeed, I have been told that a gentleman from this city visited the Asylum at Hartford, witnessed the methods of teaching reading to the deaf and dumb there pursued, and suggested the importance of having a book prepared for Primary Schools, on the same plan. Whether the "Mother's Primer" was made in accordance with that suggestion or not, I am unable to say; but such a book was published, and introduced into the Boston Primary Schools, November 7, 1837. This is the origin of the system in the Boston schools. It seems to have been suggested by the modes of teaching reading to an unfortunate class of our fellow-beings. Now while none shall go before me in commiserating the condition of the deaf and dumb; while none shall rejoice more heartily that they can be taught to read, difficult though the process may be, yet I protest against treating all children as though they were deaf and dumb. On the same principle, and with about as good reason, might one urge the general adoption of a book prepared with raised letters for the blind, because the sense of touch quickened as if to supply that of sight, they are able, at great disadvantage, to feel out the words and read a few books.

We have gone to great lengths to document the origin of the sight-vocabulary method, for the simple reason that up to now its conceptual origin was totally unknown. Up to now it had been impossible to explain the process whereby our sound-symbol system of writing had been converted to an ideographic system by the advocates of whole-word teaching. Now we know. And we also know why it does not work with normal children. *It was conceived for the deaf and dumb.*

Mann wrote a *Reply to the Rejoinder*, but it did not have the convincing tone of his earlier arguments. Greene's case for the letters-before-words approach was unassailable, and what he revealed about

151

Gallaudet's primer must have made many Boston educators stop and think. It certainly put the authors of the whole-word primers on the defensive. In any case, the Boston masters, insistent on having the final word, published *Penitential Tears, or a Cry from the Dust by the Thirty-One Prostrated and Pulverized by the hand of Horace Mann.* It is perhaps one of the most eloquent and impassioned defenses of conservative educational principles ever written in this country. This following excerpt is the epitome of their argument:

> Education is a great concern; it has often been tampered with by vain theorists; it has suffered much from the stupid folly and the delusive wisdom of its treacherous friends; and we hardly know which have injured it most. Our conviction is, that it has much more to hope from the collected wisdom and common prudence of the community, than from the suggestions of the individual. Locke injured it by his theories, and so did Rousseau, and so did Milton. All their plans were too splendid to be true. It is to be advanced by conceptions, neither soaring above the clouds, nor groveling on the earth,—but by those plain, gradual, productive, common-sense improvements, which use may encourage and experience suggest. We are in favor of advancement, provided it be towards usefulness. . . .
>
> We love the secretary, but we hate his theories. They stand in the way of substantial education. It is impossible for a sound mind not to hate them.

What did Gallaudet think of all this? He had read the *Seventh Annual Report* and found it all praiseworthy except for Mann's remarks on deaf-mute instruction in Prussia. Mann had been greatly impressed by the oralist school of instruction, in which the deaf were taught to articulate. Consequently, he devoted about twelve pages of his Report describing in detail how this miracle was accomplished.

> With us, the deaf and dumb are taught to converse by signs made with the fingers. There, incredible as it may seem, they are taught *to speak* with the lips and tongue. That a person, utterly deprived of the organs of hearing,—who indeed never knew of the existence of voice or sound,—should be able *to talk*, seems almost to transcend the limits of possibility; and surely that teacher is entitled to the character of a great genius as well as benefactor, who conceived, and successfully executed, a plan, which, even after it is accomplished, the word will scarcely credit.

152

He then described the techniques used in teaching the deaf to speak, remarking:

> Such is a very brief outline of the laborious processes by which the wonderful work of teaching the dumb to speak is accomplished; and so extraordinary are the results, that I have often heard pupils, in the deaf and dumb schools of Prussia and Saxony, read with more distinction of articulation and appropriateness of expression than is done by some of the children in our schools who possess perfect organs of speech, and a complement of the senses.

Gallaudet, a passionate teacher of the language of signs, disagreed with Mann. In a letter to Mann dated May 13, 1844, he wrote:

> I am free to say that I deeply regret the very strong language which you use in your report, so interesting and admirable in most of its features, when you say that the schools for the deaf and dumb in Prussia, Saxony, and Holland seem to you *decidedly superior* to anything in this country; because, in order to say this, as I think, understandably, you ought to be thoroughly acquainted with the system of discipline and instruction pursued in our Asylum, and other American institutions, in its details and practical results; for how else can a fair comparison be made?

There is a tremendous irony in this entire dispute. Mann favored adapting Gallaudet's hieroglyphic methods to the teaching of normal children to read, yet he clearly believed that these methods when used to teach the deaf were inferior to the oralist methods used in Prussia. Mann, however, was not aware of the inconsistency in his thinking. He went on in his *Report* to defend the new whole-word method of teaching normal children to read. Gallaudet, of course, agreed with Mann's defense of the new whole-word method, but we have found no evidence at all that he rose to challenge the criticism of the Boston schoolmasters. After all, Gallaudet's methods of teaching the deaf were already considered outmoded and inferior in most of Europe, and a challenge to the Boston schoolmasters would have only put the spotlight on the whole-word method as an offshoot of an outmoded deaf-mute instruction which Mann himself had labeled inferior. As for the other textbook writers who had copied Gallaudet, their defense of the whole-word method was weak. They were not as intimately aware of its conceptual origins as was Gallaudet who, by 1844, might have begun to have second thoughts about his sight-vocabulary techniques being used on normal children.

Gallaudet was not at all aggressive in promoting his method, and after his death there was scarcely any mention anywhere of his *Mother's Primer* or of its significance in the Mann-schoolmasters dispute. In 1838 Gallaudet had been offered the position of secretary to the Connecticut Board of Education, but declined it. In July of that same year he accepted the position of chaplain to the Retreat for the Insane in Hartford, a position he held until his death in September 1851. In a tribute to Gallaudet, Henry Barnard, who became secretary to the Connecticut Board of Education, wrote:

> In later life, at least on ordinary occasions, his power as a preacher was weakened by his habit of simplifying his thoughts, and extending his illustrations for the deaf and dumb and for children. . . .
>
> He was cautious to an extent, which in the opinion of some of his best friends, abridged his usefulness. . . . But I have had many occasions to admire his wise, forecasting prudence, in keeping aloof from schemes, which although plausible, he could foresee must fail. This caution may have abridged his activity, but it prolonged the day of his usefulness.

A deeply religious man, Gallaudet devoted his life to the service of the unfortunate. He was not the kind of man to have capitalized on his new method, and he did nothing to stop others from adopting it and calling it their own. Thus, we can only assume that the sight-vocabulary primers that followed Gallaudet's simply copied his methods without crediting him or being fully aware of its conceptual origin. One year after the Mann-schoolmasters dispute, John Russell Webb published a primer in Watertown, New York, called *The New Word Method* and claimed to have "discovered" the new method.

Gallaudet left no record of his views of the Mann-schoolmasters dispute. The details certainly must have been known to him since his name was mentioned throughout, and he must have had some second thoughts about his methodology. We shall probably never know what they were. It is also strange that it is impossible to locate a copy of the Gallaudet primer, a book that was used by the primary schools of Boston for at least eight years and of which thousands of copies must have been printed. It would be amusing to see if the actual Dick and Jane story line originated in that very primer. Certainly the dog Spot is there. If, of course, the Dick and Jane story line originated with Gallaudet, the people who adapted it to its modern version would be hesitant to broadcast its origin. In searching for the primer, I discovered this interesting observation in the third edition (1934) of Charles F. Heartman's *Bibliographical Check-list of The New England Primer*:

> The most curious fact is the impossibility of locating some New England Primers sold during the last thirty years. They seem to have vanished for all efforts to locate some of them have proven futile. A number of copies located in the first and second edition of this book cannot be found now. Some have disappeared even from libraries, probably due to the crime wave which spread, a few years ago, over all the libraries in the country.

So there you have the mystery. If anyone can come up with a copy of Gallaudet's *Mother's Primer*, they will have an item of substantial historical interest in hand.

The aftermath of the Mann-schoolmasters dispute proved to be a defeat for the whole-word method, albeit a temporary one. The alphabet was restored in the Boston schools, and interest in the word method declined. Men like Samuel Greene rose to prominence in the academic world, while Horace Mann left Boston in 1848 to become a United States Senator. In 1853 Mann became president of Antioch College in Ohio. In 1859 he died. George Combe had died the year before. In his last letter to Combe, Mann had said:

> There is no man of whom I think so often; there is no man of whom I write so often; there is no man who has done me so much good as you have. I see many of the most valuable truths as I never should have seen them but for you, and all truths better than I should otherwise have done. If I could do it, I would make a pilgrimage to see you; and, if you would come to America, I would take care of you till one or the other of us should die.

When Mann died he was eulogized for helping to create America's public education system. The great debate over the teaching of reading was largely forgotten. Meanwhile, the memory of Thomas H. Gallaudet was perpetuated by the creation of Gallaudet College for deaf-mutes in Washington, D. C. Samuel Greene went on to a professorship at Brown University and the presidency of the American Institute of Instruction in 1870. He remained influential until his death in 1883.

But the whole-word method did not die. It went underground and spread like a virus throughout the educational system of the country. Divorced from its origins at the Hartford Asylum for the Deaf and Dumb, the method was used here and there with modifications.

However, most of the country relied on Webster's spelling books and McGuffey's readers, which were based on the traditional alphabet method. By the mid-1870s, however, a new generation of educational reformers were on the move to resurrect the whole-word method for the new progressive era. This time, instead of phrenology to provide the pseudoscientific justification for a change in methods, it was socialism and modern psychology. The principal individuals involved were Colonel Francis W. Parker, G. Stanley Hall, and John Dewey. The faces were different, but there was little difference in the ideas. As John Davies comments in his book, *Phrenology, Fad and Science*:

> The aims and techniques of phrenology applied to education, taken as a whole, sound today remarkably like those of twentieth-century "progressive education."

The sight-word method survived the long drought and by the 1880s was once more considered a legitimate way to teach reading. It would eventually return to public education on the back on a general reform movement, in the same vehicle that brought "progressive education" into the public schools. The theory behind progressive education was that life adjustment, or the development of the proper social spirit, was really the primary purpose of education and that the traditional academic approach in which the tools of learning were first mastered was not appropriate for the new age of social consciousness. The word-method fitted the new curriculum and the new permissive outlook.

It is interesting that the three leading men behind the new progressivism were native New Englanders. Francis W. Parker was born in 1837 in New Hampshire. He was something of a primitive, having had very little higher academic training. Yet eventually he rose to become, in 1899, the director of the School of Education at the University of Chicago. John Dewey, a Vermonter, had established his Laboratory School at the University of Chicago in 1896. He had been greatly influenced by Professor G. Stanley Hall, who had established a psychological laboratory at Johns Hopkins University when John Dewey was working there for his Ph.D. Hall had been born in Ashfield, Massachusetts, in 1844 and had received his Ph.D. at Harvard.

All three men advocated the use of the sight-word method more on philosophical grounds than pedagogical ones. Hall fortified his opinions with the latest psychological studies indicating that adults read words as wholes. Neither Parker, Hall, nor Dewey indicates that he had any idea as to the word method's conceptual origins. Yet these men readily

156

accepted the notion that words were to be learned and read as ideo-graphs rather than "phono"-graphs. For example, in his *Supplementary Reading for Primary Schools* (1880), published when he was supervisor of schools in Boston, Parker made the following statements in the preface:

> Learning to read is learning a vocabulary. A word is learned when it instantly recalls the idea of which it is a sign, in whatever relation it may be.
>
> A word is learned by repeated acts of association of the word with the idea it represents, and with other words recalling other ideas.

Thus, according to Parker, a printed word was not a collection of sound-symbols but a single idea-symbol. To him there was no difference between the numeral 5 and the word five. This is exactly what the word was for Gallaudet's deaf and dumb pupils: an idea-symbol.

The most eloquent advocate of the word method, however, was Edmund Burke Huey, who had studied educational psychology under G. Stanley Hall at Clark University. In his book *The Psychology and Pedagogy of Reading* (1907), Huey argued emphatically that words should be looked at ideographically and not phonically. He referred to all sorts of psychological studies proving that adults read words as wholes. Besides, he argued, children learned to read too well too early, and this wasn't good for them. He felt they shouldn't be taught to read until they were at least eight years old. As for the six-year old:

> The child has not at this stage developed the logical and idea-tional habits that most printed language demands, any more than had primitive man when he used pictographs and gestures. Let the child linger then in the oral stage, and let him use the primitive means of expression and communication as he likes to do; this at least until we have developed a body of genuine child reading-matter. He must not, by reading adult grammatical and logical forms, be exercised in mental habits that will violate his childhood and make him, at the best, a prig.

This point of view adhered to progressive education's new curriculum in which the full enjoyment of childhood was to supersede the dry mastery of skills for future adult use. Then Huey introduced a new argument for whole words, a sort of racial mysticism based on evolution:

157

The history of the languages in which picture-writing was long the main means of written communication has here a wealth of suggestions for the framers of the new primary course. It is not from mere perversity that the boy chalks or carves his records on book and desk and walls and school fences, not from chance that a picture-book is of all-absorbing interest. There is here a correspondence with, if not a direct recapitulation of, the life of the race; and we owe it to the child to encourage his living through the best there is in this pictograph stage as a means both of expression and impression, before we pass on to the race's late acquirements of written speech and phonic analysis.

Were these arguments any better than the pseudoscientific ones of the phrenologists? At least Huey was honest enough to state quite plainly that children should be taught to read English as if it were Chinese: ideographically. He knew exactly what a sight vocabulary was—a form of hieroglyphics. But it was the height of pedagogic nonsense to suggest that a child be taught to read ideographically so that he could recapitulate the "life of the race" in his various stages of education. What a waste of time to learn a method of reading long discarded because of its inferiority to the alphabet method merely for sentimental racial reasons and a misplaced nostalgia for the stone age. Huey assumed that after the child learned to read ideographically, that somewhere along the line, he would "pass on" into "phonic analysis," as if this were a sort of organic evolution occurring in the child's brain. There is no indication that such an evolution takes place in the child's brain. Of course, Huey was unaware of the conceptual origins of the sight-vocabulary method. He knew nothing about Gallaudet. In summing up the history of the word method, he wrote:

> The word method, beginning with the "Orbis Pictus" of Comenius, 1657, and taught by various reformers, notably by Jacotot in France and Worcester and Horace Mann in America, was very little used in America until 1870, when progressive teachers began using it in various parts of the country.

Thus, the whole Boston experience had been forgotten between 1845 and 1905 and the new reformers were proceeding on the premise that it had never taken place. That crucial bit of history was merely gathering dust in the archives. Huey knew of Mann's *Seventh Annual Report*, but there is no indication that he knew anything about the dispute it created. Perhaps he did but thought that the Boston schoolmasters were merely the reactionaries of Mann's day and therefore should be forgotten.

Huey's book contained a chapter for parents who wanted to teach their children to read at home by the new method. In recommending books for them to use, he added:

> Besides the large picture atlases already mentioned, such books as the "Illustrated Primer" by Sarah Fuller, used in the Horace Mann School for the Deaf, give a large number of pictures of familiar objects, with the names just below each.

Need more be said? Huey was being quite consistent in his belief that normal children could be taught to read with materials devised for the deaf. Huey had arrived at Gallaudet's point of view without even having known of Gallaudet's work, which shows how consistent the modern apostles of the sight-vocabulary method are with the method's conceptual origins. We reserve for last, however, the following passage from Huey, which probably has the most graphic description of the new approach to teaching reading the progressives have ever offered with a straight face:

> It is not indeed necessary that the child should be able to pronounce correctly or pronounce at all, at first, the new words that appear in his reading, any more than that he should spell or write all the new words that he hears spoken. If he grasps, approximately, the total meaning of the sentence in which the new word stands, he has read the sentence. Usually this total meaning will suggest what to call the new word, and the word's current articulation will usually have been learned in conversation, if the proper amount of oral practice shall have preceded reading. And even if the child substitutes words of his own for some that are on the page, provided that these express the meaning, it is an encouraging sign that the reading has been real, and recognition of details will come as it is needed. The shock that such a statement will give to many a practical teacher of reading is but an accurate measure of the hold that a false ideal has taken of us, viz., that to read is to say just what is upon the page, instead of to *think*, each in his own way, the meaning that the page suggests.
> . . . Until the insidious thought of reading as word-pronouncing is well worked out of our heads, it is well to place the emphasis strongly where it really belongs, on reading as *thought-getting* independently of expression.

This is about as direct a statement as has ever been made by a whole-word advocate on whole-word methodology. However, parents have never been presented with the argument in quite those terms, or given a choice in the public schools. They have never been asked whether they wanted their children to be taught as Huey suggested or by the method tested by three thousand years of experience. Neither Huey, nor Parker, nor Hall, nor Dewey had tested the word method extensively enough to know whether it was any good or not, and in 1905 no one had ever heard of dyslexia. The Boston schoolmasters at least had had eight years of experience with the word method before they criticized it. But the progressives had nothing to go on at all but their own philosophical instincts and some observations of the eye movements of adults while reading. The new method *had* to work because it was "progressive."

There was one more writer after Huey whose pedagogical work was of great importance to the writers of the whole-word basal readers to come. He was Dr. Arthur I. Gates of Columbia Teachers College. John Dewey had set up shop at Columbia University in 1904 after leaving the University of Chicago, and Columbia became the new fountainhead of progressive education. Gates's book, *The Improvement of Reading*, published in 1927, listed thirty-one experimental studies justifying the new sight-word reading program. Study number 20 was entitled "An Experimental Study of Teaching the Deaf to Read." In describing it, Gates wrote:

> Two brief statements of the theories underlying a method tried experimentally with deaf-mute subjects as a severe test of the intrinsic merits of the procedure and the possibilities of teaching reading without articulation or phonetic instruction. A full report concerning subjects, methods, materials, and results are given in the following: 21. Thompson, Helen, An Experimental Study of the Beginning Reading of Deaf-Mutes, a Doctor's dissertation to be published in 1927 by the Teachers College Bureau of Publications.

Gates's book contains a detailed description of Dr. Thompson's study. However, he summed up the results as follows:

> A more convincing demonstration of the value of the new method appears in the comparison of the attainments of the deaf group with the achievement of normal first grade pupils in the public schools. The deaf-mute group obtained a score almost identical with the average attainments of pupils in Detroit schools on the Detroit

Reading Test and the scores on the preliminary forms of the three Gates Reading Tests are as good as, if not a trifle superior to, the average achievements of normal New York pupils.

Naturally deaf children would do as well as, if not better than, normal children under a method which had been originally devised for their use. But Gates interpreted this as conclusive proof that the method would work wonders with normal children. After all, if deaf children did so well with it, normal children could be expected to do even better.

By 1920, the sight-word method was being used in the new progressive private schools, which were trying to implement John Dewey's ideas. One such school was The Little Red School House founded in New York in 1921. In Agnes de Lima's book about the school, there is this description of the method used in teaching the children to read:

> We make the approach to reading as natural as possible. A child may take a picture of a boat or a train and he or the teacher may say, "It is a big boat" or "It is a big long train." The picture then may be hung on the wall and under it the teacher may write on a strip of paper level with the children's eyes, "This is a big boat." The teacher reads this also, and so do the children. Then the teacher asks the children if they can pick out the parts on the two strips of writing which are alike. Sheets of paper bearing these same words may be distributed and the children asked to match them to the charts on the walls and to read them after they have matched them. Besides matching words or sentences, we may match words and pictures, sentences and pictures, or we may complete a sentence by choosing one word from a group of words phonetically related. Or again we may find words which have the same beginnings or the same endings; we might find small words in larger ones.

Such techniques of teaching were all right for small private schools but they were not very practical for teaching reading in the large public schools. There had to be new textbooks or primers written and published based on the word method. Scott, Foresman Company was one of the first to fill the need. For years Scott, Foresman had published the Elson Basic Readers authored by William Harris Elson, a prolific textbook writer. It is said that Scott, Foresman sold about fifty million copies of Elson's books. Elson's books were all quite traditional until 1930 when, under the general heading of Elson Basic Readers, the first Dick and Jane Pre-Primer and Primer were published. The *Teacher's Guidebook* was authored by William S. Gray and Edna B. Liek. By

1930 Elson was seventy-four-years old and it is unlikely that he had much to do with the new Dick and Jane books. Gray had been dean of the University of Chicago College of Education from 1917, and obviously Scott, Foresman felt that it had placed the authorship of its new whole-word Pre-Primer and Primer in the best pedagogical hands.

The Dick and Jane Pre-Primer bears a 1930 copyright and a notice that it is a revision of The Elson Pupil's Handchart, copyright 1921, 1927. I have not been able to obtain a copy of the Handchart, but I have read through the 1930 edition of Dick and Jane, the *Teacher's Guidebook for the Elson Basic Readers, Pre-Primer and Primer.* The preface outlines in detail the entire sight-word, controlled-vocabulary methodology. But its authors were no more aware of its conceptual origins than were Huey, Dewey, Hall, Gates, or Parker. Most teachers who write textbooks refer to earlier textbooks for guidance. Did the authors of Dick and Jane use Gallaudet's *Primer* as a model? We won't know until we find a copy of it.

It is interesting to compare the 1930 edition of the Dick and Jane Pre-Primer with the 1951 edition analyzed in the earlier chapters of this book. Apparently the Dick and Jane books were so successful that they warranted new updated editions. Two very interesting contradictory developments took place between those two editions which are important to examine. The first was the apparent commercial success of Dick and Jane which not only encouraged new competitors to enter the field, but catapulted Dick and Jane into first place in public school use. The second was the obvious pedagogic failure of the new method despite its commercial success. We can measure that failure by simply comparing the two editions.

In 1930 the Dick and Jane Pre-Primer taught 68 sight words in 39 pages of story text, with an illustration per page, a total of 565 words and a *Teacher's Guidebook* of 87 pages. In 1951 that same pre-primer had been expanded to 172 pages, divided into three separate pre-primers, with 184 illustrations, a total of 2,613 words, and a *Guidebook* of 182 pages to teach a sight vocabulary of only 58 words! How much more evidence was needed to prove that the method was a pedagogic failure?

In 1930 the word *look* was repeated eight times in the pre-primer. In 1951 it is repeated 110 times. In 1930 the word *oh* was repeated twelve times, in 1951, 138 times. In 1930 the word *see* was repeated twenty-seven times, in 1951, 176 times!

Thus, even the authors of the Dick and Jane Pre-Primer were quite aware that children did not learn a sight vocabulary as easily as expected. Otherwise the later revisions would not have taken the shape they did and they would not have had to add the *Guess Who* review Pre-Primer for children who couldn't learn the first fifty-eight words by the completion of the regular pre-primers. Despite this incredible failure, entire public school systems were converting to the sight-vocabulary method with complete disregard for its long-range effects. The result was that a whole remedial reading industry was needed to correct the failures of the method, all run by the same educators writing the new sight-vocabulary basal readers and teaching the virtues of this methodology to all the new young teachers. If ever there was a fraud perpetrated on the American people, on a scale of unprecedented proportions, with consequences enormously damaging to millions of children, this was it. And it was all being carried out in the name of progressive education.

8

From Rudolf Flesch to Jeanne Chall

The period between 1930 and 1965 is probably the sorriest chapter in the history of American education. It was a period in which entire school systems adopted the new methods of teaching reading without the slightest awareness of what their long-range effects might be on the children subjected to them. As long as the new methods had the "progressive" label and were endorsed by such great, all-knowing philosophers and lovers of children as John Dewey, it was assumed by the lowly grade-school teachers and highly impressionable school boards that they were good. If it was "progressive," it had to be good, classroom evidence to the contrary notwithstanding.

The classroom evidence began to make itself known quite early. To get an idea of how much of it there was, all we have to do is peruse the *Education Index* for those years to see what was being written about the reading problem in the various educational journals. From January 1929 to June 1932 we find thirty articles listed under the heading of "reading difficulties" and fifty-eight devoted to "remedial teaching." Two years later, in the period between July 1935 and June 1938, we find ninety-two articles on "reading difficulties" and 117 on "remedial teaching." Ironically most of the articles about the reading difficulties were written by the very educators who were pushing the methods which created the difficulties. They included E. W. Dolch, Ruth Strang, Arthur I. Gates, Emmett A. Betts, William S. Gray, Guy L. Bond, and Paul A.

Witty. Dolch was an indefatigable compiler of word lists for the sight vocabularies of the new basal readers. Ruth Strang was an expert on remedial problems. Gates was the leading authority on the word method and author of the Macmillan readers. Betts specialized in remedial problems and produced his own Betts Basic Readers for the American Book Company. Gray, of course, was the senior author of Dick and Jane. Bond was another remedial specialist and authored a basal series for Lyons and Carnahan, and Witty became D. C. Heath's leading basal author. In all this, there were no traditionalists in the manner of the Boston schoolmasters voicing dissenting opinions. The progressives had so completely taken control of teacher education and pedagogical theory, that opposition was either passive or token at best.

The only article we came across in that period indicating that the whole-word method could cause problems was entitled "The 'Sight Reading' Method of Teaching Reading as a source of Reading Disability," in the February 1929 *Journal of Educational Psychology.* It was authored by Dr. Samuel T. Orton, a physician, who was almost apologetic in the way he approached the subject. After all, Harold Rugg, an associate of Dewey, edited the journal, and Arthur Gates served on its editorial board. Nevertheless, what Orton had to say was extremely important:

> I feel some trepidation in offering criticism in a field somewhat outside of that of my own endeavor but a very considerable part of my attention for the past four years has been given to the study of reading disability from the standpoint of cerebral physiology. This work has now extended over a comparatively large series of cases from many different schools and both the theory which has directed this work and the observations garnered therefrom seem to bear with sufficient directness on certain teaching methods in reading to warrant critical suggestions which otherwise might be considered overbold.
>
> I wish to emphasize at the beginning that the strictures which I have to offer here do not apply to the use of the sight method of teaching reading as a whole but only to its effects on a restricted group of children for whom, as I think we can show, this technique is not only not adapted but often proves an actual obstacle to reading progress, and moreover I believe that this group is one of considerable educational importance both because of its size and because here faulty teaching methods may not only prevent the acquisition of academic education by children of average capacity

166

but may also give rise to far reaching damage to their emotional life.

The sight reading method (or "look and say" of the English) has been credited with giving much faster progress in the acquisition of reading facility than its precursors and this statement I will not challenge if the measure of accomplishment be the *average* progress of a group or class. Average progress of large numerical units, however, makes no allowance for the study of effect in individuals, particularly if certain of them deviate to some degree from the others in their methods of acquisition and therefore in their requirements. To the mental hygienist whose interest is focussed on the individual and his problems rather than on group progress the results as determined by average accomplishment are of little value whereas the effect of a given method on the individual child is all important.

Orton went on to point out that some children could not learn to read via the whole-word method. They reversed letters or parts of words or syllables. Their "disorder" ranged in severity from the slightly normal to extreme cases which were described as "congenital word blindness." The physiological reason for this phenomenon was not entirely clear, but he offered a solution:

> . . . kinesthetic training by tracing or writing while reading and sounding and by following the letters with a finger (a method under taboo today) to insure consistent direction of reading during phonetic synthesis of a word or syllable.

It is easy to see why the *Journal of Educational Psychology* was not too disturbed by the doctor's article. The article had suggested the notion that the sight-reading technique was perfectly all right for the average child, but that a small number of "abnormal" children could not learn to read by this method because of something which was wrong with *them*, not the method. In time, the progressives developed this notion further to suggest that there was something wrong with anyone who couldn't learn to read by sight-reading techniques. Advocates of the sight-reading basal programs were the first to list all the things that were wrong with children who could not learn to read via their methods. In the April 1935 *Elementary English Review*, William S. Gray listed a few of the things that were wrong with children having trouble learning to read via Dick and Jane: mental deficiency or retardation; defective vision; auditory deficiencies; congenital word blindness, which he pointed out was also known as developmental alexia, congenital aphasia, dyslexia, congenital alexia, strephosymbolia, and inability to learn to read; cerebral dominance, also known as handedness, eyedness, ambidexterity, mirror-writing; emotional instability; constitutional, nervous and emotional disorders. That included just about everyone.

Other writers added their own exotic terms to the growing lexicon of reading-disability diseases: binocular imbalance, lateral dominance, word-deafness, word-blindness, acuity dominance, sinistral and mixed manual-ocular behavior, eye-muscle imbalance, poor fusion, social maladjustment, personality maladjustments, directional confusion, eye maturation, minimal brain damage, axial rotation, ocular blocks, endocrine disturbances, lateral preferences, vertical rotation in visual-motor performance, perceptual retardation, dyslexaphoria, prenatal and paranatal factors, monocular vision, neural confusion, sociopathic tendencies, ocular-manual laterality. One writer related the blood picture to reading failure, another related a child's first memories of accidents to reading failure. There was no end to the things that were wrong with children who couldn't learn to read via the whole-word method.

But of course Dr. Gray knew that the method was at fault, not the children, otherwise he would not have revised the Dick and Jane pre-primers and primer as he did from the 1930 edition to the later ones. The kinds of revisions indicated quite clearly that the average child was having considerable difficulty learning to read by sight-reading techniques. But the commercial success of the sight-reading basal systems was so great, that the method had to be "improved" to meet the insatiable demand of the school systems for something so progressive.

Meanwhile, the progressives were doing an effective public relations job on the parents. For example, *Parents* magazine of April 1931 carried an article by Dr. Gates on "New Ways of Teaching Reading." The magazine explained: "Parents puzzled by modern methods of teaching will find this article helpful." In it, Gates characterized the new method as "natural" and "undistorted," the old as "barren" and "formal." It all sounded wonderfully progressive and it was also good sales promotion for the basal readers. However, parents were apparently still not satisified, for *Parents* magazine published another article in January 1935 by Lydia K. Gerhardt on "How Children Are Learning to Read." The magazine explained: "Parents concerned because children do not know their letters will be interested in this explanation of the modern approach to reading." Miss Gerhardt explained to the parents:

When you and I went to school we learned to read in the following order: alphabet, syllables, words, phrases, and sentences.

Today, more rather than less attention is given to each of these steps, but the order is exactly reversed. This change has come about after a careful analysis of what constitutes effective reading in the intermediate and upper grades and in adult life.

Despite such assurances, the situation continued to get worse. By 1944 *Life* magazine could publish an article on dyslexia which, when you read it today, indicates the incredible lengths to which educators had gone to find fault with the children who could not learn to read. It characterizes the pedagogical climate of the time more graphically than anything else I've come across. You have to read it to believe it:

Millions of children in the U.S. suffer from dyslexia which is the medical term for reading difficulties. It is responsible for about 70% of the school failures in 6- to 12-year-age group, and handicaps about 15% of all grade-school children. Dyslexia may stem from a variety of physical ailments or combination of them—glandular imbalance, heart disease, eye or ear trouble—or from a deep-seated psychological disturbance that "blocks" a child's ability to learn. It has little or nothing to do with intelligence and is usually curable.

To analyze and cure reading difficulties Chicago's Dyslexia Institute, in Wesley Memorial Hospital on the downtown campus of Northwestern University, has set up a clinic equipped with Man-from-Mars machines that amuse the young patients while diagnosing their ailments. After a series of exhaustive tests, the Institute's specialists get together to determine the causes of the trouble and the treatment needed.

To most children the Dyslexia Institute is a wonderful place of gadgets, pictures and games. Like little Ruth Moyers (pictured in the article) they read before an ophthalmograph, eye-movement camera which produces a strip of movie film. Graphs on this film reveal reading habits. For good readers the movie graph proceeds evenly as the eye lingers for proper intervals on each word, then sweeps back to read the next line. A bad reader's graph is jerky. Its steps are uneven, showing faults like fixation (lingering too long on word) and regression (going back to read word again). Reader takes too long to read single line.

The children also make phonograph records of their voices to test phonetic troubles and play telephone with an audiometer to test their hearing. They play with blocks and tell a sympathetic man all about the mean kids who live next door. Thus the institute pain-

169

lessly uncovers the physical and psychological troubles of its patients.

About halfway through her tests, Ruth Moyers got to the stereoscope. In it she saw what she thought was a single clear picture of a rabbit, porcupine, butterfly, bird and grass. Since this was in reality two slightly different pictures, she thereby proved that she had perfect fusion and stereopsis.

In her intelligence tests, Ruth also proved to have an I.Q. of 118. She is typical of the children at the Institute, who are almost all endowed with good eyes and minds. Ruth needed—and got—thyroid treatments, removal of tonsils and adenoids, exercises to strengthen her eye muscles. Other patients may need dental work, nose, throat or ear treatment, or a thorough airing out of troublesome home situations that throw a sensitive child off the track of normality. In the experience of the institute these range from alcoholic fathers to ambitious mothers who try to force their children too fast in school.

How thyroid treatments or an adenoid operation are supposed to improve a child's ability to read is not explained. One expects to find some specialists suggesting a prefrontal lobotomy as a cure for reading disability. If I characterize this period as the sorriest in American educational history, the reader will see that I hardly exaggerate. One wonders who was worse, the schoolmasters of old who whipped their pupils with birch rods or those of the 1940s, '50s, and '60s who submitted them to the psychological tortures and induced disorders of the whole-word method. One wonders about the teachers who went along with this refined form of institutionalized sadism. An article by Amy Porter in the November 30, 1946 issue of *Collier's* gives us a glimpse of the attitude prevalent among teachers at the time. Entitled "Why Can't They Read?" the article answered, "A third of all school children are illiterate." Then Miss Porter elaborated:

> It's nothing new, it's been going on for years. It is common knowledge among educators that at least one third of our school children lag behind their age and grade in reading, all the way through school. Thousands emerge from high school totally unable to read and comprehend so much as the daily paper. As for reading for pleasure—only a lucky minority ever learn to do that.

The reading problem was obviously becoming a full-blown national crisis, with teachers quite well aware of it. An article in the November

170

1947 *Education Digest* described the problem's effects on the high school level:

> The wail of the high-school teacher is heard throughout the land. She moans that sophomores cannot read their textbooks and hence are failing in their English, history, and health classes.

Six years later, in the May 1953 issue of *High Points*, a periodical for high school teachers published by the Board of Education of New York City, we find an article entitled "America's Reading Problem," which declares:

> America's reading problem involves—and this may seem somewhat incredible—millions of people who have gone to school for years, and for some reason read poorly, or not at all. From twenty to thirty percent of our population now suffers from dyslexia, as reading difficulties are technically called, and the situation seems to be getting worse.
> What are the causes of this falling-off in reading? There is no agreement among educators on that score.

All of the articles of that period about the reading problem written by teachers all had the same thing in common. None of them could identify the cause of the problem. Educators simply refused to believe that their methods could be causing such incredible disability. Yet the changeover to the new methods of teaching reading and the subsequent widespread development of reading disability should have led any sensible educator to an investigation of the new methods to see if they were responsible for the problem. But it never happened. It took a noneducator, a professional writer, to finally bring the whole matter of methods to public attention and scrutiny. That writer was Rudolf Flesch whose *Why Johnny Can't Read* was published in 1955. To gain a somewhat helpful perspective of the period, one might compare the circumstances of Dr. Flesch's dissent from the prevailing view with the dissent of the Boston schoolmasters of 1844. At that time the debate was among educators, and the traditionalists or conservatives were not confronted with a mammoth liberal establishment which could withstand their opposition. But in 1955, the situation was quite different. Flesch, a noneducator, was attacking the citadel of institutionalized public education. He was attacking an establishment representing the most respected professors in the nation's most prestigious colleges of education. These men were also the authors of the most widely used basal readers

171

throughout the public schools of the country, backed by the largest text-book publishers in New York and Chicago. It was more than any one man or one book could oppose, and that is why Flesch's book was merely the first shot in what was to become a long protracted war between the proponents of the phonics and look-say methods. But he said what had to be said and what no teacher had dared to say:

> The teaching of reading—all over the United States, in all the schools, and in all the textbooks—is totally wrong and flies in the face of all logic and common sense.

It was a clear, ringing declaration of war, and the look-say establishment knew it. No one before this had blamed teaching methods for the reading problem. All blame had been placed on the children. Little wonder then that the public responded favorably to the book, realizing that in Flesch they had someone who understood their sense of frustration. Reviewer William Morris echoed this sentiment in the *Saturday Review* of July 30, 1955:

> If enough American parents read and follow the precepts that Mr. Flesch so effectively sets forth "Why Johnny Can't Read" may well be ranked the most important contribution to the betterment of public-school teaching methods in the past two decades. Hundreds of thousands of parents, inarticulate in the face of pompous and condescending "explanations" of the educators, have at last found a highly articulate and very well-informed spokesman.

In that same issue of the *Saturday Review* Emmett A. Betts, in an unfavorable review, characterized Flesch as "a master of histrionics."

"In his effort to present his case for phonics," he wrote, "Flesch has introduced confusion regarding what reading is." Most of Betts's review criticized the last section of Flesch's book which instructed parents in how to teach their children to read by phonics. Clearly, Betts found that section to be the greatest threat to himself and the other authors of basal readers.

The look-say establishment particularly disputed Flesch on the concept of what reading is. Flesch had made his definition of reading quite clear: "By reading I mean getting the meaning of words formed by letters on a printed page, and nothing else." Helen M. Robinson, writing in the *Elementary School Journal* of October 1955, spoke for all of the look-say advocates:

This reviewer, like most educators in this country, is unwilling to accept this definition. Actually she doubts, in view of his earlier writings, which have emphasized presenting materials in readable language, that Dr. Flesch himself has such a narrow conception of reading.

Dr. Robinson, a close associate of William S. Gray, knew however that the Flesch book would have a considerable influence on parents, and this is what worried the look-say establishment most of all. She wrote:

> The book is likely to have wide appeal to parents whose children are making slow progress in reading. It will comfort them because of the dogmatic statements the author has made. Unfortunately parents may put great pressure on school personnel to adopt Flesch's plan. However, most educators have learned to read critically and to distinguish between scientific factual findings and emotional appeals.

Look-say authors and experts were certain that they could convince the members of their own profession that Flesch was wrong. Their counterattacks in the leading educational journals reached the teachers, not the parents. Paul Witty, professor of education and director of the psychoeducational clinic at Northwestern University, was interviewed by *Nation's Schools* in July 1955. Dr. Witty had been one of those pedagogues singled out by Flesch as an important whole-word advocate. The magazine prefaced the interview with this paragraph:

> How does one tell a gullible public that it is being exploited by a biased writer—as in the case with Rudolf Flesch and his book "Why Johnny Can't Read"? It will take time and patience for parents to learn that Mr. Flesch has mixed a few half-truths with prejudices to capitalize on two misconceptions. The first is his superficial notion as to what reading really is. The second is his misrepresentation as to how reading is taught.

Besides debating Flesch on the matter of defining what reading is, the look-say experts also contended that Flesch had misrepresented their methods. This was the same complaint Horace Mann had voiced against the Boston schoolmasters. They had misrepresented him, he said, although they had actually quoted his own words, just as Flesch

173

had quoted from the works of the leading look-say experts. It is interesting that several of the look-say defenders referred back to Horace Mann in their defense. For example, Dr. Witty said:

> No man in the history of education is more revered or respected than Horace Mann, who was the first secretary of the Massachusetts Board of Education. Stacking his words against the accusations of Mr. Flesch, we hear Mr. Mann reporting, in 1838:
> "I have devoted especial pains to learn, with some degree of numerical accuracy, how far the reading in our schools is an exercise of the mind in thinking and feeling, and how far it is a barren action of the organs of speech upon the atmosphere. . . . The result is that more than eleven-twelfths of all the children in the reading classes, in our schools, do not understand the meaning of the words they read; that they do not master the sense of the reading lessons, and that the ideas and feelings intended by the author to be conveyed to, and excited in, the reader's mind, still rest in the author's intention, never having yet reached the place of their destination."

That quote was from Mann's *Second Annual Report*. But Witty had not taken it from the original source. He took it, according to a footnote reference, from an article in the April 1948 issue of *High Points*. We doubt that Witty had ever read Mann in the original or was familiar with the Mann-schoolmasters dispute. Also, Witty missed the obvious point of what Mann was complaining about. The children had all learned to read. It was a matter of what they were doing with that skill once they had mastered it. Flesch complained that the children weren't being permitted to master that skill, and therefore any talk about reading for meaning before they knew *how* to read was patently ridiculous. In the same interview Witty quoted from Francis W. Parker, also from a secondary source, to substantiate his look-say arguments. But simply because Parker was just as mistaken as Mann did not mean that Witty's arguments were any better or improved by the reference. But it revealed much about the lack of historical knowledge professors in the highest levels of our schools of education have.

Witty was not the only prominent educator who revealed his ignorance in this manner. Professor Virgil M. Rogers, dean of the School of Education at Syracuse University, did likewise in an article in the December 1955 *Atlantic Monthly* entitled "Dr. Flesch's Cure-All":

> As to Dr. Flesch's contention that the United States itself had no problems until "phonics was abandoned in favor of the word

174

method," one can only wonder how he could have missed such a landmark as Horace Mann's Seventh Annual Report as Secretary of the Massachusetts Board of Education, covering the year 1843. Mann was describing a word method which he had been fascinated to observe in German schools. His enthusiastic description suggests that it was a combination of word and phonic and kinesthetic methods.

One wonders how Professor Rogers could have missed the great debate that the *Seventh Annual Report* provoked and the subsequent return to the alphabet in the Boston schools after that debate was over. But simply because a man is a dean of a school of education doesn't mean that he knows very much about the history of education.

Of course, Flesch was also unaware of the Boston experiment that took place during Horace Mann's administration. But Flesch, as his look-say critics pointed out derogatorily, was not a professor of education, nor even a school teacher. So we can excuse Flesch, but not the professors. It is their job to know the history of their own profession thoroughly and intimately.

Professor Gates was another of the look-say experts who had been strongly criticized by Flesch. His reply, "Why Mr. Flesch Is Wrong," appeared in the September 1955 issue of the *National Education Association Journal*. He characterized Flesch as "a popular writer . . . whose doctor's degree in adult education represents no considerable experience or training in the teaching of elementary-school reading." That was enough to convince most teachers that Flesch was not an authority on reading, but that Gates, Witty, Gray, Betts, Robinson, and the others were. Gates also echoed the cry that Flesch had misrepresented them:

> By placing the American system in a false position, it is of course easy to attack it. Most teachers and all students of reading instruction would vigorously disapprove of the methods which Flesch falsely ascribed to them. In many instances he has attributed to investigators and writers the very views they have severely criticized.

What Gates meant was that the whole-word basal readers did indeed teach phonetic skills or generalizations as clues to word recognition. And he hoped that parents would not know the difference between this and phonics. But obviously the phonetic skills or rules as taught in the basal readers were not the same as phonics in the sense that Flesch wrote about it. Flesch had not misrepresented them at all. In the areas where he had been inaccurate—in identifying the origins of the whole-word method, or in evaluating the reading situation in Europe—his inaccuracy was because of simple lack of knowledge. But when it came to the whole-word method as it was being taught through the basal readers, Flesch was accurate. His analysis of the whole-word method was not very deep, but he understood the most important feature of it: that it was an ideographic approach to the teaching of a phonetically constructed written language. That was all that was necessary to point out to a public which was completely lacking of any such understanding. Most parents hadn't the faintest idea what the new methods were like—no more than they know what the new math is like. They merely assumed that the new methods were better than the old ones. Thus, for many of them, what Flesch had to say was shocking news.

The whole-word experts, however, concentrated most of their criticism on Flesch's primer in the back of his book. After all, if a child could be taught to read by merely using that simple, inexpensive primer, they'd have no need for the elaborate, expensive basal systems. The *Saturday Review* of September 11, 1954 painted a rather remarkable picture of how these systems had become the monsters they were in merely two decades:

> The first Basal Readers were the idea of Dr. Arthur I. Gates of Teachers College, Columbia University, who, in the 1920s, assembled a list of words which every child at certain periods of reading ability should know. These lists are known as controlled vocabularies. . . .
>
> These lists have resulted today in the seventy-five books and aids —which carry the child through the eighth grade—known as The Macmillan Readers; in the more than forty books known as the Betts Basic Readers, published by the American Book Co.; in the seventy-two books and pamphlets known as the Ginn Basic Readers; in the hundred or so known as The Scott-Foresman Curriculum Foundation Series, which take a child right up to college level; and in the 120 books, pamphlets, film strips, picture-and-word cards published by Row, Peterson & Co., and called the New Alice and Jerry Series. . . .
>
> Much of this lag (in updating the vocabularies) is due to the fact that the publishers of these books, whose manufacturing costs are high, must, in order to meet these costs, sell the same series for five to ten years without the expense of revisions.

176

Thus, as a tremor of fear went through the publishing houses, the attack on Flesch's phonics primer had to be swift and to the point. Dr. Witty wrote:

> The use of this type of phonic system is extremely difficult for most 5 or 6 year old children. Children using such systems frequently become hopelessly confused and discouraged—often become clinic cases.

That, of course, was pure and simple hogwash. The reading clinics had all grown out of whole-word methodology. The article in the May 1953 issue of *High Points* on the reading problem had described the new world of remedial reading which had come into existence:

> Nearly every university in the United States now operates a "reading clinic" staffed by psychiatrists, psychologists, and trained reading technicians, and equipped with novel mechanical devices such as the metronoscope, the ophthalmograph, and the reading rate accelerator. . . . In addition, an entirely new professional group of private practitioners has arisen, whose specialized training in the field justifies their hanging out shingles as "reading counselors" and rating large fees for consultation and remedial treatment.

There was a dyslexic clinic in Dr. Witty's own university which *Life* magazine had described for all America to read about, and Dr. Orton had made it clear as far back as 1929 that sight-reading caused reading disability. In addition, Horace Mann did not have to complain about any reading clinics in any of his annual reports, no matter how much he disliked the alphabet method.

Nevertheless, the specious arguments of the whole-word experts were circulated throughout the teaching profession with the help of the publishers, so that teachers everywhere could be prepared to answer the inquiries of irate parents. The preface to Gate's article described what was being done to meet the emergency:

> He [Gates] has prepared a longer article which the Macmillan Company [New York] is printing in anticipation of quantity orders. Another criticism of Mr. Flesch's book, prepared at the University of California (Berkeley), can be obtained for $1 per 100 from the California Teachers Association. . . . Still another statement by Arthur F. Corey titled "Johnny *Can* Read!" (reprinted from the San

177

Francisco *Examiner*) is available from the National School Public Relations Association. . . .

Time magazine of January 9, 1956 summed up rather neatly the impact Flesch's book had made on the country:

> If 1955 was notable for anything as far as the U.S. public schools is concerned, it may be that it will be remembered as the Year of Rudolf Flesch. . . .
>
> American education closed ranks against Flesch, and when educators were not denouncing the "Devil in the Flesch," they were damning the "Flesch peddlers." Nevertheless, though *Johnny* was marred by flagrant exaggerations, it remained on the bestseller list for thirty-nine weeks, and thousands of parents—and teachers —found in Flesch the angrily dramatic spokesman they had been waiting for.
>
> More than 125 newspapers across the nation ran the book as a serial. When the Detroit *Free Press* published its series, one distraught father wrote in to describe the plight of his son in high school. "They are trying to expel him," he said, "or in some manner rid themselves of him. You know why? Because he cannot read. How in the hell he got as far as 10B . . . is beyond my means of comprehension." In Louisville, a mother reported on her third-grader's typewriting: "He typed the letters very easily . . . But after typing the letters B-O-W-L across the page about ten times, he called it *pot*." To such parents, Flesch's book touched a sensitive nerve.

Despite the uproar created by the book, the look-say establishment merely consolidated its position, and no change in methods took place in most of the public schools. The look-say authors had formed the International Reading Association in 1956 and their hold over the elementary teaching profession for the next ten years was to be as great, if not greater, than it had been before the publication of the Flesch book. One would have thought otherwise in a free country, but one tends to underestimate the power that institutionalized vested interests can have in a country with the kind of public school system we have. Phonics made headway in the private schools and in some isolated public schools which had phonics-oriented teachers. But the look-say method continued to dominate the public schools through the use of the basal readers, and the reading situation continued to deteriorate.

Other books critical of the whole-word method by Arthur Trace,

Charles Walcutt and other phonics advocates followed Flesch's, but they said little that was new or had not been previously argued. Their influence on the teaching profession was minimal. If any teacher wanted to get ahead, he or she had to tow the line of the International Reading Association or remain in the backwater. No teacher could buck the powerful combination of professors of education, authors of basal readers, the publishing companies, the educational journals controlled by the IRA or pro-look-say progressives, organizations like the National Council of English Teachers, plus the whole remedial reading community. A parent got nowhere. He either had to teach his child phonics at home or put him in a private school where it was taught. Few parents bothered. If a parent went to the school and complained, he was told, "But we do teach phonics." What kind of phonics was never adequately explained.

However, Flesch's book had planted a seed of doubt in the minds of many teachers, publishers, and reading experts, and although the look-say establishment maintained and perhaps even increased its formidable power and position for the next ten years, a kind of pedagogical guerrilla warfare continued during that period in which phonics advocates slowly chipped away at the look-say structure. There was a small but increasing demand for beginning basal readers based on phonics, and more schools were interested in experimenting with phonics. Even the most pro-look-say educational journals had to open their pages to such experiments. Thus, the December 1957 issue of *Elementary English*, edited by John J. DeBoer, one of Gray's graduate students, published an article by Robert L. Filbin entitled "Prescription for the Johnny Who Can't Read," in which he took up the problem of the child having difficulties with look-say. Mr. Filbin wrote:

> The storm which was created by Rudolph Flesch has somewhat subsided, and those people charged with reading instruction in our schools have had time to look at the situation more objectively. Flesch's exclusive phonics approach for all children has been roundly denounced and without doubt quite justly.
>
> On the other hand many people who are constantly evaluating what they are doing have raised some questions about the techniques they are using because they have discovered that they do not teach *all* children to read. . . .
>
> Let's diagnose the child who is having difficulty. He is often ambidextrous, sometimes stutters or has some other speech impediment, is often good in arithmetic—frequently reverses words (*was* instead of *saw*) not only in reading but spelling. He falters in oral

reading, fails to get proper attacks, makes impossible guesses, and usually ends up in a complete state of flustered confusion. It is here that the problem must be dealt with realistically—and the teacher must know how to proceed.

These children can be taught successfully by an alphabetic approach. In the method developed by Anna Gillingham, she teaches the child a few letters comprising one or two short vowel sounds and consonants that have only unequivocal sounds and forms which do not become letters if reversed (as *b* and *d*). When these letters are known by their names and sounds they can be made into words—synthetic phonics. Slowly new letters and letter combinations are introduced and new words are added and finally used in sentences.

Can this method of teaching be used in the classroom? Yes, it can, and is being used successfully in the Peterborough Consolidated School in Peterborough, New Hampshire. . . .

The Peterborough program, which is completing its second year, was set up as an experimental project in two classrooms, a second and third grade. The results have been astonishing. Where children had been stymied at pronouncing words, they themselves were amazed when they could sound out words beyond their grade level. Other children in the same room who were learning by the normal method became interested and begged to read the word cards and to write the sounds on the board as the other children did. . . .

The project at Peterborough is considered to be an experimental one. So far it has worked successfully with the children participating. They are learning to read by this method where other methods have failed. . . .

Does this mean that all children should be taught in this manner? It is obvious that this is not necessary. If other children can learn to read successfully by the sight method, as the majority can, then it is not necessary to teach them in this way. Nevertheless, let us recognize these other children and give them the help they need to learn to read.

Filbin's article elicited a letter from Anna Gillingham, which was published in the February 1958 issue of the magazine. It is a long letter, and because it is the best statement on beginning reading I have found after studying fifteen years of issues of *Elementary English* and *The Reading Teacher*, it is eminently worth including in this book. If the reader knew how rare such clear, interesting statements are in the professional teaching journals, he would appreciate the sense of discovery

180

I experienced when I came upon it. It is, of course, noteworthy that it was published as a letter, not an article:

In the December issue of *Elementary English* there appeared an article by Robert Filbin entitled, "prescription for the Johnny who can't read."

Since his prescription involves the application of my technique, I was naturally much interested and genuinely grateful for the appreciation Mr. Filbin expressed. It seems to me, however, that there are some points which should be further explained and amplified. Also, teachers interested in my technique should be made familiar with some of the trends widening the application of this technique.

The first of these points is the connotation of Specific Language Disability. Increasingly, as these words are used to denote the cause of a child's reading difficulty, it has become more and more common to make unfavorable comparisons between the "afflicted" child and his "normal" classmates. As I use this term it signifies nothing pathological or "abnormal," most certainly nothing subnormal, for many of our reading cases are very bright children. It means rather that the difficulty in reading and spelling under consideration is not due to visual or auditory defects or to low mentality, but specifically to the language pattern of the individual. . . .

In the long eons of evolution the language pattern has been perfectly established in a very small percentage of individuals. An occasional John Stuart Mill reads in his cradle and an occasional Edward L. Thorndike cannot remember ever misspelling a word. Such persons deviate from the "normal" by being supernormal. The great majority of us "average" "normal" people manifest some degree of language difficulty. Some are inaccurate readers; some reverse letters or words in spelling, as when a well-educated woman suddenly wrote dry-taw for tawdry; some people are never quite sure, when writing, whether or not it will turn out to be mirror writing, or made up of letters of almost illegible form. Eloquent testimony to such deviations from the conventional language pattern can readily be demonstrated in any group of unselected "normal" adults, if the topic of reading or spelling is introduced.

Ten to twenty percent of "normal" children of school age have sufficiently severe difficulty in reading or spelling to constitute a real block in their school progress.

For the last twenty years, as a pioneer in the field, I have been administering Prereading Tests to kindergarten children to discover

181

those who, in all reasonable probability, will have difficulty with reading and spelling unless taught by the Alphabetic Approach; and on the other hand, to determine those who can perhaps safely risk being taught by the Sight-Word Method.

It has been my experience that a group of children with average or superior intelligence and no visual or auditory defect, assigned to the Alphabetic Technique, will succeed by this procedure; difficulty in its success is with borderline cases. It may happen that a pupil will safely attempt this reading of words as ideograms and later he may fail signally in spelling. For example, one child with an I.Q. of 165 did so well in the visual recall tests that he was placed in the Sight-Word Group. He learned to read very readily, but by the end of the third grade had to have remedial training in spelling and penmanship.

In other words, the imperfectly established Language pattern may reveal itself in one area only as in reading; in several tests—reading, spelling, penmanship, speech, or in a combination, as spelling and handwriting. It would seem to be impossible to draw a sharp line of demarcation between those who would profit greatly by this technique and those who can learn in no other way. The idea of teaching each child according to his needs is alluring, but there are conflicting beliefs as to those needs.

Another point that in my opinion should be accorded more space and greater stress than is given by Mr. Filbin is the attitude of the child's world.

Twenty years ago I, as a pioneer, was experimenting with the selection of kindergarten children who would probably have trouble with reading, unless taught by the technique already found successful with older Remedial pupils. I shared the anxiety of many teachers and parents, that being set apart in a special group would cast a stigma upon its members. However, by the time the experiment had been tried for two or three years, we found our fears groundless. Instead of resenting the placing of their children in a separate group, mothers came and asked for the privilege of having their children taught as a cousin or neighbor had been taught last year, "because he learned so much better." Instead of looking with scorn or ridicule upon their classmates sent out for this special kind of reading, the class manifested envy as of a privileged group. Children asked, "Miss Blank, am I going on this same way with you next year? It's a lot nicer than what the other children are having." By the time the project was in its third year, the rest of the class began to recognize the advantage the special group was experienc-

182

ing. A third grade boy said, "Those kids learn a great deal that we don't know. We know a lot of words, but when we don't know a word we have to ask, and they can work it out for themselves." Another third grade boy who had always read fluently in the Sight-Word reading group, asked his teacher wistfully, "If I read this very well, may I go with Miss Blank's class? Those children in that special group know so much more." Children asked their mothers, and mothers asked us, what could be done so that all might receive the privileges of the Special Group.

A fifth grade girl, who was an excellent speller, was excused from the class with two other children to work on a delightful art project. Meanwhile, her entire class was having spelling by the Gillingham Technique. After a few days she went to the teacher with the request, "I can do this painting at home. Mayn't I please be in the class for spelling? It is so much fun to learn the rules and the history of words and all the rest that we have been doing. It is so much nicer to know the reason than just to remember the spelling of words and not be sure that we are remembering them correctly or why they are that way." Numerous similar expressions could be quoted from all the schools in which the experiment has been tried. Pity was felt by some teachers for the children of the Special Group who must go over and over the "dull Drill Cards." To the astonishment of these critics, however, there were protests by the children if, for any reason, the Cards were omitted on a particular day. To the genuine surprise of the teachers, parents not infrequently asked to buy the Cards because the child wished them for Christmas or birthday, or, "so that I can teach my cousin, because in his school they don't have them. He doesn't know the sounds!"

Those teachers learned a lesson greatly needed in many other fields, namely, that it is the teacher and not the pupil who is bored by drill and repetition. The child feels delight in definite progress in which he can see tangible evidence of success. "See me gain, see me gain!" exulted one child.

Recently I had the privilege of observing a second grade selected group being taught by the Alphabet Approach. They had been clamoring for a new dipthong Card for which the teacher had declared them not yet ready. On this day she announced that they might have it. "And it is a tough one!" she warned. Hands were noiselessly clapped and several youngsters joggled up and down in their seats. "May I try it, may I try it?"

Another point which should be made clear in the mind of any

183

teacher attempting to use my technique is the distinction between this approach and what is usually accepted as "phonics."

Teachers not infrequently tell me that they are using my method, that they "always did believe in phonics." They usually mean "analytical" or "functional" phonics. By this method several words are taught from one of the delightful primers that have been carefully constructed to introduce the same word in a good many situations. After a considerable number of words (perhaps one hundred) are recognized on sight, they are gradually broken down into their phonetic units. In the hands of a skilled teacher this, the current method, attains apparently satisfactory results with many pupils. Others fail because they cannot learn the preparatory group of sight words. Whether or not this method is desirable is a matter of opinion. The positive statement to be made here is that this method of teaching phonics is not to be confused with the Gillingham Technique.

The Sight-Word Method and the Alphabetic Approach are based upon two distinct and mutually exclusive concepts. When men first began to attempt to communicate with each other at a distance by written messages, they drew pictures. Their communications were, in fact, pictorial narratives. Gradually these pictures became conventionalized into characters bearing less and less resemblance to objects. Thus we find Chinese characters and Egyptian hieroglyphics, each standing for a word or even for a phrase or short sentence. There are many words in any language and a scholar who had many ideas to communicate had to learn many thousands of ideograms—a laborious task.

About three thousand years ago it dawned upon some genius or group of geniuses in the Eastern Mediterranean region that it would be easier to have a character (letter) stand for a speech-sound. Then these letters, few in number (English has 26), could be combined and recombined thousands of times to form words. As long as a language developed by itself, it was perfectly phonetic. It was only when two languages mixed through conquest or migration that there came to be silent letters or more than one sound for a letter, or more than one letter for a sound. This general approach to written language prevailed in Europe and in America until something less than one hundred years ago. It is upon this concept of combining letters to form words that the Gillingham Technique is based.

Late in the 19th Century there came a return to the ancient ideogrammatic concept. A word was to be learned in its totality as an ideogram, disregarding the letters of which it was composed. In the extreme form of this method the letters are not learned at all. This Sight-Word Approach swept over America and has worked havoc with reading and spelling. Several of my older Remedial Reading pupils have told me gravely that until they had learned my Drill Cards they had no idea that the letters in a word had anything to do with its pronunciation! Here we have a clear demonstration of the mutual exclusiveness of the two concepts.

A pupil who is trying to remember a certain word as an ideogram cannot at the same time be sounding the letters in series to work out the pronunciation of the word. He may remember the wrong word, just as I may confuse the names of Mrs. Jones and Mrs. Smith met at a tea. Such a pupil may say garden for basket (both words having been previously encountered in the same story), or bird for robin (words seen as labels to pictures).

The value of introducing Phonics while the child is being exhorted to remember words as sight units is controversial, but such an introduction of the sounds of the letters as an aid to learning words as ideograms must not be confused with the Alphabetic Approach.

And now we come to my last point. It seems to me important that teachers interested in my technique should be made familiar with trends in the widening application of the Alphabetic Approach.

At least a dozen years ago teachers began to inquire, "Since this Alphabetic Approach is the means of saving from failure those who would otherwise have failed, or is the best Remedial Technique for those who have already experienced the frustration of failure, why would it not be the best way to teach all children?" For some time my voice gravely joined the chorus of conventional answers. "If a child can learn to recognize ideograms (Sight-Word Method), he should have the privilege of learning this way. The Alphabetic Approach would slow down his potential speed." But as the years went by I wondered more and more. This was not a flippant question. It was asked by some of our best and most experienced teachers. For example, Mary Davidson, former head of the Primary Department of the Fieldston Lower School in New York, asked it with purposeful interest, and is now using the Alphabetic Approach with whole classes in the Oakwood School in North Hollywood, California.

More and more emphatically it was forced upon my attention that there is no sharp line between the potential reading failure and the child who learns with a slight degree of success. If the

Alphabetic Approach is necessary for Jimmie, why is it not good for Harry whose test results show only a slight difference? With the almost universal uproar about poor spelling, we can afford to give some training in the kinesthetic and auditory aspects of the language pattern at the beginning. Only a few supernormal children never misspell. These are too few in number to have a school policy made for them. Experience proves more and more that the Alphabetic Approach is slower for only the first weeks or very few months. After that, the progress of children thus taught is often more rapid than that of their Sight-Word Method classmates. Since there is no sharp line between the children supposed to need the Alphabetic Approach and those for whom the Sight-Word Method is preferable, it begins to appear that the Alphabetic Approach may eventually come to be regarded as best for all. . . .

Anna Gillingham

Miss Gillingham confirmed, through twenty years of first-hand classroom experience and in language no one could have possibly misunderstood, everything Rudolf Flesch had said in his book. She pointed out the important distinction between the "phonics" as taught by the sight-word basal readers and the phonics taught in the alphabetic approach. But perhaps most important of all, she identified the "risk" one took in exposing a child to the sight-word method. Why should any method have been used in the schools which had as one of its built-in shortcomings an element of risk, especially when there already existed a method, used for centuries, which entailed no such risk? Dr. Orton had warned of this back in 1929. It was nothing new. Yet, in 1957 Filbin had contended that most children could be taught to read successfully by the sight-word method. But if this were so, why were there so many functional illiterates among young adults fifteen years later and such a deterioration of the literary intelligence among college students in 1970? Obviously, those "successful" sight readers of the elementary schools of 1957 did not measure up to an acceptable standard of literary success when they entered college in 1970. Also, it is interesting to contrast Miss Gillingham's approach to reading disability with the approach exhibited by the Dyslexia Institute in that *Life* magazine article. Although the little girl in the *Life* article was apparently no different from Miss Gillingham's pupils, she was subjected to thyroid treatments, a tonsillectomy, the removal of adenoids, and eye-muscle exercises to improve her reading ability. No one in the clinic suggested teaching her the alphabet!

As rare as Miss Gillingham's letter was in the pages of the professional journals, it merely indicated that the controversy between phonics and look-say—or the alphabetic approach and the sight-word method—continued to rage beneath the surface. Even within the International Reading Association, which had been created by look-say people for look-say people, there were a number of members more interested in getting to the bottom of the reading problem than protecting the vested interests of the controlling clique. They formed their own dissenting group. Perhaps the word "dissenting" is a little strong. They were simply more willing to test Flesch's arguments than to reject them as out of hand. One of these independents was Dr. Jeanne Chall, a remedial reading specialist from the City College of New York who later joined the faculty of the Harvard Graduate School of Education. She decided to ask the Carnegie Corporation for a grant with which to conduct an extensive investigation into the methods of teaching reading—to determine finally, once and for all, as scientifically and objectively as possible, if the phonics, alphabet-first approach was better than the look-say, whole-word approach. Miss Chall was awarded the grant, and her labors began in 1962.

Meanwhile, among the rank-and-file teachers there was great confusion and fear of speaking out. An interesting insight into the frustrating situation was given by Dr. Hilde L. Mosse, a psychiatrist who had written an article on the American reading problem for a West German educational journal. The article was widely distributed among educational circles in West Germany. In November 1962 *The Reading Teacher*, the IRA's official journal, reprinted the article in translation so that it could be more easily refuted. Dr. Mosse recounted the following:

The pressure exerted on educators since the appearance of Rudolf Flesch's book, and devastating statistics like those I have mentioned, have slowly led to a sporadic reintroduction of the synthetic phonetic method. But the teachers themselves do not learn phonetics any more and therefore cannot teach it.

I myself experienced only recently how much fighting still rages about the whole-word method. In May 1960, I attended the congress of the International Reading Association. Teachers, reading specialists, school principals and administrators were present in our discussion group. But a discussion did not get started. I finally said that as a psychiatrist I felt I could discuss something they seemed so anxious to avoid. I spoke about the whole-word method as a cause of reading disorders. The reaction was astonishing. It was as though a floodgate had opened, and teachers and others spoke freely, openly, and passionately. They described how they (especially the older teachers) had been aware of the great harmfulness of the whole word method for a long time, but that they had been completely helpless and powerless. They were being forced to use this method. Those who, in desperation, had the courage to teach phonetics had to do so secretly. Some even had to tell the children to do something else quickly whenever someone entered the classroom.

Despite such alarming views as held by Dr. Mosse, Anna Gillingham, and others concerning the potential harmfulness of the whole-word method, the look-say basal readers, in a variety of revised editions, continued to be shoved down the throats of American schoolchildren for another ten years. For every article or letter by a Mosse or Gillingham, there were dozens, supporting the basal readers and their stepped-up phonics. The establishment could reply to the critics that they were teaching phonics. But they would not say how effective it was to impose phonetic generalizations on sight-word techniques. However, in the January 1963 issue of *The Reading Teacher*, Theodore Clymer, senior author of the Ginn basal readers, published an article on that very subject entitled "The Utility of Phonic Generalizations in the Primary Grades." He listed forty-five phonic generalizations which the child had to remember in order to use as attack skills. How useful were these generalizations? He reported:

> The most disturbing fact to come from the study may be the rather dismal failure of generalization 1 to provide the correct pronunciation even 50 per cent of the time. As one teacher remarked when this study was presented to a reading methods class, "Mr. Clymer, for years I've been teaching 'When two vowels go walking, the first does the talking.' You're ruining the romance in the teaching of reading!"

Expecting a child to remember phonetic generalizations which did not apply in half the cases when he was confronted with unknown sight words was not phonics. The whole-word basal authors knew it, but insisted that they had been misrepresented, that they did teach phonics. It was this kind of arguing that confused so many teachers over phonics and look-say, and led parents to believe that their children were being taught phonics when they weren't. If the teachers were confused, how confused must the parents have been?

Meanwhile, those who were not confused continued to do their work in promoting alphabetic principles in the teaching of reading. In 1961, a group of citizens in New York organized the Reading Reform Foundation, a volunteer endeavor "with the aim of restoring the alphabet (phonics) to its proper place as the basis of elementary reading instruction throughout the nation." It was the first effort on the part of phonics advocates to organize in order to fight more effectively the power of the IRA and the educational establishment it had such monolithic influence over. That it had to be created by noneducators—a prominent New York attorney, Watson Washburn, was its president—indicates to what degree the professional teaching establishment was committed to look-say methods. In seeking educator support for the new organization, the founders discovered a reservoir of such support in some of the private independent secondary schools which were often called upon to repair the damage done to children in the elementary public schools.

During the early sixties, the demand for phonics instruction began to increase, and some publishers were beginning to answer the need. In England, shortly before the publication of *Why Johnny Can't Read,* two educators, J. C. Daniels and Hunter Diack, coauthored a new phonics-oriented basal series, *The Royal Road Readers.* The reading situation in Britain had become almost as bad as it was here. In the United States, J. B. Lippincott Company, publishers of the Hay-Wingo *Reading With Phonics,* the only phonics textbook to be published during the period of total look-say dominance, came out with a new phonics-based reading series in 1964 by McCracken and Walcutt, entitled *Basic Reading.* Lippincott was the only major American publisher that had decided to go all the way with phonics. Among the prominent IRA members to swing to phonics was Donald A. Durrell, whose book, *Speech-to-Print Phonics: A Phonics Foundation for Reading,* coauthored with Helen A. Murphy, also appeared in 1964. Durrell, dean of the Boston University School of Education, had made studies in 1958 which convinced him that a knowledge of the alphabet was important for beginning reading success. Durrell's findings contradicted the beliefs of his colleagues in the IRA, however his book was reviewed favorably in *The Reading Teacher* of March 1966 as a supplement to any basal sight-vocabulary series and for remedial use.

The early sixties saw most publishers of basal reading series coming out with revised editions, with more phonics instruction introduced earlier, but still with the sight-vocabulary concept still prevailing. The child was still required to remember a sight vocabulary before he was taught anything about letters, the vocabulary was controlled, and the whole gamut of word-recognition and word-attack skills had to be learned if the child was ever to become an "independent" reader.

Also in the early sixties, a new linguistic approach to the teaching of reading began to be widely discussed in the educational journals. Linguistics is sometimes described as the science of language analysis or simply and more modestly as the study of language. The linguist who turned the attention of linguistics to the problem of teaching children to read was Leonard Bloomfield, a professor at Yale University, whose book, *Language*, published in 1933, had become a standard text and reference book in the field. Bloomfield found that the methods used to teach children to read were in complete violation of the findings of linguistics, and he elaborated on this view in a long essay in the April and May 1942 issues of the *Elementary English Review*. His view could be summed up simply as follows: (1) English as represented in its written form is an alphabetic language as opposed to Chinese which is ideographic. (2) The spoken language is composed of a limited number of identifiable, distinctive sounds, which he called *phonemes,* each of which is represented in the written language by a *grapheme*. In teaching a child to read, it was necessary to first teach him the *phoneme-grapheme* correspondences. Since there are approximately 46 phonemes in our language and an alphabet of 26 letters to represent them, some graphemes are composed of one or more letters including letters which may be silent. (3) Because English spelling is so highly irregular, the phoneme-grapheme relationships should be taught by presenting the child with one-syllable words from regular spelling patterns first, and introducing the irregular spelling patterns after the regular ones have been mastered. The letter sounds should not be taught in isolation, because they were not used as such in ordinary speech. The sounds of the letters should be inferred by the learning of one-syllable words in regular, easily recognizable spelling patterns.

Actually, Bloomfield's views of the language were not too different from those of the Boston schoolmasters of 1844. They, too, clearly understood the difference between an alphabetic writing system and an ideographic one. However, Bloomfield's unique contribution was in classifying words into regular and irregular spelling patterns and suggesting that the regular ones be taught first.

While Bloomfield's approach was close to phonics methodology—in that it was alphabetic and stressed the need to learn the sound-symbol system—he criticized the kind of phonics instruction which required the child to learn the sound of the letters in isolation. This gave the child the erroneous impression that the letters came before the spoken language, not vice versa.

The whole-word establishment found no solace in the new linguistic approach which, of course, was highly critical of the word method. But there was no hostility toward it in the pages of the IRA's journals. The reason for this is probably because the linguistic approach was still in the early developmental stages, might be no more than a passing fad, and would not be introduced into the schools for a good many years. Nevertheless, some of the basal reader publishers thought it wise to add a linguistics consultant to their editorial staffs. The linguists, of course, had had little or no experience in elementary school teaching, and therefore their expertise, based on theory alone, was considered limited.

Another interesting innovation in beginning reading instruction of which a great deal was written during the 1960s was the development of i.t.a., the initial teaching alphabet. Devised in England by Sir James Pitman, i.t.a. was a special teaching alphabet in which each sound of the spoken language was represented by a single written symbol—forty-four symbols in all. It was expected that children would learn to read much faster and more easily by this completely consistent sound-symbol system than by way of our highly irregular orthography. When the child learned to read fluently via i.t.a., he was then transferred over to T.O., the traditional orthography. The i.t.a. symbols were sufficiently like the regular alphabet letters to minimize the difficulties of this transfer. Nevertheless, the transfer problem was the method's greatest drawback. Some American educators found merit in this approach which was basically an alphabetic one, even though it could be used with any of the basal readers. However, the look-say establishment saw little chance that Americans would adopt i.t.a. on any large scale.

The most important event of the mid-sixties as far as reading pedagogy was concerned, however, was the completion of Jeanne Chall's study in 1965 and its publication in book form in 1967 under the title *Learning to Read: The Great Debate*. Three years of extensive research confirmed what phonics proponents had known all along, that "a code-emphasis" method (alphabetic) used in the beginning of reading instruction with children produced better readers than methods which began with a "meaning emphasis" (whole words). However, Chall wrote:

> I cannot emphasize too strongly that the evidence *does not endorse any one code-emphasis method over another*. There is no evidence to date that ITA is better than a linguistic approach, that a linguistic approach is better than a systematic-phonics approach, or that a systematic-phonics approach is better than ITA or a linguistic approach. Neither do we have any evidence to date that one published code-emphasis program is superior to another, although some undoubtedly are.
>
> Nor can I emphasize too strongly that I recommend a code

191

emphasis only as a *beginning* reading method—a method to start the child on—and that I do *not* recommend ignoring reading-for-meaning practice.

The look-say establishment greeted these findings none too happily. After all, they vindicated what Rudolf Flesch had said twelve years earlier. But since Chall was a respected member of the IRA, an educator, a professional in her field, they could not criticize her credentials. They did criticize how she had evaluated some of the studies she reviewed. The reviewer in the January 1969 issue of the *Journal of Reading* wrote:

> What prevents Chall's study from achieving respectability is that many of her conclusions are derived from a consideration of studies that were ill-conceived, incomplete and lacking in the essentials of suitable methodological criteria. In her eagerness to clarify these studies she allowed her personal bias toward a code emphasis to color her interpretations of the data. . . .
>
> It seems rather odd that a researcher intent upon dispelling confusion should have allowed herself to be moored on a reef of inconclusiveness and insubstantiality.

Dr. Chall herself had pointed out the inadequacies of many of the studies that had been made. A good many of the sixty-seven research studies she and her staff had reviewed were prepared by researchers anxious to buttress their already established views on a particular method. Chall wrote:

> One of the most important things, if not *the* most important thing, I learned from studying the existing research on beginning reading is that it says nothing consistently. It says too much about some things, too little about others. And if you select judiciously and avoid interpretations, you can make the research "prove" almost anything you want it to.

Therefore, she had to use her own judgment in interpreting many of these research studies, and this is where the look-say establishment found her "biased." They ignored the hundreds of classrooms she visited and the numerous interviews she had with teachers, administrators, authors and publishers. Ruth Strang, the only one of the establishment old guard to review Chall's book, wrote in *The Reading Teacher* of March 1968:

While recognizing its contribution to the analysis of previous research in reading, I am in serious disagreement with some of its major conclusions and recommendations. . . .

To begin with the synthetic or code-emphasis method may 1) decrease the child's initial curiosity about printed words as he encounters and uses them, 2) deprive him of the experience of discovering sound-symbol relationships in words for himself, 3) give him the wrong initial concept of reading, and 4) if pursued too extensively and too long, interfere later with speed of reading and maximum comprehension. The Analytic or meaning method, starting with wholes, gives the child reinforcement of his learning not only from his success in the task itself, but also in the meaning gained from the short, attractive stories now available in increasing numbers for beginners.

Dr. Strang only reiterated all the excuses for nonteaching which fill the pages of the look-say guidebooks. If you taught the child the sound-symbol system, you would deprive him of the "experience of discovering" the system for himself. In our analysis of the look-say pre-primers in the early chapters of this book we pointed out how the pre-primers seemed to have been written deliberately to make it as difficult as possible for the child to discover the alphabetic principle for himself. This was obviously done to prevent the child from becoming too independent too soon. What good was a controlled vocabulary if the child could figure out the sound-symbol system for himself, break out of the controls, and thereby read anything he wanted?

Another unfavorable review appeared in the *Grade Teacher* of May-June 1968, written by Blanche Scheman, a reading specialist:

> As could have been predicted, Dr. Jeanne Chall's new book . . . was greeted with acclaim by many, but most enthusiastically of all, by the staunch and vocal critics of our schools. They have long been engaged in attacks on education and have been pleading for a return to the simple teaching of the 3R's in the "good old fashioned way" (spelled "phonics"). Now they finally feel justified and upheld in the area of reading, by no less than a leader of the establishment. By simple distortions, exaggerations, removal of sentences from context, plus wishful thinking, such groups as the Reading Reform Foundation have used Dr. Chall's findings to come to some fantastic conclusions. . . .
>
> The principal danger in Dr. Chall's book is already bearing fruit. Reason and fact are disregarded while emotion and prejudice take

over. The fact that most children come to school with some sight vocabulary is ignored. The fact that phonics is taught as early as the pre-primer is also side-stepped. The fact that there are many ways to crack the code, and that some children work best with one and some with another is overlooked entirely. The fact that it is the teacher—not the system—that determines reading success is lost almost entirely in Dr. Chall's work and the publicity that has been attendant on it.

Another critical view of the Chall book appeared in *Elementary English* of May 1969. The reviewers, Richard Burnett and Wallace Ramsey, both professors of education at the University of Missouri, said:

> Very few voices were raised publicly to suggest that Chall's book did not clarify anything, but did, in fact, confound the issues and perpetuate the debate. . . .
> The book is written as an odyssey which reflects the heroic efforts of a troubled mind wandering through a chaotic mass of confused thinking and conflicting research findings in an attempt to emerge with some kind of absolute statement regarding how children should be taught to read.
> The picture presented of the state of confusion which exists is an honest one. The author calls reading research "shockingly inconclusive" and points out that researchers came up with conclusions not warranted by their research. . . .
> One of the major faults of the book is that the author is guilty of the same practice in research which she finds deplorable in others—oversimplifying the problem. Like Rudolph Flesch, Chall attributes the controversy in reading to a simple issue. She couches the issue in more sophisticated terms than Flesch did—not a phonics versus a sight approach, but a "coding emphasis" or a "meaning emphasis."

It was inevitable that Chall's book would be compared to Rudolf Flesch's. In essence it did the same thing as the Flesch book. However, this time the monolithic consensus which had denounced the Flesch book was lacking. The leading lights of the look-say establishment had grown old, or died, or retired. William S. Gray had died in 1960. Dolch had also died. Gates was retired.

The favorable reviews were perhaps more important than the unfavorable ones, for they showed to what extent serious disagreement on basic

194

issues divided the reading establishment. Nancy Larrick, who had been second president of the IRA but had no connection with a look-say basal series, praised the Chall book in glowing terms in the *Saturday Review* of January 20, 1968. Much of the review, however, was devoted to Chall's devastating analysis of the most widely used basal readers. As an important member of the reading establishment, Miss Larrick's own comments were particularly interesting:

> Since research points to the need for code emphasis in beginning reading, why do those responsible for teaching reading ignore the evidence? Dr. Chall answers by citing "the influence of the prevailing climate of opinion" and the American educator's passion for consensus. It has become fashionable to stress meaning rather than mere sounding of letters, so we all do it. . . .
>
> This kind of mass thinking is created to some extent by the multimillion-dollar textbook industry with salesmen and teacher-demonstrators covering the country like the dew.

What Miss Larrick and even Dr. Chall did not mention was that the publishers' best salesmen were the authors of the basal readers themselves who were in positions to influence the opinions of teachers through their control of educational journals, organizations, and colleges of education. It is important, of course, to understand the publishers' role in all this. But it is also important to understand that publishers rely on the expertise and knowledge of their educator-authors for the final product which they must then sell to the educational community.

Another favorable review appeared in the March 1968 *Phi Beta Kappan*. The reviewer, Carl B. Smith of Indiana University's department of reading, wrote:

> *Learning to Read—The Great Debate* took a mountain of courage to write and may well live up to John Gardner's prediction that it is the most important book about education in 10 years. . . .
>
> Hopefully, the strength and wisdom that shine through the book will inspire researchers, caution educators, and reassure parents that much good science and skill are operating to help their children with their education.

Robert W. Wilson, professor of education at the University of Maryland, wrote in the May 1969 *Elementary English:*

195

I see the book as a springboard for future research. . . .

To this reviewer's knowledge, she has no vested interests, commercial or otherwise, in either side of the argument.

If this book changes some readers' thinking, let it. They should use this book as a point of departure, not for more argument, but for further research.

Mr. Wilson was the only reviewer who referred to the unmentionable "vested interests." That he should have voiced this in an educational journal was somewhat remarkable. His obvious inference was that Dr. Chall had no vested interests but that others within the establishment had. How many other educators shared his views but were afraid to speak out about them?

Perhaps the most significant review in terms of the future effects of the book was by Eldonna L. Everetts, the assistant executive secretary of the National Council of Teachers of English, an organization which in 1955 had denounced Rudolf Flesch. She wrote in *National Elementary Principal* of January 1968:

This is, indeed, an excellent book which could only have been produced by a good staff and a capable director. . . .

Although Dr. Chall advocates the code-emphasis approach as a beginning reading method, she does not present details on the concepts of language principles on which such a program can be based. Phonics means different processes to different persons. . . . Before phonics can become a widely accepted basis for instruction, it must be adequately described in terms of what is presently known about the nature of language.

Beyond doubt, the debate in reading has not been concluded. The "heat" for such discussions continues to exist: attempting to define the goals for beginning reading instruction, shifting of goals when rejecting some research findings, and turning to recognized leaders for interpretation. . . .

At times readers will be excited and alarmed, but perhaps they will agree with me that the conclusion constitutes a prophesy of what is going to be the "new" look in beginning reading instruction.

The "new" look in beginning reading instruction. We can imagine the editorial meetings that must have taken place in the board rooms of the various textbook publishers after the Chall book had been thoroughly digested. There would be much confusion as the look-say establishment would resist the changes that would force them to admit

196

that they had been wrong for forty years. But publishing houses that were not committed to any sight-vocabulary basal series would have the freedom to move ahead with all deliberate speed. In the commercial world, where sales are the supreme arbiter of what is to be produced, ideology takes second place. If the public wanted phonics, the public would get phonics. But if the public did not know what kind of phonics it wanted or how much of it or when, there was a tremendous potential for confusion. As Miss Everetts wrote, "Phonics means different processes to different persons." Thus, every publisher would start selling phonics, but many buyers would still be confused as to what phonics really meant.

Thus, in the early seventies, we find ourselves in a period of great pedagogical confusion, which does no good whatever for the children who must be taught to read. This confusion has led to a new consensus in the reading establishment, a new view which tries to accommodate Jeanne Chall's findings with the sensitive interests of the look-say establishment.

9

The Present Turmoil, the Coming Change, and What a Parent Can Do About It

Although the sight-vocabulary establishment, or what's left of it, would like to stop, or at least slòw down, the changes underway in beginning reading instruction, there is no question but that the field of reading instruction is on the verge of great changes. The changes are taking place from within the academic community. During the last five years, the Chall book has reached the teachers colleges in a way that the Flesch book never did. Fifteen years more of the debilitating whole-word method had much to do with the professional world's receptivity to Chall's book. In addition, the thrust of the linguistic movement is now so strong that its influence is being felt in reading pedagogy and the language arts all the way from grade one through high school and into college. This new interest in linguistics in conjunction with the language arts may mean a rebirth of literacy in America, a greater interest in the writing and reading of the language, a new enthusiasm for literature. For the first time in fifty years, millions of students will become aware of the beauties of language rather than its obstructions. They will find language facilitating thought rather than thwarting it. They will find language expanding their minds rather than retarding them. But all of this is still in the future. It is a happy prospect, but it is not here yet.

The publishers, of course, are anxious to meet the demands of the market, but it takes time before books are written, published, and find their way into the classroom. The changes that are taking place promise to restore sanity and logic to the teaching of reading. But it is obvious that in a country as large as ours, the changes will take place faster in some areas, more slowly in others. Teachers will have to be retrained, new textbooks adopted, new concepts learned and absorbed. All of this cannot be done overnight. It will take years. How many? No one can say.

Meanwhile, there is a tremendous amount of confusion, conflicting claims, and a continued debate about methods among teachers, teachers of teachers, textbook writers, educational psychologists, behavioral scientists, and other members of the elementary educational establishment. New words are being used to describe old methods: *decoding* is now the term used to describe anything from teaching the alphabet to the linguistics-phonics approach. The basal sight-vocabulary reader is now known as the *eclectic* basal reader, eclectic being the new code word for sight vocabulary. Letter sounds are now *phonemes* and written letters are now *graphemes*. Despite the new terminology, which is meant to provide greater descriptive accuracy in some cases, greater obscurity in others the basic issues are the same: sound-symbol reading versus sight-vocabulary reading. There is basically little difference between the issues as they were presented in 1844 in the dispute between Horace Mann and the Boston schoolmasters and the issues as they have been disputed in the last twenty years by Flesch and the reading establishment, or more recently by Chall and her allies the linguists and the crumbling sight-vocabulary establishment. It is surprising how little has changed in over a hundred years.

However, if you are a parent about to enroll your child in school, you will not want him to be a victim of this turmoil, another victim of the look-say method while the local school authorities decide which way to go. Thus, it is up to the parent to have enough understanding of the situation to guide him through the pedagogical confusion that now exists in elementary education. As of this writing, the majority of schools are still using eclectic basal sight-vocabulary readers written and published in the 1960s. These basal readers largely follow the methodology reviewed in the first four chapters of this book. Despite all the claims of the publishers that the revised editions of the sixties are better than those of the fifties, the updated revisions of the basal readers are *essentially* no different from the one we analyzed in the early chapters of this book. They all start with a sight vocabulary, and therefore all adhere to the whole confusing, contradictory methodology of word attack, which includes word-form, contextual, and phonetic clues. If you start teaching a child to read *from the very beginning* on alphabetic principles, you can dispense with the whole complicated pedagogical mess that goes with learning a sight vocabulary. You will have saved your child untold agony.

It is important for the parent to know the sequence of what his child is being taught. Because of Chall's book, some schools will supplement the basal sight-vocabulary program with more intensive phonics started earlier. But the sequence in which phonics is taught in conjunction with a sight vocabulary is so crucial, that it is important for a parent to know how his child is being taught. The way to find out is to ask your child's teacher. Ask him or her this simple question: "Is my child being taught a sight vocabulary?" If she answers, "Yes, but . . ." that means yes, period. Find out the title and publisher of the basal reader being used, and check it against the list in the appendix to this book. *Under no circumstances should you permit your child to be taught a sight vocabulary.* The sight vocabulary is the thalidomide of modern elementary education, and you run the risk of turning your child into a sorry dyslexic by subjecting him to sight-vocabulary methodology, no matter how much phonics they may teach in conjunction with it. Remember, learning a sight vocabulary is by definition learning words as wholes without knowing the sound-symbol components or letters or phoneme-grapheme correspondences that make up the words being "read." He begins the process of word-guessing from the very beginning, and this may lead to letter reversals, described by Dr. Orton and Anna Gillingham, reading words from right to left, and other assorted bad habits.

If the teacher tells you that your child is being taught a sight vocabulary, you have a job to do at home. The primer in the final chapter of this book will tell you how to instruct your child. However, to be on the safe side, it is wise to instruct your child in the sound-symbol system *before* he gets to school. If the school is using an eclectic basal reader with a sight vocabulary, you will have prepared your child in advance to read on sound-symbol principles. If the school is using an alphabetic-phonics or linguistics method, your home instruction will have given him a good head start.

If your child is beyond the first grade and in a sight-vocabulary basal reading program, you *must* start converting him to sound-symbol reading. The primer in the final chapter can be used for that purpose. It can also be used with adults who were taught to sight read and have always had a reading problem as a result. The conversion process may take a very long time for some students. The bad habits ingrained by the sight-vocabulary technique in the first grades can be very difficult to change. But the effort should be made, and it should be made in the home. There are not enough reliable remedial teachers to go around, and they can be expensive. A rather stark assessment of the present remedial situation was given by Frank Vellutino, director of the Albany Study Center for Learning Disabilities, in an article in the March 1971 issue of *The Reading Teacher*. He wrote:

It is clear that not only is reading retardation of epidemic proportions; it is even more prevalent in the inner-city. . . . Reading specialists in particular are overwhelmed by the many children requiring remediation. The number of youngsters, however, who need assistance far exceeds the number of trained professionals available.

Thus, you had better do the job at home, for it is unlikely that your child will be converted from sight reading to sound-symbol reading by anyone in his school.

With reading retardation reaching "epidemic proportions," parents have a right to know why the situation was allowed to get this bad before a change of methods could take place. We explained in the previous chapter how the institutionalization of vested interests made the necessary changes impossible. Millions of more children have had to suffer needlessly as a consequence. If anything, this situation should make us look closely at the institutions of public education which have made such widespread suffering inevitable. If one wanted to focus on the group most responsible for the literacy disaster we have today, one would have to single out the teachers of teachers. The teachers of teachers are a somewhat remote group of professionals, many of them with doctoral degrees, who have had a minimum amount of experience teaching children. They deal mainly with theory, which may look good on paper but often does not work in a classroom situation. These teachers of teachers do not work with children, they do not teach children, and in many cases they probably don't even like children. They teach adults. Yet they control all of the educational journals dealing with elementary teaching. Their dry, bloodless, remote articles fill issue after issue of the journals teachers read. It is rare that *The Reading Teacher* or *Elementary English*, or any similar journal devoted to elementary reading contains an article by a teacher relating classroom experiences with actual children with individual personalities. Most of the research studies deal with children clinically, in statistical groups, as if they were guinea pigs. The teaching profession, unfortunately, is dominated by a professional group vying for honors and royalties as textbook writers and authorities on pedagogical theory. Their professional status is so far above the lowly grade-school teacher who does the actual teaching that the latter is forced to believe that the teacher of teachers knows more about teaching children than the teachers of children themselves.

It is important to understand the dominant position that the teachers of teachers hold in the world of public education. Their influence is enormous. Yet their remoteness from the children in the schools permits them to look at these children in an abstract way, as statistics, as guinea pigs. Yet, since these are the professionals whose *un*literate writings fill the educational journals, their bloodless, affectionless, emotionless attitude toward children no doubt infects the young teachers who are taught to look at children clinically instead of as living, feeling, interesting young persons.

If some children develop a hatred for the public schools and a disrespect for their teachers, it must partly be due to this clinical attitude that teachers unconsciously project toward their students. When millions of real individuals are treated like statistics and guinea pigs, their resentment will eventually be felt.

Of course, the teachers of teachers resent the intrusion of the parent and layman into their professional world. That is why it was so easy for the teaching profession to dismiss Rudolf Flesch in 1955. They could not dismiss Jeanne Chall in 1967. As she puts it: "The reading field must find a way to avoid a situation like the one that produced a *Why Johnny Can't Read.*" Her solution?

> With more than one thousand reading research studies completed each year, it is understandable that no one person can keep up with the evidence. The summaries of research are quite useful, but they are not sufficient. The field, it seems to me, is prolific and important enough to warrant a computerized storage and retrieval service. Such a service can help pull together the relevant research for a periodic synthesis of findings on crucial issues; it can also produce a monthly or bimonthly journal of reading abstracts to serve researchers and college teachers of reading.

It would appear that Dr. Chall is asking for more of what they have had for the last forty years: more dry, bloodless research by Ph.Ds, which is seldom read or worth the paper it is printed on. What the teaching profession needs is fewer teachers of teachers, fewer researchers, but more teachers of children. We cited Vellutino's findings that there weren't enough trained professionals to handle all of the children who need remedial help. Why don't some of these Ph.Ds get into the classrooms and help undo some of the damage they are responsible for? I repeat: the country needs fewer teachers of teachers and more teachers of children. But being a teacher of teachers is a lucrative profession. You earn a professor's salary, occupy a position of prestige, and get asked to write textbooks which can supplement your income in a big way. Then, of course, once you have written a textbook or several textbooks, you can teach the young teachers how to use them when they get into their classrooms, thus promoting the sales of your own books.

There is an obvious conflict of interests involved here, which members of the teaching profession, particularly those in the teachers colleges, have been very reluctant to admit exists. Authors of the basal readers are an excellent case in point. They have used their prestige and position to push their own pedagogical theories and ideas among their students in the face of legitimate opposition and much evidence that their methods were faulty. Their economic interests were so great that they should have disqualified themselves as teachers of teachers. Yet how could they have been expected to do this? Their positions as teachers is what supposedly qualified them to write the basal textbooks in the first place. Yet one can only shake one's head as one turns the pages of an IRA publication filled with the advertisements for books written by the editors of the publication or officers of the organization. This was particularly in evidence in the late fifties and early sixties when ads for Betts Basic Readers, the Dolch games, the Macmillan Readers by Gates, the Sheldon Basic Reading Series, or the D. C. Heath reading series by Witty could be found liberally interspersed with articles and commentaries by these very same authors. One flagrant example of such unabashed huckstering involved the editor of *The Reading Teacher* himself, Russell G. Stauffer. The January 1960 issue of that IRA publication carried a full-page ad for the Winston Basic Readers authored by Stauffer, and the September 1960 issue carried a very favorable review of these same books. Where do professional ethics end and commercial interests begin? It is a difficult question to answer, but it is obvious that such professional and commercial interests in a subject area where different methods are in competition for school adoption should be acknowledged for what they are: in conflict with each other. Professors of education who become the authors of best-selling basal textbooks—and some authors have made *millions* in royalties—have a vested interest in perpetuating their methods and seeing their books adopted. It is impossible to divorce the phonics-look-say controversy from the question of vested interests. But the authors of the basal readers would tell you that there is no conflict of interests. Their professional and commercial interests coincide beautifully.

Of course, it would be ridiculous to forbid teachers and professors from pushing their own books. They have as much right to promote their own ideas as other writers do. And publishers often find that their best salesmen are their own authors. But how does one deal with the problem of vested interests in public education? No one wants to deprive teachers of the right to write textbooks and earn a little extra money or even a lot of money or the right to form professional organizations. But we do think that teachers should be aware that when they become surrogate book salesmen and create an authors' guild in the guise of a professional organization, they are not being teachers. The teachers of teachers, of course, can get away with it easily enough. Their island of professionalism is so remote from the world of the layman, that they can influence or even intimidate their own colleagues with impunity.

It is this appalling situation which makes it absolutely imperative for lay educational organizations to keep watch over the teaching profession. The teachers cannot police themselves, and the teachers of teachers are authorities unto themselves—the real untouchables in the educational world. They are responsible to no one.

Who can possibly offset the negative influences of the teachers of teachers? Other teachers? Hardly. Or the few like Dr. Chall who take lay criticism to heart? Perhaps. But there are not enough of them. A better watchdog would have to come from outside the profession. And that is where the lay educational organization can play a very vital and crucial role in our society. The Reading Reform Foundation is an excellent example of such an organization. At its inception in 1961, its 210-member National Advisory Council included such prestigious names as Jacques Barzun, John Dos Passos, Max Eastman, Rudolf Flesch, Harry Golden, Russell Kirk, Joseph Wood Krutch, Phyllis McGinley and Samuel Eliot Morison. Its objectives were clearly stated in its brochure, *The Reading Crisis:*

> It is the Foundation's purpose to enlighten teachers, parents, public authorities, and the nation generally on the nature and extent of the reading crisis, its cause and cure; to coordinate and encourage the numerous local reform movements already active; and to create an informed national public opinion in favor of quickly eradicating from all our schools the cancer of configurationism; to the end that every child may soon have the opportunity to appreciate as early in life as possible the richness of the English language and the beauties of English literature, and to progress in a logical and orderly way to the other departments of education, of which reading ability is the indispensable basis.

Through its yearly conferences, regional seminars, and phonics workshops, the Foundation has been able to reach hundreds of teachers who would have never known what phonics was all about or how to teach reading on alphabetic principles. Even more important has been the local parental effort the Foundation has encouraged. Such local efforts could sometimes have extremely effective results in the face of strong professional opposition. An example of one intelligent parent whose efforts came into direct conflict with such professional opposition is that of Mrs. Mary Johnson of Winnipeg, Canada, a member of the RRF's National Advisory Council.

Mrs. Johnson, a music teacher, had accidentally stumbled onto the reading problem in 1956 when one of her pupils, an eleven-year-old girl, read *minuet* for the word *mimic*. The child could read a piece of music only after six months of piano lessons, but could not read a simple title to a song after four and a half years of schooling. Mrs. Johnson became so curious about this situation that she asked her own nine-year-old son to read aloud to her. She discovered that he did not know what a vowel was and could not sound out the simplest words which he had not memorized at school. He too had had no trouble learning how to read musical notation, yet he could not read some of the simplest words in his own language. Mrs. Johnson spent the winter tutoring her son in the letter sounds until he was able to read any word he encountered.

This whole experience started Mrs. Johnson off on a one-woman crusade to change the reading instruction methods—*Dick and Jane*—used in the schools of Manitoba. Her incredible struggle to get straight answers from the professionals is duly recorded in her book, published in 1970, *Programmed Illiteracy in Our Schools*. In it she describes the cooperation she got from some of the teachers at the lower levels of the system and the universal rebuffs she got from the superintendents and other higher-ups. Nevertheless, in the face of this opposition, she did her homework, tested children in their reading, submitted a brief to the Royal Commission on Education, and made headlines in Winnipeg. Yet, that was only the beginning of a more than ten-year struggle to change reading instruction methods in Manitoba schools. As of 1970, the Manitoba schools were still teaching children a sight vocabulary. Concerning lay-parental interest in education, Mrs. Johnson wrote:

> When parents were silent about educational problems they were accused of apathy; when they presented proof of a problem and wanted to discuss it they were told it was too technical; when they persisted they were told that education was not their business.

Mrs. Johnson's experience belied the oft-stated views of so many educators that they welcomed parental interest in public education. The truth was the very opposite. "The most significant outcome of the controversy, however," wrote Mrs. Johnson, "was that many more parents began to teach basic phonics at home. My investigations and the resulting publicity had helped to expose the complacent attitude of key educators in Manitoba, and parents could see that they might have to wait a long time for change to be instituted by school authorities."

Is it any wonder that parents and the lay public have lost confidence in the professional educators? Every time Mrs. Johnson made headway in arousing parental indignation, the publishers of the basal sight readers would inundate the teachers with pamphlets defending the sight-reading method, and the IRA would sponsor meetings with prestigious guest speakers to defend *Dick and Jane*. Concerning the IRA's pervasive influence within educational organizations, Mrs. Johnson commented:

> Officials in the Department of Education were known to complain privately about the pressure which was exerted on them by lay critics like myself. Ours was a weak voice indeed, however, in competition with the might and power of the IRA. It was to the IRA's strong voice that the Department listened: there was certainly more professional security to be gained by heeding the advice of this pressure group than from agreeing with the critics of the *Dick and Jane* method. And it might have been courting professional disaster for the Department of Education to defy the IRA and implement the Commission's recommendation that Manitoba school children be told the sounds of the letters.

It wasn't until 1971 that Mrs. Johnson could finally report to the annual conference of the Reading Reform Foundation, that a phonics-based reading program—*Language Patterns*, published by Holt, Rinehart and Winston—had been put on the approved list by the Manitoba educational authorities. The offical educational door had finally been opened to phonics, which could now compete with the other sight-vocabulary basal programs being used. It was a giant step in the right direction.

Of course, it took the Chall book and the linguistic movement to bring about the change. Educational officialdom had been able to resist parental and lay criticism indefinitely. They had changed their views only because the educational establishment had been changing them from within. However, there is no telling how many children had been saved from dyslexia, reading disability, and emotional agony by parents who had become aware of the problem through the efforts of the Mary Johnsons, the Reading Reform Foundation, and the many local groups for the improvement of education throughout the country. It was a sorry commentary that millions of children were forced to learn reading by way of defective methods while the educators were engaged in their great debate—some of them counting their royalties on the way to the bank. But better late than never.

Another area where the teachers of teachers have failed miserably has been in their knowledge of educational history. I found no evidence within any of the journals on reading that any doctor of education was even remotely aware of the whole-word experiment which had taken place in Boston during Horace Mann's time, although many invariably quoted Mann—second-hand, of course—to defend their positions. No one within the reading establishment or among the teachers of teachers, all of whom write dissertations at the drop of a hat, could accurately identify the conceptual source of the sight-vocabulary method. Mitford M. Mathews, in his book *Teaching to Read* (1966), came close to it. He mentioned Gallaudet's contribution to this new methodology, and it was this lead which led me to investigate Gallaudet's role more closely. Perhaps the reason why that excellent historian missed the significance of Gallaudet's original contribution was an unfamiliarity with the details of whole-word pedagogy as it is practiced by teachers using the guidebooks. It was my close analysis of the Dick and Jane Guidebooks which made me curious about the conceptual origins of a teaching method which flew so completely in the face of all logic. It was difficult to understand how such confusions could have replaced logic in elementary pedagogy. And when I investigated Gallaudet, it became obvious where the original confusion had started: in Gallaudet's mind. Gallaudet confused the teaching of reading with the teaching of language. To prove how completely this original confusion became a part of whole-word methodology, let me quote from an article in the March 1972 issue of *The Reading Teacher* by Kenneth S. Goodman, professor of elementary education at Wayne State University:

> We have been teaching children who are competent users of oral language as if they were beginners in language learning.

Professor Goodman wrote that without any knowledge of where it had all started: in Gallaudet's mind, based on the latter's experience with deaf children. But that initial confusion, divorced from its original source, is at the heart of whole-word methodology as it has been practiced in our schools for the last forty years. When I finally identified the source of the sight-vocabulary concept, I realized why it made no sense in the teaching of normal children. Yet, a gross ignorance and neglect of educational history made it possible for a group of teachers' teachers to subject millions and millions of normal American children to reading instruction as if they were deaf! But, I would have never been able to discover this for myself, had I not first made a minute, detailed analysis of the whole-word method itself as it was being used. It is one thing to denounce the whole-word method as illogical. It is another to know why it is not only illogical, but also insane—that is, unhealthy. It was the utter insanity of the method, as outlined in the Guidebook lessons, which made me curious enough to want to identify its conceptual origins. I wanted to know in whose mind such insanity could have originated. Perhaps some far-out phrenologist had thought it up.

But when the evidence indicated that it had originated in Gallaudet's mind, it was obvious that it was the honest confusion of an honest man. Gallaudet thought he had discovered a great new way of teaching normal children how to read based on his experiences with the deaf. It is probable that he was as disappointed in the final results in the Boston schools as were the Boston schoolmasters, which might account for why he wrote nothing to defend his method after it had been so brilliantly demolished by Samuel S. Greene. Gallaudet was interested in getting children to read, not in defending an indefensible method. Those who adopted his method after it had been divorced from its conceptual origins, eventually had something else to defend in the face of criticism: their pedagogical status and their textbook royalties. They had done what Gallaudet had never done. They built a whole complex system of instruction on the original confusion and carried it to insane lengths.

It is important to understand the confusions that have made reading instruction for the last forty years the most illogical in history. The first confusion concerns the process of learning how to read and the process of learning language. When Gallaudet was teaching the deaf children to read, he was teaching them language for the first time. These children had no concept of language since they could not hear nor speak language. As a result, their thinking and intellectual processes were virtually undeveloped. When Gallaudet taught them to recognize words, to read, he actually started teaching them language. This was the process which started these deaf children on the road to some intellectual development. Their vocabulary consisted solely of their reading vocabulary, and each word had to be learned not only for the way it appeared on paper, but for its meaning. That is how "reading for meaning" began. The deaf child had to read every word for meaning, because he previously knew none of them. In addition, because of his hearing deficiency, language for the deaf child became sight-associational, that is, words were associated with visual pictures, not sounds. The normal child with perfect hearing, however, comes to the first grade with a speaking vocabulary of between three and four thousand words, all of which he has learned through his ears, and with a considerable intellectual development as a result of that knowledge. Through the use of spoken language he has undergone a considerable mind expansion in a very short time. He is ready for much more. He already knows the meanings of *look, run, see, jump,* etc. He does not have to be taught their meaning as if he had never heard these words before.

At this point it is important to understand the role of language in intellectual development, or to put it more simply, in developing the uses of the mind. When men lived in caves and spoke in a kind of grunting language, their ability to communicate with one another was limited and imprecise. As language developed, so did the speed and accuracy of communication. So did the thinking process. Language serves as a tool of communication. But it also serves as the tool of thought. We think in terms of language. When we think we internalize speech, we debate internally, we talk to ourselves. It is this internal verbal exercise which expands our mind's capacity. When we add to our own thoughts the thoughts of others, we increase the expansion of our minds tremendously. Thus, the basis of all thinking is language, and language is, by definition, spoken, the word language itself referring to the tongue.

The alphabet was a perfect means of recording the spoken language on paper by way of a sound-symbol writing system. Before that men had not recorded language per se. They first drew pictures of objects, which then evolved into complex characters representing words. The leap from character writing to alphabet writing was a tremendous intellectual advance, and in reality it started man on the road to modern civilization. It was the key intellectual tool which permitted mind expansion on an unprecedented scale. Some ancients were so overwhelmed by the alphabet that they considered it of divine origin.

We identify the Greeks as the starting point of Western civilization. The Greeks were the first to use the alphabet for intellectual purposes. The inventor of the alphabet, a Phoenician, seems to have invented it for commercial reasons, although we really are not sure. But the invention of the alphabet represented an incredible piece of mental work. It meant pinning down and identifying the separate and distinct sounds of a language and designating a set of written symbols to represent them. Not an easy thing to do. Yet, it was done because man's intellectual requirements forced him to invent a better method for mind development than had been previously used. Character writing was simply too inadequate for the purpose, and man's mind was bursting beyond the limitations set by so inadequate a system.

When writing of the inventor of the alphabet, most historians refer to "the man or men." I like to think that it was invented by one man, merely because it is the kind of intellectual discovery or invention which only one mind, figuring out things for itself, could hit upon. Of course, there were primitive elements of sound-symbol writing in hieroglyphics, but the inventor of the alphabet realized that the entire hieroglyphic system had to be scrapped and a new system, completely based on sound-symbol principles, devised to replace it.

It is vitally important to understand that the thinking process is carried out in terms of the spoken language, and until a written language was invented which could represent that spoken language precisely, accurately, and as a fluid continuum, man's mental development would be hampered. Even the teachers of the deaf recognized this connection of the thinking process with the spoken language and developed the school of articulation, to get the deaf to speak, so that their minds could think and develop further. Thinking is internalized speaking.

There is also a confusion between thinking, dreaming, and daydreaming. Dreaming is a free flow of mental images stimulated by emotional associations while we are asleep. Daydreaming is a more controlled version of the same process which occurs when we are awake. In both dreaming and daydreaming elements of speech are present along with mental imagery. But both dreaming and daydreaming are characterized by their free-associational flow. Control is absent in dreaming and very relaxed in daydreaming. However, in the process of thinking, control is the sine qua non, and it is carried out in terms of the spoken language. That does not mean that there are no mental images in thinking. But the mental images are stimulated by the spoken language rather than by the emotions as they are in dreams. Emotions can stimulate outbursts in terms of spoken language—when we shout in anger or communicate our strong feelings to others. But that is not thinking. Thinking, as an intellectual process, is a very specialized form of mental activity which follows certain logical rules. It is a learned process, a process which can be developed with effort—control always requiring effort, but it is a language process.

It is easy to see how the invention of the alphabet could facilitate the thinking process. In the first place it made it possible for man to reproduce as accurately as possible his spoken language, and in the second, it made it possible for men to communicate their thoughts with one another in as accurate a way as possible. This was most crucial for intellectual development, for it made it possible for one man's mind to use the best insights and thinking of other men's minds, thus speeding up the learning process enormously. If each one of us personally had to go through the laborious processes which have produced the greatest breakthroughs in knowledge, learning would be a very slow, tedious process. But we develop on what other men have already done, and the only way we do this is by *reading* what other men have said and thought. That is the meaning of reading as an intellectual tool. It opens the door to other men's minds, thoughts, insights, inventions. The printed word is the avenue whereby intellectual exchange is carried out. Your mind cannot grow and expand unless it has access to the thoughts of others, and only books provide us with that access. Therefore, the ability to read is vital to intellectual growth and mind expansion. The inability to read can stifle intellectual development. It can be an enormous source of frustration for an active intelligent mind. The "dyslexic" child with an intelligent mind has been pitifully crippled by teaching methods used in the earliest days of his education.

Some teachers cannot understand why some intelligent children cannot figure out the sound-symbol system for themselves despite the obstacles placed in their way by the sight-vocabulary method. But as we pointed out in the earlier chapters, and as Dr. Orton found out in the 1920s, some children, despite high intelligence, cannot learn to read our written language when it is taught pictographically—or sight associationally. This is perfectly normal. My conviction is that *no* child actually learns how to read our written language in that way, and our colleges are full of the new illiterates to prove it. These college students have probably learned more from the mere use of spoken language than from the written language. But their deficiencies are quite apparent to the college professors. You simply cannot expand your mind or learn adequately enough by way of the spoken language alone. You can pick up a lot of stray information in that way, but organized learning can only occur with the aid of books, and books require many hours of reading, quiet concentration, and absorption.

Whole-word advocates would argue that they do teach children to read—to read for meaning—and that phonics people are only creating "word callers." They disputed Rudolf Flesch on his definition of reading. It seems to me that the confusion here is between two entirely different processes: that of *learning how* to read and that of reading. They are two distinct processes and the sight-vocabulary basal textbooks hopelessly confuse them. Learning how to read is a highly specialized intellectual feat. It consists primarily of mastering the sound-symbol system of which our written language is composed. Learning how to read is not reading. It is an entirely different process and should be considered and treated so.

The sound-symbol system is one of the great intellectual achievements of mankind. Because we have had the alphabet for so long, its recognition as an incredible feat of human genius is often overlooked. It was quite an achievement for someone to have been able to isolate the separate sounds of speech and to designate separate symbols to represent them on paper. When you teach a child this system, you impart to him some of the intellectual excitement of this great achievement —the idea that each sound of the language can actually be isolated and represented by a symbol! What a tremendous insight that gives him into the nature of both the spoken and written language and the relationship between the two.

Although the human race has been in existence for perhaps a million years, it was only three thousand years ago that man had reached the intellectual and cultural development enabling him to invent the alphabet. It was the revolutionary work of a brilliant mind and has probably had more influence on the further development of civilization than any other single invention. A child cannot help but feel the excitement and sense of achievement that the mastery of such an enormously useful tool will give him. For a child who has already mastered several thousand words in his speaking vocabulary, the mastery of the sound-symbol system immediately gives him an intellectual power of tremendously greater dimension. To deprive a child of this mastery is criminal, especially in a complex industrial world where he must have it to survive.

Therefore, we can say that the whole-word method has been built on two great confusions: the first, that learning to read is the same as learning the language; the second, that learning how to read is the same process as reading. A method based on such confusions will have a very debilitating effect on the minds of children exposed to it. That is why one can characterize a sight vocabulary as the thalidomide of modern elementary education, because of the crippling effect it has on the minds of some children. In the first confusion, the child is taught as if he were deaf and knew no language. In the second, the natural order and sequence of learning is reversed so that the logic in language and the sound-symbol system is destroyed. The child assumes that written language is a mess of arbitrary symbols, requiring a photographic memory to visualize as word forms and the memorization of numerous dull rules in order to learn the right phonetic clues. What a totally false understanding of what an alphabetically written language is.

It is interesting how despite the fact that the conceptual origins of the whole-word method as a means of teaching the deaf to read have not been known until the publication of this book, others have detected in the whole-word methodology exactly those confusions that go right back to its origin. We have cited Professor Goodman's observation earlier. Mary Johnson's book provides further awareness that this is so. In describing her home remedy for converting sight-readers to sound-symbol readers, she writes:

213

If an older child finds oral spelling, even of three-letter words, discouragingly difficult, it helps to explain to him that this is because he has not learned to think with his ears. He has been spelling and reading just with his eyes—and his ears haven't been doing their share of the work. Once his ears have learned to co-operate they will be able to help his eyes and this will make reading and spelling much, much easier.

This probably explains why so many sight-readers have such difficult reading comprehension problems. A sound-symbol reader "thinks with his ears" and therefore more easily hooks up reading to thinking, because, as we have shown, thinking is internalized speech and writing is thinking on paper. A sight-reader, however, is trying to think with his eyes, which simply cannot be done. The thinking process is a direct extension of the speaking process, and you short-circuit or break up the smooth flow of the process by inserting a sight-reading technique between the written language and the thinking mind. In sight-reading, the child associates words with ideas rather than with sounds. Therefore, the process of reading and thinking is constantly interrupted by sight associations.

We can get an idea of what the interruptive process is like if we had to read a sentence like the following: "The # of $ & ¢ I have is a small % of the total." The sentence is easy enough to read because the symbols are common ones, quite distinctive in appearance, and are few and frequently used. But the symbols $ & ¢ do not convey what the words *dollars and cents* convey in terms of fluent, accurate spoken language, that is, if you know what the letters stand for in terms of sound. But imagine what it must be like for a child trying to learn to look at each word as if it were a whole distinctive symbol like a dollar sign, especially words which look so much alike as *dad, bad, bab, dab, hid, bid, bib, did, lid,* etc. When such word symbols must be memorized by the thousands, or figured out on the basis of phonetic clues, the child is hopelessly lost. He is back in the pre-alphabetic period when man's mind was handicapped by an inadequate method of writing. And he is even more handicapped than a learner of hieroglyphics because our words were never meant to be read as characters and therefore are not distinctive enough.

Yet we have forced millions of children to read as if the alphabet had never been invented. And we have seen an entire educational system perverted to accommodate the illogic and confusion of a defective teaching method. It is easy to see that the neural disorganization which some dyslexic children exhibit is a result of imposing a sight-association method on a sound-association writing system. The mind can get so mixed up trying to reconcile two irreconcilables, that it ceases to function properly at all. And this is why no parent should permit his child, under any circumstances, to be taught a sight vocabulary. It is inimical to healthy associational organization—which is what every child's mind requires for the proper and orderly absorption of knowledge.

Some pages back we mentioned that even the teachers of the deaf recognized the connection between thinking and speaking and developed the oralist school of articulation in direct opposition to the manualist school, the school of methodical signs or sign language to which Gallaudet adhered. The connection between the development of the intellect and the spoken language was so crucial, that the deaf had to learn to "speak" and read phonetically even though they could not hear. Samuel Heinicke, the German teacher of the deaf who developed the oralist school, described its genesis in 1781 in a letter to the Abbé de l'Epeé, who had founded the manualist school in Paris where Gallaudet later studied:

> As I went about teaching written language to deaf-mutes for a number of years, I came to see that they did not think in that language at all, but rather in methodical signs. During the very process of learning, they found themselves forgetting, sometimes partially, sometimes totally. Signs were the only things that they retained. I tried them in spoken language and then set them to work part-time in written language. They still retained more concepts in speech than in writing. Finally I became quite discouraged and wanted to throw up the whole business. But I thought the matter over very carefully, and set about studying the human understanding of both hearing and deaf people, as based upon successive acts of speech and its influence upon, and union with, thinking. In this way happily I came upon psychological phenomena which I had not previously thought of, heard about, or read about. And the result was that I built up and put into practice an entirely new type of teaching.
>
> . . . Now I am on the right path. My pupils learn to read and speak clearly and with understanding. They think in their articulate speech waking and dreaming; anyone can speak with them if he will only speak slowly. Their written language rests on their spoken language, which, it is true, they do not hear, but rather grasp through another sense, which does equally well. In this process,

the beginning is always a pitiable sing-song, but in two or three years they speak well and intelligibly, and in the end they also learn to declaim.*

Thus was born the articulation or oralist school of teaching the deaf to read phonetically by teaching them to speak. If even the deaf must learn to read by a sound-symbol method in order to advance intellectually, how much more important must it be for a normal child to learn that way? Heinicke's method was not the method Thomas Gallaudet brought back with him to America. He brought back the manualist method of the Paris school, from which he later developed the sight-vocabulary method for teaching normal children to read. The manualist method, which Heinicke considered to be a form of hieroglyphics, was clearly inferior to the oralist method, and its introduction in America by Gallaudet retarded the development of deaf-mute education in this country for quite a number of years. When Horace Mann had toured Europe he was greatly impressed by the oralist schools for the deaf and he praised them in his *Seventh Annual Report*. We pointed out in an earlier chapter how Gallaudet took issue with him on this particular section of the report. It is interesting that Mann could understand the need for teaching the deaf to read by sound-symbol methodology, but could not understand its necessity for normal children. At least Gallaudet had been consistent in his approach, generalizing that both deaf-mutes and normal children could be instructed in the same manner.

There is a remarkable similarity between the debates that went on between the manualists, who considered theirs the "natural method," and the oralists, whose method was called "artificial," and the debates which have continued to take place between the look-say ("natural") and phonics ("synthetic") advocates. Both, essentially, dealt with the same problems of sight-reading versus sound-symbol reading. But the teachers of the deaf solved their problem in favor of logic—the sound-symbol approach; while the teachers of normal children went back three thousand years to the time before the alphabet. The irony is that the whole-word method is not only based on Gallaudet's method of teaching the deaf to read, but on a method which has since been discarded by the teachers of the deaf themselves as outmoded and inadequate!

Oddly enough, it was Gallaudet's son, Edward Miner Gallaudet, head of the National Deaf-Mute College in Washington, D.C., who brought

---

* Christopher A. Garnett, Jr., *The Exchange of Letters Between Samuel Heinicke and Abbé Charles Michel de l'Epée* (New York: Vantage Press, 1968).

the oralist school to the United States. Edward had been trained in the manualist school by his father and he loyally adhered to it until he toured Europe in 1867 and saw the oralist schools for himself. In Maxine Boatner's biography of Edward Gallaudet there are some graphic descriptions of his school visits which began with skepticism but ended with enthusiasm:

> The boys' school for the deaf in Brussels was visited and Frere Cyrille took him around. There were 43 boys. The Prussian System had been adopted and signs were abandoned, yet the use of natural signs were allowed when necessary. Frere Cyrille showed a decided preference for the oral method, and the pupils seemed anxious to learn to articulate. Although some born deaf could read lips and speak well, Edward still felt that as a means of easy and rapid communication between the teachers and his pupils articulation and lip-reading failed completely. . . .
> Edward made a return trip to Frere Cyrille's school and selected a paragraph in the elementary French reader for each pupil to read aloud. With the book before him he could see that every pupil had been enabled to form distinct sounds for the syllable uttered. Had he not had the book before him, however, he would have failed to comprehend some of the passages.

So the deaf were reading phonetically! Something which twentieth-century American children with perfect hearing would be unable to do. From Brussels Edward went on to Paris to visit his father's old school which had gone oralist with some interesting innovations of its own:

> Mr. Vaisse introduced Edward to something new in the classroom. Instead of using his organs of speech he employed written characters; each represented a certain sound, its form having a likeness to the position of the mouth when the sound is given forth. Mr. Vaisse had invented this system of written signs, and the *modus operandi* of the exercise is understood when it is explained that the sounds are first expressed phonetically and then the proper etymological order is given. Edward copied examples of this in his Journal. Edward was surprised that the different positions of the organs of speech, in uttering different sounds, could be so accurately presented to the mind through the medium of the eye, enabling the deaf student to imitate the sound with a good degree of accuracy.

In Vienna Edward was even more impressed:

> At the Jewish Institution in Vienna, Edward found the ability
> of the children to read from the lips greater than in any school
> he had visited. Their ability to write from dictation and with speed
> on the blackboard was amazing.

The upshot of all this was that when Edward Gallaudet returned to
the United States in 1867 he too issued a famous report on a European
tour, in which oralism (phonics) triumphed over sign language (hieroglyphics). He recommended:

> That instruction in artificial speech and lip-reading be entered
> upon at as early a day as possible; that all pupils in our primary
> department be afforded opportunities of engaging in this until it
> plainly appears that success is unlikely to crown their efforts; that
> with those who evince facility in oral exercises, instruction shall
> be continued during their entire residence in the institution.

Why was it so important for the deaf to learn how to articulate and
read via a sound-symbol system instead of a sight-reading system?
Because the spoken language was the medium of thought, and a deaf-
mute could not expand his mind without the use of the spoken language,
even though he could not hear it. Heinicke had made the point quite
clear in 1782:

> Clear thinking is possible only in spoken language. Written let-
> ters are only signs for articulations. With both types of signs we
> admittedly form concepts, but the articulate signs are the core of
> the written ones. The latter are an abstraction neither serviceable
> for thinking nor praying. Also they are quite evanescent. Indeed,
> if we had no articulate signs, we would likewise have no written
> signs at all. We would have no German writing if we had no Ger-
> man speech. It would be a mistake to believe that it is more weari-
> some to teach deaf-mutes spoken language and written language
> at the same time, or one before the other. A shadow is never possi-
> ble without a body, and the written word is not even the shadow
> of speech. It is quite natural that the written word is much more
> rapidly forgotten, since it is only a sign of previously known, and
> past conscious articulations. Words will remain more firmly
> anchored in the memory if the letters and syllables can be inwardly
> named (by sound) before they are outwardly represented.

We need not belabor the point. Let the professors of education do a little useful homework on their own. And let Messrs. Gates, Betts, Witty, Artley, and the like, who have subjected millions of normal American children to reading instruction based on an outmoded method of teaching the deaf, answer to the parents of America.

When one begins to think of the incalculable damage done to the young minds of America through defective teaching techniques, one can scarcely contain one's anger. Flesch was accused of writing in anger by his critics, as if anger were an inappropriate reaction to gross pedagogical malpractice which has had a ruinous effect on the literacy of millions of children. Even Jeanne Chall was unable to restrain her anger in some of her biting criticism of the basal readers, and heaven knows she made every effort to keep her professional cool. If it bothers you to see children suffering and failing needlessly because of defective teaching methods obstinately adhered to against all criticism, you will become angry. If it makes no difference to you, you won't care one way or another.

While researching this book I have been amazed at the coolness of the leading members of the sight-vocabulary establishment, the detached way in which they have been able to catalog and discuss all of the things that were wrong with normal children who couldn't learn to read by way of an outmoded method discarded by the deaf. If there is one thing these teachers have lacked it is humility, and a teacher without humility is no teacher at all. Their stupidity has only been excelled by their pride and their greed.

I am not the only writer to feel this strong sense of indignation and anger. George Riemer, in his book *How They Murdered the Second "R"*, is just as angry at pedagogical malpractice. Who murdered the second "R"? He points the accusing finger at the "reading specialists who dominate the primary grades" and the English departments who "not only look the other way when the evil is being done but conduct a graduate school of crime showing teachers how to kill." Strong language indeed. But why not, when the situation warrants it?

Meanwhile, what can we expect from the reading establishment in the next ten years? The establishment's point of view was best expressed by Ernest Hilton of Harcourt Brace Jovanovich, the textbook publisher, in *The Elementary School Journal* of April 1971. He wrote:

There is no one best way to teach reading, and programs in the '70's will continue to use various methods and materials.

Method is always a central concern in elementary-school curriculum practice, and in no subject is it more centrally a concern than in reading. . . . The literature—research reports, theoretical discussions, speculation—is so extensive that it seems to defy orderly review. Yet, out of it all has emerged no clear case for the superiority of a given method or a given set of materials, in terms so convincing that one can say, "This, at least, is the way to teach reading."

. . . One of the most debated issues has been that of the place of what is commonly called "phonics." If the differences in viewpoint are thought of in terms of extremes, on the one end of the scale is what we may call the "look and say," or "whole word" method; on the other, an approach that insists on "decoding" by knowledge of sound-symbol relationships as the method. Materials on decoding either impose a rigorous control in introducing sound-symbol relationships or use an artificial (augmented) alphabet in reading to achieve "regularity."

The realities of general practice, however, seldom reflect extreme positions. Moreover, as many have said, any general method must accommodate itself to concerns other than decoding, as, for example, the concern that what children are asked to read be expressed, insofar as is practicable, in "natural" language patterns. Another concern, and surely one worthy of serious consideration, is with the content and the quality of what is to be read—in plain terms, concern that what is to be read is worth reading. It is not easy to bring these concerns together. For example, it is difficult, if not impossible, to use "natural" language and at the same time control sound-symbol relationships.

There is a mainstream position in which the several concerns are accommodated—a method that strongly emphasizes the decoding skills and at the same time emphasizes reading for meaning. It seems quite safe to assert that this position will prevail through the '70's.

What Mr. Hilton means is that the "mainstream" basal series will continue to teach children a sight-vocabulary regardless of the risks involved to the child. It is strange that he should characterize teaching an alphabetic writing system alphabetically as an "extreme position." When the inventor of the alphabet discarded hieroglyphics for a sound-symbol system, he was not taking an "extreme position." He was replacing an inadequate, outmoded system of recording language with a completely new system based on sound symbols which created a new smoother, more direct, more precise associational flow between reading and thinking, between thinking and writing. Simply because American pedagogues of the twentieth century have confused the two systems of writing is no reason to believe that a compromise is either possible or desirable.

It has been proven by forty years of experience, which has produced the greatest epidemic of reading disability we've ever had, that there is only one way to teach a sound-symbol system—the way it was taught for three thousand years before American pedagogy lost its head.

Hilton also confuses the process of *learning how* to read with the process of reading. He is worried about giving first-graders something "worth reading." He seems to forget the order of priorities: that the child must first *learn how* to read before he can read anything worth reading. In the process of learning how to read—by mastering the sound-symbol system—the child should not be distracted by a story requiring "interpretation." Mastering the sound-symbol system is a highly technical intellectual task in itself which requires the full concentration of the child. It can be made as interesting and stimulating as the publisher would like to make it. There is enough intellectual excitement in the process to keep any normal child highly motivated—and if deaf children can do it, so can normal children.

But perhaps the most important sentence in Hilton's article is the one where he states that out of all the research and studies conducted up to 1971 there has been "no clear case for the superiority of a given method or a given set of materials, in terms so convincing that one can say, 'This, at least, is the way to teach reading.' " Mr. Hilton has done this writer a great service by explaining why this book was written: to make the case clear in terms so convincing that not only Hilton but also the one and a quarter million elementary school teachers will understand that an alphabetically based writing system must be taught alphabetically from the very beginning. Frankly, we don't understand why Flesch's book was not convincing enough to people like Hilton. But then almost the entire educational establishment rejected it. But what about Jeanne Chall's book? Wasn't that convincing enough? Perhaps it wasn't. Chall's book had several notable failings: one, she did not clearly differentiate between an alphabetic system of writing and a hieroglyphic one. By defining the great debate in beginning reading instruction in terms of a decoding emphasis vs. a meaning emphasis, she inadvertently fell into a confusing semantic trap. The man who invented the alphabet was very much concerned about reading for meaning. In fact his system was invented particularly to facilitate reading for meaning—with a much greater degree of accuracy and ease. Dr. Chall fell into the trap that whole-word advocates have been in since they went down their pedagogical road to ruin: confusing *learning how* to read with reading. Everyone who learns to read is expected to read for meaning. Why else do we learn how to read? But before you can read for meaning, you must know *how* to read, and that process consists of mastering the sound-symbol system of which our written language is composed. If Mr. Hilton were learning Russian, he would not be expected to read whole words and sentences in Russian without first learning the Cyrillic alphabet and the sounds the letters represented. He would expect to be taught first things first. He would not want to be bothered with the meaning of the sentence before he even knew how to read it. But a child in grade one being taught a sight vocabulary does not know what should be taught first. He accepts what the teacher tells him, even though she may have reversed the natural order of learning. I use the phrase "natural order of learning" because people like Mr. Hilton are so concerned with the child's "natural" language being used in the first reading lessons. The "naturalness" of the vocabulary is not an issue in teaching the child the sound symbols. Nonsense syllables can be just as effective in helping a child master the sound-symbol system. What is far more important pedagogically is the "natural order of learning," the sequence of what is learned.

Which brings us to the second failing in Dr. Chall's book: her lack of understanding of the look-say method's contribution to reading disability. If we have characterized a sight-vocabulary as the thalidomide of elementary education it is because there is overwhelming evidence in the sheer number of remedial cases that imposing a sight-associational technique on a sound-associational system can create in perhaps one out of three or four children a severe case of associational confusion—or dyslexia, reading disability," or whatever else you want to call it. The severity of such cases is legendary, and some children have had to undergo remedial training for years at great expense to their parents in order to undo the associational confusion caused by Dick and Jane. A good example of such hard-core cases was given by Dr. Gladys L. Persons speaking before the Reading Reform Foundation conference in 1963:

> Another angle on this problem of rehabilitation of the youngsters, to whom reading is just one vast confusion, is the time it takes to do this job. Have you ever considered how long a twelve-year-old boy with a good mind but no skill must be under systematic retraining? I can think of two—both 12 years old and reading on second-grade level when we took them. Both are established now—Danny was one whose parents kept him with us *five* years and at the end of that time all subjects by test measurements were on high-school levels except spelling, which never was above fifth-grade level. And S.P. is another one over whom we labored for four years, summer and winter. . . . I need not stress the costs

222

of retraining; but can say that it takes more than money to accomplish it.

Such is the damage which can be done by teaching a child a sight vocabulary. Dr. Orton warned of it in 1929, but his warning went unheeded. It is surprising that in these forty years not one parent has sued a school or a publisher for pedagogical malpractice to recover the costs of remedial retraining and for the emotional damage done to the child. In the food industry, if one can of soup poisons a customer, the federal government can put a whole soup company out of business. If the Food and Drug Administration merely suspects that cyclamates or hexachlorophene can cause harm, products which use these ingredients are withdrawn from the market. When the auto industry produces faulty cars, they are recalled for adjustment. When thalidomide was found to cause alarming birth deformities, the drug was withdrawn, the pharmaceutical house sued, and the executives of the company tried on charges of criminal negligence.

It is true that no child has died of reading disability or dyslexia. But of the one thousand or so teen-agers who commit suicide each year, reading disability may contribute to the loss of self-esteem and subsequent depression which leads to suicide. Certainly the dropout problem is a part of the reading problem—and drugs and delinquency are part of the dropout problem. As Dr. Chall puts it: "Publishers of reading programs have an obligation, similar to that of pharmaceutical companies manufacturing drugs, to test out their materials, not only for anticipated effects but also for unanticipated consequences." Authors and publishers of sight-vocabulary basal readers have had their books used for over forty years by millions of American children, with the result that we now have a reading disability problem of "epidemic proportions." The epidemic is so great that the federal government has had to step in with its Right-to-Read program. The very existence of and need for the program is in itself an indictment of the educational system which made the program necessary. It was a very clear slap in the face of the reading establishment, which nevertheless welcomed the program not with a sense of shame over the establishment's enormous failure, but with a sense of glee over the millions of dollars which would now be spent to buy more defective books written by the same IRA authors. Wrote Donald L. Cleland, president of the IRA, in the November 1971 issue of *The Reading Teacher:*

> The International Reading Association, the most prestigious single organization in its field, through its Commission on Quality Teacher Education and other appropriate scholars stands ready to

lend its expertise to the United States Office of Education in the launching of improved teacher-education programs, both preservice and inservice.

If the "expertise" of the IRA had been any good to begin with, there would be no need for a Right-to-Read program. But since the federal government has decided to intervene in what has become a national disaster, we strongly recommend that the Department of Health, Education and Welfare do the following: (1) issue an order requiring all schools to cease using sight-vocabulary basal programs, and to have such textbooks removed from the schools at once; (2) supply sufficient funds to replace all sight-vocabulary reading programs with programs based on the alphabetic, sound-symbol principle; (3) provide funds for the retraining of all reading teachers who do not know how to teach reading on sound-symbol principles.

These are the minimal drastic measures which are called for if we are to stop creating dyslexics with every new class of children who enter the first grade. We have cited enough evidence in this book—based on an analysis of the whole-word method, an investigation into its conceptual origins, an examination of the causes of reading disability, and an exposure of the professional and commercial conflict of interests involving leading members of the reading establishment—to make it absolutely imperative that the federal government act in behalf of the parents of this country and the millions of school children who will be exposed to pedagogical thalidomide during the next ten years. Nothing short of such intervention will put an end to such widespread educational malpractice and restore some measure of faith in the educational system. It would be criminal, in the light of the information presented in this book, for the federal government to permit one more American child to be exposed to the dangers of the sight-vocabulary method in a public school.

Walter W. Straley, chairman of President Nixon's National Reading Council, pointed out the American public's loss of faith in its institutions at the IRA convention in 1971. He said:

> There is in our nation a decreasing faith in our own institutions. . . . Across the country, more than half of last year's school bond issues were defeated in confrontation of often angry voters. Taxpayers strike against their schools, teachers strike against school boards. Administrators cut staff and curricula. Many schools must close before normal terms are ended. Probably a million children will strike out this year by simply dropping out, many to drugs and decay.

224

Obviously much of this loss of faith in the public schools is a result of the schools being unable to divest themselves of entrenched error. Too many authors, teachers and publishers have a vested interest in error with the result that the public is becoming less and less willing to support public education. Who can blame them? How else can they get back at the vested interests?

An idea of the kind of double-talk the public gets from its educators was given in an interview of Dr. Theodore L. Harris, president of the IRA for 1972, in *Reading Newsreport* of January 1972. Dr. Harris was asked: "Recent psychological experiments suggest that the letter is the key unit in word perception. What implication does this have for beginning reading methods?" Dr. Harris's answer:

> Among the many possible implications, the critical implication, in my estimation, for beginning reading instruction is that it must develop a set of discriminations of the comprehensive words from the outset as well as for word forms and for a new association with word forms.

That is the kind of pedagogical double-talk and evasion the public and a lot of teachers are sick of. Forty years of it are more than enough. Why should any parent have to put up with it any further? Why should a child's education be ruined because of it? If our public institutions lack integrity, it is because the people who run them have none. It should be noted that *Reading Newsreport*, the publication that asked Dr. Harris such a direct question, is not controlled by the IRA. It is an independent publication serving that segment of the teaching profession which has stopped reading the unliterate, unreadable, bloodless research reports which pass for articles in the IRA journals. It is easy to cover up error with unreadable articles written in a professional jargon which only the initiates can understand. If nobody can understand what you are talking about, nobody can accuse you of being right or wrong, and you can go on doing what you are doing indefinitely.

In the next ten years approximately forty million children will be exposed to beginning reading instruction. Some will be taught to read from the very beginning on alphabetic principles. They will be the lucky ones. Most children, unfortunately, will be given a good strong dose of educational thalidomide—the sight vocabulary—unless a drastic curriculum change is instituted without delay. Only the federal government can institute such a change. This book has provided enough of a basis to make the Department of Health, Education and Welfare act. The mental health of those children is at stake, their educational progress, and ultimately their welfare. No single writer, no single book, no single

225

school can do what desperately has to be done in *every* public school in the country. This is a task which only the federal government can undertake—simply because it is nationwide in scope, concerns public institutions, and requires enormous funding.

It is, of course, true that changes for the better are already taking place. Even *The Reading Teacher*, under its new editor Lloyd W. Kline, is improving and was more readable in 1972 than it was in 1971. But the changes are coming much too slowly. There is no reason why any child should be subjected to reading instruction based on an outmoded method of teaching the deaf to read when there are in print excellent reading instruction textbooks based on sound alphabetic principles. We are still waiting for a cure to cancer. But the preventive cure of reading disability exists *now*. There is no earthly reason why any American child in any American public school should be given anything else.

Even if we switch all schools over immediately to sound-symbol reading instruction, we shall still have the problem of what to do with all of those children beyond the first grade right up into high school who labor each day under severe reading handicaps. How do we undo the damage done three, four, five, and six years ago? This is a problem for the educators to grapple with. Let them deal with real problems. Let them finally really teach instead of pretending to do so. If I have been harsh on the professional educators in this book, it is for good reason. They are responsible for the education of our children. For years they have resisted the legitimate criticism of informed laymen and the desperate pleas of frantic parents. Some contend that the nature of public education, the institutionalization of vested interests, makes educators impervious to outside influences. But ultimately public education will stand or fall on the ability of public educators to perform in the true interests of their charges. If through professional pride, greed, and arrogance they fail in their responsibilities, public education will have failed with them. I have pointed out earlier that a teacher without humility is no teacher at all, just as a writer without humility is no writer at all. I have not written this book to put publishers out of business, embarrass educators, or stir up public indignation against public schools. I have written this book for three very simple reasons: to spare millions of children unnecessary suffering, to increase their enjoyment and knowledge of the written word, and to make this country once more a fountainhead of literary greatness.

10

How to Teach Your Preschool Child to Read at Home: A Primer

Teaching your preschool child to read at home is not a difficult task, but it does require three basic elements: time, patience, and organization. Learning how to read consists of your child learning to master the sound-symbol system of which our written language is composed. It therefore takes time to achieve such mastery. How much time? How long would it take you as an adult to master the Morse code or Pittman shorthand? It would depend on how readily you picked it up. You might find it easy, others might find it tough going. Similarly, your child's mastering the sound-symbol system depends on how quickly he learns and how well you impart the information to him. Therefore, do not set any particular time limit. *Take as much time as is needed* until he masters what has to be mastered. That's where patience comes in. What you will be teaching your child will be the foundation of a lifetime of reading and learning. Therefore, the foundation must be a good one, a solid one. Some children require more time than others during this foundation building period. The situation is comparable to that of laying the foundation for a skyscraper. For example, the Back Bay area of Boston is composed of soft landfill, and when the John Hancock Tower, the tallest building in Boston, was being erected there, it required two years to lay the foundation. For months, hundreds of steel piles were driven deep down to bedrock, and then tons of concrete were poured before the foundation was ready to support the sixty-five story structure.

On the other hand, on Manhattan Island, which is virtually one big solid rock, it takes half as much time to lay the foundation for a comparable skyscraper. In both cases, regardless of the land conditions, the foundations are built according to what they must support in the future, and not according to any other criterion. Thus, if because of soft landfill it takes two years to lay an adequate foundation, it must take two years. There can be no possible shortcut if the structure which is to be built on that foundation is to be secure.

The ability to read is the foundation on which a lifetime of educational and intellectual achievement is built. Therefore, the foundation must be a solid one, based on thorough understanding. Some children, for a variety of reasons, learn more quickly than others. Some learn very slowly. But all of them, regardless of how long it may take, can master the sound-symbol system which is the foundation of reading ability. Take as much time as you need to lay the foundation. Once the foundation is solid, the structure that rises on it will be equally secure and solid.

The first step in teaching your child to read is to teach him the alphabet. By teaching him the alphabet, we mean teaching him to recognize all twenty-six letters by name and to be able to print them and write them when asked to do so. Once he has learned to identify the letters of the alphabet by name and can write them down, then he is ready to learn their sound values. He does not have to know the alphabet letter-perfect before you start teaching him the sounds, for the simple reason that he will be learning the letters better as he uses them. Therefore, as soon as he has a fairly good acquaintance with all of the letters, you can proceed into the sound teaching phase.

How old should your child be when you teach him the alphabet? Old enough to understand what you are doing. As soon as your child has developed a sufficient speaking skill he should be ready to learn how to read. A child's preschool vocabulary indicates to what extent he has picked up the spoken language used around him. Deaf children can be taught to read without having heard a word of the spoken language. Thus, if your child can jabber away intelligibly, he has already expanded the use of his mind considerably and is ready to learn to read.

Before teaching your child the alphabet, tell him that a knowledge of the alphabet is necessary in order that he may learn to read. Tell him that it is the first step. Thus he will understand that learning to read is a process that takes time. A child who has learned to speak several thousand words all by himself is quite an intelligent human being, and you should acknowledge this intelligence by explaining to your child in terms he can understand how he is going to be taught to read. Children at the preschool age are forever asking questions. They are very inquisitive, and there is no reason not to give as understandable an answer as you know to any question your child may ask.

Since your child is constantly surrounded by alphabet letters—on cereal boxes, television, billboards, in reading materials at home—he will be curious about them. Tell him that once he knows the letters by name, he and they will be life-long friends, for he will be using them all of his life. So we introduce him to the alphabet in alphabetical order. There is no good reason to do it in any other way, since he will have to know them alphabetically in order to be able to use a dictionary or a phone book some day.

You introduce each letter by name. You point to the letter and tell the child, "This letter's name is *ay*." Then you point to *B* and tell him, "This letter's name is *bee*." Teach him several letters at a time. The reason why I write the names of the letters out is to remind you of the important distinction between the letter names and the letter sounds. For example, the letter *A* has four sounds, and the *ay* sound is only one of them. That sound also happens to be the name of the letter. The sound of the letter *B* is not *bee* but *buh*. Notice how impossible it is to give the sound of a consonant without adding a vowel element. In your own mind, however, the distinction between the letter sound and the letter name should be quite clear. The name is important, because the names are a means of identifying the letters, just as the names of individuals are used for that purpose. However, many people tend to confuse the letter names with the letter sounds because of their close similarity in English. In Greek the letter names—alpha, beta, gamma—are quite distinctive and there is no way of confusing them with their sounds. However, in the transfer of the alphabet from Greece to Rome, these distinctive names were lost and new names quite similar to the letter sounds were adopted.

However, there is no reason to confuse your child. He is learning the letter names and their individual shapes so that he can identify them and know one from another, just as he knows his friends by their names. If his friends had no names, how would he identify them? It would be awkward to remember them by some physical feature alone. He talks about his friends easily by referring to them by name. Thus, he will be able to talk about the letters and their distinguishing shapes by their names. Remember also that our letter names contain an element of each letter's sound, so that the letter names will also be important reminders of the letter sounds when we get to that phase.

In teaching your child the letters, teach him to print them in capital and lower-case forms as well as to write them. Such printing and writing

229

practice makes him learn the shapes of the letters more thoroughly. Also, he must get used to the idea that reading and writing are inseparable skills. One goes with the other. When you learn the Morse code you learn how to send messages as well as receive them. When a stenographer learns shorthand, she learns how to take dictation as well as read it back. It is the same with the alphabet. The inventor meant it to serve as a way of encoding or putting down the spoken word on paper as well as a way of decoding or translating back into spoken words the written words on paper. Thus, reading and writing, or decoding and encoding, are two parts of one skill, and both should be learned simultaneously, for the learning of one reinforces the other. In addition, it teaches the child that the alphabet is to be used as a means of conveying his thoughts in writing to others as well as a way of reading the thoughts of others. It is important that he should be an active sender of messages as well as a receiver. He is talker and listener, not just listener, and he should be able to transcribe his talk into written words with ease. Thus, we start writing from the very beginning.

There are a number of pleasant and playful ways in which the child can be taught to recognize different letters. He can cut letters out of magazine and newspaper advertisements and paste them on the blank pages of an artist's pad—each page devoted to a particular letter. This can be his own personal alphabet book, and hunting for new letters to add to his collection can teach him to recognize the letter shapes more quickly. If he asks about words, point to the different letters in the words and tell him that he will be able to read the words after he is taught the letter names and then their sounds. Tell him, "You will be able to read any word you want to after you know the letters and their sounds."

I believe that any child is quite capable of understanding that learning is an orderly process and proceeds in logical steps. When you proceed in this way, you are teaching your child something about the learning process, which is as important to know as what he is being taught in that process. It develops an orderly approach to learning which he will be able to apply in all of his schoolwork ahead of him.

Teaching the alphabet can be fun. You can use blocks. You can use alphabet books. I would discourage the use of pictures in conjunction with learning the alphabet. The picture he should be looking at is the *letter itself*, not an apple, or a ball, or an elephant. I make this point because shortly after he knows the letters, he will be taught to identify them with sounds, and that is very crucial. A letter is a symbol of a sound. It is not the symbol of anything else. Thus, it is important for the child to see the letter as symbolizing sound, a noise. The letter is supposed to stimulate his mouth, lips and tongue to shape themselves into a particular sound. It is not supposed to make him think of an apple or an elephant. He must translate groups of letters into speech, and he will do this more easily the better he associates the letters with sounds.

The child sees lots of pictures around him. The letter is simply another picture among them. But he must know that the letter stands for something. It has a meaning. It means a sound, not an object. Sound, *nothing else.*

When the inventor of the alphabet identified each distinct sound in his language and devised a system of symbols with which each sound could be represented, his purpose was to create a direct association between a symbol and a sound. In designating a name to each symbol, he included its sound element. But it was still a matter of remembering which letter represented which sound—and the name of the letter is a much better clue to the letter's sound than a picture of an elephant or bumble bee. It was easier to commit the letters to memory in a set alphabetical order. However, as has been pointed out, the child will learn the letters better as he uses them.

Some teachers believe it better to teach the child only a few letters at a time and to start using those letters to create words. I suppose this is as good a way to do it as any. But I think there is a virtue in taking each step at a time, so that the child develops a certain sense of logic. Learning to read is the child's first real intellectual work, and therefore it should be as logical, organized and non-confusing as possible. While learning to read he should be also learning something about method and procedure. This will set the pattern for future learning habits. The child does not have to know the alphabet letter perfect before going on to the sounds, but he should be fairly familiar with most of the letters, being able to name them and write them.

When you are ready to teach the letter sounds, you tell the child: "Now we're going to learn the sounds each letter stands for so that you can put the letters together into words." That is the essence of what you want to convey to the child: that letters stand for sounds, and that when you put them together, they make words.

In teaching the child the letter sounds, we must always remember that the alphabet was invented by an adult for use by adults, and it was easy enough at that time to teach an adult to isolate the distinct sounds of the language and indicate which letter represented which sound. And obviously, the alphabet was invented by a man who spoke clearly and heard clearly and could distinguish between the fine differences of speech sounds, between the *t* and the *d*, between *s* and *z*.

231

But a child's attunement to speech sounds is quite different. His words run into one another, and he may talk child-talk or baby-talk. So the approach must be scaled down to the child's ability to grasp the knowledge you wish to impart. *Take as much time as you need to do the job.* There is no rush. Your three-, four-, or five-year old has all the time in the world in which to learn how to read. What is important is not how fast he learns but how thoroughly and accurately. Remember, there are no shortcuts. The whole-word method was meant to be a shortcut. It has produced disasters. A whole remedial reading industry has grown out of this "shortcut." Shortcut to what? What's the big hurry? Why is there a need for a shortcut? The whole-word experts thought that if a child could not read words the first day he was in school, he'd never want to read a book for the rest of his life. Nonsense. Your child will want to read if he knows *how* to read, and if your child knows that learning how to read is an orderly process involving several preliminary steps, he will be quite happy to cooperate with you. Today's notorious adult nonreaders were taught the whole-word method. That inadequate method turned them away from books because it did not teach them to master the sound-symbol system, how to translate printed words into sounds instantly and automatically.

As we have pointed out, the alphabet is perhaps the greatest single intellectual invention of man. The sound-symbol system is an exciting piece of work and an exciting system to learn when you know that it is going to open up the entire world of literature to you and permit you to express your own thoughts in a durable, lasting way. How do you convey such intellectual excitement to a child? By being excited about it yourself. "Did you know that every sound you speak can be put down on paper?" you tell your child. That's exciting. "And that's what we are going to learn to do—put down every sound you make with your voice on paper."

By telling the child this, you've established the concept in his mind of being able to represent speech sounds on paper. That is the association you want to establish in his mind—that letters on paper stand for sounds which he can make with his voice, and that the sounds he makes can be put down on paper by way of letters representing them.

I have worked out the following sequence of instruction because it seems to me to be the most logical and easiest to accomplish what we want: an orderly understanding of the relationship between letters and voice sounds, an ability on the part of the child to hear the differences in spoken words and to translate them into written symbols.

Before proceeding into lesson one, however, a short word about the special problem our written language poses. While our written language is about 85 percent consistent in its sound-symbol correspondences, there are enough irregularities to warrant a very careful step-by-step procedure to minimize possible confusion. Since the child's own speaking vocabulary has a very large number of irregularly spelled words, we can make use of only a few of them in the early stages of instruction. That is why the child should be told that he is learning *how* to read, and that he will be considered a reader when he can read and write any word in his spoken vocabulary.

In the course of learning the sound-symbol system, however, the child will learn a lot of new words simply because these words fall into the most common and regular spelling patterns and best illustrate the alphabetic principle. They will represent a considerable expansion of his own vocabulary. After the child has shown that he can read these words, it is not necessary to spend too much time on their meaning just yet, since he will not be using these words in his own speaking vocabulary for a while. Emphasis on comprehension and meaning should not begin until *after* the child has mastered the sound-symbol system and can read and write with ease every word in his own spoken vocabulary. When this is done, the emphasis can then be shifted to the comprehension of new words and the general expansion of the child's vocabulary.

The plan of instruction is quite simple, based on the special characteristics of our sound-symbol system. We have forty-five sounds in our language, twenty-one of which are vowel sounds. Since there are only six vowel letters in our alphabet—a, e, i, o, u and part-time y—which must represent twenty-one vowel sounds, most of the difficult work in learning to read is in mastering the vowel-symbol correspondences. They are best learned in spelling family groups. So we begin with the five short vowels in combination with the consonants. The spelling patterns in these vowel groups are the simplest and most regular in our written language. They are easy to learn, and they teach the child the basic principles of the sound-symbol system. From there we move into the various consonant blends of our language. Finally, we learn the rest of the vowel sounds along with all of the important irregularities.

By the time the child has completed his final lesson he should be able to read any word he encounters. He may mispronounce some of the words he has never heard. But this is understandable. It should never be forgotten that the written language is merely a shadow of the spoken language and that the spoken language is one's basic guide to the pronunciation of the written word. In most cases the written word provides sufficient indication of stress and accent. But in multisyllabic words, the reader's knowledge of the spoken language becomes an indispensable requisite to correct pronunciation. The dictionary, of course, helps us determine how an unknown word is pronounced. However, a child learns it better by hearing it spoken. So pronounce all of the words clearly.

(Note: The division of the instruction into numbered lessons is for the sake of convenience and to provide a guide to the proper sequence of skill acquisition. You can cover as many lessons as you want in one session. However, set your pace according to your child's learning speed. Each lesson represents additional material to be mastered or a review of what has already been learned.)

Lesson 1: We start by telling the child that now we are going to learn what the letters mean: the sounds they stand for. We know the letter names and their shapes, now we are going to learn their sounds. Tell the child: "There are twenty-six letters which stand for forty-five sounds, and we are going to learn them all, one by one. So we have a lot of exciting work to do. When you know all of the sounds the letters stand for, you will be able to read any word you see." You start with the short sound of the vowel *a*. You explain to the child that there are two types of letters: vowels and consonants. The vowels are the most powerful letters in the alphabet, because you can't have a word without one. Consonants must always have vowels with them. They can never stand alone. You needn't go into detail at this point. Merely establish the fact that there are two classes of letters: vowels and consonants. Identify the vowel letters as *a, e, i, o, u*. All the rest are consonants. He will learn what you mean as he learns to use the different letters.

Tell the child that he is going to learn two words with the short vowel sound *a: am* and *at*. Ask him if he can hear the difference between *am* and *at*. Draw his attention to the fact that both words sound alike at the beginning, but end with a different sound. Then print them: *am* and *at*. The idea to get across to the child is that each word is composed of two sounds represented by two letters, a vowel and a consonant. The letter *a* stands for the short *a* vowel sound, and the *m* and *t* are consonants. Spell *am* and *at* out loud, and ask the child to spell them also. Pronounce the word *am* and ask the child if he can hear the *m* sound at the end of the word. Pronounce the word *at* and ask the child if he can hear the *t* sound. You might say: "The letter *m* stands for the *mmm* sound. The letter *t* stands for the *tuh* sound."

Then ask the child: "How do we make different sounds with our mouths?" If he can't answer, show him how we do it by shaping our lips and tongue in different ways to get different sounds. The purpose of this is to get the child to understand how we isolate sounds, so that

234

he can see how we can identify a *t* sound and an *m* sound. Do not expect the child to repeat the sounds in isolation at first try, but let him hear you say them. You can tell by how a child speaks how well he can discriminate the different sounds. He has never before considered the idea that a word is composed of one or more different sounds. But as he sees the word written down, he becomes aware of that fact, simply because he sees that a word is composed of more than one letter, and he now knows that each letter stands for a sound.

Lesson 2: Now take the word *am,* erase the *m* and replace it with *n.* By doing this, we show the child how the beginning sound is retained, but how the final sound is changed. Play around with this concept by replacing the second letter in the word *am* to produce these different words: *am, at, an, ax, as.* This should begin to give the child the idea of the interchangeability of letter sounds. He is learning to identify the sounds of five different consonants combined with the short sound of the vowel *a.* Tell him that he has already learned six different letter sounds. Let the child write these five words himself. These are five perfectly good English words which he will be reading and writing for the rest of his life. Let the child see the sound-symbol construction of the word. Arrange them in column form, so that he can see more graphically the beginning short *a* sound. Ask him to read the different words down the column. In this way he learns to associate the letters with sounds, and sounds with letters as you dictate the words back to him and ask him to write them down. By writing he also learns the left-to-right sequence of sound symbols in words. The letters follow the same sequence as the spoken sounds.

Do not at any time introduce any pictures into these exercises. The important task is to get the child to associate written letters with spoken sounds and vice versa. Pictures only disrupt this sound-symbol association process. The written word only represents sounds. It is the spoken word which represents an object or an idea. Therefore, in the writing or reading process, the smooth transcription of sounds into sound symbols and sound symbols back into sounds should not be disrupted by the intrusion of pictures of any kind. The contemplation of a picture is an entirely different process and has absolutely nothing to do with reading.

By now you've taught the child the short *a* sound and the consonants *m, t, n, x,* and *s.* In the word *as,* the soft *s* sounds more like *z.* But at this point that fine distinction need not be stressed. We shall bring the child's attention to that later when we deal with the two sounds of *s* and the letter *z.* The point is not to make a fuss over such very minor distinctions. In time, the child will realize that in English spelling there is not always a perfect symbolic representation of spoken sounds, and that the ultimate guide in pronunciation is not the written word by itself, but the spoken word as it is used in everyday speech.

Drill: Put the words on cards and flash them to the child until he can easily recognize them. A few minutes a day is all you need of drill.

Lesson 3: Arrange the words *am, at, an, as, ax* on the top of the page or blackboard and tell the child that you are going to make some new words for him. Directly under *am* write *Sam,* under *at sat, an man, as has,* and *ax tax.* Thus we've used the consonants we already know, added the *h,* and expanded our written vocabulary to ten words. You can write the sentences: *Sam has an ax. Sam sat.* But before you do that, make sure the child grasps the principle of word building, that he sees how each letter's power is used. This is the time to study the consonant sounds: *m, n, t, x, s, h.* Now use the *h* to create *ham* under *Sam, hat* under *sat.* When the child is thoroughly acquainted with these twelve words, can write them and read them and spell them, introduce the consonant *d* by changing *man* to *Dan* and *Sam* to *dam.* Introduce the consonant *w* by adding *wax* under *tax.* Drill the new words with flash cards.

Lesson 4: Take the *d* and add it to *an,* making *and.* This is our first final consonant blend. Explain how you've changed the word by adding the *d,* but do it in terms of speech first. Say *an, and,* and ask the child to tell you if he hears the difference and what it is. He should hear the difference before he sees it on paper or the blackboard. Once he understands this, write: *Sam and Dan, man and ham, tax and wax.* Now take the *h,* put it in front of *and* and ask the child if he can figure out what the word is: *hand.* Put an *s* in front of *and* and show him how it becomes *sand.* Introduce the consonant *l* by adding it to *and* to make *land.* Now you can play a game and see how many sentences the child can write with the nineteen words he now knows how to read:

am	Sam	ham	dam
an	man	Dan	
as	has		
at	sat	hat	
and	hand	sand	land
ax	tax	wax	

Suggested sentences: Explain that a sentence always begins with a capital letter and ends with a period or question mark.

Dan has an ax.
Has Dan an ax?
Sam has ham.
Has Sam ham?
Dan has sand.
Has Dan sand?
Sam sat.

Also arrange the words in columns so that the child can see more graphically the similarity of sound-symbol construction in word families:

am	an	as	at	ax	and
dam	man	has	sat	tax	hand
ham	Dan		hat	wax	sand
Sam					land

Then add these four new words to the appropriate columns: *Max, mat, Nat, tan.*

So far, the child has learned the short *a* sound and the consonants *d, h, l, m, n, s, t, x, w,* and the final consonant blend *nd.* The child should by now have grasped how the sound-symbol system works, how he can transcribe the sounds of his voice into symbols on paper, and how he can translate symbols on paper back into spoken words. At this point you might play a game of creating nonsense words just to see if he understands the principle of sounds being put into sound symbols and vice versa. All the while, the child should be writing the words he is learning. He must know that decoding-encoding, reading-writing is a two-way process. One cannot be learned effectively without the other. Continue to use drill techniques to reinforce automatic recognition of words.

Lesson 5: Teach the child the consonant *b.* This will give him these additional words: *bat, ban, band, dab, tab.* Introduce the consonant *c* as its *kuh* sound. This will expand the word list to include: *cat, cab, can.* Next, introduce the consonant *f.* This will expand the word list to include: *fab, fat, fan.* Introduce the consonant *p.* This will give us: *Pam, pan, pat.* Next, comes *r* to make: *rat, ran, ram.* Next, introduce *v* with *vat* and *van*. Then, introduce *g* with *gas, gap, gag, gab; j* with *jam, Jan, jab; y* with *yap, yam; z* with *zag*.

Lesson 6: (Review) The child has now covered the short *a* sound in combination with consonants: *b, c, d, f, g, h, j, l, m, n, p, r, s, t, v, w, x, y, z,* plus the final consonant blend *nd*. His reading and writing vocabulary can be expanded to include:

am	an	at	ax	as	and
Sam	ban	bat	Max	has	band
dam	can	cat	tax	gas	hand
Pam	Dan	fat	wax	*was*	land
ram	fan	hat			sand
jam	Jan	mat			
yam	man	Nat			
	pan	pat			
	ran	rat			
	tan	sat			
	van	vat			

cab	bad	bag	cap	Al
dab	cad	gag	gap	gal
fab	dad	lag	lap	Hal
jab	fad	nag	map	pal
lab	had	sag	nap	Sal
nab	lad	tag	rap	Val
tab	mad	wag	sap	
	pad	zag	tap	
	sad		yap	
	Tad			

These words can also be arranged alphabetically to illustrate more graphically the sound values of consonants at the beginnings of words:

add	bad	cab	dab	fab	gab	had
Al	bag	cad	dad	fad	gag	hag
am	ban	cap	dam	fan	gal	Hal
an	band	cat	Dan	fat	gap	ham
as	bat				gas	hand
at						has
ax						hat

238

jab	lab	mad	nab	pad	rag	sad
jam	lad	man	nag	pal	ram	sag
Jan	lag	map	nap	Pam	ran	Sal
	land	mat	Nat	pat	rap	Sam
	lap	Max			rat	sand
						sap
						sat

tab	Val	wag	yam	zag
Tad	van	*was*	yap	
tag	vat	wax		
tan				
tap				
tax				

An endless number of simple sentences can be made from the words above. Also, continue to use drill techniques to create automatic recognition of the word the child has learned.

Lesson 6a: Irregular word *was*. Explain to the child that some words are not pronounced exactly as they are spelled. The word *was* is one of them. Illustrate this with such sentences as: Jan *was* sad. Pam *was* mad. This inconsistency should not trouble the child at all and no special fuss should be made over it. It should be noted that the only inconsistency is in the sound of the vowel *a*, not the two consonants.

Lesson 6b: Review the two *s* sounds. Explain that sometimes the *s* has a harder sound and sometimes a softer sound, as in these words: *gas, has, sad, as, sand, was*. He can only tell which sound to say by hearing in his mind the word as it is spoken. Also, special drills with these words on cards will help develop instant recognition of the words.

Lesson 6c: Nonsense syllables. To test how well your child is picking up sound distinctions and associating them with the proper letters, you might give him some nonsense syllables to read and then dictate back to him. This would be a pure exercise in sound-symbol understanding and mastery. It will show you where the child is weak in sound discrimination and needs practice. Unless your child has a hearing problem he should be able to recognize the different sounds with little or no trouble as long as you pronounce them clearly. You can make a game of "Phony words" using such nonsense syllables as: *bam, bap, bax, cag, cam, dag, dat, fam, fal, fax, gan, gat, jav, jap, lab, lav, mag, nan, sab, tam, vam, zam*. Notice that most of these nonsense syllables are parts of multisyllabic words which the child will be learning as he progresses. So his ability to hear them, write them, and read them will help him in his spelling later on. However, if your child is picking up the sound-symbol system rapidly and without any problems, you need not spend time on nonsense syllables. If your child finds it difficult to discriminate between subtly different sounds, take the time to train him to hear the differences and to speak the differences. You can show him how your lips and tongue are set in a different position to make a different sound. In any case, narrow down his sound discrimination difficulties and work on them in a playful, casual way. Never, under any circumstances, show impatience, and never force anything. Let him advance at his own pace.

Lesson 7: Introduce the *ck* consonant combination ending. Make the words: *back, hack, Jack, lack, Mack, pack, rack, sack, tack.*

Lesson 8: Introduce the short *e*. Start with the word *Ed*. Accustom the child to recognize the short *e* sound as distinguished from the short *a* by comparing *Ed* with *ad*. Then expand *Ed* into: *bed, fed, led, Ned, red, Ted, wed.* Introduce the word *egg*, pointing out that the double g sounds the same as a single g. From there expand into *beg, keg, leg, Meg, Peg.* The child will not be at all troubled by the inconsistency between *egg* and *leg*. He doesn't expect perfect consistency. In fact, the reason why he will be able to understand and master the sound-symbol system is because it does have a very high degree of consistency. This basic consistency between written symbols and spoken sounds is the great intellectual lesson he is learning. So the exceptions that make the rule should neither be ignored nor overly stressed, but merely pointed out. *By pointing out the occasional exceptions and irregularities, the basic consistency of everything else is reinforced.*

Next take the word *and* and change it to *end*. Emphasize the difference in sound between *and* and *end*. Ask the child to say the two words and write them down from dictation. Now expand *end* into *bend, lend, mend, send, tend.* Show how *bat* can be changed to *bet; mat* to *met; pat* to *pet; sat* to *set; vat* to *vet; ban* to *Ben; Dan* to *den; man* to *men; tan* to *ten*. Go through the following list of words with the child:

	Ed	egg		
web	bed	beg	deck	den
	fed	keg	heck	Jen
	led	leg	neck	Ken
	Ned	Meg	peck	Len
	wed	Peg		men
				pen
				ten
				yen

bend	bet	bell	gem	pep
lend	get	cell	hem	
mend	let	dell		yes
send	met	fell		
tend	net	hell		Rex
	pet	sell		Tex
	set	tell		vex
	vet	well		
	wet	yell		
	yet			

In reviewing the words *bell, cell, dell,* etc., point out that the double *l* has the same sound as the single *l*.

Lesson 8a: Consonant *c* as *s* sound. Explain that *c* has both a *k* and an *s* sound. Illustrate with the words *cat* and *cell*. Consonant *g* as in *gem*.

Lesson 8b: Explain that so far we have learned three ways of writing the *k* sound: *K*en, *c*at, de*ck*, *k*eg, *c*an, sa*ck*.

Lesson 9: The name game. Since many simple names illustrate the short *a* and *e* sounds in a variety of consonant combinations, a game can be devised in which the child makes a list of those whom he would invite to his birthday party. He can choose from: *Pam, Sam, Dan, Jan, Nat, Van, Pat, Max, Tad, Hal, Sal, Val, Al, Ned, Ed, Meg, Peg, Jen, Ken, Len, Jack, Mack.* Let him practice writing such simple combinations as:

Jack and Dan.
Meg and Peg.
Van and Sam.
Max and Ed.
Pam and Mack.
Ned and Nat.

Names are also good for dictation purposes and spelling tests. Also, place names on drill cards for short drill practice.

Lesson 10: Many sentences can be made from the words already learned. These sentences are for the purpose of helping the child master the sound-symbol system. No story interpretation is needed or even desirable at this point. The child should be totally absorbed in the challenging job of mastering the sound-symbol system. The sentences are quite obvious in meaning, and you can think up many more:

Jack has let Mack get wet.
Pam fed Ted.
Dan and Ben met Val and Al.
Jan has wax.
Peg was fat.

Make up other sentences if you feel that additional work is necessary before moving on to the short *i*.

Lesson 11: The short *i*. Begin with the words: *if, in, is, it, ill*. Compare *a* as in *at*, *e* as in *Ed*, and *i* as in *it*. Let the child hear the difference. Let him say all three vowel sounds and feel the difference in the way he shapes his mouth when saying them. Then expand the five words as follows:

if	in	is	it	ill
	bin	his	bit	Bill
	fin		fit	dill
	pin		hit	fill
	sin		kit	gill
	tin		lit	hill
	win		mitt	Jill
			pit	kill
			quit	mill
			sit	pill
			wit	quill
				rill
				sill
				till
				will

Further expand your short *i* words to include the following:

fib	bid	big	dick	dim	dip	Dix	hiss
rib	did	dig	hick	him	hip	fix	kiss
	hid	fig	kick	Jim	Kip	mix	miss
	kid	gig	lick	Kim	lip	nix	sis
	lid	jig	Mick	rim	nip	pix	
	mid	Mig	Nick	Tim	pip	six	
	rid	pig	pick	vim	quip		
	Sid	rig	quick		rip		
		wig	Rick		sip		
		zig	sick		tip		
			tick		zip		
			wick				

Lesson 11a: Introduce the consonant *q* and explain how it is always followed by *u* as in: *quit, quill, quip, quick*. Explain *ss* as in *kiss*, etc.

Lesson 11b: Suggested sentences for practice:

Quit it.
Bill is ill.
Kim is ill and Nick fed Kim an egg.
Fix it.
Mix it.
Will Bill win? Will Jill kiss Bill?

Lesson 11c: Introduce the name *Phil*. Explain that *ph* together is pronounced as *f*. Compare *Phil* with *fill*. Acquaint the child with the idea that often two different words that sound alike are spelled differently. Expand *Phil* into *Philip*.

Lesson 12: The short *o*. Begin with the words *on* and *ox*. Let the child hear the distinction between short *a*, short *e*, short *i*, and short *o*. Expand *ox* into *box* and *fox*. Then expand *on* into *Don* and *Ron*. Further expand your short *o* words to include the following:

Bob	cod	of	cog	on
cob	God		dog	Don
gob	mod		fog	Ron
mob	nod		hog	son
rob	rod		log	ton
sob	sod			won
	Tod			

cop	cot	mom	ox	cock
hop	dot	Tom	box	dock
mop	got		fox	hock
top	hot		pox	lock
	jot		sox	mock
	lot			pock
	not			rock
	pot			sock
	rot			tock
	tot			

Lesson 12a: Irregular pronunciations: point out that *dog* is pronounced as the spoken word. Also take up the word *of*. Point out that it too is pronounced as it is spoken.

Lesson 12b: Irregular pronunciation of the words *son, ton, won*. Explain these exceptions as the previous ones have been explained. Suggested practice sentences:

Ron is his son.
Don won.

If you feel the child needs additional practice before proceeding any further, make up sentences using the new words with the short *o*. Also, use drill card techniques for developing quick word recognition.

Lesson 13: Introduce the word *a*, as in *a box, a dog, a mop, a cop, a kit, a hill,* etc.

Lesson 14: Introduce the word *the*, as in *the box, the dog, the mop, the cop,* etc. Explain the *th* sound. Take the words *at, in,* and *is,* and make them into *that, thin,* and *this*. Note that there is a soft *th* sound as in *the* and a hard *th* sound as in *thin*. Also add *th* to *em* and make *them*. See if your child can read the following:

That thin cat has that fat rat.
This cat has that rat.
This cat is red.
Dan has fed them.
Bill sat on a hill and fed a cat.
The cat sat on the box.
Jim sat on the red box and fed the tan fox.

Lesson 14a: Introduce the apostrophe *s*: Bill's dog. Dan's cat. Pam's hat. Suggested practice sentences:

Rick has Tim's dog.
Peg's cat is sick.
That is Don's pig.

Lesson 15: The short *u* sound. Start with the words *us* and *up*. Compare the initial sounds of *as*, *is*, and *us*. Expand *us* into *bus*, *fuss*, *pus*. Expand *up* into *pup* and *cup*. Have your child read the following short *u* words:

cub	bud	bug	cull	gum	bun
dub	dud	dug	dull	hum	fun
hub	mud	hug	*full*	mum	gun
pub		jug	gull	sum	nun
rub		mug	hull	yum	pun
sub		rug	*pull*		run
tub		tug			sun

up	us	but	lux	duz
cup	bus	cut		
pup	fuss	gut		
	Gus	nut		
	pus	*put*		
		rut		

Lesson 15a: Irregular pronunciation of the words *full*, *pull*, *put*. Numerous sentences for practice reading can be made up from the words the child already knows. Include irregular words. Here are some suggestions:

Jack put the pup in the box.
The pup sat on the rug.
The cup is on top of the box.
The jug is full.
The cat is in the tub.
Can Jack pull the log?
Tom's dad is a cop and has a gun.

Lesson 16: General Review. We have covered the five short vowel sounds, *a, e, i, o, u,* all of the consonant sounds, and *ph, th, qu,* and *nd.* Now would be a good time to see how well your child has mastered this much of the sound-symbol system and to give him general practice with what he already knows. You can do this by having him read mixed word lists, giving him spelling tests, and dictating sentences to him. It cannot be emphasized too strongly that encoding, or spelling, should be taught at the same time with decoding, or reading. One reinforces the other. It also shows the child that he can actively make words instead of merely passively reading them. He can use the sound-symbol system to communicate his thoughts to others as well as have the thoughts of others communicated to him. We build in him a double sense of mastery and independence in being able to handle the sound-symbol system in both active and passive capacities: as a sender of information as well as a receiver. This is the kind of confidence we want the child to acquire.

Also, in having mastered this much of the sound-symbol system, he will eagerly want to master the rest. He has seen how new knowledge builds consistently and logically on old knowledge and how it all makes sense, how it all fits logically together. Words are no longer a mystery to him. He can't as yet read them all, but he knows that he can read many of them, and that eventually he will be able to read all of them with the same ease with which he now reads those he already knows.

Lesson 17: Adding *s* to words, which makes them plural or changes tense. You needn't go into the details of verb tenses. The child changes verb tenses in his speech all the time without being technically aware of what he is doing. We want him merely to recognize the sound change on paper as he does when he hears it:

cab	cabs	cup	cups
bed	beds	kiss	kisses
wag	wags	cat	cats
rock	rocks	box	boxes
bell	bells	hand	hands
yam	yams	egg	eggs
run	runs		

Suggested practice sentences:

Bill had six boxes of eggs.
Dick has six cats.
Rick picks six kids.

Lesson 17a: Contractions. Take the words *is not, can not,* and *has not* and explain how they can be contracted into *isn't, can't,* and *hasn't.* Also, contract *it is* and *let us.*

is not	isn't	it is	it's
can not	can't	let us	let's
has not	hasn't		

Suggested practice sentences:

Is Bill sad?	Has Jill a cat?
Bill isn't sad.	Jill hasn't a cat.
Can Ken run?	Is this Bob's jug?
Ken can't run.	This isn't Bob's jug.
Is this Peg's dog?	Let us run. Let's run.
This isn't Peg's dog.	It is big. It's big.

Lesson 17b: Two-syllable words. There are a good many simple two-syllable words made up of two regular short-vowel pronunciation units. See how many your child can read on his own. Help him if he needs it. The point is to show how two syllables are put together to make one word. Discuss the meaning of the words he does not know. After he can read them, use them in a few simple sentences with other words he knows. The exercise is still primarily to advance his mastery of the sound-symbol system in regular multisyllabic words.

napkin	lentil	nitwit	suntan
relic	pencil	vivid	husband
tidbit	comet	civil	magic
habit	puppet	Nixon	sudden
rapid	upset	dental	wagon
gallon	mimic	until	unfit
candid	public	vomit	hatbox
basket	picnic	tonic	exit
Ex-lax	kidnap	mascot	goblin
helmet	linen	hotrod	sunset

velvet	visit	boxtop	Philip
tomcat	rabbit	camel	robin

The next series of lessons is devoted to final consonant blends with regular short vowels in one-syllable words. This will teach the child to recognize the written symbols for two consonant sounds blended together at the ends of words.

Lesson 18: Review of the double consonant endings *bb, gg, ll, ff, ss, tt.* The child should be taught that although the letters are doubled, the sound is the same as though there were only one final consonant:

bell	Matt	doll	fill
ebb	well	muff	puff
hill	Bill	kill	less
egg	Webb	fell	dull
cuff	mill	kiss	tiff
hull	Jeff	will	hiss
lass	yell	miff	sell
Jill	mess	pass	miss

Lesson 18a: The sound of *a* followed by double *l*. Explain the difference in sound between *Al* and *all*. Expand *all* into *ball, call, fall, gall, hall, mall, pall, tall, wall.*

Lesson 19: Final consonant blend *ng.*

ang	ing	ong	ung
bang	bing	bong	hung
dang	ding	dong	lung
gang	king	gong	rung
hang	ping	pong	sung
pang	ring	*song*	
rang	sing		
sang	wing		
	zing		

Mixed *ng* list:

bang	dong	lung	rung	wing
bing	hung	ping	rang	sang
dang	gang	pong	gong	zing
dong	king	pang	ring	bong
ding	hang	ring	sung	bang

bing-bang	ping-pong
ding-dang	bing-bong
Hong-Kong	ding-dong

Lesson 19a: Explain how adding *ing* to many words gives us new words. Note how the consonant following a short vowel is doubled:

fan	fanning	fix	fixing
nap	napping	rob	robbing
send	sending	run	running
get	getting	rub	rubbing
let	letting	dig	digging
yell	yelling	sing	singing
pack	packing	ring	ringing
kid	kidding	hang	hanging
pick	picking	pass	passing

Suggested practice sentences:

Jan is singing a song.
Bill is ringing a bell.
Ken is getting all wet.
Rick is calling his dog.

Lesson 20: Final consonant blends *nd, nt*.

and	rant	Kent	land
tent	fond	fund	rent
bend	dent	tint	tend
bent	hand	end	punt
wind	gent	lent	sand
hint	send	bond	sent
band	bunt	hunt	mend
went		rend	

Lesson 21: Final consonant blends *ct, ft, pt*.

act	pact	lift
kept	apt	duct
fact	left	raft
aft	tact	gift

Lesson 22: Final consonant blend *nk*.

bank	mink	hunk	wink
link	*monk*	ink	tank
honk	dunk	rank	punk
bunk	lank	sink	rink
Hank	pink	junk	sank

Lesson 22a: Irregular pronunciation: *Monk* rimes with *junk*.

Lesson 23: Final consonant blends *sh, sk, sp, st*.

ash	dash	ask	asp	last	must	vest
mesh	wish	desk	lisp	best	fast	just
cash	lush	risk	gasp	fist	lest	zest
dish	gash	task		rest	list	vast
sash	mush	mask		bust	west	pest
gosh	lash	dusk		cast	rust	
fish	rush	wisk		jest	mast	
rash	mash	tusk		gist	nest	
hush	gush			test	mist	

Lesson 24: Final consonant blends *th, ch, xt, nch*.

bath	rich	next	ranch
Beth	such		bench
with	much		inch
math			pinch
path			lunch

Lesson 25: Final consonant blends *lb, ld, lf, lk, lm, lp, lt*.

bulb	held	bulk	*calf*	elm	help	belt	quilt
	meld	sulk	*half*	helm	yelp	felt	tilt
	gild	milk	elf	film	gulp	melt	cult
	bald	silk	self		pulp	pelt	
		talk	golf			hilt	
		walk	gulf			jilt	

Lesson 25a: Irregular pronunciation: *talk, walk, bald.* Note also that in the words *calf, half, walk* and *talk* the *l* is silent.

Lesson 26: Final consonant blend *mp*.

camp	romp	hump	lump
hemp	limp	pomp	limp
bump	dump	jump	hemp
damp	lamp	ramp	pump

Lesson 27: Final consonant blend *tch*.

batch	itch
etch	botch
catch	pitch
fetch	hutch
hatch	witch
hitch	patch
latch	dutch
dutch	match

Lesson 28: Final consonant blend *dge*. Explain that the *e* is silent.

badge	Madge
edge	hedge
ridge	podge
hodge	fudge
budge	ledge
lodge	wedge

Lesson 29: Final consonant blends *nce, nse*. Explain that the *e* is silent.

fence	mince	*once*
since	dance	
tense	hence	
dense	rinse	
sense	dunce	

Lesson 29a: Irregular pronunciation: *once* rimes with *dunce*.

Lesson 30: General review of final consonant blends. These words can also be drilled on cards.

batch	kept	desk	hunt	next	belt
left	duct	last	went	path	self
fund	link	pest	dance	itch	help
ring	cash	lisp	much	film	milk
jump	fudge	half	with	sing	fond

Lesson 30a: Two-syllable words with regular short vowels and known consonant blends:

disgust	vanish	polish	Kenneth	within	fishnet
witness	rubbish	dentist	Nashville	contact	bathtub
suspect	content	after	conduct	often	offense
enrich	dancing	withheld	consent	selfish	punish
sandwich	enlist	absent	compact	engulf	dustpan

The next series of lessons is devoted to teaching the child initial consonant blends in words with known short vowel sounds and final consonant blends. Work on those words first which are in your child's speaking vocabulary. Then let him try the others. At this point, we are still more concerned with his mastering the sound-symbol system than expanding his vocabulary. However, if he shows an interest in the meaning of a new word, explain the meaning to him.

Lesson 31: Initial consonant blend *bl*.

blab	bled	blink	block	blunt
black	blend	bliss	blond	blush
bland	bless		blop	
blank			blot	
blast				

Lesson 32: Initial consonant blend *br*.

bran	bred	brick	broth	brunt
brand		brig		brush
brash		bridge		
brass		brim		
brat		bring		
		brink		

Lesson 33: Initial consonant blend *ch*.

chap	check	chin	chop	chum
chat	chest	chip		chug
chance		chick		chuck
		chill		chunk
		chink		

Lesson 34: Initial consonant blend *cr*.

crab	crest	crib	crop	crud
cram		crisp		crum
crack				crux
crank				crush
crass				crutch

Lesson 35: Initial consonant blend *dr, dw*.

drab	dress	drip	drop	drug	dwell
drag	dredge	drift		drum	
draft		drill		drudge	
		drink			

Lesson 36: Initial consonant blend *fl*.

flab	fled	flit	flog	flub
flag	flesh	flip	flop	flunk
flat		flint	flock	flush
flack				
flash				

Lesson 37: Initial consonant blend *fr*.

Fran	Fred	frill	frog
France	fret	fridge	frost
Frank	fresh		froth
	French		

Lesson 38: Initial consonant blend *gl*.

glad	glen	glib	glob	glum
glass			glop	glut
gland			gloss	

Lesson 39: Initial consonant blends *gr* and *gw*.

grab	Greg	grid	grub	Gwen
grad		grim	grudge	
gram		grin		
grand				
grant				
grass				

Lesson 40: Initial consonant blend *pl*.

plan	plop	plug
plant	plot	plum
plank		plus
		pluck

Lesson 41: Initial consonant blend *pr*.

prance	prep	prig	prod
		prim	prom
		prick	prompt
		prince	
		print	

Lesson 42: Review of initial consonant *qu*.

quack	quest	quit
		quill
		quick

Lesson 43: Initial consonant blends *sh, shr*.

sham	shed	ship	shot	shun
shack	shell		shock	shut
shank				

shrank	shred	shrimp		shrug
		shrink		shrunk

Lesson 44: Initial consonant blend *sl*.

slab	sled	slid	slob	slum
slam		slim	slot	slush
slat		slit	slosh	
slant		slick		
slash		slink		

Lesson 45: Initial consonant blends *sm, sn*.

smack	smell	smog	smut	snip	snob
smash				snick	

Lesson 46: Initial consonant blend *sp, spr*.

spam	sped	spin	spot	spud
span	spell	spit		spun
spat	speck	spill		sprung
spank	spend	spick		
sprang	spent	spring		

Lesson 47: Initial consonant blends *st, str*.

stag	stem	stiff	stop	stub
stab	step	stick	stock	stud
Stan	strep	stink	stomp	stuck
stack		sting		stump
stank		stint		stunk
strap		strip		strut
strand		string		

Lesson 48: Initial consonant blend *sw*.

swam	swell	swim
swan		swish
		swift

Irregular pronunciation: *swan*.

Lesson 49: Initial consonant blends *sc, scr, sk*.

scab	skid	scum	scrub	scrod
scan	skim	scuff	scrunch	
scant	skin	skunk		
scat	skip			
	scalp	skit		
		skill		

Lesson 50: Initial consonant blend *th*. Note that there is a soft *th* sound as in *than* and a hard *th* sound as in *thick*.

than	then	thin	thus
that		think	thrush
thank		thick	thrust
		thrill	

Lesson 51: Initial consonant blend *tr, tw*.

tram	treck	trip	trod	truck	twin
trap	trend	trick	trot	trunk	twit
trance				trust	twig
				trudge	twill
					twist
					twitch

Lesson 52: Initial consonant blend *wh*.

whip	when
whim	
which	

Lesson 53: General review of short vowel words with initial and final consonant blends. These words can be used in making up new sentences, in spelling tests, in dictation.

truck	quick	blond	task	dwell	witch
skip	grudge	fudge	sash	slack	jump
swift	glass	dump	lisp	spring	bless
then	frill	edge	bank	trick	bring
spun	flag	golf	king	France	chance
slosh	cliff	elm	fond	hitch	flash
shrimp	crux	dutch	hint	next	plus
shack	draft	with	act	rich	grin
plum	chest	pest	lift	lunch	class
prom	bridge	dish	kept	patch	stink

Lesson 54: Show the child how by adding *s, ing,* or *ed* to many words, you can change the tenses:

hint	hints	hinting	hinted
lift	lifts	lifting	lifted
act	acts	acting	acted
miss	misses	missing	missed
pass	passes	passing	passed
jump	jumps	jumping	jumped
dump	dumps	dumping	dumped
vanish	vanishes	vanishing	vanished
visit	visits	visiting	visited
zigzag	zigzags	zigzagging	zigzaged

The next series of lessons is devoted to the remaining vowel sounds to be learned as written symbols. The long vowel sounds are not quite as regular in their written forms as the short ones, and they can be spelled in more than one way. However, despite the higher number of irregularly pronounced words to be found among the spelling families of the long vowel sounds, there is still a very high degree of consistency, and your child should have no problem mastering both the regular and irregular words. As we pointed out earlier, the occasional exceptions and irregularities merely confirm the basic consistency of everything else. Again, take time, have patience, and let your child learn at his own rate. There is no hurry.

Lesson 55: Introduce the long *a* sound. Explain to the child that the long *a* sounds the same as the name of the letter. Let the child hear the difference between *at* and *ate*. Both words have two sounds each—a vowel and a consonant. But one has the short *a* and the other the long *a*. In written English we find the long *a* represented by several spelling forms. We shall take up the most common one first: the *a* followed by a consonant followed by a silent *e*.

Take the word *at*, add an *e* to it, and tell the child that the word is now *ate*. Let him hear the long *a* sound and ask if he knows of any other words which begin with a long *a*. If he can't think of any, suggest: *Abe, ace, age, ale, ape*. Write them down and tell him that the silent *e* is there to tell us that the *a* is a long *a*. It's a signal to us to say *ay* instead of *aa*.

Now expand the six words as follows.

257

		Abe	ace	age	ale	ape	ate
		babe	face	cage	bale	cape	date

lace	page	dale	gape	fate
pace	sage	gale	tape	gate
race	wage	hale	drape	hate
grace	stage	male	grape	Kate
place		pale	scrape	late
space		sale		mate
trace		stale		rate
brace				crate
				grate
				plate
				state

When the above words are learned, add the following:

fade	safe	bake	came	cane
jade		cake	dame	Dane
made		fake	fame	Jane
wade		Jake	game	lane
blade		lake	lame	mane
grade		make	Mame	pane
trade		quake	name	sane
		rake	same	crane
		sake	tame	plane
		take	blame	
		wake	flame	
		brake		
		stake		
		shake		
		flake		

bare	base	cave	daze
care	case	Dave	craze
dare		gave	graze
fare		have	maze
hare		pave	
mare		rave	
rare		save	
ware		wave	
share		brave	
stare		crave	
are		grave	
		slave	

Lesson 55a: Irregular pronunciations: *are, have.*

Lesson 56: The next most common letter symbols for the long *a* sound is the *ai* combination. Introduce the words *aid* and *aim* and *air*. Explain how *ai* represents the long *a* sound. Expand *aid, aim,* and *air* as follows:

aid	aim	air
laid	maim	fair
maid	claim	hair
paid		pair
raid		chair
said		Clair

When these are mastered, add the following:

bail	Cain	bait
fail	gain	wait
Gail	lain	trait
hail	main	
jail	pain	
mail	rain	
nail	vain	
pail	brain	
rail	chain	
sail	drain	
tail	grain	
wail	plain	
frail	slain	
trail	Spain	
	stain	
	strain	
	train	
	twain	

Lesson 56a: Irregular pronunciation: *said.* Rimes with *red.*

Lesson 57: The next most common spelling form for the long *a* is *ay* as found in the following words:

bay	may	clay
day	nay	gray
Fay	pay	play
gay	quay	pray
hay	ray	slay
jay	say	stay
Kay	way	tray
lay		stray
		sway

Lesson 57a: Irregular words. A few words spelled with *ey* are pronounced as *ay*, as in *they* and *grey*. *Gray* and *grey* are two different spellings for the same word.

Lesson 58: Another, less common, way of writing the long *a* is with *ei*, as in the words *vein, veil, heir,* and *eight.* Explain that sometimes two different words like *vein* and *vain*, which sound alike but mean two entirely different things, are spelled differently so that the reader can tell which meaning is intended by the writer. The same is true of *veil* and *vale, heir* and *air, eight* and *ate.* Point out that the *h* in *heir* is silent. As for the word *eight*, which sounds exactly like *ate*, point out that the *gh* is silent and is found in other words which are taken up in later lessons.

It is not necessary for your child to remember everything you tell him about irregular words. Most of them are our most common words and he will get to know their spelling and pronunciation peculiarities through repeated use of them in reading and writing.

Lesson 59: General review of long *a* words:

face	grace	tail	heir	main
vain	scrape	dare	fake	flame
way	paid	brave	stain	grade
plate	chair	brain	care	cake
cage	say	stake	gate	bay

Lesson 59a: Two- and three-syllable words composed of known short and long vowel units:

payday	explain	waitress	raining	tailgate
railway	complain	cake-mix	painful	graceful
airplane	mailman	enslave	embrace	engage
careful	inkstain	grateful	away	maintain
	engagement		complaining	

Lesson 59b: Suggested sentences for practicing the long *a* in its various spelling forms:

The train is late but on the way.
Dave is complaining that it's raining.
Clair and Ray went away on the same airplane.
The mailman came late.
Jane said, "If it rains let's take the train."

Explain the use of quotation marks when quoting the speech of a person. Make up more sentences if additional practice is needed.

Lesson 60: Introduce the *a* sound as in *all, Paul, jaw.* Teach the following words:

all	halt	balk	haul	gaunt
ball	malt	calk	maul	haunt
call	salt	*talk*	Paul	jaunt
fall		*walk*	Saul	taunt
gall		*chalk*	fault	launch
hall			vault	staunch
mall				
pall		Maud		
tall		fraud		
wall				
stall				

cause	awe	hawk	bawl	dawn
pause	jaw		brawl	fawn
	law		crawl	lawn
	paw		drawl	pawn
	raw			yawn
	saw			brawn
	claw			drawn
	draw			
	flaw			
	thaw			
	straw			

Irregular pronunciation: Note that in *talk, walk, chalk* the *l* is silent.
Irregular spelling: Take up the following group of irregularly spelled words all of which rime with *taut.* Note the silent *gh* and the mixed

pattern of *au, ou* spellings.

ought	fraught
bought	nought
caught	sought
fought	taught
brought	thought

In learning these words, it is obvious that the child will have to devote some practice to reading them and writing them. The important thing is not to make any great fuss over them, except to point out that they are unusual spellings and represent something of a challenge in mastering them. Again, these irregularities merely confirm the consistency of everything else.

Lesson 60a: Suggested practice sentences:

Tall Paul caught the ball.
Small Paul hit his jaw.
Saul walked and talked with Paul.
Paul taught Saul a lesson.

Lesson 61: Introduce the *a* sound as in *arm, art, ah, ma, pa.* Words with this *a* sound include the following:

bar	bard	scarf	ark	arm
car	card	*wharf*	bark	farm
far	hard	*dwarf*	hark	harm
jar	lard		lark	*warm*
par	yard		mark	
tar	*ward*		park	
war			Clark	
			spark	

barn	carp	art	farce	ah
darn	harp	cart		ma
yarn	tarp	dart	carve	pa
warn	*warp*	*heart*	starve	
		mart		
		part		
		tart	Marx	

wart
quart
quartz

Irregular spelling: *heart*.

Irregular pronunciation: Notice the similar pronunciation of the *a* in *war*, *ward*, *wharf*, *dwarf*, *warm*, *warn*, *warp*, *quart*, *quartz*.

Lesson 62: Introduce the long *e* sound by comparing such words as *bet* and *beet*, *fed* and *feed*. Show the child the *ee* as the most common written form of the long *e* sound. Show how *ee* can be expanded into *bee*, *fee*, *see*, etc. Then introduce the word *eel*. Expand *eel* as shown:

ee	eel
bee	feel
fee	heel
gee	peel
Lee	reel
see	steel
free	
tree	

Then create additional words with the long *e* sound spelled as *ee*:

heed	beef	leek	deem	*been*
deed	reef	meek	seem	seen
feed		reek	teem	teen
need		seek		queen
reed		week		green
seed				screen
weed				
breed				
creed				
greed				

beep	beer	beet	breeze	sleeve
deep	deer	feet	freeze	
keep	jeer	meet		
Jeep	peer	greet		
peep	cheer	sweet		
seep	queer	tweet		

weep	steer
creep	
sleep	
steep	
sweep	

Irregular pronunciation: The word *been* is pronounced as if it were spelled *bin*.

Lesson 62a: There is a group of short common words in which the long *e* is spelled with a single *e*, as follows:

be
he
me
we
she

Lesson 63: Another way in which the long *e* sound is written is *ea*. Introduce the words *eat, ear, each*. Expand them as follows:

eat	ear	each
beat	*bear*	beach
feat	dear	peach
heat	fear	reach
meat	gear	teach
neat	hear	preach
peat	near	
seat	*pear*	
cheat	rear	
treat	sear	
sweat	tear	
wheat	*tear*	
	wear	
	year	
	swear	

Irregular pronunciations: The word *sweat* rimes with *wet*. The following words rime with *care: bear, pear, tear, wear,* and *swear*. Point out that regular *tear* (as in *teardrop*) is an entirely different word from irregular *tear*, which means to rip apart.

Additional words with the long *e* sound written as *ea:*

pea	bead	*deaf*	beak	deal	beam
sea	*dead*	leaf	leak	heal	ream
tea	*head*		peak	meal	seam
	lead		teak	peal	team
	lead		bleak	real	cream
	read			seal	dream
	read			veal	stream
	bread			weal	
				zeal	

bean	heap	east	ease	eave
dean	leap	beast	cease	leave
Jean	reap	feast	lease	heave
lean		yeast	tease	weave
mean			crease	
clean			please	

Irregular pronunciations: The following words rime with *red: dead, head, lead, read, bread.* Explain that there are also regular pronunciations to *lead* and *read* which have different meanings from the words which rime with *red.* The word *deaf* rimes with *Jeff.*

Lesson 64: Sometimes the long *e* sound is spelled *ie,* as in the following words:

niece	thief	pier	field	siege	sieve
piece	chief	tier	yield		
	grief	pierce	shield		
		fierce			

Lesson 65: The long *e* is also commonly written as *y.* This usually occurs at the end of a two-syllable word or name, as follows:

Abby	daddy	taffy	saggy	Billy
baby	caddy	daffy	baggy	silly
Tabby	paddy	jiffy	Maggy	Sally
Libby	Teddy	puffy	Twiggy	hilly
lobby	giddy	stuffy	foggy	Molly
	muddy		Peggy	Polly
			muggy	Dolly
				bully
				chilly

265

mammy	Danny	happy	Harry	messy
mommy	Fanny	pappy	carry	fussy
mummy	Benny	poppy	Perry	sissy
tummy	Jenny		Terry	
Tommy	Lenny		merry	
Timmy	Kenny		hurry	
	penny		sorry	
	bunny			
	funny			
	sunny			

easy	batty	hazy
busy	fatty	lazy
	ratty	crazy
	catty	dizzy
	city	fuzzy
	pity	
	pretty	
	nutty	

Irregular pronunciations: *Pretty* rimes with *city. Busy* rimes with *dizzy*.

Lesson 66: There are also a few words in which the long *e* is followed by a consonant and a silent *e*, as in *gene, here, mere, these*. However, *there* and *where* rime with *care; were* rimes with *fur;* and *eye* is pronounced the same as the name of the letter *i*.

gene	here	eve
	mere	Steve

Lesson 67: Review of words with the long *e* sound represented symbollically by *e, ee, ea, ie, y,* or with a consonant and silent *e*.

tea	please	steal	meet	treat	eve
week	queen	feet	tease	cheer	weep
gear	reach	eel	here	fear	tree
niece	sweet	ease	near	chief	breeze

beet	sea	clear	greet	mean	Steve
see	field	city	Pete	need	Jean
easy	she	beach	feel	bean	believe
feast	steer	read	she	seat	Jeep
jeer	greasy	dear	thief	these	leave
meat	hear	he	feat	we	leaf

Lesson 68: Suggested practice sentences:

Pete and Steve are sleeping on the beach.
Peggy ate a pretty peach.
The busy airfield is near the city.
A green leaf fell from the tree.
Jean ate a piece of greasy meat.
He drank a cup of sweet tea.

Lesson 69: To further explain why there is more than one way to write a sound, show how different words which sound alike are spelled differently to help us tell them apart. Here are some examples:

week	weak	seem	seam
meet	meat	feet	feat
beet	beat	see	sea
peek	peak	heel	heal
reed	read	reel	real

Lesson 70: Introduce the long *i* sound. Tell the child that the long *i* sounds the same as the name of the letter *i*. First teach the word *I*. *I am.*

I am
I take
I make
I have
I had
I met
I ran

Next, show how the most common way to write the long *i* is with a consonant followed by a silent *e*. Illustrate with the word *ice* and the name *Ike*. Expand *ice* and *Ike* as follows:

ice	Ike
dice	bike
lice	dike
mice	hike
nice	like
rice	Mike
vice	pike
price	spike
slice	strike
twice	

Teach these additional words in these spelling families:

bribe	bide	life	bile	dime	dine
tribe	hide	wife	file	lime	fine
	ride	rife	mile	mime	line
	side	*knife*	Nile	rime	mine
	tide	strife	pile	time	pine
	wide		tile	chime	vine
	chide		vile	crime	wine
	bride		smile	grime	brine
	pride		while	prime	shine
	slide		aisle	slime	spine
					swine
					twine
					thine

pipe	dire	rise	bite	dive	size
ripe	fire	wise	kite	five	prize
wipe	hire		site	*give*	
gripe	mire		trite	hive	
swipe	sire		quite	jive	
stripe	tire			live	
	wire			*live*	
	spire			chive	
				drive	
				strive	
				thrive	

Irregular words: The *kn* in knife is pronounced *n*. The *s* in *isle* is

268

silent. The *s* in *aisle* is silent, the *ai* is pronounced as long *i*. Both *isle* and *aisle* are pronounced the same as *ile*. Explain the difference in meaning of the two words. *Give* and *live* are pronounced as if they were spelled *giv* and *liv*, with short *i* sounds. Note the difference in meaning between *live* (short *i*) and *live* (long *i*).

Lesson 71: The long *i* sound is also sometimes written as *ie*, *y*, and *uy*, as in the following simple words:

die	by	buy
lie	my	guy
pie	ply	
tie	sly	
vie	cry	
	dry	
	fry	
	pry	
	try	

In the past tense, the *y* is changed to *ied:*

die	died		cry	cried
lie	lied		dry	dried
tie	tied		try	tried

Lesson 72: In some words the long *i* sound is also found in combination with a silent *g* or *gh* as in:

sign	high	fight
	sigh	light
	thigh	might
		night
		right
		sight
		tight
		bright
		fright

Irregular spelling: The word *height* rimes with *light*, not *eight*.

Lesson 73: Review of short *i* pronunciation units in two-syllable words:

reply	defy	delight	admire
decide	inside	beside	assign
refine	define	sublime	alive
rely	imply	astride	alike
abide	devine	design	advice
desire	retire	advise	reptile

Lesson 74: Introduce the long *o* sound. Say the words *oak, old, oat* to make sure the child identifies the sound. Then tell him that the long *o* sound can be written in a number of ways and that it is easy to learn them all.

The most common way of spelling the long *o* is with a consonant and a silent *e*, similar to the way the long *a* and the long *i* are spelled. Show him how *rob* is changed to *robe* by adding the silent *e*, *cod* to *code*, *rod* to *rode*. Then show him the words *Dave* and *dive* and show how inserting an *o* in place of the *a* and *i* makes it *dove*, the past tense of *dive*. Present him with the following words:

robe	ode	coke	hole	dome
	code	joke	mole	home
	mode	poke	pole	Rome
	rode	woke	role	chrome
		broke	sole	*come*
		choke	whole	*some*
		smoke		
		spoke		
		stoke		

one	cope	ore	dose	note
bone	dope	bore	hose	vote
cone	hope	core	nose	quote
lone	mope	fore	pose	
tone	pope	more	rose	
zone	rope	sore	chose	
phone		tore	close	
done		yore		
none		chore		
gone		store		
		swore		

```
            cove        doze
            dove        froze

                  dove
                  love
                  move
                  rove
                  wove
                  clove
                  drove
                  grove
                  stove
                  glove
                  shove
```

Irregular pronunciations:

> *come, some* rime with *hum.*
> *one, done, none* rime with *fun.*
> *gone* rimes with *Don.*
> *dove, love, glove, shove* are pronounced as if they were spelled
> *duv, luv, gluv, shuv.*

Lesson 75: Review of words with long *a, e, i,* and *o* sounds spelled with consonants and the silent *e.*

cake	Dave	grave	Jake	lane
coke	dive	grove	joke	line
	dove			lone
cane	drive			
cone	drove			

mare	male	pale	ride	whale
mere	mile	pile	rode	while
mire	mole	pole		whole
more			rise	
			rose	

made
mode

make
mike

Lesson 76: A second common way in which the long *o* is spelled is *oa* as in the following words:

load	loaf	oak	coal	foam
road		soak		roam
toad		cloak		

soap	oar	boast	oat
	roar	coast	boat
	soar	toast	coat
		roast	goat
			moat
			float
			gloat

Lesson 77: A third way of writing the long *o* sound is with *ow* as in the following words:

bow	blow	own
low	crow	blown
row	flow	grown
sow	grow	shown
tow	show	
	slow	
	snow	

Lesson 78: A fourth way in which the long *o* is written is in combination with a consonant blend as in these words:

old	host	cord	cork	dorm
bold	most	ford	fork	form
cold	*cost*	lord	pork	norm
fold	post		York	
gold	*lost*			
hold				
mold				
sold				
told				

born	fort	horse	boss	or
corn	Mort	Norse	loss	for
adorn	port	Morse	moss	nor
horn	sort		toss	
morn				
torn				
worn				

Irregular pronunciation: Note that *cost* and *lost* sound like *boss, loss, moss, toss,* all of which have a slight variant of the long *o* sound, close to *aw* as in *jaw*.

Lesson 79: In a few simple words, the long *o* is simply spelled with an *o,* as follows: *go, no, so, quo, yo-yo.* The pronunciation of these words will be obvious to the child when he encounters them in reading. He should become aware of the exceptions in this group, namely *do, to, who,* and *two.*

Lesson 80: Introduce the *oo* sound as in *good* and *food.* There is a a slight difference between the two sounds, but the spoken language is always the guide to the word's pronunciation.

coo	boob	brood	goof	kook
boo		food	roof	spook
moo		mood	proof	book
too		good	hoof	cook
woo		hood		hook
zoo		wood		look
		stood		nook
				took
				brook
				crook
				shook
cool	boom	boon	boop	boor
fool	doom	moon	coop	*door*
pool	moon	noon	loop	moor
tool	noon	soon	hoop	poor
wool	soon	spoon	poop	
drool	spoon		stoop	
	swoon			
	loose	boot	ooze	booth
	moose	coot	booze	tooth
	noose	foot		
choose	hoot			
	loot			
	soot			
	root			
	toot			
	zoot			

Irregular pronunciation: *door* rimes with *more*.

Special group: the following group of irregularly spelled words also rime with *good: could, would, should*. After you explain their meanings, explain also that these words are often contracted with *not* to make: *couldn't, wouldn't, shouldn't*.

Lesson 81: Introduce the *ow*, *ou* sound as in *cow* and *ouch*. There are many common words in this vowel group, as shown below:

bow	owl	*own*	browse	ouch
cow	*bowl*	down		couch
dow	cowl	gown		pouch
how	fowl	town		*touch*
now	howl	brown		vouch
pow	jowl	clown		
sow	growl	crown		
vow		drown		
wow		frown		

loud	gouge	ounce	noun	
proud		bounce		
cloud		pounce		
		flounce		
		trounce		

bound	count	our	douse	out
found	fount	*four*	house	bout
hound	mount	hour	louse	lout
pound		sour	mouse	pout
round		*tour*	rouse	rout
sound		*your*	souse	tout
wound		flour		clout
wound				flout

ground				*doubt*
				trout

bough	
plough	

Irregular pronunciations:

> *bowl* rimes with *role*.
> *own* rimes with *tone*.
> *touch* rimes with *much*.
> *four* and *your* rimes with *or*.
> *tour* rimes with *poor*.
> the *ou* in *wound* sounds like *oo* in *moon*.

Irregular spelling: *bough, plough.* Silent *gh*.

Irregular spelling: *doubt.* The *b* is silent.

Lesson 81a: Here are some simple two-syllable words with *ow, ou* sounds which the child should be able to read quite easily:

dowry	Bowery	downtown	Mounty
towel	dowel	flounder	bow-wow
county	bounty	tower	foundling
flower	voucher	vowel	counsel
council	lousy	*country*	pow-wow

Irregular pronunciation: *country.* The *ou* sounds like *u* in *hunt*.

Lesson 82: Introduce the *oy, oi* sound as in *boy* and *oil*. Here are some words in that sound group:

boy	void	oil	coin	joint	noise	hoist
coy		boil	join	point	poise	foist
joy		coil	loin			moist
Roy		foil				
soy		spoil				
toy		broil				

Lesson 83: Introduce the long *u* sound. Illustrate by pronouncing such words as *use, June, cube, mule.* These words are spelled with *u* followed by a consonant and silent *e* as follows:

275

cube	dude	huge	cuke
lube	Jude		duke
Rube	nude		juke
tube	rude		Luke
	crude		puke
	prude		

mule	fume	dune	dupe
rule	plume	June	
Yule		tune	
		prune	

cure	fuse	cute
pure	muse	jute
sure	ruse	lute
		mute
		brute
		chute
		flute

Irregular pronunciation: The *s* in *sure* is pronounced *sh*.

Lesson 84: Review of long vowel sounds as spelled with consonants and the silent *e*:

Dane	fame	Jane	lake
dine	fume	June	like
dune			Luke

male	pike	pride	tame
mile	poke	prude	time
mole	puke		tome
mule			

Lesson 85: Here are some two-syllable words with long *u* pronunciation units which your child should be able to read with little or no trouble:

cupid	assure	ice-cube
Yuletide	refuse	duty
jukebox	prudent	rebuke
dilute	Neptune	tuneful
amuse	pupil	jury
tubeless	ruler	student

Lesson 86: The long *u* is also spelled *ue* and *ui* as in the following words:

cue	blue	juice
due	clue	fruit
hue	flue	bruise
rue	glue	cruise
Sue	queue	
	true	

Lesson 87: The long *u* is also spelled *ew*, *eu* and *ue* as in the following words:

dew	blew	flew	news	feud	duel
few	brew	grew		deuce	fuel
Jew	chew	stew			cruel
Lew	clew	view			
mew	crew	screw			
new	drew				
pew					

Lesson 88: The *er, ear, ir, ur* sounds. Note the similarity, as in the following words. A few *or* words have the same sound.

her	search	fir	fur	word
jerk	heard	sir	cur	work
clerk	learn	bird	purr	worm
germ	yearn	gird	curd	worst
term	earth	firm	hurd	worth
fern	dearth	girl	urge	
Bert		whirl	purge	
pert		dirt	splurge	
terse		flirt	curl	
verse		shirt	hurl	
berth		squirt	furl	
Perth	birth	urn		
nerve	girth	burn		
serve	mirth	turn		
verve	first	Burt		
swerve	thirst	Curt		
Merv	dirge	hurt		
	smirk	curse		
	quirk	nurse		
		purse		
		burst		
		curve		

Lesson 89: Your child should be able to read the two-syllable words made up of *er, ear, ir, ur,* and *or* pronunciation units joined with other known sounds.

perfect	herself	terminal*
nervous	Mervin	searchlight
birthday	mirthful	thirsty
unfurl	return	auburn
Bertram	expert	reverse
learning	affirm	dirty
further	current	urgent
Burton	confirm	worthwhile

* try this three-syllable word

Lesson 90: Many common English words have an *le* ending. These words will familiarize your child with this common construction:

able	apple	battle	ample
cable	grapple	cattle	sample
fable	paddle	rattle	simple
gable	faddle	little	dimple
table	fiddle	brittle	rimple
sable	saddle	settle	pimple
stable	coddle	mettle	temple
maple	riddle	kettle	gentle
staple	peddle	tattle	fumble
idle	hobble	tittle	bumble
bridle	bubble	turtle	humble
eagle	babble		mumble
beagle			rumble
			grumble
			stumble
			tumble
			jumble
			nimble
			thimble
			handle

278

jungle	dazzle	hustle
juggle	fizzle	bustle
struggle		rustle
oggle	raffle	wrestle
bungle	ruffle	pestle
wiggle	piffle	
wriggle		
wrinkle		
crinkle		
jingle		
jangle		
strangle		
bangle		
single		
dangle		

Lesson 91: Show how these multisyllabic words are derived from the above words:

wrestler	settler	unstable	cobbler
wrinkled	rustler	littlest	babbling
juggler	fizzled	ruffled	dazzling
struggling	tumbler	gently	unsettling
simply	gentleman	pimply	paddling
strangler	rattler	handling	tattler

Lesson 92: Many common English words have an *er* ending. These words will familiarize your child with this common sound-symbol:

better	lower	upper	zipper	summer	dinner
rubber	lumber	bitter	farmer	gutter	trigger

higher	winter	butter	sitter	chatter	father
other	letter	later	maker	bumper	fewer
bigger	dreamer	shimmer	slipper	faker	fever
baker	hiker	rather	mother	brother	heater
teacher	preacher	pitcher	slumber	number	rover
sister	blister	corner	over	dealer	owner

Lesson 93: Introduce the child to the silent *k* and *kn* with the following words:

knack	knap	knave	knee
knight	knit	knob	knock
		known	knowing

kneel	knelt	knickers
knot	know	knowledge
knuckle		

Lesson 94: Introduce the silent *g* in these words beginning with *gn*:

gnarl   gnarled   gnat   gnaw   gnawing   gnome   gnu

Lesson 95: Introduce the child to the silent *w* and *wr* with the following words:

wrack	wrangle	wrap	wrapping	wrath	wrathful
wreath	wreck	wrench	wrestle	wrestler	wriggle
wright	wring	wrist	write	writer	writing
wrong	wrote	wrought	wry	wren	wretch

Lesson 96: Introduce the child to the silent *b* as in the following words:

dumb	thumb	plumber	limb	climb	numb	debt
lamb	comb	crumb	dumb	thumb	bomb	bombing

Lesson 97: Introduce the silent *t* with these words:

castle	hustle	nestle	rustle	often	listen
whistle	hustling	hasten	jostle	soften	wrestle
whistling	bristles	hastening	rustling	moisten	wrestling
gristle	christen	thistle	jostling	moistening	softening

Lesson 98: We have already learned the silent *g* and *gh* in relation to the long *i* in such words as *sign* and *sight*. The silent *gh* is found in other common words as well. The following is a review of such words:

ought	taught	caught	thought	wrought	slaughter
bought	fraught	naughty	daughter	nought	eight
straight	weight	weigh	eighty	neighbor	eighteen
freight	height	bright	light	lightning	frightened
frightening		frightful		brighten	

Lesson 99: The *h* is silent in some words, as follows:

honor   hour   ghost   honest   ghastly   ghetto   ghoul

Lesson 100: Review of *ph* and *gh* as *f* sound:

phantom	Ralph	rough	cough	laugh	laughter
graph	pharmacy	phase	Phoenix	Philip	phone
tough	phony	photo	graphic	physic	phrase
emphasis	physical	phrase	photograph		Philadelphia

Lesson 101: There are many words of Latin origin in which the *ce, se, ci, ti, xi, sc, si, su,* and *tu* are pronounced like *sh, ch,* or *zh.* Here are some of them the child can become familiar with:

ocean	ancient	nation	mission	sure	nauseous
insure	fission	fraction	measure	treasure	issue
special	racial	facial	conscious	anxious	atrocious
station	ration	patient	bastion	section	question
fracture	rapture	capture	pleasure	leisure	tissue
fissure	fusion	traction	obnoxious	musician	physician
initial	crucial	ration	motion	patience	picture

Glossary of Terms

affix - a syllabic unit which, when added to a word, modifies the meaning of the word. There are three types of affixes: prefixes, suffixes, and inflectional endings.

alphabet - a set of graphic symbols (letters) representing the speech sounds of a given language, the purpose of which is to permit the speaker to record (write) his words and thoughts in a manner as closely resembling his actual speech as possible and to permit the reader to translate back into sound the precise spoken words of the writer.

antonym - words having opposite meanings, such as hot-cold, big-small.

auditory discrimination - the ability to distinguish by ear the subtly different sounds of the spoken language so that they can be accurately identified by the proper written symbols.

basal reader - a textbook in a structured series used for the purpose of teaching children to read. Vocabulary is controlled throughout the series so that the ability to read the advanced readers depends on the pupil's knowledge of the vocabulary in the pre-primers and primer of the series.

configurationism - a concept by which one learns to recognize a whole word by its total overall shape rather than by the sound values of its individual letters.

consonant - an elementary irreducible speech sound produced by stopping and releasing the air stream, or stopping it at one point while it escapes at another, or forcing it through a loosely closed or very narrow passage.

consonant digraph - two alphabet letters representing one consonant sound, such as *th, sh, ch, ph, gh,* etc.

context clues - a means by which a reader determines the meaning of a word by its relationship with the other words in a sentence. Same as context cues.

decoding - a means of determining the sound of a written word by translating the letters into spoken sounds. Sounding out a word. The term is also loosely used by eclectic basal series authors to describe any technique to determine the meaning of a word.

dipthong - two vowel letters together in the same syllable representing one sound in which both vowels are heard, such as in b*oi*l, s*ou*nd, b*oy*.

dyslexia - a term widely used to describe the inability to learn to read by sight-vocabulary techniques. The causes of dyslexia are widely disputed within the remedial reading community, but they include mixed dominance, ambidexterity, or simply poor memory of word forms.

eclectic basal reader - a current euphemism for sight-vocabulary basal textbooks in which no one method of teaching reading is singled out as being better than any other. Usually combines techniques of sight reading with phonetic clues. Some current eclectic basal series now feature linguistic decoding instead of incidental phonics.

encoding - writing.

grapheme - a representation by alphabet letters of a phoneme, or distinct irreducible speech sound.

hieroglyphic - a picture, character, or graphic symbol representing a word, syllable, or sound in which some sound-symbol correspondences may be present, but which depends mainly on a meaning association rather than a sound association for interpretation. Some hieroglyphics are pure ideograms, such as numerals and the dollar sign, others represent whole words, parts of words, or pronunciation units. Was considered a cumbersome, inaccurate, difficult system for recording spoken language and was replaced by alphabetic writing. The alphabet was specifically invented in order to overcome the serious shortcomings and handicaps of hieroglyphic writing which had become a serious bottleneck to intellectual development.

homographs - words spelled alike but with different meanings and pronunciations, such as *wind-wind, convict-convict.*

homonym - words which sound alike but with different meanings and, sometimes, spellings: *one, won; air, heir; bare, bear; bear, bear.*

ideogram - a graphic symbol representing an object or idea such as the numeral 5 or such symbols as %, $, ¢, , #, +, −.

inflectional ending - an affix at the end of a word to form plurals, possessive cases, comparisons, tenses of verbs, etc., as in: boy*s*, boy*'s*, big*gest*, talk*ed*, walk*ing*.

i.t.a. - initial teaching alphabet devised to create perfectly consistent letter-sound correspondences between spoken and written English so that a child can learn to read without having to learn irregular spellings. Eventually the child is transferred to t.o., traditional orthography.

linguistics - the study of language, in spoken and written forms.

look-and-guess method - a description of the look-say method by some of its critics.

look-say method - synonomous with sight-vocabulary, whole-word, and sight-word method whereby a child is taught to read by remembering the appearance of the whole word rather than by learning the sound values of the individual letters. It is a hieroglyphic technique of reading applied to a sound-symbol system.

manualism - school of deaf-mute instruction in which sign language, the manual alphabet, is used as the chief means of communication and learning among the deaf. This is a hieroglyphic system since it involves sight symbols and associations only.

mixed dominance - a condition in some children associated with ambidexterity which makes them read words in reverse in sight reading.

morpheme - the smallest unit of meaning in written language.

oralism - the school of deaf-mute instruction in which the student is taught to articulate in order to gain a concept of spoken language and to read phonetically.

orthography - spelling, or the study of spelling.

phoneme - a distinct, irreducible language sound.

phoneme-grapheme correspondences - the sound-symbol correspondences of a spoken language and its written counterpart. The phoneme is a distinct, irreducible language sound and the corresponding grapheme is its representation by one or more written letters.

phonemics - a linguistic term referring to the study of the specific sounds of a specific language, as opposed to phonetics, which is the study of language sounds in general.

phonetic alphabet - a system of language sound symbols in which each distinct sound feature of the language is identified by one separate symbol. A phonetic alphabet for the English language as it is spoken in different parts of the world with different accents would require well over 100 separate graphic symbols. The phonetic alphabet for English in most American dictionaries numbers about 44 or 45 symbols.

phonetics - the study of language sounds and their representation by written symbols. It covers the complete range of sound differences producible by the human vocal apparatus for the purpose of speech.

phonics - the application of phonetics to the teaching of reading and spelling.

phonography - the written representation of the sounds of speech; phonetic spelling or transcription. Also, any system of shorthand based on a phonetic transcription of speech.

phonogram - a sign or symbol representing a word, syllable, or sound, as in shorthand. Also used to describe certain regular graphemes found in common spelling families in written English. Also referred to as a graphemic or graphonic base in some textbooks.

prefix - an affix at the beginning of a word, modifying the meaning of the basic word, such as *pre*fix, *re*done, *un*do.

pictograph - a picture representing an idea as in primitive writing and hieroglyphics. Widely used in road signs and traffic signs.

pre-primer - the first and most elementary reading textbook in a basal series. It is generally used to introduce the child to a basic sight vocabulary.

primer - generally, a book whereby a child is taught how to read. In whole-word parlance, it is the first textbook reader of a basal series, following the pre-primers, incorporating all of the sight words learned in the pre-primers.

reading for meaning - a method of reading instruction whereby a child is taught to associate a whole written word with its meaning. In reading for meaning a child may misread the word *father* for *daddy*, or vice versa, since he has not been taught the relationship between written symbols and spoken sounds. He associates the whole word with an idea, a meaning. In some reading-for-meaning instruction, phonetic clues are introduced early enough so that the most blatant misreadings are avoided.

reading readiness - a concept regarding the readiness of a child to learn how to read. Phonics advocates suggest that a child is ready to learn how to read when he has an adequate speaking vocabulary and can distinguish between subtly different speech sounds. Sight-vocabulary advocates suggest the need to develop visual discrimination skills before a child is ready to learn how to read. Sight-word readiness programs teach picture reading, shape configurations, then word-picture associations.

remedial reading - a course of instruction to help poor readers improve reading proficiency. Methods vary according to the teacher's preference and training.

reading disability - general term applied to children who, for a variety of reasons, cannot learn to read with any proficiency via the sight-vocabulary method.

schwa - the unstressed, central vowel sound of most unstressed syllables in English, such as the *a* in *a*go, *a*bove, the *e* in ag*e*nt, tak*e*n, the *i* in penc*i*l, the *u* in circ*u*s, etc. Sometimes referred to as the muttering vowel.

sight-word method - synonomous with look-say, whole-word, or sight-vocabulary method, whereby a child is taught to read by remembering the appearance of the whole word rather than by learning the sound values of the individual letters.

sight vocabulary - words which a child has learned to read or recognize on the basis of their overall appearance and configuration before he has learned the alphabet and the sounds the letters stand for.

silent reading - a concept, sometimes advocated to extremes, in which children are trained to read silently without moving their lips so that printed words are associated with mental images rather than speech sounds.

sound-symbol system - the alphabetic means of writing and reading, whereby one uses written letter-symbols to represent speech sounds.

strephosymbolia - a term coined by Dr. Samuel T. Orton to describe the habit of reversing letters and of reading words backwards which plagues children with mixed dominance who are taught to read via a sight-word method.

structural analysis - the use of meaning units in the recognition of sight words of more than one syllable.

suffix - an affix at the end of the word: saf*ely*, force*ful*, teach*er*.

synonym - words that have the same or nearly the same meaning: *love, adore; careful, cautious; car, automobile.*

vowel - a voiced speech sound characterized by generalized friction of the air passing in a continuous stream through the pharynx and opened mouth, with relatively no narrowing or other obstruction of the speech organs. In written English the vowels are represented by the letters *a, e, i, o, u,* and *y* in cases where the latter substitutes for one of the other letters.

vowel digraphs - two vowels together in one syllable representing only one or a new vowel sound, such as in rec*ei*ve, b*ea*m, d*oe*s, ag*ai*n, p*ai*l, l*ea*ther.

whole-word method - a hieroglyphic method of learning to read English by associating whole-word configurations directly with pictures or meanings. Synonomous with sight-word, sight-vocabulary, and look-say method.

word forms - whole words seen as hieroglyphics in which the parts of the word are visually studied as one would study a Chinese character.

word attack - the technique of figuring out the meaning of a word by its configuration, relation in context with other words, structural analysis, phonetic rules, and letter-sound correspondence clues. It is a development of sight-word methodology, whereby hieroglyphic reading techniques have been applied to the reading of a sound-symbol writing system.

Appendix I: Textbook Evaluations

Textbooks are never reviewed by the general press and yet they are some of the most important and most widely read books in the country. Parents and interested laymen, therefore, have no way of knowing whether a textbook being used by their children in a public or private school is any good. Parents assume that all textbooks used in schools are good because they have been approved by the school authorities. Unfortunately, school authorities are far from infallible, and their choices in textbooks often leave much to be desired. This is particularly true of the basal readers, which are used in thousands of elementary classrooms across the nation. The purpose of this appendix, therefore, is to provide the parent, in as clear and concise a form as possible, a review or evaluation of the various basal reading instruction textbooks now being offered by the nation's textbook publishers and being used in the classrooms today. The review is limited to only the first books in basal series—the readiness, pre-primer, and primer textbooks—where the crucial matter of reading instruction methodology is our central concern.

Textbook adoption in public education is a complex process and varies from state to state. Some states have a state-wide adoption system whereby a textbook committee selects a number of books which the individual schools can choose from. Other states leave textbook adoption up to the local school districts. In some states and school districts, one book is chosen for a particular subject and grade level. In other states and school districts, several books covering the same subject and grade level may be approved and each school permitted to choose the particular book or books they want to use.

Some state textbook adoption committees hold open hearings during which interested parents and laymen can state their views concerning the various textbooks being proposed for adoption. However, it is difficult for a parent to review a textbook before the state has adopted it for use. The public's access to school textbooks, new or old, is limited. They are not to be found in the public libraries. Only a few very extensive reference collections have them. Most colleges of education have libraries of textbooks, and if there is one in your community, you may be able to use their facilities to review books. However, they will not have the new textbooks on hand, the textbooks which have not yet been adopted but are being considered for adoption.

The way to find out what new reading instruction textbooks are being offered is to write to the publishers for their latest catalogs and brochures, which describe the new textbooks. Then, at least, you will have some information about the new books being offered instead of no information at all. Sometimes the descriptive literature is sufficient to give you an adequate idea of what the new books are like. But in this period of transition and pedagogical confusion, the descriptive literature can often be very misleading.

The most crucial books in any reading instruction series are the starters: the readiness books, the pre-primers, and the primer. If you have a child about to enter school for the first time, it is important to know what textbooks will be used to teach him how to read. Go to the school and ask to see the books yourself. As a parent, taxpayer, a citizen of a free country, you have a right to do so. Jot down the name of the series, the authors, the publisher, the copyright date. Check them against the evaluations in this appendix. If your child is being taught to read via one of the well-known sight-vocabulary basal series, you had better start teaching him how to read at home via the primer in the final chapter of this book. If he is being taught to read via a sound-symbol method (phonics or linguistics), you can check his knowledge and progress by having him go through the primer in this book. It will reinforce whatever he is being taught in school.

Any child who is exposed to the sight-vocabulary method risks becoming a dyslexic or a disabled reader requiring laborious, painful remedial reading instruction later in his school career. The Food and Drug Administration forces cigarette manufacturers to label the danger inherent in cigarette smoking, but HEW does not force publishers to label the danger inherent in the sight-vocabulary method. Thus, it is up to the parent to make sure that his child is not exposed to educational malpractice. It is unfortunate that parents should have to do this job, but until HEW issues an order to remove all sight-vocabulary pre-primers and primers from the public schools, parents will have to either complain to the school authorities for a change of methods or teach their children to read at home.

Note: In reviewing the textbooks I have not always had access to the latest editions. But it is obvious that most of the basal readers now being used in the classrooms of America were written and published in the mid or late 1960s. I have, however, reviewed some of the new basal series of the major publishers which will no doubt find their way into many classrooms within the next few years. Some of them represent improvements in reading instruction suggested by Jeanne Chall in *Learning to Read*. Some, however, are very complicated and confusing, with completely new linguistic terminology obscuring questionable pedagogy. Parents should not subject their children to instruction techniques based on the authors' confusions, compromises, and poorly digested concepts. There is a tremendous amount of just plain bad, inept pedagogy in today's elementary reading instruction, and it takes more expertise than most parents have to separate the good from the bad.

In addition, I have reviewed the teacher's editions of the various text-books, in which the methodology of the particular series is fully explained for the teacher's benefit. Most teachers follow the instructions quite slavishly. Some may deviate from the prescribed sight-vocabulary course and teach bootleg phonics. But we must assume that the average teacher will follow the instructions of the manuals and guidebooks as closely as possible. It is important to be aware of this, for parents may have access to the textbooks their children bring home, but they will not have access to the teachers' editions, manuals, and guidebooks which tell the teachers how to teach.

EVALUATIONS

Title of series: The Ginn Basic Readers, 100 Edition
Authors: David H. Russell and Odille Ousley
Publisher: Ginn and Company, A Xerox Education Company, 191 Spring Street, Lexington, Mass.
Date of copyright: 1964, 1966
General description of series: Sight-vocabulary basal series.
Evaluation of readiness, pre-primer, and primer programs:

The readiness program is completely pictographic, preparing the child for a sight-vocabulary approach to printed words. Words are considered symbols, like pictures, representing ideas not speech sounds. The child is taught to associate words with pictures, not sounds. He is not taught the letter names or letter sounds. The authors' approach is summed up as follows: "Even the most immature child must be led to realize that reading is the written expression of ideas. . . . Before learning to read, children must have many clear and vivid concepts. This is necessary if they are to learn to associate with ease and understanding the printed symbols known as words, and the ideas which the symbols represent. . . . Pictures are important in helping the child to associate meaning with spoken words."

Nowhere is the child given to understand that our writing system is a sound-symbol system. He is taught that it is ideographic.

The three pre-primers (*My Little Red Story Book*, *My Little Green Story Book*, and *My Little Blue Story Book*) introduce the child to 62 sight words and follow the Dick and Jane format but with a different cast of characters. The 1966 edition (100 Edition) is racially integrated; the 1964 edition is not. The methodology is described in the teacher's manual as follows:

> The program of the Ginn Basic Readers, as outlined in the primary manuals of this series, does not depend upon any one method of attack on words. The identification and recognition of words are thoroughly developed in the primary grades through a variety of methods:
> 1. Recognition through general configuration or unusual characteristics of the word.
> 2. Recognition through similarities to known words—common elements.
> 3. Use of picture clues.
> 4. Use of phonetic analysis.
> 5. Use of context clues.
> 6. Use of structural analysis.

In these pre-primers, sight words are matched with pictures not sounds and are associated directly with meanings. Children are taught to make word blocks, that is, to frame whole words so that their general configurations can be studied. This is the worst sort of sight-reading instruction. A few initial consonant letters are identified and their sound values learned as phonetic clues. But context clues are considered much more important. There is some of the worst sort of hieroglyphic deaf-mute instruction in this program. For example, on page 275 of the teacher's manual, there is this exercise in "associating meaning with sight words":

> Display the word card *funny* and say, "If you know this word, you may tell the group about something that is funny." Give several children an opportunity to identify the word *funny* and to tell a humorous incident or describe a picture or object that is funny.

The assumption in this sort of exercise is that the child doesn't know the meaning of the word *funny*. The fact is that he does know it. He only wants to know how to read it. But as a sight word, it must be identified in his mind with the idea of funny, while in actuality, the written word *funny* is merely a sound-symbol representation of the spoken word *funny*. It is the latter which represents the idea, not the written word. This sort of confusion in the minds of the authors can cause serious associational confusion in the mind of the child.

The primer (*The Little White House*) provides more of the same hieroglyphic methodology, with much emphasis on context clues, word blocking, sight-word recognition. On page 100 of the teacher's manual (1966 edition) there is this ludicrous exercise in associating meaning with a sight word—the word *guess*:

> To help children associate meaning with the recognition of sight words, ask the children to close their eyes. Place a small toy in a large paper bag and tie a string around the opening. Say: "Open your eyes. This sentence tells what I want you to do." Write *Guess what this is*. After a child has read the sentence he may lift, feel, or shake the paper bag. While he is trying to find out what is in it, write on the chalkboard *I can guess what it is*. Have the child read the sentence, tell the group what he thinks the toy is, and open the bag to see if he guessed correctly. Continue the activity by using other small toys in the same way.

Again, this exercise seems to have been conceived not so much to teach the child how to read the word *guess* but to understand the spoken word, as if he had never heard it before. This is pure deaf-mute instruction. It is obvious that this methodology can cause dyslexia, strephosymbolia, associational confusion, and other severe reading disabilities.

Title of series: Reading 360
Authors: Theodore Clymer, Virginia L. Brown, Billie Parr, Bernice M.

Christenson; consultants: Roger W. Shuy (Linguistics), E. Paul Torrance (Creativity)

Publisher: Ginn and Company, a Xerox Education Company, 191 Spring Street, Lexington, Mass.

Date of copyright: 1969

General description of series: Reading instruction program with emphasis on letter-sound relationships but retaining many aspects of sight-vocabulary methodology.

Evaluation of Levels 1, 2, and 3:

It is a pity that after spending so much money on this new reading program, the publishers should have come up with this schizoid product. The authors have decided that, indeed, written English is a sound-symbol system, but they have also decided to retain some of the unfortunate methodology of whole-word pedagogy. Obviously influenced by Jeanne Chall's work, the authors have "linguisticized" their approach to beginning reading instruction by emphasizing "decoding" in the first three levels. Nevertheless, the authors have violated basic linguistic principles by the use of powerful, distracting illustrations throughout the beginning books, and by teaching the letter-sound correspondences in the kind of piecemeal way associated with earlier sight-reading programs. They first teach the consonant letters by way of the initial consonants in whole words. The child is helped to identify the whole word by way of word-picture associations. This is a hieroglyphic method of teaching word recognition.

The sound-symbol is used as a phonetic clue. For example, on page 44 of the Teacher's Edition of *My Sound and Word Book* (Level 2) in which the words *Bill, Lad, runs* are being taught, the teacher is instructed as follows: "Help the pupils understand that the beginning letters serve as clues for reading these words. . . . Explain that beginning letters serve as clues, but a reader must look at a whole word to see whether or not he can read it." The child, of course, has not been taught the sound values of the other letters in the words, therefore he must either identify the word by way of its configuration beyond the initial consonant or by a picture clue. The word *this* is taught as a whole word in Level 2 with these instructions to the teacher: "Do not call attention to the phoneme-grapheme correspondence *th*, as it will not be taught until level 5." Then why ask the pupil to read the word at level 2 if he has to wait until level 5 to be taught the letter-sound correspondences?

The vowels are not taught until level 3. To teach the vowel sounds, the authors have contrived an unnecessarily complicated way of doing it using completely new terminology. There is no such thing as a short

294

or long vowel any more. There are now "glided" and "unglided" vowel sounds. The glided vowel sound is introduced on page 73 of the Teacher's Edition (Level 3) in this way:

Repeat the word *kite*, emphasizing the medial vowel sound. Identify this sound as a glided vowel sound. Help the children understand that "glide" means to move smoothly from one place to another—the way a sailboat moves across the water, or the way a skater moves across the ice.

Demonstrate the meaning of a glided vowel sound by slowly pronouncing /ay/ to show that the sound slides from /a/, as in *father*, to /iy/, as in *me*. Tell the children that the English language has several glided vowel sounds, and /ay/, as in *kite*, is one of them.

Encourage the children to pronounce /ay/ several times, so they can hear the sound glide from /a/ to /iy/ and feel the jaw move as the sound is being pronounced. Reinforce awareness of this sound by asking the children to repeat the following: /ay/ *ride*, /ay/*side*, /ay/*white*, /ay/*dime*.

If there are children who have difficulty in identifying the vowel sound /ay/, provide additional practice for them at a convenient time.

This jaw-stretching method strikes us as not only being *not* an improvement over the traditional way of teaching the long vowel *i*, but of needlessly complicating it. If the child has to think of his jaw sliding every time he hears a "glided" vowel, it might produce some uncomfortable results. This highly questionable approach is applied to the teaching of all the vowel sounds. Simple short vowels are taught as complicated "unglided" vowels. The silent *e* is now called the "*e* marker," and a syllabic unit is now called a "graphemic base." We do not find that the new terminology in any way improves the teaching of sound-symbol relationships. The fragmented way in which the sound-symbols are taught, along with whole words, makes this basically an instruction program with a hieroglyphic approach.

In short, while the Ginn Reading 360 program is an improvement over the Ginn Basic Readers, it has some serious shortcomings, namely, the overreliance on distracting illustrations, the piecemeal approach to the sound-symbol system using whole words, the overcomplicated new terminology which makes no improvement over traditional terminology. The authors seem to be confused between the two notions of "reading" and "learning how to read." This basic confusion seems to prevail among the authors of all basal reading programs using the hieroglyphic approach. Also, it seems obvious that the authors do not fully understand the difference between a purely alphabetic system of writing and a hieroglyphic one. This becomes obvious in their definitions of the terms reading, decoding, encoding, etc. Their broad definitions indicate that they look at written English as a hieroglyphic system rather than an alphabetic one. This, of course, is due to their reluctance to make a clean break from whole-word methodology and their insistence on retaining some of the hieroglyphic features of the sight-vocabulary programs. We cannot, at this point, say what kind of reading disabilities can result from this schizoid approach. However, it is probable that some children will be confused.

Title of series: Scott Foresman Reading Systems
Authors: Ira E. Aaron, A. Sterl Artley, Kenneth S. Goodman, Charlotte S. Huck, William A. Jenkins, John C. Manning, Marion Monroe, Wilma J. Pyle, Helen M. Robinson, Andrew Schiller, Mildred Beatty Smith, Lorraine M. Sullivan, Samuel Weintraub, Joseph M. Wepman
Publisher: Scott, Foresman and Company, Glenview, Illinois 60025
Date of copyright: 1971
General description of series: Eclectic reading instruction without Dick or Jane.
Evaluation of Levels 1, 2, and 3:

This is Scott, Foresman's successor to Dick and Jane, who are being phased out. Dick and Jane are gone and so is the repetitive, insipid vocabulary, but the sight-word methodology is basically the same. The approach is pictographic, ideographic, with a very incidental piecemeal approach to the sound-symbol principle. This hieroglyphic approach to written English will cause as much dyslexia, strephosymbolia, associational confusion and other reading disabilities as Dick and Jane.

The authors equate teaching a child to read with getting an astronaut to the moon and have concocted probably the most confusing, needlessly complex reading instruction program on the market. All of the terminology of the Dick and Jane guidebooks has been discarded and replaced with a new jargon. "Word attack skills" have been replaced with "comprehension strategies," which is even worse than word attack, if that's possible. The idea that a child has to employ a host of "comprehension strategies" to translate written sound symbols back into spoken sounds indicates how far Scott Foresman's methodology is from the sound-symbol principle. Note this complex definition of reading given in the Level 1 Manual Glossary: "Reading: The interaction between the reader and written language through which the reader tries to reconstruct the message from the writer. Learning to read involves the acquisition of the concepts, skills, and comprehension strategies needed to understand, use, enjoy, and evaluate the messages communicated in various kinds of written language." The definition applies to the "reading" of a primitive pictographic system or a sophisticated hieroglyphic system, but does not apply at all to the reading of a pure sound-symbol system, which is what we have. The alphabet was invented so that man could dispense with "comprehension strategies" and simply limit the reading task to translating written sound symbols back into spoken sounds. By even concocting a term like "comprehension strategies," the Scott Foresman authors have simply announced that they have gone further back to hieroglyphic methodology.

Thus, the Dick and Jane terminology has been changed, but the basic method is the same. Picture clues and context clues are now called picture cues and context cues. Phonetic clues are now letter-sound relationship cues. I suppose the latter change was made in deference to linguistics. A good summary of the system's pedagogy can be found in the brochure about the system. It reads:

> There are so many different cues to meaning. In Scott Foresman Reading Systems, teaching children to read is teaching them how to recognize these cues and use them as strategies.
>
> Pictures provide cues to meaning in books. At early levels pictures are used, often with the initial consonant, to provide the cue to a word. . . .
>
> The context of what children are reading can provide many hints that help with the unfamiliar. If the word *scolded* on the third line of the right-hand page gives children trouble, their teacher points out the information that the context gives them: "Lisa frowned at the grompet and said, 'Don't be silly!' What's another word for *said* that explains she sounded cross?"
>
> In providing further help for the word *scolded*, if needed, a teacher should help children eliminate guesses such as "angry talking," or "yelled" by reminding pupils of what they know about letter-sound relationships. Pupils have been working with consonants since Level 2, with vowels since Level 3. By Level 8, most children will be fairly proficient at using their knowledge of letter-sound relationship cues. However, there is plenty of additional practice available for youngsters who still need it.

That by Level 8, a child could possibly misread the word *scolded* as *angry talking* or *yelled* is enough to indicate that the Scott Foresman system will do nothing to solve the incredibly bad reading problem this country now has. On the contrary. It will only compound it.

Title of series: The New Basic Readers (Curriculum Foundation Series)
Authors: Helen M. Robinson, Marion Monroe, A. Sterl Artley, Charlotte S. Huck, William A. Jenkins; W. Cabell Greet, Linguistic Advisor.
Publisher: Scott, Foresman and Company, Glenview, Illinois 60025
Date of copyright: 1962
General description of series: This is the Dick and Jane sight-vocabulary basal series. The 1962 edition is a direct revision of the edition evaluated in chapters 2, 3, and 4 of this book.
Evaluation of readiness, pre-primer and primer programs:

The readiness program is designed to prepare the children for Dick and Jane and consists of "reading" pictures ad nauseam. The child also learns to recognize the names Dick, Jane and Sally by word-picture association. The three pre-primers—*Sally, Dick and Jane, Fun With Our Family, Fun Wherever We Are*—are revisions of the three pre-primers evaluated in this book. There is still the belabored teaching of a scant sight vocabulary. Ten initial consonants are introduced in the second and third pre-primers, a concession to *Why Johnny Can't Read*. But this is basically the same hieroglyphic system of reading with phonetic clues introduced a bit earlier than in the previous edition. The business of chopping up words into three nonphonetic parts seems to have been discarded. The pre-primers and primer have enough story interpretation to choke a horse. The transition from pictures to words is so painstakingly slow, that the child must be bored to tears before he gets there. This sight-vocabulary series can cause dyslexia, strephosymbolia, associational confusion and other reading disabilities.
Evaluation of the 1965 edition:

This is the "integrated" or multi-ethnic edition of the Dick and Jane sight-vocabulary basal series, in which Mike, Penny and Pam, the children of a black family, join Dick and Jane in their antics. Aside from the addition of these new characters, the reading instruction methodology is the same as in the 1962 edition.

Title of series: The Harper & Row Basic Reading Program
Authors: Mabel O'Donnell; Byron H. Van Roekel, Educational Consultant.

298

Publisher: Harper & Row, Evanston, Ill.

Date of copyright: 1966

General description of series: Sight-vocabulary basal series. Instead of Dick and Jane, Miss O'Donnell has given us Janet and Mark, successors to Alice and Jerry.

Evaluation of readiness, pre-primer and primer programs:

The readiness program is completely pictographic. The child is not taught the alphabet. Children are introduced to Janet and Mark and learn to read their names by word-picture associations. No inkling is given whatever that written English is a sound-symbol system. In the pre-primer workbook all words are associated with pictures. In the four pre-primers, which teach a total sight-vocabulary of 78 words, the rebus, or small pictures, are actually interspersed in the text in place of words. Thus, the child is trained not only to look at words as pictures, but pictures as words. The Teacher's Edition states: "The introduction of the rebus into the line of print makes the picture a functional part of the reading process and supplies a much-needed step between the reading of the large-page illustration and a complete line of type." Thus, the authors reveal their complete confusion concerning how one reads a hieroglyphic system as opposed to a sound-symbol system.

Objects in the story illustrations are also labeled so that the child can make direct word-picture associations. Initial letter sounds are taught incidentally as phonetic clues. But word recognition relies mainly on word-picture associations, context clues, word configurations, and initial letter-sound clues. This is a pure hieroglyphic approach to the teaching of a sound-symbol writing system and about as close to manualist deaf-mute instruction as you can get. It can cause associational confusion, dyslexia, strephosymbolia, and other reading disabilities.

Title of series: The Alice and Jerry Basic Reading Program

Author: Mabel O'Donnell

Publisher: Row, Peterson and Company, Evanston, Illinois

Date of copyright: 1957

General description of series: Sight-vocabulary basal series.

Evaluation of readiness, pre-primer, and primer programs:

This series is no longer in print, having been replaced by Miss O'Donnell's Janet and Mark books. However, some schools may still be using them. This is a hieroglyphic approach to a sound-symbol written language, with a liberal use of the rebus throughout and much word-picture associations. Letter sounds are taught only as phonetic clues, along with context clues, configuration, etc. This methodology can cause associational confusion, dyslexia, strephosymbolia, and other reading problems.

Hillel Black, in his book, *The American Schoolbook*, tells us that Alice and Jerry have earned Miss O'Donnell $2,700,000 in royalties since 1936.

Title of series: Sheldon Basic Reading Series
Authors: William D. Sheldon, Queenie B. Mills, Merle B. Karnes, Bess M. Saddoris
Publisher: Allyn and Bacon, Inc., Boston, Mass.
Date of copyright: Readiness books, 1957; pre-primers 1963
General description of series: Sight-vocabulary basal series closely following the methodology of Dick and Jane.
Evaluation of the readiness and pre-primer programs:

The readiness books are purely pictographic. The second book introduces the characters of the pre-primers, Bill, Linda, and Ricky. Their names are learned by word-picture association and configurational word-blocking. The pre-primers follow the Dick and Jane format in text and pictures quite closely. The sight vocabulary is learned by use of configurational word-blocking and word-boxing, context clues, picture clues, and phonic analysis. Concerning the latter, the authors write: "Phonic analysis is one of several methods children can and should be taught to use as aids in attacking words independently." Therefore, the approach is basically hieroglyphic. Imposing a hieroglyphic reading instruction program on a sound-symbol writing system can cause associational confusion, dyslexia, strephosymbolia, and other reading disabilities.

Title of series: Betts Basic Readers, Anniversary Third Edition
Authors: Emmett A. Betts and Carolyn M. Welch
Publisher: American Book Company
Date of copyright: 1965
General description of series: Sight-vocabulary basal series featuring Jimmy and Sue, modeled after Dick and Jane.
Evaluation of readiness, pre-primer, and primer programs:

An incredibly disorganized approach to phonics is interspersed in a sight-vocabulary program of reading instruction which starts out as primitive pictography in the readiness level and graduates to complex hieroglyphics in the primer level. The unfortunate child who is exposed to such pedagogical confusion can only become hopelessly confused himself unless he has a perfect photographic memory. The readiness pro-

300

gram puts a tremendous emphasis on picture reading, word-picture associations, and word blocking. The pre-primers and primer are in the Dick and Jane tradition, with piecemeal phonics. This confused, illogical program of instruction can easily cause associational confusion, dyslexia, strephosymbolia, and other reading disabilities. Dr. Betts, incidentally, is a leading specialist in remedial reading.

Title of series: Reading for Meaning
Authors: Paul McKee, M. Lucille Harrison, Annie McCowen, Elizabeth Lehr, William K. Durr
Publisher: Houghton, Mifflin Company, Boston, Mass.
Date of copyright: 1966
General description of series: Sight-vocabulary technique with stress on initial consonant sounds as phonetic clues.
Evaluation of readiness, pre-primer, and primer programs:

Although the authors give the impression that they understand that written English consists of a sound-symbol system, they then justify not teaching it to the child as such. The authors describe their own technique as follows in the Pre-Reading Program manual:

> A sensible technique or key to be taught to the child is a simple one. Any child can use it to call quickly to mind the unfamiliar spoken word for which the strange printed form stands. It consists of using together (1) the context (the sense of the reading matter), and (2) the beginning sound of the word and, to the extent that they are needed, some of the sounds following the beginning sound.

Thus, the child is expected to learn a considerable sight vocabulary on the basis of initial consonant sounds and context clues. Vowel sounds are not taught. Pupils, we are told, "will ordinarily not need to use letter-sound associations for the vowels in unlocking strange printed words. Pupils will learn that the sense of the context in which a word appears indicates the sound that the vowel in that word stands for."

The result is that the child will not learn to spell very well via this system, nor can he learn much about syllabic pronunciation units, for consonants are learned without vowel accompaniment. Because the sound-symbol system is taught in so fragmented a manner, this is basically a hieroglyphic system of reading instruction. Any system of reading instruction which mixes fragments of the sound-symbol system with contextual word-guessing is essentially hieroglyphic. The unusually heavy emphasis on context clues is bad teaching. The search for context clues, in a sound-symbol system of writing, is only valid when dealing with homographs. Otherwise, one should have no more need to hunt for context clues to understand a written word than one does in understanding a spoken word. The child understands the meaning of the written word as he understands the meaning of the spoken word—in the context of speech—not writing. Looking for context clues as a means of "reading for meaning" negates the idea that written language is a sound-symbol reflection of spoken language. The child should not "read" for meaning, but *listen* for meaning, for when he reads he listens. Hieroglyphic writing is read for meaning. It is not listened to. The distinction is quite important in differentiating how one reads alphabetic writing as opposed to hieroglyphic or ideographic writing. The importance of that difference is what made the invention of the alphabet so significant.

Title of series: The Developmental Reading Series
Authors: Guy L. Bond, Marie C. Cuddy, Kathleen Wise
Publisher: Lyons and Carnahan, Chicago, Illinois
Date of copyright: 1962
General description of series: Sight-vocabulary basal series.
Evaluation of readiness, pre-primer, and primer programs:

This looks like a poor man's Dick and Jane, with characters Jane, Ann, Billy and pets Skip and Rex. All beginning instruction is in the form of association of words with pictures. The child looks at the words, then looks at the pictures to find out what the words say. The only virtue this series has over Dick and Jane is its greater brevity. Story interpretation is not carried to the preposterous lengths one finds in Dick and Jane and other series. Nevertheless, this sight-vocabulary methodology can cause associational confusion, dyslexia, strephosymbolia, and other reading disabilities.

Title of series: The Macmillan Reading Program
Authors: Albert J. Harris, Mae Knight Clark
Publisher: The Macmillan Company, New York, N.Y.
Date of copyright: 1970
General description of series: Eclectic basal series with a hieroglyphic technique of word identification.
Evaluation of readiness, pre-primer, and primer programs:

Although at least thirty sight words are taught through word-picture associations in the first level of the reading readiness program, the

302

authors claim that theirs is not a sight-vocabulary series because they start analyzing words in the pre-primer from the very beginning. Yet the child is expected to learn to read words like *policemen* and *cowboy* in the first pre-primer on the basis of an initial consonant sound and word-picture associations. If that isn't sight reading, then it is at least hieroglyphic reading. No alphabetic writing system should be taught in that way. The authors cover the initial and some final consonants in the pre-primers and don't get to the vowel letter sounds until the primer. The justification for this variant of the Dick and Jane method is that the authors want their pupils to start reading stories of high interest with lots of irregular words from the very beginning. But this simply indicates that the authors do not understand the difference between learning how to read and reading. They expect the child to gain the immediate benefits of the experienced reader without having first to learn how to read.

The authors, unfortunately, are really deceiving the children. It's not the written words which contain the high interest for the children in these elementary books, but the pictures. This series, like all of the other eclectic sight-word readers, are illustrated to the point of nausea. You hardly need words with so many pictures which are so much more colorful and interesting to look at than the few sickly words under them. The pictures get much more attention in the course of story interpretation than the words. Besides relegating words to their inferior, colorless status on the page, the authors expect the child to use "strategies for word identification," which include context clues, beginning and final letter sounds, and looking through the word for "familiar elements." Thus, this is basically a hieroglyphic system of instruction. Imposing a hieroglyphic system of instruction on a sound-symbol writing system can cause associational confusion, dyslexia, strephosymbolia, and other reading disabilities.

Title of series: Winston Basic Readers - Communications Program
Authors: Russell G. Stauffer, Alvina Treut Burrows, Mary Elizabeth Coleman
Publisher: John C. Winston Company, A Division of Holt, Rinehart and Winston, Inc., New York, N.Y.
Date of copyright: 1960
General description of series: Sight-vocabulary basal series which follow the Dick and Jane physical format and pedagogical formula quite closely.
Evaluation of readiness, pre-primer, and primer programs:
    The readiness program starts with a picture book—*Ready to Go*—then

303

graduates into another picture book—*Ready to Read*—in which the characters of the pre-primers, Susan, Bill and Nancy are introduced and their names learned by word-picture association. No instruction in alphabet letters or sounds is given. The pre-primer program teaches 56 words. The authors write: "Skill in word recognition means that a pupil has the ability to use context (meaning) clues, phonetic (sound) clues, and structure (sight) clues to read and understand a word. Since the ability to attack and to recognize a word is a skill, training in that skill must be provided." Further, the authors write: "The basic and most important clues to word attack are context or meaning clues. Context clues are inherent in the natural logic of the language used to communicate a thought. Words stand for things or ideas. They are used to represent experiences. They communicate identical meaning whether spoken or written. A child learns to use meaning clues to recognize the printed word in much the same way that he learns to use meaning clues to recognize and interpret the spoken word. Throughout this series meaning clues are given priority in word-recognition training because meaning clues or logical association clues promote functional recall and remembering."

Finally, the authors write: "Structure clues or sight clues are another means of attacking words. The initial training in this skill develops quick recognition of visual differences in the size, shape, and color of objects. Then the emphasis is shifted to words. Every reader uses visual clues or form clues to distinguish one word from another. The beginning reader totally relies upon this skill to recognize the difference in the first few words he learns in their printed form."

It is obvious from these quotations from the teacher's edition of the pre-primers that the authors are using a hieroglyphic approach for the reading of an alphabetic system of writing. The letter sounds are taught as phonetic clues along with the context and structure clues. In fact, the authors consider the context clues to be the most important of all. The confusions here are obvious. The authors do not understand the difference between written and spoken language, especially when that written language is a pure sound-symbol system. In addition they do not know the difference between a hieroglyphic system of writing and a sound-symbol system. This approach can cause associational confusion, dyslexia, strephosymbolia, and other reading disabilities.

Title of series: The Bank Street Readers
Authors: Prepared by the Bank Street College of Education. Senior editor, Irma Simonton Black; managing editor, Carl Memling; associate

editors, Joan W. Blos, Betty Miles; Teacher's Guide editor, Elsa Joffe; skills consultant, Frances M. Kerr
Publisher: The Macmillan Company, New York, N.Y.
Date of copyright: 1965
General description of series: Sight-vocabulary basal series.
Evaluation of readiness, pre-primer, and primer programs:

The Bank Street Readers were created primarily to provide a basal series for urban children who could not identify with the suburban family setting and such middle-class characters as Dick and Jane, Mark and Janet, Tom and Betty, etc. Aside from this sociological difference, and a great reliance on the experience chart technique in the readiness program, the reading instruction is based on whole-word methodology, with a great deal of word-picture associations. Some scanty instruction in initial letter sounds to be used as phonetic clues is given. No vowels are taught at all through the first reader. Thus, this is one of the most blatant of the sight-vocabulary reading-instruction programs on the market. Can cause associational confusion, dyslexia, strephosymbolia, and other reading disabilities.

Title of series: Reading for Living Series
Authors: William H. Burton, Clara Belle Baker, Grace K. Kemp
Publisher: Bobbs-Merrill Company, Inc., Indianapolis, Indiana
Date of copyright: 1959
General description of series: Sight-vocabulary basal series.
Evaluation of pre-primer program:

This is another Dick and Jane imitation. Here is what the authors have to say about acquiring a sight vocabulary:

"In the beginning a child has no real foundation for learning to recognize word symbols except his oral vocabulary. For the most part he must learn to associate the configuration of a printed word with the sound and meaning of the same word in his oral vocabulary. He must repeat the association sufficiently to identify the printed word almost instantaneously at sight. On this basis he can learn a fairly sizable sight vocabulary with which to start reading. This sight vocabulary is fundamental, not only as·a foundation for initial reading but also as a foundation for learning methods of word attack. The 'Reading for Living Series' provides a systematic program for helping the child to acquire an adequate sight vocabulary."

In other words, hieroglyphic methodology is imposed on a sound-symbol system. This can lead to associational confusion, dyslexia, strephosymbolia, and other reading disabilities.

305

Title of series: Phonetic Keys to Reading, A Basic Reading Series
Authors: Theodore L. Harris, Mildred Creekmore, Margaret Greenman
Publisher: The Economy Company, Oklahoma City, Oklahoma
Date of copyright: 1964
General description of series: Phonics-oriented beginning reading instruction.
Evaluation of the pre-primer program:

The authors state: "This series is designed to . . . help the pupils understand that written symbols convey meaning by representing speech sounds and language patterns." Thus, written English is taught as a sound-symbol system. There are three pre-primers: *Tag, Dot and Jim,* and *All Around with Dot and Jim.* The authors describe their method as follows: "*Tag* is the first book of the Phonetic Keys to Reading Series. The two parts of this book incorporate the audio-readiness program and the preprimer. The first part, pages 2-70, introduces the long and short vowel sounds, the consonant sounds, and a few phonetic principles. The second part, pages 71-96, contains stories on the pre-primer level. The vocabulary in these stories has been carefully controlled to permit the use of the phonetic principles learned in the readiness section and to provide for the gradual introduction of additional principles. This vocabulary is composed of words commonly used in other reading series."

Thus, the authors hoped to mesh their phonics-oriented beginner's course with the sight-vocabulary primers of the major publishers. The result is that the pre-primer stories read a lot like the Dick and Jane type books, with the same "See Spot run" literary quality. In addition, like the Open Court Basic Readers, the sequence of letter sounds learned starts with the long vowels. No explanation is given why the authors start with the more difficult long vowel sounds instead of the simpler short vowels.

Title of series: Open Court Basic Readers
Author: Priscilla L. McQueen
Publisher: Open Court Publishing Company, La Salle, Illinois
Date of copyright: 1963
General description of series: Beginning reading instruction based on phonics.
Evaluation of the first three books:

It is firmly understood by the author of this series that written English is a sound-symbol system and she goes about teaching the child to read on that basis. She has developed her own phonics approach, known as

306

the McQueen Method. The sounds of the English language and the spelling of these sounds are introduced in a sequential manner. The sequence is as follows: *T*, long *o* (as spelled *oe, oa, ow*), *b*, long *e* (as spelled *ee, ea, e-e, y*), *s, p*, long *i* (as spelled *igh, i-e, y*), etc. Why she begins with the long vowel sounds and their variety of spelling patterns rather than with the simpler short vowels is not explained. In addition, Miss McQueen teaches the letter sounds before teaching the letter names. She explains: "Classroom experience has demonstrated it is most efficient *to relate the groups of letters* that usually do have the same sound *directly* to the *sound itself,* by-passing the confusion caused by naming letters and using clue words."

Obviously the English sound-symbol system can be approached in more than one way. Its high degree of irregularity and inconsistency requires that the approach be as logical and orderly as possible. There is no law that says you must begin with the short vowel sounds. But their simplicity and regularity of letter-sound correspondances would suggest that one would do better to start with them than with the long vowel sounds and their variant spellings. While this reading instruction program is infinitely superior to any sight-vocabulary system, it may not be the best series, using the sound-symbol approach, available on the market. A new edition was published in 1971.

Title of series: Basic Reading
Authors: Glenn McCracken and Charles C. Walcutt
Publisher: J. B. Lippincott Company, Philadelphia, Pa. 19105
Date of copyright: 1963
General description of series: Basal series based on sound-symbol principles.
Evaluation of beginning program:

The authors of this series base their instruction on the premise that written English is a sound-symbol system. "Reading," they write, "is first of all, and essentially, the mechanical skill of decoding, of turning the printed symbols into the sounds which are language. . . . In the earliest stages of learning to read, there is very little need for thinking or reasoning on the part of the child. What he needs is practice in mastering a decoding skill, and the thinking will come along quite some time later."

The letters and their sounds are learned in the pre-primer in a sequence beginning with the short vowels and covering a number of consonants and consonant clusters. The primer and first reader cover the rest of the letter-sound correspondences. On the whole, the sound-symbol system is very logically taught with reading materials appropriately written to give practice to what the child has learned. This is a well-organized, sensible, pedagogically sound approach to beginning reading instruction and is highly recommended. Its only possible shortcoming is the presence of too many unnecessary and distracting pictures.

Title of series: The Merrill Linguistic Readers
Authors: Charles C. Fries, Rosemary G. Wilson, Mildred K. Rudolph, Lorene B. Hull, Miriam M. Fuller
Publisher: Charles E. Merrill Publishing Co., A Division of Bell Howell Company, 1300 Alum Creek Drive, Columbus, Ohio 43216
Date of copyright: 1966
General description of series: Linguistics-oriented beginning reading program.
Evaluation: This is a complete beginning reading instruction program based on linguistic principles as outlined by Charles C. Fries in his book, *Linguistics and Reading*. The beginning reading program starts with an alphabet recognition training book and includes six basic readers with supplements for the primary grades. A promotion brochure describes the program as follows:

"Primarily, the linguistic approach to reading instruction is built upon the very high degree of phonemic (spoken) and graphemic (written) *regularity* in present-day English. The linguistic approach exposes pupils to basic words which both look and sound alike but for one basic difference. This smallest difference is known as *minimum contrast*. For example: *mat - fat*; *mat - man*; *mat - met*; *mat - mate*.

"Awareness of minimum contrasts leads pupils to recognize *spelling patterns* of the English language and so to develop the ability to decode. They soon realize that the English language, despite its many irregular constructions, is really quite predictable. Thus, pupils learn to expand their decoding ability and anticipate minor variations in word patterns, which in turn allows them to read many words they were never formally taught at the very early stages of reading instruction.

"We know from experience that children dislike memorizing rules. Rote memorization only dampens interest and hampers learning. So we do not confront the child with dull (and contradictory) rules. Instead, after the Merrill Readers—and especially the alphabet book—have familiarized the pupil with letter shapes and names, he is led systematically through stories with controlled reading vocabulary based on English spelling patterns. In addition, a small number of necessary "sight" words—words, such as "the" and "of," that don't fall within a pattern—are included in these stories. With repeated practice in seeing, speaking, and spelling, the child easily learns how to use the words and what they mean. And he is never really concerned about the educational process in which he is engaged.

"We also know through experience that pictures can easily distract pupils, lead them to guess at word meanings, and hamper true creativity. Perceptive reading experts have long recognized this fact. So we have deliberately omitted pictures from the Merrill Linguistic Readers. Without pictures, the pupils can come to grips with the structure of words and sentences. By reading words—not pictures—and by intuitively understanding the structure of the language, he becomes a confident, independent reader."

That basically sums up the pure, linguistic approach to beginning reading instruction as conceived by Leonard Bloomfield and further developed by Charles C. Fries. It differs from phonics in that the child is not taught one-for-one letter-sound correspondences. Writes Fries: "Instead of the approach trying to match individual letters and separate sound units, we must develop the automatic habits of responding to the contrastive feature *of spelling patterns as identifying the word-patterns* they represent. . . . The spelling-pattern approach here employed does develop the connections between alphabetic signs of reading and the sound-patterns of talk. This spelling-pattern approach also does treat the 'words' as wholes. The significant identifying criteria used in the spelling-pattern approach differ greatly from those used by any common 'phonics' method or by any common 'word' method."

Thus the linguistic approach to beginning reading instruction is neither a phonics method nor a sight-word method, yet it has elements of both. It is based on the premise that written English is a sound-symbol system, but it believes that the letter-sound correspondences can be learned through exposure to contrastive spelling patterns. It is, of course, very easy to add phonics instruction to such a method, should the teacher or parent desire to do so.

Title of Series: The Linguistic Readers
Authors: Jack E. Richardson, Jr., Henry Lee Smith, Jr., Bernard J. Weiss, Eugene P. Williams
Publisher: Benziger, Inc., New York, N.Y.
Date of copyright: 1971
General description of series: Linguistic-oriented beginning reading program.

Evaluation of pre-primer and primer programs:

According to the authors, the major purpose underpinning The Linguistic Readers is to give the beginning reader a reliable relationship between the principal English sound units and the English writing system. Thus, theoretically, the methodology used is based on sound-symbol principles. However, the authors have essentially followed the lesson format of a sight-vocabulary basal program, with considerable story interpretation to go with each page of picture and text, no matter how scanty the text. This is a tedious process which delays the teaching of the sound-symbol system. Consonant letter sounds are learned in their initial positions in whole words, as in the Ginn Reading 360 program. The result is a hieroglyphic approach, in which the child is expected to learn to read words of which he may only know one letter-sound relationship. The vowel letter-sound correspondences are not taught explicitly. The child figures them out by seeing them used in recurring spelling patterns. It is assumed that the child will master the sound-symbol system via this approach, but since it is totally new in reading pedagogy, we shall have to wait a few years before we can evaluate the results of the method. It should be noted that this linguistic series is much closer to the Ginn approach than to the Charles Fries (Merrill Linguistic Readers) approach.

Title of Series: The READ Series (Reading Experience and Development)
Authors: Marjorie Seddon Johnson, Roy A. Kress, John D. McNeil
Publisher: American Book Company, New York, N.Y.
Date of copyright: 1968, 1971
General description of series: Nongraded basic reading program.
Evaluation of the readiness, pre-primer, and primer programs:

This is an eclectic basal reading program in which sight-reading techniques are heavily mixed with linguistic decoding techniques. The child begins reading whole words before he learns anything about letter-sound correspondences. In describing the readiness program (*Before Reading* 1 and 2, *First Step* and *Second Step*) the authors write:

> *First Step* and *Second Step* are designed to help with the development of selected prerequisite skills for success in beginning reading. Correct use of the materials will enable the young learner to acquire competency in using intellectual tools for learning to read.
>
> Examples of these prerequisites for reading are: (a) the ability

to comprehend the language of instruction, such as the terms "same" and "different," (b) the ability to interpret pictures, (c) the ability to order events in a story, (d) the ability to draw inferences and make analogies, and (e) the ability to identify constituent sounds in spoken words. More than fifty-six specific skills and abilities are introduced in *First Step* and *Second Step*.

Thus, the authors are rather "eclectic" in their approach. In *Before Reading 2 (Second Step)* the child is introduced to the letters and their names. In the *Third Step* the child learns to identify letters in isolation and in words.

In the pre-primers the child is introduced to a "basic recognition vocabulary," that is, a sight vocabulary. However, whereas the old Dick and Jane sight vocabulary deliberately obscured the alphabetic principle, this sight vocabulary has been chosen to help the child discover sound-symbol relationships. The authors describe their technique as follows:

> At the Pre-primer level, for instance, he [the child] acquires a basic recognition vocabulary by meeting concurrently several words which fall into a definite pattern. The four skill pages preceding each story provide the child with an opportunity to contact the new vocabulary before he is called upon to read the story. Each new word is accompanied by pictorial aids and is introduced in a psychological and/or verbal setting. The teacher will find in the insert pages, marginal notes, and in the overprint for these pages specific suggestions for directing the child's perception of these words through using appropriately his language-conceptual background.
>
> *Mastery of Patterns*. As words which fall into a new phoneme-grapheme pattern are introduced, pattern boxes are provided on the skill pages with suggestions for ways to direct the child's attention to the pattern. As new instances of the pattern occur, they are presented in boxes with "known" words from that pattern so that the child can be aided in using his analytic skills and then synthesizing the results of his analysis to master the "new" word. This constant review of previous learnings continues through successive levels until mastery is virtually assured for every child.

Reduced to laymen's terms this means that the child must basically teach himself the letter-sound correspondences. He is, of course, given help by the phoneme-grapheme pattern approach, which is essentially a syllabary approach to our sound-symbol system, whereby our written letters are taught as representing spoken syllables rather than individual sounds. Thus the simplicity and logic of the alphabetic approach is not taken advantage of at all.

While the READ system is an improvement over the sight-reading basal series of the past in that it recognizes that written English is a sound-symbol system and it teaches the alphabet in the readiness program, it still retains many undesirable features of the hieroglyphic approach. These include too many distracting pictures, a strong emphasis on story interpretation, the teaching of whole words before the letter sounds are known, and a syllabary approach to the sound-symbol system. It is hard to say how well children will learn to read via this hybrid product.

Title of series: SWRL Beginning Reading Program
Authors: Southwest Regional Laboratory for Educational Research and Development (Inglewood, California). Program Director: Dr. Howard Sullivan, assisted by Dr. Fred Niedermeyer, Leslie Bronstein, Carol Labeaune, Dr. Suzanne Baker
Publisher: Ginn and Company, a Xerox Company, Lexington, Mass. 02173
Date of copyright: 1972. Materials pass into public domain January 1, 1978.
General description of series: This is a kindergarten reading program consisting of 52 12-to-14-page story books, designed to teach children to read about 100 words by sight before they enter first grade.

Evaluation of the program: This is a product of the new eclectic approach to reading instruction in which the basic Dick and Jane technique of sight reading—repetition of sight words—is augmented by a linguistically oriented choice of vocabulary and a simultaneous introduction to some letter sounds. For example, in the first book, in which the child is taught to read the words "I see Sam" by sight, the child is also taught the names of the letters s, m, e in lower case and capitals and to know the sounds of s and m. Thus, before the child has been formally introduced to the alphabet as a set of symbols with specific meanings, he is introduced to whole words, some letter names and some letter sounds in a way that may confuse him. The emphasis in this book and the others in the program is in the story, the animal characters, and pictures. The letter names are taught in conjunction with the words used in the stories, and some letter sounds are taught.

At completion of the program, the child is expected to read 100 words and to know the names of all the letters of the alphabet, but not in alphabetical order, and to know the sounds of consonants *s, m, t, n, d, w, f, r, l, n, h, b,* and consonant digraphs *th* and *sh.* He is also expected to grasp the vowel sounds of *a, i, e,* and *u* in such syllables or word elements as *at, it, eet, an, ad, ill, am, et, ut, eed, en.* The vowel sounds, for some unknown reason, are taught as parts of word elements rather than as individual letters. This is a syllabary approach to the teaching of the vowels.

The basic problem with the approach of this program is that it sets up conflicting learning habits. Sight reading requires a hieroglyphic approach to words and alphabetic reading requires a sound-symbol approach. By trying to blend the two approaches in one primary course of instruction the child can become confused as to what reading is, what words are, and what the nature of the alphabet is. The confusion is inherent in the methodology and no child of kindergarten age is equipped to figure out for himself what the true nature of alphabetic reading is when the adults who conceived the program are obviously not too sure of it themselves.

Title of series: The Bookmark Reading Program
Authors: Margaret Early, Marian Y. Adell, Elizabeth K. Cooper, Nancy Santeusanio
Publisher: Harcourt Brace Jovanovich, Inc., 757 Third Avenue, New York, N. Y. 10017
Date of copyright: 1970
General description of series: Eclectic basal series combining sight and phonetic methods.
Evaluation of beginning reading program:

Of the new eclectic basal reading programs, this one pays the most lip-service to the alphabetic principle but then proceeds to violate it with blatant hieroglyphic methodology. Thus, although the child is introduced to the alphabet letters by name in a curious nonalphabetical order, he is required to learn a vocabulary of thirty-two words in the first pre-primer on the basis of only eleven initial consonant sounds. The result is that the child is forced to learn what is, essentially, a sight vocabulary by way of configuration and context clues. The initial consonants merely serve as phonetic clues. The program's method lacks logic and consistency and, in fact, contradicts itself. The following quotations from the teacher's edition will give the reader an idea of the schizoid approach taken by the authors:

"Meaning is considered primary in this program. Because children encounter words in meaningful context, they are able to decode many words which are only partially consistent with the one-to-one phoneme-grapheme correspondence. They use context and initial consonant knowledge to decode words that contain vowel letters that represent other than the so-called short vowel sounds."

"At the Preprimer level, the most broadly applicable technique is the use of sound-letter knowledge with context clues. To establish children's understanding of sound-letter relationships, the vocabulary of the Pre-primer provides a high percentage of regularly spelled out words. These words suggest to children that a large body of English is consistently phonetic; that English is an alphabetic language. At the same time, the Preprimers introduce a smaller percentage of words that represent seeming inconsistencies in spelling patterns. The presence of these words suggests to children that phonics is a useful but limited tool for identifying words."

Either written English is an alphabetic language or it isn't. Apparently, the authors of this program can't make up their minds, and their confusion is thus passed on to the children. Thus, the child is forced to apply both hieroglyphic and phonetic techniques to figuring out the words in an alphabetic writing system. This makes beginning reading needlessly more complicated than it has to be. At the completion of the first pre-primer the child has been introduced to eleven initial consonant sounds—*s, b, w, g, m, r, l, h, d, p, t*—and has learned thirty-two words. Obviously a knowledge of eleven initial consonants is hardly sufficient for a child to be able to read thirty-two words alphabetically. So he must rely heavily on configuration gimmicks and context clues. The thirty-two words are, in order of instruction: *Bing, Sandy, and, the, was, sun, up, good, morning, in, ran, after, rabbit, met, away, log, bug, little, a, grass, big, bee, went, hid, hill, lost, grasshopper, hop, down, duck, pond, turtle.* The words are all learned on the basis of initial consonants and configuration and context clues, except for words beginning with vowels which are learned purely as sight words.

Mixing hieroglyphic and alphabetic methods is bound to create confusion in the minds of some children. One of the most important things a child must learn in an alphabetic system is that the sequence of letters in the *entire* word has meaning, and this the Bookmark program fails to teach in its beginning reading program.

Appendix II:
"Modes of Teaching Children to Read"

[This essay, written in 1844, is the first critique of the sight-vocabulary or whole-word method ever published. It was written by Samuel Stillman Greene (1810-1883) in behalf of the Association of Boston Masters for their *Remarks on the Seventh Annual Report of the Honorable Horace Mann, Secretary of the Massachusetts Board of Education.* This was the opening salvo of a dispute which was to go on for over a year and finally reveal the fact that Thomas H. Gallaudet was the originator of the new sight-vocabulary method. At the time of the dispute, Greene was principal of the Phillips Grammar School in Boston. In 1851 he became professor of didactics at Brown University. He also became known for his excellent textbooks on English grammar.]

Reading, justly deserves the first rank among the studies of our schools. As an accomplishment alone, it possesses intrinsic excellence; but, considered as fundamental to other departments of learning, its value cannot be too highly estimated. In judging, therefore, of the merits of any system by which this branch may be taught, *remote, as well as immediate effects should be duly regarded.* A child, even at the threshold of his education, should be subjected to any delay, which the formation of correct habits may require. He should never be hurried over difficulties, at first concealed, yet, in his progress, unavoidable, simply to make his entrance into the temple of learning, easy and agreeable. A system of instruction is subjected to an unworthy test, when the chief excellence claimed for it consists in *smoothing* the path of the learner. To ascertain where the *true* path lies, and to exhibit what, to us, seems erroneous, are the objects of the following discussion.

Though differing from Mr. Mann, upon this subject, we would, by no means, be supposed to undervalue his efforts in the cause of education, or detract aught from the benefits his labors have conferred. Our dissent from his views arises from an honest conviction that, if adopted, they would retard the progress of sound learning. His opinions on the method of teaching reading, may be learned from the following quotations, taken from his second and seventh annual reports, and from his "Lecture on Spelling-Books, delivered before the American Institute of Instruction, August, 1841."

> "I am satisfied that our greatest error, in teaching children to read, lies in beginning with the alphabet;—in giving them what are called the 'Names of the Letters,' *a,b,c,*&c."... "Although in former reports and publications I have dwelt at length upon what seems to me the absurdity of teaching to read by *beginning* with the alphabet, yet I feel constrained to recur to the subject again,—being persuaded that no thorough reform will ever be effected in our schools until this practice is abolished."—*Seventh Annual Report,* pp. 91, 92.

> "Whole words should be taught before teaching the letters of which they are composed."—*Lecture on Spelling-Books,* p. 13.

> "The mode of teaching words first, however, is not mere theory; nor is it new. It has now been practised for some time in the primary schools in the city of Boston,—in which there are four or five thousand children,—and it is found to succeed better than the old mode."—*Common School Journal,* Vol. I. p. 326.

> "During the first year of a child's life, he perceives, thinks, and acquires something of a store of ideas, without any reference to words or letters. After this, the wonderful faculty of language begins to develop itself. Children then utter words,—the names of objects around them,—as whole sounds, and without any conception of the letters of which those words are composed. In speaking the word 'apple,' for instance, young children think no more of the Roman letters which spell it, than, in eating the fruit, they think of the chemical ingredients,—the oxygen, hydrogen, and carbon,—which

316

compose it. Hence, presenting them with the alphabet, is giving them what they never saw, heard, or thought of before. It is as new as algebra, and, to the eye, not very unlike it. But printed names of known things are the signs of sounds which their ears have been accustomed to hear, and their organs of speech to utter, and which may excite agreeable feelings and associations, by reminding them of the objects named. When put to learning the letters of the alphabet first, the child has no acquaintance with them, either by the eye, the ear, the tongue, or the mind; but if put to learning familiar words first, he already knows them by the ear, the tongue, and the mind, while his eye only is unacquainted with them. He is thus introduced to a stranger, through the medium of old acquaintances. It can hardly be doubted, therefore, that a child would learn to name any twenty-six familiar words, much sooner than the twenty-six unknown, unheard, and unthought-of letters of the alphabet."—*Ibid.*

"The practice of beginning with the 'Names of the Letters,' is founded upon the idea that it facilitates the combination of them[?] into words. On the other hand I believe that if two children, of equal quickness and capacity, are taken, one of whom can name every letter of the alphabet, at sight, and the other does not know them from Chinese characters, the latter can be most easily taught to read,—or, in other words, that learning the letters first is an absolute hindrance." . . . "The 'Names of the Letters' are not elements in the sounds of words; or are so, only in a comparatively small number of cases. To the twenty-six letters of the alphabet, the child is taught to give twenty-six sounds, and no more."—*Seventh Annual Report*, p. 92.

"But, not only do the same vowels appear in different dresses, like masqueraders, but like harlequins they exchange garbs with each other."—*Ibid*, p. 95.

"In one important particular, the consonants are more perplexing than the vowels. The very definition of a consonant, as given in the spelling-books, is, 'a letter which has no sound or only an imperfect one, without the help of a vowel.' And yet the definers themselves, and the teachers who follow them, proceed immediately to give a perfect sound to all the consonants. If a consonant has 'only an imperfect sound,' why, in teaching children to read, should not this imperfect sound be taught them? And again,

317

in giving the names of the consonants, why should the vowel be sometimes prefixed, and sometimes suffixed?"—*Ibid.*

"For another reason, the rapidity of acquisition will be greater, if words are taught before letters. To learn the words signifying objects, qualities, actions, with which the child is familiar, turns his attention to those objects, if present, or revives the idea of them, if absent, and thus they may be made the source of great interest and pleasure."—*Common School Journal*, Vol. I. p. 326.

For the sake of distinction, and from its recent origin, this mode of teaching reading is called the new method. To whom belongs the honor of its discovery seems not to have been fully ascertained. Miss Edgeworth, in the opinion of Mr. Pierce, was the first to recommend it. "It is practiced," he says, "by Mr. Wood, late principal of the Sessional school, Edinburgh; by Jacotot, the celebrated teacher of the Borough school, and others. It is founded in reason and philosophy; and it must become general."

The plan of teaching, as developed by the publications of the secretary, by Mr. Pierce's "Lecture on Reading," and by various other publications, is substantially as follows: whole, but familiar words, without any reference to the letters which compose them, are first to be taught. The alphabet, as such, is kept entirely concealed. Some three or four words are arranged on a single page of a primer prepared for the purpose, or are written on the black-board several times, and in various orders, as follows: cat—dog—chair; dog—cat—chair; chair—cat—dog. These are pointed out to the child, who is required to utter them at the teacher's dictation, and to learn them by a careful inspection of their forms, as whole objects. After these are supposed to be learned, new words are dictated to the pupil, in the same manner as before. This process is repeated, till the child has acquired a sufficient number of words to read easy sentences in which they are combined. To what extent this mode of learning words should be carried, is, nowhere, definitely stated. Mr. Pierce says: "When they are perfectly familiar with the first words chosen, and the sentence which they compose, select other words, and form other sentences; and so on indefinitely." He then proceeds to recommend several books, as containing suitable sentences for this purpose. Of these, one prepared by Miss Peabody, now Mrs. Mann, contains, he says, "a full illustration of the whole method, with words and sentences." Since this book is also recommended, by the secretary, as containing the best exemplification of the whole plan, it may be taken as a standard, by which to form an estimate

318

of the extent to which the friends of the new system would carry this process of teaching words.

More than a hundred words, having little or no apparent connection with each other, and arranged in the manner above described, occupy the first twenty or thirty pages. Then follows a reading lesson, in which these words, with many more, are joined together in sentences. Subsequent to this lesson, and arranged as before, is another set of words followed by another reading lesson, and so of the remaining part of the book, save some fifteen pages containing the alphabet, a few lessons in spelling, and a few cuts for drawing. The whole number of words in this "Primer" does not differ materially from seven hundred. Derivative words, though differing but slightly from their primitives, are, in this reckoning, to be counted, because this minuteness of difference enhances the difficulty of acquisition. "When the scholars," says Mr. Pierce, "have reached this stage of advancement," by which, it is supposed, he means, have learned all the words contained in this or other books which he recommends, "you may teach them the *name* and the *power* of the letters, especially the latter; though I can conceive no great disadvantage from deferring it to a still later period;" that is, till they have learned more words. It appears then, that at some period in the child's progress, after learning either seven hundred, a thousand, or two thousand words, he is to commence the laborious and unwelcome task of learning "the unknown, unheard, and unthought-of letters of the alphabet." Here, if ever, it is supposed, he begins to learn how to combine letters into words; that is, learns how to spell; and thus, by a new process, acquires the power of uttering words, without having them previously pronounced by the teacher.

As this system is somewhat new, and has not been well tested by experiment, although its immediate adoption is earnestly recommended by high authority, it cannot be reasonably supposed that a system by which the present generation were taught to read, a system as prevalent as is the mode of alphabetical writing, and one which, from its long and uninterrupted use, has become venerable with age, will be abolished, unless good and substantial reasons can be given for such change. Indeed, change itself, is undesirable. If the new system can be shown only to be equally as good as the old, no change should take place. Positive proof of its superior advantages alone, should be considered, or, at least, the *probabilities* of a successful issue, should so far exceed the chances of a failure, as to amount to a good degree of certainty. As, until quite recently, the secretary has presented, rather than strongly advocated the claims of the system, his opinions, have called for nothing more than a passing consideration. But, as his personal and

319

official influence is now exerted for its adoption, that our silence may not be construed into assent, we feel impelled to express a respectful dissent from his views.

Aware that this position is to be sustained against prevailing usage, he has given his reasons for believing, "that no thorough reform will ever be effected in our schools until this practice [of beginning with the alphabet] is abolished." These reasons are drawn,

1st.—From what he conceives to be the *natural order* of acquisition.

2d.—From the anomalies of the alphabet.

3d.—From an impression which he has, that "the rapidity of acquisition will be greater, if words are taught before letters."

With us, as teachers, the main question is, whether or not we approve of the new system, and can recommend its universal adoption.

In assuming the negative of the question, it is first to be shown that the arguments urged in favor of the system, fail to make it even *equal* in value to the old, much more *superior;* and, then, that there are reasons of a positive character, which are adverse to it, and serve to show it vastly *inferior* to the old system.

Before entering upon a consideration of the separate arguments which have been urged in its support, some general remarks will be necessary, in order to remove whatever is irrelevant to the question, and to restrict it within its appropriate limits.

1st.—Whether words should be taught before letters, is a question which should be confined strictly to written language.

That much irrelevant matter, employed in the secretary's argument, arises from confounding written with spoken language, appears from the following passage in his lecture: "The advantages of teaching children, by beginning with whole words, are many. . . . What is to be learned is affiliated to what is already known." So in the quotation at the beginning of this article, he says: "But if put to learning familiar words first, he [the child] already knows them by the *ear*, the *tongue*, and the *mind*, while his *eye* only is unacquainted with them. He is thus introduced to a *stranger*, through the medium of old acquaintances." The principle here claimed for the new system, is that of passing from the *known* to the *unknown*. The principle is good; it is of its application that we complain. The secretary speaks of *"familiar words;"* the question arises, *What* is familiar? *What* is known? When we speak of words, we may mean either the *audible*, or the *written* signs of our ideas. The term *word* is, therefore, ambiguous, unless it be so qualified as to have a specific reference. In speaking of familiar words, nothing can be meant except that the child can *utter* them; he knows them only as *audible* signs. To say that *printed* words are familiar to a child's tongue, can have no other meaning than that he is accustomed to the taste of ink; to say that such words are familiar to his *ear*, is to attribute to that ink, a tongue; and to say that they are familiar to the mind, is to suppose the child already able to read. *Now, as reading aloud is nothing less than translating written into audible signs, a knowledge of the latter, whatever may be the system of teaching, is presupposed to exist, and is about as necessary to the one learning to read, as would be knowledge of the English language to one who would translate Greek into English.*

To illustrate. Take the printed word *mother*; when pronounced, it is familiar "to the ear, the tongue, and the mind." Does this familiarity aid the child in the least, in comprehending the printed picture? Can he, from his acquaintance with the audible sign, utter that sign by looking upon the six unknown letters which spell it?

The truth is, in all that belongs, appropriately, to the question under consideration, the word is unknown; unknown as a whole, unknown in all its parts, and unknown as to the mode of combining those parts. *The question, when restricted to its appropriate limits, is simply this; 'What is the best method of teaching a child to comprehend printed words?'* All that is said about the familiarity of the child with the audible sign, and the thing signified by it, is claimed in common by the advocates of both systems, and is, therefore, totally irrelevant in the discussion of this question; since what belongs equally to opposite parties can have no influence in a question in which they differ.

What though "printed names of known things are the signs of sounds which their [the children's] ears have been accustomed to hear, and their organs of speech to utter, and which may excite agreeable feelings and associations, by reminding them of the objects named?" Is the rose any the less agreeable to the mind of the child, or, is the word *rose*, when pronounced, any the less familiar to his organs of speech or to his ear, because its printed sign is learned by combining the letters r-o-s-e? Or does the mere act of telling the child to say *rose*, while pointing to the picture, formed of four unknown letters, in any way enhance its agreeableness?

The question, then, is not whether a child shall be "introduced to a stranger through the medium of old acquaintances," for, in fact, by the new system, this introduction is made through the medium of the teacher's voice.

The true question at issue is, whether the child shall be furnished with an attendant to announce the name of the stranger, or whether he shall be furnished with *letters* of introduction by which, unattended, he may make the acquaintance, not of some seven hundred strangers merely, but of the whole seventy thousand unknown members of our populous vocabulary.

2d.—The question must be confined not merely to written language, but to written language of a particular species.

When the secretary, in speaking of a child after the first year of his life, says that, then, "the wonderful faculty of language begins to develop itself," he undoubtedly refers to spoken language. And well may that be called a wonderful faculty by which, through the agency of the vocal organs, we can so modify *mere sounds*, as to send them forth freighted with thoughts which may cause the hearts of others to thrill with extatic delight, or throb with unutterable anguish. And no wonder that there should have existed, early in the history of the world, a desire to enchain and represent to the eye these evanescent messengers of thought. Hence the early and rude attempts at writing, by means of pictures and symbols. But these, unfortunately, were representatives of the *message*, not the *messenger*; of the idea, not the sound which conveys it. *At length arose that wonderful invention, the art of representing to the eye, by means of letters, the component parts of a spoken word, so that now, not merely the errand, but the bearer stands pictured before us. The grand and distinctive feature of this invention is, that it establishes a connection between the written and the audible signs of our ideas.* It throws, as it were, a bridge across the otherwise impassable gulf which must ever have separated the one from the other. The hieroglyphics and symbols of the ancients, performed but one function. To those who, by a purely arbitrary association, were able to pass from the sign to the thing signified, they were representatives of ideas—and ideas *merely;* hence they are called ideographic characters, and that mode of writing has been denominated the *symbolic*, and is exemplified in the Chinese language.

On the other hand, words written with alphabetic characters perform two functions. Taken as whole pictures, they, like Chinese characters, represent ideas; but taken as composed of alphabetic elements which represent simple sounds, they conduct us directly to the audible sign which, in the case of common words, we have from childhood been accustomed to associate with the thing signified. Owing to the last office which these words perform, namely, that of representing sounds, this mode of writing is called the *phonetic*. It has been said with truth, that "the art of writing, especially when reduced to simple phonetic alphabets like ours, has, perhaps, done more than any other invention for the improvement of the human race." If any one wishes still further to be convinced of the difference between the two, *let him compare the figure 5, which is purely a symbol, with the written word five;* the one gives no idea whatever of the *spoken word,* whereas the other conducts us directly to it. Here the contrast is too striking to be misapprehended. A person might read Chinese, without knowing a single sound of the language, simply because Chinese characters were never intended to represent sounds.

The new system of teaching reading, abandons entirely this distinctive feature of the phonetic mode of writing, and our words are treated as though they were capable of performing but one function, that of representing ideas. The language, although written with alphabetic characters, becomes, to all intents and purposes, a symbolic language. *Now we say, as ours is designedly a phonetic language, no system of teaching ought to meet with public favor, that strips it of its principal power.* And we confess ourselves not a little surprised that the secretary, who cherishes such correct views of the inferiority of the Chinese language, should urge us to convert ours into Chinese. He says, in his second annual report, (*Com. Sch. Journal*, Vol. I., pp. 323, 324:) "It is well known that science itself, among scientific men, can never advance far beyond a scientific language in which to record its laws and principles. An unscientific language, like the Chinese, will keep a people unscientific forever." Besides losing the vantage ground which we now possess, of passing with ease from the visible to the audible sign, and the reverse, we meet with another objection to the proposed change. As our language was written with alphabetic characters, our words are too long and cumbrous for becoming mere symbols. A single character would be vastly superior to our *trissyllables* and *polysyllables.* If the new system prevails, we may soon expect a demand for reform in this respect. As it now is, the child must meet with all the difficulties that necessarily accompany the acquisition of the Chinese language, and these greatly increased by the forms of our words.

The defenders of the new system seem to lose sight of the nature and design of the alphabetic mode of writing, as an *invention.* To understand an invention, we must first know the law of nature which gave rise to it, and then the several parts of the invented system, as well as the adaptation of these parts, when combined, to accomplish some useful purpose. Thus, to explain the steam-engine, the chemical law by which water is converted into steam must first be understood, and in connection with it, that of elasticity, common to all aeriform bodies. Then follows—what constitutes the main point in this illustration—the explanation of the several parts of the machine, with the modes of combining them, so as to gain that immense power, which is found so valuable in the arts. Take another illustration, more nearly allied to the subject under consideration. It was discovered a few years since, that a piece of iron exposed, under given circumstances, to a galvanic current, would become a powerful magnet, and that it would cease to be such, the instant the current was intercepted. Little was it then thought, that this simple discovery would give rise to an invention by which the winged lightning, fit messenger of thought, could be employed to enable the inhabitants of Maine to converse with their otherwise distant neighbors in Louisiana, with almost as much ease, as though the parties were seated in the same parlor.

Now, no one will pretend, that to make use of the steam-engine successfully, all that is necessary is to gain an idea of it, as a *whole*. The several parts, with their various relations and combinations, must be explained. Equally necessary is it, in managing the magnetic telegraph, for the operator to be familiar with the laws of electricity, and the adaptation of the several parts of the machine, to accomplish, by means of that agent, the object proposed. But who would think of interpreting the results of its operation, the dots, the lines, the spaces, by looking upon them as constituting a single picture?

To apply these illustrations. *It was discovered, ages ago, that Nature had endowed the organs of speech with the power of uttering a limited number of simple sounds. From this discovery originated the invention of letters to represent these elementary sounds. Letters constitute the machinery of the invention. They are the tools by which the art of reading is to be acquired;* and a thorough knowledge of letters bears the same relation to reading, as does a thorough acquaintance with the parts of a steam-engine, or of the magnetic telegraph to a skilful use of these instruments. The new system proposes to abandon, for a time at least, all that is peculiar to this invention; all that distinguishes it from the rude and unphilosophical system of symbolic writing, which, centuries ago, gave place to it, throughout every portion of the civilized world. *Now, since such an estimate was placed upon this invention by the ancients, as to secure its adoption to the exclusion of all other methods of writing; and since a trial of many centuries has served only to confirm mankind in the belief of its superiority over every other system; we can but protest against the adoption of a mode of teaching, that subjects the child to such inconvenience and loss.*

3d.—Mr. Mann has not been more unfortunate in blending spoken with written language, than in confounding the names of letters with their powers.

All his remarks, therefore, which proceed upon the supposition that the defenders of the old system advocate a plan of teaching, by which the *name-sounds* of letters are to be joined, as "l-e-g" into "elegy," can have no weight in the discussion of this question.

The word *letter*, as applied to the alphabet, is ambiguous, unless accompanied by some term, or explanatory phrase, to show what is intended. In referring to one of the elementary sounds which enters into the formation of a *spoken* word, we call that *sound* a letter; so, in speaking of the conventional sign, which represents that sound to the eye, as the character *h*, seen in a *printed* word, that sign we call a letter; both the sound and the sign, take the *name aitch*, for example; this *name*, in turn, is called a letter. Now, to prevent confusion, these three things, the power, the character, and the name, should be kept entirely distinct from each other. In a *spoken* word, elementary *sounds* are combined; in a *written* word, elementary *characters:* in neither written nor spoken words, are the *names* of letters joined, except in those instances, where the name and power are the same, as in the case of the long sounds of the vowels.

A perfect alphabet would require that the thirty-five elementary sounds of the language, as given by Dr. Rush, should have each one representative, and no more. With such an alphabet, the transition from the written, to the audible sign, would be made without the possibility of a mistake; and, equally certain would be the passage from the sound of a word, to its written sign, in which consists the art of spelling. *But we have not such an alphabet. Ours is imperfect. A single letter has several different sounds; the same sound is represented by different letters and combinations of letters, and many of the letters in some of their uses become silent. These anomalies are the cause of inconveniences as sensibly felt by the defenders of the old system, as by those who, to effect, for the child, a temporary escape from one difficulty, would thrust him into others equally great. The defenders of both systems agree that these difficulties must, at some time, be met and mastered.*

Were a language reduced to writing by means of a perfect alphabet even, it is not difficult to see how, in time, that alphabet would become corrupted. It is probable that, at the time of the invention of letters, it was intended that each character should represent but one sound. But, as the sounds of the language to be written were better analyzed, either new letters, as among the Greeks, were added, or, the same letter was made to represent more than one sound.

Again, different nations have adopted the same alphabetic characters; but in applying them to the elementary sounds of their respective languages, the rules of uniformity were disregarded; thus, the sound represented by e in English, is represented by i in French, and so of others. Then, as the words of one country, like its citizens, may emigrate to, and become naturalized in another, retaining, in the latter, their original orthography and pronunciation, new sounds must inevitably be attached to the same letter; hence, the French sound of *i* in *fatigue*. In the same way, many equivocal words have been introduced into our language; thus, *bark*, derived from a Saxon word, means the noise made by dogs; so, again, the same word, derived from the French *barque*, signifies a vessel, while the Danish word *bark*, signifying the covering of a tree, has been introduced, unchanged, into the language; all of which give three widely different meanings to the same word. Add to these circumstances, the mutations to which every language is subject, from age to age, and it is easy to account for such changes as are seen in the words, *could, would, should,* and others, in which the *l* was sounded by the generation before us; so also, usage requires us to retain the silent letters of such words as *catarrh, phthisic,* and many others derived from the ancient languages, that their etymology may not be lost.

These various changes have created the necessity of referring to the same alphabetic *character* and *name* some two, three, or more elementary sounds; thus *ce* is the *name* of the character *c*; to this name and character we are obliged to refer a hissing sound, which is also represented by *s*; another sound represented by *k*; and still a third, represented by *z*. Another evil arising from such mutations, is, that many letters, having become silent, must be retained in the formation of the written sign, although worse than useless in determining the audible.

Such being the three-fold meaning to be attached to the word letter, and such being the condition to which various circumstances have conspired to reduce our alphabet, let us inquire, if Mr. Mann has not been led astray, by neglecting to make these necessary distinctions.

He says, on page 92:

> "The advocate for teaching the letters asks, if the elements of an art or science should not be first taught. To this I would reply, that the 'Names of the Letters' are not elements in the sounds of words; or are so, only in a comparatively small number of cases. To the twenty-six letters of the alphabet, the child is taught to give twenty-six sounds, and no more. According to Worcester, however,—who may be considered one of the best authorities on this subject,—the six vowels only, have, collectively, thirty-three different sounds. In addition to these, there are the sounds of twenty consonants, of diphthongs and triphthongs."

Before proceeding to show that the secretary has confounded those things which should be kept distinct from each other, it is necessary

326

to correct an erroneous statement which he has made, respecting the number of different sounds in the language. It is not true, nor does Worcester, anywhere, as we can find, assert, that "the six vowels only, have, collectively, thirty-three *different* sounds." It *is* true that he assigns to *a*, seven sounds,—to *e*, five,—to *i*, five,—to *o*, six,—to *u*, six,—and to *y*, four; and that these several numbers when added, amount to thirty-three. But if any one will take the pains to compare the sounds of *y* with those of *i*, those of *a* with those of *e*, and so on, he will find an illustration of what we have already said; that the same sound is represented by different letters; and if he will go still further, and select from Worcester's table of vowel sounds, the *different* ones *only*, he will find less than half thirty-three. A little further on, he proceeds to say that "it would be difficult, and would not compensate the trouble, to compute the number of *different* sounds which a good speaker gives to the different letters, and combinations of letters, in our language,—not including the changes of rhetorical emphasis, cadence, and intonation. But, if analyzed, they would be found to amount to hundreds." Here, it seems, he has fallen into the same error; and his statements are calculated to mislead the reader. The greatest number of elementary sounds in our language does not exceed forty-three. Barber gives the number forty-three; others, forty-one. But Dr. Rush, who probably gave more time and thought to the analysis of the human voice, than any other person, fixes the number at thirty-five. Never, before, have we known it placed as high as hundreds. We have been the more careful to make these corrections, that the reader may see how much weight to attach to Mr. Mann's remarks on the 97th page of the report, where he makes use of these erroneous statements, to show a want of analogy between teaching reading, on the one hand, and written music, on the other. He says:

"Some defenders of the old system have attempted to find an analogy for their practice, in the mode of teaching to sing by first learning the gamut. They compare the notes of the gamut which are afterwards to be combined into tunes, to the letters of the alphabet to be afterwards combined into words. But one or two considerations will show the greatest difference between the principal case and the supposed analogy. In written music there is always a scale consisting of at least five lines, and of course with four spaces between, and often one or two lines and spaces, above or below the regular scale; and both the name of a note and the sound to be given it can always be known by observing its place in the scale. To make the cases analogous, there should be a scale of thirty-three places at least, for the six vowels only,—and this scale should be enlarged so as to admit the twenty consonants, and all their combinations with the vowels. Such a scale could hardly be crowded into an octavo page. The largest pages now used would not contain more than a single printed line each; and the matter now contained in an octavo volume would fill the shelves of a good-sized library. If music were taught as unphilosophically as reading;—if its eight notes were first arranged in one straight vertical line, to be learned by name, and then transferred to a straight horizontal line, where they should follow each other promiscuously, and without any clew to the particular sound to be given them in each particular place, it seems not too much to say, that not one man in a hundred thousand would ever become a musician."

Here the reader will see that Mr. Mann has compared an erroneous conception of the elements of our language, with an erroneous conception of the elements of written music. A scale of *thirty-three* places, at least, for the six vowels only! And this scale so *enlarged* as to admit the twenty consonants, and all their *combinations with the vowels!* It will suffice to say, concerning this scale, that it must be very much reduced; so that he need not be alarmed at the cumbrous size to which our books may attain. But, Mr. Mann seems to be entirely unacquainted with the nature and difficulties of written music, or, at least, he has given, if any at all, a very imperfect and erroneous exhibition of them.

In the science of Music, the Natural or Diatonic scale, consists of eight sounds or tones. The five intermediate tones furnished by the Chromatic scale, added to these, increase the number to thirteen different sounds.

The compass of the human voice, if cultivated, is sufficient to embrace about two and a half octaves, or from thirty to thirty-five different sounds. With instruments, the number of different sounds may be extended almost without limit. We are concerned, however, with the human voice It will be seen that the number of sounds which are to be represented by visible symbols, in music, is about the same as the number of elementary sounds in our language. It will be seen, moreover, that it is not one "scale," [staff?] with its added lines, that can represent these thirty or thirty-five different sounds. There is a staff for the Base, one for the Tenor, and one for the Alto and Soprano. Besides, it should be understood, that a note on a given line or space, affected by a flat or sharp, is sounded in the former case, half a tone higher, and in the latter, half a tone lower, than it otherwise would be; or, in other words, it can have, without changing its position in

328

the staff, three different sounds. But, it is not in this particular, that the principal difficulty consists. A note placed on the letter C, for example, will, in all cases, receive the same absolute sound. It now stands as 1, or the key note, and the syllable *do*, is applied to it. Let F be sharped, and then, although this note still has the same sound as before, its relation to the other notes is entirely changed. It now becomes 4 of the scale, and the syllable *fa* is applied to it. Let C now be sharped, and the note still remains unchanged on the staff, but the original sound is lost from the scale; the note which then represented it, becomes 7 of the scale, and is called *si*. Next, let D be sharped, and a similar change takes place, and so on, till all the notes are sharped. Again, taking the scale as at first, let B be affected by a flat, and the original key-note becomes 5 of the scale, and is called *sol*; then let E be flatted, and so on, till all the notes have been flatted, and changes of relation will take place for every successive flat. Now, a change of this kind, affects the relation, not of one merely, but of every note of the scale, and the number of changes far exceeds the highest number of sounds attached to any letter of the alphabet. If any one will take the trouble to estimate the whole number of such changes, for all the notes, he will discover some of the difficulties to be overcome by the pupil in this branch of science. Each transposition of the scale is equivalent to giving a new sound to each note; it does give a new name, and a new relation. The only point, therefore, in which the analogy fails, is this: the number of changes which a note may undergo, is much greater than the number of sounds represented by any letter; and the labor of acquiring the notes of music, is very *much* greater than that of learning the letters of the alphabet. Such, certainly, is the opinion of the ablest professors of music in our country.

In respect to emphasis, pauses, and expression, reading and music are analogous; and so, in regard to the elements, in all essential points, they resemble each other. So much has been said, to correct an erroneous statement, and the conclusion drawn from it. Let us now inquire, if the secretary has not fallen into an error, equally inexcusable, from a misconception of the several functions of a letter. We understand him tacitly to concede the principle, that "the elements of an art or science should be first taught." But, in his subsequent remarks, if we comprehend their design, he denies, that the defenders of the old system are entitled to this conceded principle, because the *names* of the letters are not elements in the sounds of words. We never supposed, nor do we know of a single advocate of the old system, who ever supposed, that the *names* of letters, entered into the formation of words; as, h-a-t, into *aitchaitee*; "l-e-g," into "elegy."

Names were not given to letters for such a purpose. They were assigned to them, for the same reason that names are given to other objects, to aid us in referring to the objects themselves. One would scarcely expect to convince even a child, that there was neither pastry, fruit, cinnamon, nor sugar, in the pie he was eating, by telling him that pies are never made of such names as pastry, cinnamon, &c.

We agree with Mr. Mann, when he says that, with the exception of the long sounds of the vowels, "the 'Names of the Letters' are not elements in the sounds of words;" but we differ from him, if he denies that the *characters*, called letters, are elements in printed words, or that the *sounds* which they represent, are elements in spoken words. One, or both of these two things are implied, when it is asserted, that letters are elements in the formation of words.

The question then returns. Should not letters be taught before words; since, in two important respects, they are elements?

The argument, found upon the next four or five pages of the report, proceeds upon the supposition that the *name-sounds* of letters, are combined into words; and if it will avail the secretary anything, we are ready to grant that he has fully shown, what would have been most cheerfully admitted at the outset, that "the *names* of the letters, are not elements in the sounds of words." But when he, in apparent triumph, says, "this, surely, is a most disastrous application of the principle, that the elements of a science must be first taught," we cannot resist the conviction, that his is a most disastrous application of logic, to the true question at issue. *That the fallacy in his argument, consists in confounding the names and powers of letters, is obvious from the following:* "To the twenty-six letters of the alphabet, the child is taught to give twenty-six sounds, and no more." Now, if he means that he has discovered the fact, that instructers, everywhere, have fallen into the palpable error of teaching children, that to the twenty-six alphabetic characters, only twenty-six *elementary sounds* are attached, the wonder is, since he believes there are hundreds of such sounds, that he has not, by his journal, or otherwise, sought to correct such defective instruction. But, if he means, by the "twenty-six sounds, and no more," merely the sounds given to the *names* of the letters, he has either accused the teachers of this country of totally neglecting one essential function of the letters, or else, *he himself has failed to make the proper distinction between the name of a letter, and its power.* If the former is the meaning, and if he intended the above remark as a rebuke to teachers for neglecting to give the elements of sound, as well as the *names* of letters, we reply that, though it may, to some extent, be deserved, it is too unqualified. There are not a few instructers, who teach the children

330

to associate together, the names, the forms, and the powers of the letters. But, what surprises us most, if this be the meaning, is, that Mr. Mann should discover from such defective instruction, reasons for a *total* neglect of the alphabet, till after the child has learned to read. Some teachers may neglect to require the meaning of words. Is this a reason why words should be entirely set aside, till the child can first read whole paragraphs?

The most probable interpretation of the passage, is, that Mr. Mann did not have in his mind a clear perception of the difference between the name-sound of a letter, and its power. This explanation is rendered still more probable from the following allusion to the Greek letters: "Will the names of the letters, *kappa, omicron, sigma, mu, omicron, sigma,* make the word kosmos?" Has any defender of the old system ever asserted that they would? Yet, would the secretary have us suppose that if those names should fall upon the ear of one familiar with the Greek alphabet, he would not, at once, utter kosmos as the combination of the elementary sounds which those letters *name*.

If these quotations fail to convince the reader; let him take the following passage on the 33d page of Mr. Mann's lecture:

> "The faculty of judgment, the power by which we trace relations between causes and effects, and by which we expect the same results from the same antecedents, will be perpetually baffled if we attempt to spell words according to the vocal power, or *name sound*, as it is sometimes called, of the letters as presented in the alphabet; or, if we infer, that one word should be spelled so or so, because another is spelled so or so."

Here it will be seen that he makes the *vocal power* of a letter, and its *name-sound* identical; that is, he has defined the meaning of *vocal power*, as he understands it. The *name-sound* of a letter is the sound given to its name, as the sound of the syllable *be, ce, em,* &c.; whereas, the *vocal power* of a letter is the sound that letter receives in combination, as the sound of *b*, in *b*ut, *b*ate. The reader can determine the sound, by directing the attention to what precedes the sound of *ut*, in the former, and *ate*, in the latter example. In this instance, the blending of the *name* and *power* is not left as a matter of inference. Let any one carefully examine the pages of the secretary's report, from the 92d to the 99th, and he will find many other examples of the same error.

But, we apprehend that Mr. Mann has been induced to bring forward, once more, his theory of teaching words before letters, from what he saw in the Prussian schools. He says:

"When I first began to visit the Prussian schools, I uniformly inquired of the teachers, whether in teaching children to read, they began with the 'Names of the Letters,' as given in the alphabet. Being delighted with the prompt negative which I invariably received, I persevered in making the inquiry, until I began to perceive a look and tone on their part not very flattering to my intelligence, in considering a point so clear and so well settled as this, to be any longer a subject for discussion or doubt. The uniform statement was, that the alphabet, as such, had ceased to be taught, as an exercise, preliminary to reading, for the last fifteen or twenty years, by every teacher in the kingdom. Whoever will compare the German language with the English, will see that the reasons for a change are much stronger in regard to our own, than in regard to the foreign tongue."

Now, we have supposed the word *alphabet* to be a generic term, including all the letters of the alphabet; and that each letter has the three-fold meaning already attached to it. But, if in Prussia, it signifies simply the *names* of the letters, we will endeavor to bear that in mind. If we compare the Prussian mode of teaching children to read, as described by Mr. Mann, with the following portion of the above statement, it will be seen that alphabet, as there used, can mean nothing more than the names of the letters. "The uniform statement was," he says, "that the *alphabet*, as such, had ceased to be taught as an exercise preliminary to reading, for the last fifteen or twenty years, by every teacher in the kingdom." According to his description of their method of teaching children to read, it appears that the *forms* of the letters were first taught, then their *powers*, and finally the art of combining the forms into *written* words, and the *powers* into spoken words; so that nothing can be left for the meaning of *alphabet*, as here used, but the *names* of letters. But, we ask, if teaching the forms and powers of the letters, is not teaching the alphabet, or all in it, that is absolutely essential to *reading*? To teach the whole alphabet, as we understand it, is to teach all that belongs to it, not omitting the names of the letters, as do the Prussian teachers, at first.

It appears from the last sentence of the above quotation, that Mr. Mann thinks, if such a change as the omission of the *names* of letters was needed in Prussia, a comparison of German and English languages will show a greater demand for a change in the latter. What change, we ask? Such an one as theirs?

Let the following passage answer:

"There are two reasons why this *lautir*, or *phonic* method, [that is, the method of the Prussian and Saxon teachers, just described,] is less adapted to the English language than to the German;—first, because our vowels have more sounds than theirs, and secondly, because we have more silent letters than they. This is an argument, not against their method of teaching, but in favor of our commencing to teach by giving words before letters. And I despair of any effective improvement in teaching young children to read, until the teachers of our primary schools shall qualify themselves to teach in this manner;—I say until they shall *qualify* themselves, for they may attempt it in such a rude and awkward way as will infallibly incur a failure. As an accompaniment to this, they should also be able to give instruction according to the *lautir* or *phonic* method."

Now, how the secretary could discover, from the purely alphabetic and elementary method of teaching which he witnessed in Prussia, reasons for *such* a change, one which converts our language into Chinese, we cannot easily conceive. It is true, that he adds, "as an accompaniment to this, they [teachers] should also be able to give instruction according to the lautir or phonic method." But this seems to be only a secondary consideration; they should be *able* to do it. Besides, from the description of the new system which he has given, and sanctioned as given by others, it would seem that this kind of instruction could not well be given till the child can read easy sentences. Were it not for two reasons, which affect the question in degree, only, not in kind, Mr. Mann, it appears, would recommend that we adopt the Prussian method. But these reasons shall be considered in their appropriate place.

Mr. Mann has been led, as we believe, to recommend anew, this system of teaching words before letters—a system as wide asunder from the Prussian, as are the poles from each other—imply from confounding the names of letters with their powers. They, at first, omit the names of the letters, or, as he affirms that they say, "the alphabet." But they teach every thing else that belongs to a letter, and, probably, soon after, the names themselves.

And, now why should the *name* be omitted? *To neglect the names of letters is to destroy, at once, one of the most important exercises of the primary school; that is, oral spelling. The letters must have names to aid us in referring to them, no one will deny.* Otherwise, how could Mr. Mann have read such a passage as the following from his lecture? "*Ph* is *f*; and *c* is uniformly concealed in *s*, or sacrificed as a victim

333

to *k* or *z.*" Did he give simply the powers of the letters *f, c, s, k,* and *z*? or, did he hold up a card and point them out? or, did he speak their *names? If, then, letters must have names, why should the child be kept in ignorance of them? One of the first inquiries of a child, on seeing a new object is, "What is it?" "What do you call it?" or, in other words, "What is its name?" Shall such inquiries be silenced, when made respecting the alphabet?*

Besides, the names of the letters, in most cases, must, when spoken, differ from their powers; that is, the name of a letter and its power cannot be identical. Yet, it is evident, from the following quotation from the 96th page of the report, that there exists in the mind of the secretary an impression that the usefulness of the alphabet, in teaching reading, is very much diminished, from the want of a perfect coincidence between the powers of the letters and their name-sounds: "I believe it is within bounds to say, that we do not sound the letters in reading once in a hundred times, as we were taught to sound them when learning the alphabet. Indeed, were we to do so in one tenth part of the instances, we should be understood by nobody. What analogy can be pointed out between the rough breathing of the letter *h,* in the words *when, where, how,* & c., and the 'name-sound,' (aytch, aitch, or aych, as it is given by different spelling-book compilers,) of that letter, as it is taught from the alphabet?" Will the secretary give a name to *h,* or *p,* or *b*; or indeed to any of the consonants, which shall sound exactly like the power of the letter? We mean one that can become sufficiently audible to subserve all the purposes of a name; one that can be represented to the eye, like the name of any other object? *Why should not a letter have a name, as well as a peach? And if so, why should the name of the letter resemble that letter, any more than the name of the peach should resemble that fruit?* We can see no *necessity* for such resemblance. True, the name of a letter, when uttered, is a sound; and the power is a sound; and for the most part, a different one; so is thunder itself very different from the sound of its name; yet we never complain of that name as inadequate to call to mind the idea of thunder. The Greeks have nowhere, as we have seen, complained of any difficulty in associating their dissyllables, *alpha, beta, gamma, delta*; and trissyllables, *omicrom* and *omega,* with the elements of sound to which they refer. Yet how untoward are these names, compared with ours. *The resemblance between the names of most of our letters and their powers is so marked, as to afford no little assistance in combining letters into words. The dissimilarity, of which so much complaint has been made, might never have been mentioned, had it not been for such resemblances as now exist.* The names of the vowels, and their long sounds, with

334

the exception of *y*, are the same. The names of most of the consonants contain the elementary sound joined to a vowel, which either precedes or follows it. And here, we see again, the same want of distinction as before. "And again," says Mr. Mann, "in giving the names of the consonants, why should the vowel be sometimes prefixed, and sometimes suffixed?" So on the 98th page, he says:

"There is one fact, probably within every teacher's own observation, which should be decisive on this subject. In learning the alphabet, children pronounce the consonants as though they were either preceded or followed by one of the vowels;—that is, they sound *b*, as though it were written *be*, and *f*, as though written *ef*. But when they have advanced ever so little way in reading, do they not enunciate words where the letter *b* is followed by one of the *other* vowels, or where it is *preceded* by a vowel, as well as words into which their own familiar sound of *be*, enters? For example, though they have called *b* a thousand times as if it were written *be*, do they not enunciate the words *ball, bind, box, bug*, &c. as well as they do the words *besom, beatific*, &c.? They do not say *be-all, be-ind, be-ox, be-ug*, &c."

Since it is not the *name*, but the *power*, which enters into the combination, of what consequence is it, whether the vowel is prefixed or suffixed? We might as well have *eb* as *be*; *me* as *em*; *le* as *el*. Whatever be the name, whether *eb* or *be*, it does not enter into the formation of words, as *eb-ug*, or "*be-ug*;" so *h*, when represented to the eye as *aitch*, is the *printed* sign, or to the ear, as when pronounced, is the audible sign, of a rough breathing.

We cannot believe that even Mr. Mann himself would so disgrace the alphabet, as to reduce it to a file of *anonymous* letters, merely because their *real* names do not, at once, display all their virtues.

Such are some of the errors, at least as it seems to us, into which Mr. Mann has fallen, from a misconception of the offices performed by the letters of the alphabet.

4th—Whatever the secretary has said by way of ridicule, calculated to disparage the alphabet, ought to receive no consideration in the discussion of this question.

It is somewhat amusing that Mr. Mann should indulge in occasional merriment, even in the midst of so much confusion. We do not complain of it, but simply ask that it may receive no weight, when indulged in at the expense of the poor alphabet. In speaking of the devices which some humane teachers used to practice, he says in his lecture, page 17th: "He [the teacher] used to tell us that *a* stands for apple, to call *o*, round *o*, *s*, crooked *s*, *t*, the gentleman with a hat on;" and adds, "What manner of ejaculation would that be, which, instead of the unvarying sound of the word 'sot,' for instance, should combine the three sounds which the child had been taught to consider as the powers [?] of the letters composing it; viz. 'crooked s, round o, gentleman with a hat on?' " "Yet, this is the way," he adds, "in which many of us were taught to read." A more grave assertion.

So, in his last report, he says: "If *b*, is *be*, then *be* is *bee*, the name of an insect; and if *l* is *el*, then *el* is *eel*, the name of a fish;" that is to say, if the object named, is the same as the name itself, then that name becomes the name of an insect, or of a fish. Surprising!

All printed names of objects are formed from printer's ink. *Bee* is the printed name of an object; and since the object itself is the same as its name, it follows that this insect is only printer's ink. It is, therefore, harmless, unless it is that remarkable bee that has three stings; for we are told that—

'No *bee* has two stings,' and that, 'one bee has one more sting than no bee;' therefore, it would seem that one bee (and perhaps, this one) has three stings.

As for the *eel*, fit emblem of the logic that caught it, we will leave it to hands best able to retain it.

In his lecture before the American Institute, he says, page 16th, after giving an analysis of the sources of pleasure to a child, among which he includes form, "In regard to all the other sources of pleasure,—beauty, motion, music, memory,—the alphabetic column presents an utter blank. There stands in silence and death, the stiff perpendicular row of characters, lank, stark, immovable, without form or comeliness, and, as to signification, wholly void. They are skeleton-shaped, bloodless, ghostly apparitions, and hence it is no wonder that the children look and feel so death-like, when compelled to face them."

This, truly, is a dismal picture. How much less do the characters employed to designate numbers, deserve? And shall we neglect to teach *them* to children, because they are thus "bloodless" and "skeleton-shaped?"

So again, if such a reform is called for on account of the "bloodless" forms of our letters, we should suppose that it ought to be extended to music, requiring a similar change in teaching that science; such, for example, as teaching whole measures, or whole tunes, before notes. For, after applying nearly all the chilling epithets, which Mr. Mann employs in reference to the letters of the alphabet, one might go on further, and say of those used in music, that while some have from one to four *fangs*, others are *tadpole-shaped*, and therefore disgust by calling to mind loathsome reptiles; some are bound together in little groups, showing a degree of social affinity; others refuse all alliance whatever, and stand aloof from each other in wilful solitude; and even if they had any kindred feeling, they are kept asunder by immovable *bars*. The faces of some are *white*, while those of others are *black*; and these two classes are mingled together without distinction of color. Besides, some, in their pride, rear their heads above the lines assigned to the common classes, while others are depressed as far below the ordinary ranks of the social scale; and it is not surprising that the children, on beholding such distinctions, express themselves in *high tones* of indignation at the arrogance of the former, and in *deep-toned* sympathy at the sufferings of the latter.

Now, how can a child, whose ear is charmed with sweet sounds, and in whose soul melody is seeking for utterance, turn with other than "death-like" feelings, to such loathsome and revolting pictures, as salute his eyes in written music? Would it not be the dictate of *kindness*, to endeavor to make the path of the learner more *easy* and *pleasant*, by allowing him to read whole measures, or whole tunes, before learning the notes of which they are composed? But whether the child, after all, in reading whole words or whole tunes, will entirely escape from these "ghostly apparitions," we will leave for others to decide.

5th.—*As a final consideration, by way of restriction, let it be suggested, that the mere promotion of a child's pleasure should never form the basis of any system of education.*

If such considerations, as making the path of the learner *pleasant* and *easy*, have not formed the basis of the new system, they have, at least, had great weight in the minds of its defenders.

Let the reader refer to the whole paragraph on the 16th page of Mr. Mann's lecture, containing the last quotation, and he will see reasons for believing that a desire to promote the pleasure of the child, lies at the foundation of the system. The letters of the alphabet, "bloodless, ghostly apparitions," should at first be omitted; because, "having dimensions in a plane," merely, they are capable of affording only a small amount of that pleasure which arises simply from the love of form; a source of pleasure which, at best, he says, "is the feeblest of all." Such, certainly, seems to us a natural inference from this paragraph; and if such a principle induces him to urge the adoption of this system, it is hoped that every practical teacher, and every friend of thorough instruction, will enter against it his solemn protest. The child's pleasure to be consulted at the expense of order! at a sacrifice of first principles, the only *basis* of a thorough education! Nothing has been more productive of mischief, or more subversive of real happiness, than mistaking what may afford the child present gratification, for that which will secure for him lasting good.

It would seem that the child, in his ignorance and devotion to pleasure, is allowed to judge what is best, what is proper; what, on the whole, will result in the greatest amount of good. "How," inquires Mr. Mann, "can one who, as yet, is utterly incapable of appreciating the remote benefits, which, in after-life, reward the acquisition of knowledge, derive any pleasure from an exercise, which presents neither beauty to his eye, nor music to his ear, nor sense to his understanding?" And since the child cannot "appreciate the remote benefits" of learning the alphabet, must his caprice govern those who can, and determine them to abandon, even for a time, what they know is all-important in teaching him to read? A child is sick, and cannot appreciate the remote, or immediate benefits of taking disagreeable medicine. Will a judicious parent, who is fully sensible of the child's danger, regard, for one moment, his wishes, to save him from a little temporary disquietude? A child has no fondness for the dry and uninteresting tables of arithmetic. Shall he, therefore, be gratified in his desire to hasten on to the solution of questions, before acquiring such indispensable prerequisites? We have been accustomed to suppose that the responsibilities of the teacher's profession, consist, mainly, in his being required to fashion the manners and tastes of his pupils, to promote habits of thinking and patient toil, and to give direction to their desires and aspirations, rather than to minister to the gratification of their passion for pleasure.

If we mistake not, it was this same pleasure-promoting principle, that led Mr. Mann to interpret, as he did, the relation subsisting between the pupil and the teacher in the Prussian schools; on the part of the pupil it was, says Mr. M., "that of affection first and then duty." Here, it seems, Mr. M. would have the teacher first amuse the child, so as to gain his good-will, at any expense, and would, then, have him attend to duty as a secondary matter. This is reversing the true order of the two. Duty should come first, and pleasure should grow out of the discharge of it. We wish to be distinctly understood on this point. The teacher ought, when compatible with duty, to awaken in the child, agreeable, rather than painful feelings. He, who delights in seeing a child in a state of grief, is unfit for the teacher's office. On the other hand, he, who would substitute *pleasure* for *duty*, or would seek to make that sweet, which is of itself bitter, and to make that smooth, which is naturally and necessarily rough, is actuated by a misguided philanthropy. Hence, we dislike all attempts to make easy, and to simplify, that which is already as easy and simple as the nature of the case will allow.

The grand mistake lies in the *rank* assigned to pleasure. To *gratify* the child, should not be the teacher's aim, but rather to lay a permanent foundation, on which to rear a noble and well-proportioned superstructure. If, while doing *this*, the teacher is successful in rendering mental *exertion* agreeable, and in leading the child from one conquest to another, till *achievement itself* affords delight, it is well; such pleasure stimulates to greater exertion. But if, to cultivate pleasure-seeking is his aim, he had better, at once, abandon his profession, and obtain an employment in which he will not endanger the welfare, both of individuals and society, by sending forth a sickly race, palsied in every limb, through idleness, and a vain attempt to gratify a morbid thirst for pleasure.

But even if the promotion of pleasure were the aim of the teacher, the new system of teaching reading, is a most unfortunate mode of securing it. Pleasure springs from an active, rather than a passive state of the faculties.

The new system proposes to afford the child pleasure in the exercise of *reading words*: yet, instead of requiring him to exert, in the least, his mental faculties, in combining the elementary parts of these words, the teacher gives merely the result of his own mental processes, and exacts nothing from the child, but a passive reception of the sound, which is to be associated arbitrarily, with the *visible picture*, pointed out to him.

To this, the reply will, probably, be made, that the *idea*, not the mere act of passing from the visible to the audible sign, affords the pleasure. Such a reply is cut off by our first and second restrictions. The pleasure arising from the *idea*, can be urged, with equal force, by both parties. Therefore, in determining to which of the two systems belongs the greater pleasure, no account whatever can be made of that which arises from the *meaning* of words. We submit the question to any candid mind, which system, is adapted to afford the greater amount of pleasure? We will now grant to the defenders of the new system, for the sake of argument, all the advantage which they claim, from the association of interesting ideas, with the words which convey them. All that they can then mean, is, that the idea throws such a charm around those "bloodless and ghostly apparitions" which constitute words, that the "death-like" feeling, with which the child would otherwise "face" them, is now converted into pleasure. According to the plan of teaching, already described, however, the familiar word is first pronounced to the child; the *idea* is then in the mind, as soon as he hears the word uttered. Having received the idea, and all the pleasure it can afford, does it seem reasonable to suppose he will interest himself much, with the "ill-favored" forms that represent it to the eye? There is a little nut enclosed in a prickly encasement. The nut itself is very agreeable to children; so agreeable as to induce them, at the expense of some pain, to try their skill in removing this unfriendly exterior. Repeated trials, with the stimulus afforded by a desire to gratify the taste, gives them skill; till at length, they can obtain the nut without much suffering. Now, suppose some "humane" person, desirous of aiding the child in *acquiring* this kind of skill, and of making his task, at the same time, more *pleasant*, should begin by removing the troublesome covering without any effort on his part. Would he, in the first place, secure the object of giving the child *skill?* and in the second place, will the child, having obtained the nuts, derive much pleasure from handling the vacant burrs? and, finally, does not pleasure itself become vitiated and morbid, when unattended with effort? This illustration, will, at least, apprize the reader, of our reasons for the opinion, that the new system is the result of a misguided effort to make that pleasant, which, to some extent at least, must be disagreeable; to make that easy, which, from the nature of the case, is beset with unavoidable difficulties.

Having fixed what seem to us, the necessary limitations of the question, we will now consider whatever of argument remains in favor of the system.

The first consideration seems to arise from the fact that the child learns to utter whole sounds, the names of objects, without attending, in the least, to the elements which compose them. The following quotation from the 14th page of Mr. Mann's lecture, will explain what he means: "When we wish to give to a child the idea of a new animal, we do not present successively the different parts of it,—an eye, an ear, the nose, the mouth, the body, or a leg; but we present the whole animal, as one object. And this would be still more necessary, if the individual parts of the animal with which the child had labored long and hard to become acquainted, were liable to change their natures as soon as they were brought into juxtaposition, as almost all the letters do when combined into words." So, we are to understand that *printed* words, in like manner, should be learned as whole objects, though composed of elementary parts.

So far as this argument receives any force from its reference to the fact, that the child *utters* words, as whole sounds, we have no more to say, but would refer the reader to the first restriction of the question.

340

All that remains to be considered under this head, is that part of the argument contained in the last quotation, the general principle of which, seems to amount to this; the whole compound objects should first be taught, and made use of, as if understood; at some future period, the unknown elements which compose them, should be given, with the modes of combining them.

According to this, in teaching Numeration, all numbers, like 349, 8764, 97635, &c., should be given to the child as single objects. It is true, Mr. Mann denies the pertinency of this comparison, on the 98th page of his report; yet, it is impossible for us to see how he can escape it. The comparison fails only in one respect. Some of the letters of the alphabet do not, with unerring certainty, guide to the proper sound, while the *forms and places* of the figures, taken together, are an unfailing index of their value. Now, if our alphabet were what we have denominated a perfect one, the *forms* of the letters could never fail to lead to the correct sound. With such an alphabet, the comparison would fail in no material point.

But, if there is any meaning in the above quotation, Mr. Mann would recommend this mode of teaching words, even if they were written with a perfect alphabet. "Still more," he says, "would this be necessary if the individual parts of the animal, with which the child has labored long and hard to become acquainted, were liable to change their natures as soon as they were brought into juxtaposition, as almost all the letters of the alphabet do, when combined into words;" that is, whole words should be taught first, if each letter had but one sound; "still more," *a fortiori*, is it necessary so to teach them, since such is not the fact. And hence, we say, if words should be taught in this way, numbers, music, and every other art and science should be taught in the same way. If Mr. Mann still denies the aptness of the comparison, he makes the argument, drawn from the "natural order," as it is called, rest entirely on the imperfections of the alphabet, which forms one of the distinct arguments to be considered hereafter. The only difference which he has pointed out, certainly comes from that source; as any one will see by referring to the 98th page of the report. A denial, therefore, of the pertinency of this comparison is equivalent to giving up that part of the argument now under consideration. If, on the other hand, he acknowledges the aptness of the comparison, and recommends that the decimal system of numeration be treated in this manner, every one will see, that it loses all that gives it a superiority over the Greek or Roman numerals. The evil which would result, from the extension of this principle, to other branches of knowledge, could not be estimated.

Moreover, the illustration drawn from the animal, or a tree which is more commonly given, fails, we think, to meet all that is required in teaching a child to read. Grant, that he does not, in learning to distinguish a tree from a rock, or any other dissimilar object, form his idea of it, by inspecting the parts separately, and then by combining trunk, bark, branches, twigs, leaves, and blossoms. In learning to read, however, he is to distinguish between objects which resemble each other; and in many instances, very closely, as in the case of the words, *hand, band; now, mow; form, from;* and scores of others. To make the illustration good, it would be necessary to place the child in a forest, containing some seventy thousand trees, made up of various genera, species, and varieties, among which were found many to be distinguished only by the slightest differences. Or, if it will suit the case any better, let him be placed in a grove, containing seven hundred trees, having, as before, strong resemblances; if, then, this general survey of each of them, as a whole object, will enable him to distinguish them rapidly from each other, whatever may be their size, or the order in which he may cast his eyes upon them, we will acknowledge the aptness of the illustration. Primary school teachers, who have tried the system, testify, that when children have learned a word in one connection, they are unable to recognise it in another, especially if there be a change of type.

As Mr. Mann has, virtually, denied the right of extending the principle of teaching compound first, and the elements subsequently, to music and numeration, and, as his reasons for that denial are drawn from the present imperfect state of the alphabet, we may infer that he relies, mainly, if not solely, on the latter branch of the argument.

We will, therefore, next consider the *second* reason urged in favor of the new system. It may be thus stated. 'Such is the imperfect condition of the alphabet, that the letters, when combined into words, do not, with certainty, lead the learner to the correct pronunciation; whereas, by teaching words before letters, all this uncertainty is avoided.'

That the alphabet is imperfect, we have already conceded. The nature of these imperfections, we will repeat. 1st.—A single character may represent several different sounds. 2d.—A single sound, may be represented by several different characters, either separate or combined. 3d.—A letter may be silent. These anomalies are, to children, a source of much perplexity and doubt. We fully appreciate the difficulties arising from them, and as heartily deplore their existence, as can the authors of the proposed remedy. And here, two questions arise. The first is this; 'Is the condition of the alphabet a sufficient cause for any material change in the modes of teaching children to read?' And the second, 'Does it afford sufficient reasons for *such* a change as the one proposed?'

342

In answering the first question, we are prepared to say unhesitatingly, that the mode of teaching letters before words, is the only true and philosophical one. Letters, as we have already shown, are elements in the formation of words. That the elements of an art or science should first be taught, no one in the least acquainted with teaching, will pretend to deny. To proceed from known elements to their unknown combinations, is natural and easy; it is the only course that will ensure a thorough acquaintance with any subject. Hence, we say, no *material* change should take place. But in making the child acquainted with the letters and the modes of combining them, we are not sure that the best methods have always been adopted. A letter is not understood until its *visible symbol*, its *name* and its *power*, are associated together. It is the custom, in many primary schools, to teach at first only the *name* and *symbol*, and to leave the power to be learned by imitation or inference, when the child begins to combine letters into syllables or words. For example; the learner readily pronounces the names of the letters h-i-v-e, but being ignorant of their powers, he hesitates; the teacher says, pronounce; the child still hesitates; the teacher utters *hive*, as the combination of these four letters, and the child is then left to receive only a twilight conception of the powers of those letters. The Prussian method, it appears, consists in presenting the *symbol* and the *power*, leaving the name to be learned afterwards. This method has the advantage of bringing the *powers* of the letters, at an early period, to the notice of the child, in a manner so distinct and vivid, as to impress them indelibly upon his memory; and must give him great facility in the process of mental combination. The omission of the name, however, lies at the root of oral spelling, and endangers the acquisition of that important branch.

A third method, and one which will, we think, commend itself to the favorable regard of all who examine it, is that in which the three attributes of a letter are at once associated together. The advantages of this method, and the modes of interesting children in it, are topics which will be more fully discussed in another place. While we deny, therefore, that any material change should take place, we cheefully admit, that some such improvements as named above may be made in the manner of teaching the letters.

The second question is, 'Do the imperfections of the alphabet afford sufficient reasons for *such* a change as the one proposed?' We have already said, that no material change, in our opinion, should take place. But others think differently, and have proceeded both to devise, and strongly recommend, the plan under consideration. To this method of teaching we are opposed, for the following reasons:

1st.—Teaching whole words according to the new plan, to any extent whatever, gives the child no facility for learning new ones. Every word must be taken upon authority, until the alphabet is learned.

2d.—Since the alphabet must, at some period, be acquired, with all its imperfections, it is but a poor relief, to compel the child, at first, to associate seven hundred different, arbitrary forms with the ideas which they represent, and then to learn the alphabet itself.

Mr. Mann was sensible of this objection to his new theory, when he said, in his second annual report, (Common School Journal, Vol. I. page 327),

> "There is a fact, however, which may, perhaps, in part, cancel the differences, here pointed out. The alphabet must be learned, at some time, because there are various occasions, besides those of consulting dictionaries or cyclopaedias, where the regular sequence of the letters must be known; and possibly it may be thought, that it will be as difficult to learn the letters, after learning the words, as before. But the fact, which deprives this consideration of some part at least of its validity, is, that it always greatly facilitates an acquisition of the names of objects, or persons, to have been conversant with their forms and appearances beforehand. The learning of words is an introduction to an acquaintance with the letters composing them."

To learn to associate readily the form of a word with its meaning, is as difficult a task, for aught we can see, as it would be to associate the form and name of a letter with its power. It will be said that the former exercise affords the learner pleasure, and therefore attracts his attention and interests him. We have already expressed our sentiments on the policy of consulting the pleasure of a child, at the expense of his real good. If it can be shown, however, that, of two methods equally good in other respects, one has the additional recommendation of pleasing the child, and the other has *not*, we should by all means, choose the former. But all these remarks about the pleasure resulting from the new mode of teaching, grow out of the supposition, that learning the alphabet is totally destitute of interest.

This impression is not correct. And it is somewhat surprising, that the defenders of the new system do not see, when speaking of the alphabet, as destitute of interest, that a striking symbol, on the one hand, and the meaning of a word and its symbol, on the other.

That children are constantly uttering the elementary sounds of the language, before learning the letters, is obvious to every one. They must have some knowledge of them. So says Mr. Mann, on Page 93 of the report: "Generally speaking, too, before a child begins to learn his letters, he is already acquainted with the majority of elementary sounds in the language, and is in the daily habit of using them in conversation." It may be said of a letter, then, with as much propriety as of a word, that it is "familiar to the ear, the tongue, and the mind." The eye is not acquainted with the visible symbol. If, then, such old acquaintances can introduce the child to the stranger (the visible representative) in one case, why not in the other? If the one exercise affords pleasure, why not the other? The latter may not to the same extent, as the former. We have made these comparisons for the benefit of those who insist so much on pleasing children.

But in interesting children, much depends upon the modes of teaching. It is not necessary to teach the alphabet invariably from the vertical column. Letters may be made upon the black-board; and the children may be allowed to make them on the slate, or on the board. Again, the teacher may be supplied with small pieces of card, each containing a letter; or, with metallic letters, which may be handled. Let these be kept in a small box or basket and when a class is called upon to recite, let the teacher hold up one of these letters. One of the class utters its name; let him then be required to utter its *power* also. The same should afterwards be exacted of the whole class, in concert. The teacher should then give the letter to the successful pupil. Let this exercise be repeated till all the letters are distributed. The pupils now, one by one, return the letters to the teacher, who counts the number belonging to each, and awards praise where it belongs. Children may be deeply interested in exercises of this kind, and at the same time be laying the foundation for a thorough course of instruction in reading. Then, let the teacher present some two or three letters, so arranged, as to spell a familiar word; as *ox, cat, dog*. The pupils should be required first, to utter the names of the letters thus arranged; next their powers, then, to join those powers into the audible sign which will call to mind the object named.

3d.—Another objection to converting our language into Chinese, arises from the *change* which must inevitably take place in the modes of associating the printed word with the idea which it represents, when the child is taught to regard words as composed of elements. *Children, at first, learn to recognise the word, by the new method, as a single picture, not as composed of parts; and for aught we know, they begin in the middle of it and examine each way. It is not probable that they proceed invariably from left to right, as in the old mode. However that may be, an entire change must take place when they begin to learn* *words, as composed of letters.* The attention, then is directed to the parts of which words are composed. While the eye is employed in combining the visible characters, the mind unites the powers which they represent, and the organs of speech are prompt to execute, what the eye and the mind have simultaneously prepared for them. *The mode of association in a symbolic language, if we mistake not, is this: The single picture is associated arbitrarily, yet directly, with the idea; the idea is then associated with its audible sign; this sign being familiar to the child, is readily uttered. In a phonetic language, it is different. The attention being directed to the letters and their powers, the child is conducted immediately to the audible sign; this when uttered, or thought of, suggests the idea.* Whether or not these are the correct views, is immaterial to the argument. All that is claimed is, *that a change takes place in the modes of association, as soon as the child begins to combine letters into words. It is of this change we complain. All will acknowledge the importance of forming in the child, correct habits of association, such as will not need revolutionizing at a subsequent period in life.* On this point, we cannot forbear quoting the excellent remarks of the secretary, relating to the subject of spelling. After recommending a certain natural and simple mode of classifying words, he proceeds to say:* "On such lessons as these, scholars will very rarely spell wrong. They can go through the book twenty times while they would go through a common spelling-book once; and each time will *rivet the association,* that is, it will make an ally of the almost *unconquerable force of habit.* A connection will be established between the general idea of the word and its component letters, which it will be nearly impossible to dissolve. In pursuing any study or art, it is of the *greatest importance to have the first* movements, whether of the eye, the hand, or the tongue, *right.* The end will be soonest obtained to submit to *any delay that exactness* may require. We all know with what tenacity *first impressions* retain their hold upon the mind. When in a strange place, if we mistake the points of compass, it is almost impossible to rectify the error; and it becomes a contest which of the two parties will hold out longest, the natural points of the compass, in their position, or we in our false impressions. So if, in geography, we get an idea that a city is on the west bank of a river, when it is on the east, it is almost as practicable to transfer the city itself, bodily, to the side of the river where it seems to belong, as it is to unclench our own impressions, and make them conform to its true location. These illustrations might be multiplied indefinitely." It seems to us that, as one of these illustrations, the subject under consideration must be legitimately ranked.

4th.—The new system fails to accomplish the object which it proposes. The main design of this mode of teaching seems to be, to escape the ambiguity arising from the variety of sounds which attach to some of the letters, as well as from the variety of forms by which the same sounds may be represented.

The defenders of this system seem to forget, since these anomalies are elementary, that they must be carried into the formation of words. Thus, we can represent a single elementary sound, first by *a*, then by *ai*, and again, by *ei*; hence, we can form three different words; *as vane, vain, vein*. In a similar manner we have, *rain, reign, rein; wright, write, right, rite;* and hundreds of others. It will be seen at once, that it must be as difficult for a child to attach the same sound to four different pictures called words, as to four different pictures called letters. Hence, it is plain, that we have "harlequins" among words; as well as among letters. The only difference is, that the former are more numerous, yet the legitimate offspring of the latter. We have "masqueraders," too, among words. Let the sound represented by the four letters, r-i-t-e, fall upon the child's ear, and he may think, either, of a ceremony, of making letters with a pen, of justice, or of a workman. Again, let either the printed or spoken word *pound*, for example, be given; and he may think of an enclosure for stray cattle, of striking a blow, of certain weights, as avoirdupois, apothecaries', or Troy weight, and also, of a denomination of money. To illustrate the difficulty arising from this equivocal word, or from any other one of the hundreds in the language, we will pursue a course similar to that in which Mr. Mann shows the child's perplexity with the letter *a*, on page 93 of the report. Pound has more than seven different meanings, if we take into the account all the various weights, and moneys. But we will suppose it to have only seven. Now, if the sentences in which this word occurs be equally divided among these seven meanings, we have only to use the words *sentence, word,* and *idea,* instead of *word, letter,* and *sound;* and the secretary's own language will bring us to a result as deplorable as that to which he arrives; namely, "that he [the child] goes wrong six times in going right once."

But what shall be done, since words, as well as letters, may become "masqueraders," and "harlequins?" Shall some enthusiastic reformer, some Miss Edgeworth, come forward and tell us that no thorough reform can be effected, till the practice of teaching words, before *whole sentences,* is abolished; intimating, that at no distant period children will begin with whole *paragraphs,* and, if very small, with whole *pages?*

Thus, it would seem that the advocates of this system, in attempting to shun Scylla are falling upon Charybdis. But it will, probably, be said in reply, that the connection will aid the child in determining the meaning of such words. This we willingly grant, and at the same time, claim, what is somewhat similar to it, in teaching the use of the letters; namely, that simple analogies may be pointed out to the child, which will aid him, not a little, in determining the correct sound to be given to the letters. In monosyllables ending with *e* mute, the vowel, almost without exception, is long, or like the name-sound. So when a syllable ends with a vowel, especially if accented, that vowel is long. The vowel *a*, in monosyllables, ending with *ll*, has generally, the broad sound. A monosyllable, ending with a single consonant, contains, usually, a short vowel. These are only a few of the various analogies which may be pointed out, and which will enable the learner, in most cases, to give the correct sound.

5th.—It introduces confusion into the different grades of schools.

The elements must be taught somewhere. If neglected in the primary schools, they must be taught in the grammar schools. And thus the order of things is reversed, and disarrangement introduced into the whole school system. The teacher who is employed, and paid, for instructing in the higher branches, is compelled to devote time and attention to the studies appropriately belonging to the schools of a lower grade. This is found to be the case, to too great an extent, in the schools of our city. We do not say this to the disparagement of the primary school teachers, or from the belief, that there is a want of fidelity on their part. We believe it to be, in part, at least, owing to the system of teaching, or rather want of system, in the primary schools. The books used in these schools, according to the author's own account of them, are adapted to either system. This is equivalent to saying that they are adapted to neither; for it is impossible to see how two methods, so entirely different from each other, as those under consideration, can be embraced in one series of books. After repeated inquiries made in many of the primary schools of the city, we are persuaded, that the teachers have taken the full amount of license allowed them, by the author of the books which they use. Some begin with the alphabet; others require the children to learn eight or ten words, from which they teach the several letters, though not in the order in which they are arranged in the alphabet. Some carry the process of teaching words to a greater extent, yet require the child to learn to spell, before teaching him to read. Others, as will appear, teach the children to read, without making them at all acquainted with the letters. One evil, resulting from this want of system, is a great neglect of spelling. It is the opinion of those masters who have been longest in the service, and can therefore compare the results of the two systems, that in respect to spelling, among the candidates for admission from the primary schools, there has been a great deterioration during the trial of the new system; a period of about six years. The following instance, which occurred a few weeks since, though perhaps, an extreme case, well illustrates a large class of cases, in which there is a deplorable neglect of spelling. A girl in her tenth year, presented herself for admission into one of the grammar schools, with a certificate of qualification from the district committee. The master gave her to read, the sentence beginning with the words, "Now if Christ be preached," &c. The third word, she called "Jesus," and persisted in saying it was so pronounced. She was requested to spell it; the master, at the same time, pointing out the first letter. This letter, she called "Jesus." The first letter of the alphabet was pointed out; the pupil uttered "and"; the second letter was shown her; "but," was her response. The letter *m*, she called "man." She was sent to the assistant teachers of the school, who found her totally ignorant of the alphabet. The master sent her back to the primary school, with her certificate endorsed, "not qualified; can be admitted only by the authority of the sub-committee of the grammar school."

And, here we may remark, that the testimony of able primary school teachers themselves, who have tried both systems, is adverse to this mode of teaching reading. They declare that in the end, nothing is gained, but much is lost; that the task of teaching the alphabet, and the art of combining letters into words, are more difficult, and less satisfactory, than if the child had begun with the letters.

6th.—It cherishes and perpetuates a defective enunication.

Children so universally come to the school-room, especially from uneducated families, with habits of incorrect articulation, that the efforts of the teacher, at an early period, should be directed towards the correction of these habits. The only sure way to accomplish this, is to drill the pupils on the elements of sound. The errors in enunciation consist, chiefly, in giving either an incorrect sound to, in suppressing, or in mingling, the vocal elements. A forcible enunciation of these elements, separately, will direct the attention of the child to, and correct, those which are uttered improperly; will bring out those which have been omitted, or too feebly expressed, and will tend to keep separate those, which, from early habit, have been blended together. Nor is this all. Reading may be divided into two departments, which may be called the *mechanical* and the *intellectual*. The latter embraces all the higher excellences of reading; such as *emphasis, inflection, pauses,* and what is comprehended in the term *expression*. To prepare the pupil for this department of reading, it is of paramount importance, that all which is embraced in the former, should first be carefully taught. In this discussion, we are concerned especially with the mechanical part of read-

349

ing. It includes two particulars; first a skilful use of the *tools* employed in the art, that is, the ability of uttering with fluency the *sounds* of the words, while the eye passes rapidly over the letters which represent them; and, secondly, such a thorough training of the organs of speech, as will enable the pupil to give those sounds with clearness and force. By the new system, neither of these particulars can, to any great extent, be attended to; for they both involve a knowledge of the elements. To be able to utter the elements forcibly, when taken either separately, or combined, is not unlike the acquirement of skill on an instrument of music. That a performer can pass over rapid and difficult passages with ease and gracefulness, is the surest proof that he has been thoroughly drilled, on every *note* of those passages. He did not acquire them all in a mass, as a *whole*; and that by some fortunate movement of the fingers which cost him no effort. Such skill must have been the result of patient toil, which was but gradually rewarded with success. What if one desiring to become a skilful player upon the piano-forte, yet impatient to play a tune, because more *agreeable*, should, at first, omit the lessons for practice, and place the fingers upon the keys, regardless of order, or the rules contained in the "Book of Instructions?" The bad habits, thus acquired, might last him through life, and ever prove an obstacle to his success. But what would be thought of a professor of music, who should allow of such a disorderly beginning? *Still more*, of one who should recommend it, and affirm that no thorough reform could be effected without it? A defect in the enunciation of the elements, is a radical one, and the new system is directly calculated to perpetuate it. If there was no other argument against the system, this, of itself, would be sufficient to show its utter futility.

The *third* and last argument for the system, in the words of the secretary, is, that "the rapidity of acquisition will be greater, if words are taught before letters." This is a question of fact. It either is so, or it is not so, and facts alone, can sustain the position which Mr. Mann here assumes. If he could have adduced facts to sustain the assertion, and then have said, *I know*, instead of saying, as he does on the 92d page of the report, "I believe that if two children, of equal quickness and capacity, are taken, one of whom can name every letter of the alphabet, at sight, and the other does not know them from Chinese characters, the latter can be most easily taught to read," such facts would have done much towards effecting the desired change in the State. But where are the facts? We have seen none. It is true, the secretary does allude, in his second annual report, to the introduction of the system into the Boston primary schools, and says, "it is found to succeed better than the old mode." Here, let the reader first inquire,

350

What is the system in the Boston schools? Is it precisely the one which Mr. Mann recommends? And in the second place, What is the opinion of practical teachers concerning the results of the nearest approaches to this system, as seen in the Boston schools for the last five or six years? And thirdly, let the reader be informed that *"The Mother's Primer,"* which begins with words, was introduced, as appears from the vote of the Boston Primary School Committee, Nov. 7, 1837, and that the second annual report of the Secretary of the Board of Education, bears date Dec. 26, 1838, leaving an interval of about one year only, for the trial of the new system. Whether a trial during so short a period, amidst the novelty always attending a change, is sufficient to warrant the assertion that "it is found to succeed better than the old mode," we will submit to the judgment of any candid mind.

It is supposed, that the secretary, when he affirms that "the rapidity of acquisition will be greater, if words are taught before letters," intends to include the acquisition of the alphabet, with the modes of combining letters into words; otherwise the whole matter is unworthy of the attention of the friends of education. Such being the case, the question stands thus. Two children, in like circumstances, in every respect, commence learning to read; the first learns some seven hundred different words, as he would so many different letters; having acquired no more ability to learn the seven hundred and first, than he had at the beginning; afterwards he learns the twenty-six letters of the alphabet, including all the "harlequins" and "masqueraders," and finally the art of combining the letters into words. The other learns first, the letters; then, the art of combining them; and finally makes use of his knowledge, to acquire his seven hundred words. Now by what rule of arithmetic, or of common sense, it is ascertained that the former will advance more rapidly than the latter, is to us entirely unknown.

Such are the reasons that have compelled us to dissent from the opinions of the secretary, on this branch of education. The main question at issue, we are constrained to answer in the negative; because such a change, as that proposed by Mr. Mann and others, is neither called for, nor sustained by sound reasoning. The arguments adduced in its support are, as we believe, inconclusive. The plausibility of some, arises from considerations wholly irrelevant; others are fallacious; and others still, are based upon false premises.

On the contrary, the reasons brought against the change, and in favor of the prevailing system, are of paramount importance. Therefore, as conscientious and faithful servants in the cause of education, we feel bound to adhere to the path of duty, rather than yield to the opinions even of those who are high in authority.

Index